ELECTIONS IN CANADA

ELECTIONS IN CANADA

PEOPLE, PLAYERS, AND PROCESSES

Edited by

Tamara A. Small and Royce Koop

UNIVERSITY OF TORONTO PRESS

Toronto Buffalo London

ISBN 978-1-4875-5132-2 (cloth)   ISBN 978-1-4875-5135-3 (EPUB)
ISBN 978-1-4875-5134-6 (paper)   ISBN 978-1-4875-5136-0 (PDF)

Library and Archives Canada Cataloguing in Publication

Title: Elections in Canada : people, players, and processes / edited by Tamara A. Small and Royce Koop.
Names: Small, Tamara A. (Tamara Athene), 1975– editor | Koop, Royce, 1978– editor
Description: Includes bibliographical references and index.
Identifiers: Canadiana (print) 20240478703 | Canadiana (ebook) 20240478746 | ISBN 9781487551346 (paper) | ISBN 9781487551322 (cloth) | ISBN 9781487551353 (EPUB) | ISBN 9781487551360 (PDF)
Subjects: LCSH: Elections – Canada. | LCSH: Political campaigns – Canada. | LCSH: Voting – Canada.
Classification: LCC JL193 .E46 2025 | DDC 324.70971 – dc23

Cover design: Val Cooke

We welcome comments and suggestions regarding any aspect of our publications – please feel free to contact us at news@utorontopress.com or visit us at utorontopress.com.

Every effort has been made to contact copyright holders; in the event of an error or omission, please notify the publisher.

We wish to acknowledge the land on which the University of Toronto Press operates. This land is the traditional territory of the Wendat, the Anishinaabeg, the Haudenosaunee, the Métis, and the Mississaugas of the Credit First Nation.

University of Toronto Press acknowledges the financial support of the Government of Canada and the Ontario Arts Council, an agency of the Government of Ontario, for its publishing activities.

Contents

Part Two: The Players

Part Three: The Campaign

Part Four: The People

Figures and Tables

Figures

Tables

Acknowledgements

First, we would like to thank the contributors to this book. There are so many ways that editing a book with more than 20 chapters featuring more than 20 different scholars could go wrong, and it didn't. This project received the most positive peer reviews of our careers, and we have your excellent contributions to thank for this.

This collection would not see the light of day without the help of several people. We would first like to acknowledge the team at the University of Toronto Press, particularly our editor Rebecca Duce. Rebecca's guidance and enthusiasm has been invaluable throughout this process. Thank you to the reviewers of both the initial proposal and the final manuscript. We appreciate your time and your helpful comments that shaped the direction of the book and the individual chapters. We would not have been able to bring this through the publication phase without Janice Evans and Jenn Harris. Finally, a big thanks to Aidan Harris for his research assistance on this book.

In 2022, David Taras, Tamara's MA supervisor, passed away after dealing with cancer. This reminds us that so much of our success in this field, including this book, was made possible because of our academic mentors while we were graduate students. We dedicated this book to David Taras, Jonathan Rose, Anthony Sayers, and Ken Carty as a sign of our appreciation.

Lastly, a huge thank you to our families – Douglas (TAS) and Denisa and Mikaela (RK) – your support can never be overestimated.

TAS and RK

Introduction: The People, Players, and Processes of Canadian Elections

Tamara A. Small and Royce Koop

On the final day of the 2021 federal election, the *Beaverton*, an online news satire and parody publication, posted the following on its Twitter feed:

> @TheBeaverton "We don't technically elect a prime minister," says buzzkill polisci prof ruining all the fun #cdnpoli #elexn44

While it is debatable the extent to which political scientists are buzzkills, the tweet reminds us that there is often a lack of precision when discussing what Canadian elections are and what they do. This book seeks to clarify this by exploring elections and campaigns in Canada from a variety of perspectives. In a federal election, Canadians elect a legislature, *not* a government. That is, Canadians elect candidates in individual ridings to be members of Parliament in the House of Commons (there will be 343 seats in the House of Commons as of April 2024). From this legislature, the governor general then selects the prime minister (conventionally, the leader of the party with the largest number of seats), and the leader then forms a government.

Elections are considered by many as the defining feature of democracy (Katz 1997; Courtney 2004). But what is an election? Medvic (2021) notes that the term is often used as a catch-all to refer to the casting of a ballot but also the lead-up to the actual vote. We define an election as *a mechanism where the expressed preferences of individuals are aggregated into a decision regarding who will govern* (O'Neill 2009). Elections, therefore, are related to the individual act of voting and the counting of ballots that collectively inform who will hold public office. An election differs from forms of direct democracy such as referenda, recall, or initiatives. While all three involve casting and counting of ballots, none are concerned with filling public offices with people. Elections are central mechanisms of political accountability. Citizens consider the performance of incumbents and decide to either keep them or throw them out of office.

An election differs also from a campaign, which is the lead-up to the vote. An election campaign is *an attempt to mobilize people in support of a particular candidate or team of candidates*

(Flanagan 2010). Drawn from military parlance, the term signifies that politics is a form of combat (Safire 2008). While the practical goal of an election campaign is for parties and candidates to win votes, the democratic goal is to inform citizens of the key policy issues and debates of the day and introduce them to candidates in order to help citizens formulate their preferences.

OUR APPROACH TO CANADIAN ELECTIONS

This distinction between elections and campaigns is central to the approach we take in *Elections in Canada: People, Players, and Processes.* Elections are more than the vote, who wins or who loses. We see elections and campaigns as a process, a process that begins months, perhaps years, prior to election day. Both reflect not only the choices of voters, but also the historical context of a polity, the legal context, political actors, and the media system. That is, both how elections occur and the wider context within which elections occur matter profoundly to the outcome.

This is not the way the academic literature typically approaches the study of elections in Canada. Instead, after the votes are counted, numerous excellent studies are published on vote choice or the campaign strategies of political actors. While this literature is crucial to our understanding of Canadian elections, these studies often focus on very discrete aspects of elections and treat them as stand-alone events. For instance, Jon H. Pammett and Christopher Dornan have produced a series of excellent analyses after each federal election (for instance, 2016; 2020; 2022). These books focus heavily on the most recent election and tend to only cover the writ or campaign period. Institutional and other enduring features of Canadian elections are generally not covered in these books. In a similar vein, Alex Marland and Thierry Giasson (2015; 2022; Giasson and Marland 2020) have edited collections focusing on campaigning in the last three federal elections. These collections are unique in that many of the chapters are co-written with practitioners – individuals working in that campaign. Finally, the contributions of the Canadian Elections Study teams in studying voting behaviour are foundational to Canadian political science (for instance, Johnston et al. 1992; Nevitte et al. 1999; Blais et al. 2002; Gidengil et al. 2012), as is the *Absent Mandate* series (for instance, Clarke et al. 2019). These books typically have a single focus: they seek to explain vote choice in either a single or small series of elections.

While we owe a huge debt to these works, *Elections in Canada* takes a different approach. First, this collection is not an assessment of or reflection on the most recent election. Rather, the chapters consider how their topic (and the study of the topic) has evolved over time and draw on relevant examples and literature from the full gamut of federal elections. This collection focuses most of its attention on federal politics. While there are similarities between elections federally and provincially, there are also differences in election law, party systems, and political culture. Indeed, elections in the Northwest Territories and Nunavut are vastly different. Both have a consensus style of government where all members of the Legislative Assembly are elected as independent candidates; political parties do not play a role. Moreover, there are differences between federal elections and those elections in the more than 3,500 municipalities across the country. While some municipalities have locally based political parties, most do not. There are also differences related to boundaries, voting systems, and vote counting. Our emphasis on federal elections is not meant to detract from their importance at other levels. Rather, given that provincial, territorial, and municipal elections take so many forms, covering them adequately along with federal elections would become prohibitively complex. That said, individual chapters may draw on examples from other levels of government where relevant.[1]

This book presents a focused analysis organized by two central themes: *evolution* and *democracy*, with all contributing chapters structuring their analysis using the same guiding questions:

1   What is the election/campaign-related topic? Why is it important to an overall understanding of Canadian elections?
2   How has the election/campaign-related topic evolved over time?
3   What, if any, are the democratic implications of this topic for Canadian elections?

These guiding questions allow for a consistent discussion of the practical, empirical, and normative issues surrounding Canadian elections. Overall, *Elections in Canada* constitutes a more comprehensive approach to analyzing elections and campaigns than other books due to its historical, longitudinal, and institutional content. This book brings together knowledge, viewpoints, and expertise from senior scholars as well as new voices in research on elections and campaigns. Several of the contributors have practical experience with electoral politics, including a former chief electoral officer, a national campaign director, a boundary commissioner, and academics who have advised courts, legislatures, and other organizations on various aspects of the electoral process.

Finally, *Elections in Canada* includes a much broader array of topics beyond the typical themes of voting behaviour and the campaign. As the subtitle notes, the collection also discusses the people, players, and processes that make up Canadian elections. Following this introductory section, the collection is divided into four main sections, which we outline here.

PART ONE: THE INSTITUTIONAL SETTING

We begin our exploration of elections and campaigns by exploring the institutional setting or the rules of the electoral game. Canadian elections and campaigns operate in a highly regulated environment. Election law "regulates matters such as who can participate in elections, how campaigns are conducted and how votes are counted" (Small 2022a). Key here are the democratic rights entrenched in Canada's constitution. Section 3 of the *Charter of Rights and Freedoms* states that "every citizen of Canada has the right to vote in an election of members of the House of Commons or of a legislative assembly and to be qualified for membership therein." Unlike other sections of the Charter, section 3 cannot be overridden by section 33, the notwithstanding clause (MacIvor 2013). It is also one of the few Charter rights reserved for Canadian citizens (Department of Justice 2021). These sections are also important because it means that election law is subject to judicial review. While section 3 appears to only protect (1) the right to vote and (2) candidacy rights, several court decisions have extended the meaning of section 3 to be much more inclusive of the entire electoral system. According to Yasmin Dawood (2012, 524), section 3 includes four rights: (1) the right to effective representation, (2) the right to meaningful participation, (3) the right to equal participation, and (4) the right to a free and informed vote. The final two rights come from the interconnection between

Table 1.1. Main Parts of the *Canada Elections Act*, 2000

Part 1. Electoral Rights	Part 12. Counting Votes
Part 2. Chief Electoral Officer and Staff	Part 13. Validation of Results by the Returning Officer
Part 3. Election Officers	Part 14. Judicial Recount
Part 4. Register of Electors and Register of Future Electors	Part 15. Return of the Writ
Part 5. Conduct of an Election	Part 16. Communications
Part 6. Candidates	Part 17. Third Party Advertising, Partisan Activities, and
Part 7. Revision of Lists of Electors	Election Surveys
Part 8. Preparation for the Vote	Part 18. Financial Administration
Part 9. Voting	Part 19. Enforcement
Part 10. Advance Polling	Part 20. Contested Elections
Part 11. Special Voting Rules	Part 21. General

section 3 and section 2(b), the right to free expression (Small 2022a). Section 4 of the Charter states that unless there are extraordinary circumstances, like a national emergency, no government can stay in office for more than five years. This essentially means that an election must be held every five years. In practice and by convention, federal elections occur more frequently, typically roughly every four years. Sections 3 and 4 enshrine the democratic importance of Canadian elections.

However, to fully understand how federal elections work, one must look at the *Canada Elections Act*, 2000 (CEA). As Table 1.1 shows, the CEA spells out how elections and campaigns operate in detail. The CEA is not a static document; governments regularly fine-tune, update, and amend the law in response to changing circumstances, advice from the chief electoral officer (CEO), or court rulings. The CEO, Elections Canada, and their roles in administering elections are discussed in Chapter 2. The most recent large-scale amendment occurred in 2018 with the *Elections Moderni-zation Act*. Changes included the establishment of the official pre-campaign period, a maximum election period, the banning of foreign interference, and the registry for online advertising.

One crucial aspect of the CEA is campaign financing, the democratic importance of which is taken up in Chapter 6. Campaign financing describes the legal rules governing who can contribute to electoral actors (parties, candidates, and third parties), how much they can spend, and any rules regarding the transfer of public money to electoral actors (Young 2016). Chapter 3 and Chapter 9 will discuss campaign financing vis-à-vis political parties and third parties, respectively. Another key piece of election law is the *Electoral Boundaries Readjustment Act*, 1985. As Chapter 5 discusses, this Act outlines the process by which Canada's electoral boundaries are redrawn.

As the chapters in this section show, most of Canada's electoral rules have changed dramatically since Confederation. One area that has seen little change is Canada's voting system. In the first-past-the-post (FPTP) – also known as single-member plurality (SMP) – system, one representative is elected from each electoral district using a plurality formula where the winning candidate is the one who receives more votes than any other candidate. FPTP has been used in every federal election, and it is currently used in all provincial and territorial elections. FPTP has profound impacts on our politics and is not without controversy. As such, many Canadians – from elected leaders to academics to citizens – continually question whether we should adopt a new voting system. Chapter 4 will delve into the nuts and bolts of FPTP and discuss recent attempts to reform the system.

Overall, the institutional setting of an election matters profoundly to what happens during and after the campaign. As Courtney (2004, 5) notes, "[w]ithout procedures and machinery that are known to be fair and equitable, the electoral process itself falls into disrepute and the results are treated with contempt." The chapters that follow provide a detailed exploration through the institutional building blocks of Canadian elections (electoral administration, campaign finance, the voting system, and electoral boundaries). They will demonstrate that, in general, our electoral processes work extremely well, and Canadians have much to be proud of when it comes to the rule of the electoral game. The final chapter in this section uses survey data to demonstrate that Canada ranks very high in electoral integrity when compared to countries around the globe.

PART TWO: THE PLAYERS

The institutional setting of Canadian elections provides the field on which players compete with one another. But who exactly are the players of Canadian elections? There is little doubt that political parties – which compete against one another for power – are the crucial actors of Canadian elections (Cross 2004). But the parties themselves are multidimensional in nature, and their actions and behaviours during election campaigns cannot be understood apart from an understanding of how their different components work in unison over the course of the campaign. Further, parties compete for power across a number of discrete yet interconnected levels, and the responses of party actors are shaped in part by this setting. And while parties compete for power, there are other crucial actors that, while they themselves do not seek power, give shape to election campaigns through their activities. In this section, we devote two chapters to two aspects of political parties, as well as a chapter each to other actors: third parties and journalists.

Conceiving of Canadian parties as multidimensional in nature is crucial to understanding both what they do and why they do the things they do during election campaigns. Eldersveld's (1964) conception of stratarchy provides a jumping off point for organizational analysis of parties: according to Eldersveld, parties are characterized by different nodes of power that are mutually interdependent. Carty's (2002) conception of franchise parties applies this conception to Canadian parties; according to Carty, the crucial trade-off in power within Canadian parties during election campaigns is between national party leaders, who are permitted to identify broad themes to run on, and local candidates who must select and adapt those broad themes to local tastes within the context of a very large, diverse, and segmented country.

Since the 2000s, we have seen Canadian parties evolve campaign organizations that diverge from Carty's expectations in important ways in response to changing technological, competitive, and regulatory contexts. But the crucial distinction remains between that of the national as well as the local campaigns in each of the constituencies. These campaigns differ in their personnel, functions, and activities. Accordingly, we dedicate chapters to these two sets of actors: Chapter 7 focuses on national campaigns while Chapter 8 explores constituency campaigns.

An important area of study related to Canadian parties during election campaigns is coordination between the national and local levels, as the time when these campaigns could operate largely independently from one another is well over. Instead, we now see a range of mechanisms that parties have developed to ensure national and local campaigns are consistent on messaging and to provide local campaigns with assistance when needed (sometimes when such help is requested, sometimes when the national campaigns deem it necessary). While we allow for separate explorations of national and local campaigns, it is important to examine synchronization in light of recent emphasis on the increasing prominence of power-sharing relationships within parties (Cross 2018).

Parties compete for power, but they are not the only important actors in Canadian election campaigns (Young and Everitt 2004). Other actors, known in Canadian law as third parties, involve themselves in election campaigns to push for outcomes that favour their own goals. A third party is a person or group other than a candidate, a registered political party, or an electoral district association of a registered political party. This could be a business, union, interest group, or an individual. Third parties in Canadian elections are subject to a number of regulatory requirements that shape how they approach their goals. Indeed, the development of third-party regulations is "distinguished for being one of the most legally contested election policies in Canada" (Crandall and Lawlor 2018, 214). Third parties are discussed in Chapter 9.

The news media – including individual journalists but also all the media companies that employ them – are also important actors in Canadian election campaigns. Canadians turn to media to provide coverage of the parties and candidates for public office. Waddell and Dornan (2006, 222) describe the news media as the "representatives of the public," where journalists pose questions of politicians and raise issues on behalf of citizens. The democratic importance of the news media is found in the constitutional entrenchment of press freedoms in section 2 of the Charter (Small, Marland, and Giasson 2014). Indeed, a free media is considered essential to the free and fair electoral process.

Increasingly, however, media figures themselves have been pulled into politics and have become politicized, with figures in the parties regularly accusing journalists of bias and engaging in behaviours like granting interviews to some outlets but not others. On his first day as leader of the Conservative Party, for example, Pierre Poilievre accused a parliamentary press gallery journalist of being "a Liberal heckler" after the journalist aggressively interrupted and questioned Poilievre. The Trudeau government's financial support for several mainstream news organizations through funds such as the Local Journalism Initiative and the Special Measures for Journalism top-up seem to have aggravated the politicization of media in Canadian politics.

The news media have traditionally been understood to refer to the printed press as well as radio and television broadcasters. However, changing technology has seen a democratization of media. Tweeters and podcasters are able to shape opinion through their own followings, and there are now lower burdens of entry for tenacious new online journalists. Many of these may eschew traditional standards of impartiality but may nevertheless have significant audiences, such as *The Rebel* or *The Post-Millennial* websites. Parties are well aware of these developments in the media landscape and have adjusted their own approaches accordingly. Chapter 10 discusses the role of journalists and the news media in elections.

Overall, political parties, their candidates, third parties, and the media are all important players in Canadian elections. What they do and how they behave is essential to understanding election as a process. The players of Canadian election campaigns have changed over time. On the surface, the same old parties with the same old structures appear to take the field in every election; in reality, the organizational, structural, and internal logics of parties have shifted several times throughout Canadian history. The same goes for the new media: the old partisan newspapers that characterized the prime ministerships of John A. Macdonald and Wilfrid Laurier have been replaced many times with new forms of media and journalism. The chapters that follow partially illustrate the long histories of these players of Canadian elections.

PART THREE: THE CAMPAIGN

As mentioned, a campaign is an attempt to mobilize people to vote in support of a candidate or political party. Compared to election campaigns in the United States, Canadian campaigns are short. Given the primary system for selecting presidential candidates for the Republican and the Democratic parties, US campaigns can essentially begin more than 500 days before election day (Friedman 2016). The *Canada Elections Act* establishes the official campaign period as being between 37 and 51 days, although in 2018, the CEA was amended to establish a pre-election period, which starts on June 30 and ends on the day before the general election. In both periods, political parties, candidates, and third parties are subject to spending limits and reporting obligations for certain regulated activities. The pre-election period exists for fixed-date elections (see below). To date, the 2019 election has been the only election with a pre-election period.

There are two different interpretations of the objective of an election campaign. From the perspective of voters, the objective is to gather information and learn about political parties, their leaders, their candidates, and their policies. For many Canadians, a campaign is the one time when they give their sustained interest to politics and policy discussions. Campaigns are a time when voters can look retrospectively; that is, look back in time and assess whether the incumbent government did a good job. Voters may also look prospectively; that is, they look forward and attempt to evaluate the promises of the parties and candidates. Campaigns may also be about participation. For some citizens, they might volunteer or be involved in a local campaign, in third-party activities, or even be a poll worker for Elections Canada. From the perspective of voters, a campaign is an important democratic moment for the country.

For political parties and candidates, the objective of a campaign is very different. In general, the goal here is to win more votes than one's opponent. That said, this might be overly simplistic given Canada's multiparty system. For the two largest parties, the Liberals and the Conservatives, winning a majority government is prized, though there are likely times when achieving a minority government will do. For the smaller parties (e.g., the New Democratic Party, Bloc Québécois, or Greens), the goal might be to increase their number of seats or percentage of votes from the last election, to become an official party (12 seats in the House of Commons), or to meet the threshold to receive financial support. In 2021, for example, the People's Party of Canada did not win a seat in the House. However, the party increased their vote share by 3.3%, making it eligible for significant election expense reimbursements. While the specific goal for each party will be different (Flanagan 2010), they all seek to maximize their vote share. This might seem less noble, but it is no less important. At the end of the day, an election must result in a decision about who will govern. Regardless of the goal, parties attempt to frame their leader, candidates, and policies as the most suitable for the country during a campaign. As such, campaigns are essentially communication events (Medvic 2021) or competitions to set the agenda (Gidengil et al. 2002).

Indeed, the national campaign is sometimes described as an "air war" because messages are mediated through news media, broadcast technologies (radio and television), and, more recently, digital technologies such as social media (Carty, Cross, and Young 2001). Chapter 11 explores the ways in which Canada's parties attempt to inform, mobilize, and ultimately persuade voters using different modalities and media. The importance of political communication in Canadian campaigns is reflected in the related campaign finances. That is, campaign advertising ate up a significant share of expenses; research shows that in the five federal elections between 2004 and 2019, advertising assumed more than 50% of total election expenses for the three largest parties in each election (Rose 2016; Small 2022b).

As discussed in Chapter 12, another aspect of the air campaign are the leaders' debates. Even though Canadians do not directly elect a prime minister, at least two debates (one in each official language) are held between the leaders of the main parties. The leaders' debates very much incorporate the two different objectives of the campaign mentioned earlier. Attracting a wide viewership, the leaders' debates are an opportunity for Canadians to see all the main party leaders in the same place to discuss the very same political issues. For the leaders themselves, the debates are a strategic opportunity to contrast themselves, personally and in terms of policy, with the others.

Polling is another aspect of the modern campaign arsenal, especially for the national party organizations. Taras (1990) once described polling as the "basic antenna" that guides the campaign. While it is costly, polling helps a party maximize political support by identifying who the party should target, on which issues the party should focus, and what sort of messages should be delivered to the target audience. Chapter 13 discusses polling in campaigns in more detail.

To what extent do television ads, tweets, or debates work in changing the hearts and minds of Canadians? Answering the question of whether campaigns matter, also known as campaign effects, is complicated. Using both provincial and federal election survey data, Fournier and colleagues (2019) found that campaign activities "powerfully" affect only around 20% of voters; other voters are only moderately affected by things that occurred during campaigns. While this is not overwhelming, these authors note that in some campaigns this number is enough to tip the scales toward one party or another. Nevertheless, those working in campaigns believe that what they do matters a great deal, as evidenced by the effort put into campaigning at both the national and local levels in terms of resources (personnel and financial). Overall, the chapters in this section will explore the various techniques, strategies, and tools used by parties and local candidates in their attempts to attain the ultimate goal of maximizing electoral support.

PART FOUR: THE PEOPLE

This section focuses on the electoral participation of Canadians. It includes chapters that summarize and expand on why Canadians participate in election campaigns in the ways they do, with a special emphasis on voting behaviour. Further, one chapter explores why Canadians do not vote and how turnout rates have changed over time, as well as the implications this has for understandings of Canadian democracy. This section also reflects on electoral participation and voting behaviour by including chapters on the specific participation of women (Chapter 16), racialized communities (Chapter 17), Indigenous peoples (Chapter 18), and 2SLGBTQ+ people (Chapter 19) in elections. Both candidates and voters from these groups are addressed.

We can think of political participation as any activity that seeks to affect the outcome of an election or some party or government policy (Johnston 2020). The range of activities considered as political participation is therefore quite large. In election campaigns, Canadians may participate by volunteering to hand out literature, knock on doors, attend rallies, or get out the vote on election day. Putting one's name forward to run for office is another – perhaps the ultimate! – form of political participation. But even comparably easy activities such as following the news during election campaigns, talking with friends or family about the campaign, or trying to persuade others to vote a certain way all count as political participation.

Voting is the most foundational form of political participation. In a liberal democracy like Canada, governments receive legitimacy to govern and to implement their election promises from the votes cast during election campaigns. It therefore becomes problematic when people who have the right to vote decline to do so, and the voter turnout rate declines as a result. Turnout is covered in this volume in Chapter 15. Turnout rates have varied across Canadian history but, like those in other developed democracies, are experiencing a long-term decline: from historic highs in elections held during the 1950s and 1960s, the turnout rate in the most recent (2021) federal election was 62.2% of electors. A range of institutional and campaign-specific factors shape individuals' likelihood to vote; for example, people are more likely to turn out to vote if they feel their vote will make a difference to the overall result. Following the 2021 election, Statistics Canada (2022) surveyed Canadians and found that 43% of those surveyed who did not vote did so for "everyday life or health reasons": they were too busy or otherwise indisposed to cast their ballots. A further 32% simply were not interested enough in politics to vote.

A key question related to voting is who is entitled to vote, and is there widespread access to voting available to those with the right to do so? In Canada, access to the vote has democratized across the course of the nineteenth and twentieth centuries from being a privilege bestowed on those men who were affluent enough to own land or pay taxes to a right entrenched in the *Charter of Rights and Freedoms* that is available to almost all Canadians (Elections Canada 2020). This evolution in the franchise was driven both by increasing democratization but also by external events that jolted the status quo. World War I, for example, saw an expansion of the franchise as the government, through the *Wartime Elections Act*, extended the right to vote to women related to Canadian military members. The cynical goal was to expand the franchise to people the government thought would be favourable to its re-election. The suffragette movement pushed for full equality for women throughout the early years of Canadian history and, in 1918, the franchise in federal elections was extended to all women 21 years of age or older. However, the full voting rights of other peoples, including Indigenous peoples and Canadians of Asian origin, would only occur much later. As noted, the 1982 Charter entrenches voting rights, and it has subsequently been used to remove remaining limits on the franchise, including on prisoners and on Canadians living outside the country. The CEA thus defines an elector as "[e]very person who is a Canadian citizen and who on polling day is 18 years of age or older." Canada's franchise is extremely wide, limited only by age and citizenship. This is the case in all levels of government, though there have been proposals in some Canadian municipalities on extending voting rights to permanent residents (Pelley 2018).

In addition to whether Canadians vote, political scientists are deeply concerned with why Canadians vote for the parties and candidates they do. What can help explain why one Canadian votes for the Conservative Party while another casts their ballot for the Liberal Party? This is the study of voting behaviour in the Canadian context. In Canada, vote choice is often a regional matter, with federal parties enjoying geographically defined regions of strong support that are then amplified by the FPTP electoral system (Pruysers, Sayers, and Czarnecki 2020). Regionalized vote choice has ripple effects across Canadian politics by, for example, producing government caucuses with clear regional biases. Increasingly, as Canada has become an increasingly urban country throughout the twentieth and twenty-first centuries, there has been more attention on the divide between urban and rural Canadians, along with the consequences of this division for vote choice. Chapter 20 explores this divide in more detail.

When explaining vote choice in Canadian elections, political scientists have often followed the bloc-recursive model, which holds that some factors are more proximate to the vote than others. Long-term factors (such as a voter's social background) shape short-term factors (such as the voter's evaluations of the parties' leaders or candidates), which in turn lead to vote choice. In her recent review of the voting behaviour literature related to Canadian elections, Elisabeth Gidengil (2022) covers a range of long- and short-term factors that shape Canadians' vote choice: social background characteristics, ideological orientations, party identification, economic evaluations of the incumbent government, evaluations of both leaders and local candidates, and strategic considerations. Chapter 14 covers the voting behaviour of Canadians in detail.

Old concerns about issues such as regionalism in shaping vote choice in Canadian elections have given way to new concerns about participation – and barriers to participation – from members of previously marginalized groups in Canadian society. While there is an old and well-developed literature related to women and barriers to political participation in Canada, the same is not true for the study of other groups, including racialized Canadians, Indigenous peoples, and 2SLGBTQ+ Canadians. Accordingly, we include chapters that explore the political participation of all these people in Canadian elections, as well as barriers to participation that are specific to each of them.

PART FIVE: LANDMARK CANADIAN ELECTIONS

The final section of this volume is dedicated to comparably short reflections on several key Canadian elections throughout Canadian history. Since our approach to exploring elections in Canada is both conceptually and historically broader than most other analyses, it makes sense to go back into Canadian history and delve deeply into elections that have had particularly notable consequences for the future and direction of the country. We expand on the 1917, 1921, 1988, 1993, 2011, and 2015 elections because we believe each of these elections held consequences for the development of Canadian democracy and the future conduct of Canadian elections. Some of these cases involved party system change, in others institutional innovation occurred. In each case, we employ the broad knowledge developed in previous chapters to better understand these pivotal elections in Canadian history. Overall, this section applies in practice our approach of elections as a process.

HOW DO CANADIAN ELECTIONS HAPPEN?

While the chapters that follow will go into detail regarding many of the key components of elections and campaigns in federal politics, we conclude this chapter by starting at the beginning—that is, by sketching out the process under which a federal election happens. This process is remarkably complex. Despite our earlier conversation about the Charter and the *Canada Elections Act*, constitutional conventions are central to understanding this process. Drawn from our Westminster parliamentary heritage, conventions are widely accepted, unwritten, and informal customs that bind political actors to a traditional practice. The governor general calls an election by formally dissolving Parliament and instructing the chief electoral officer to issue the writs. In practice, the prime minister decides when an election is called by advising the governor general. This occurs under three circumstances. The first is the fixed-date election. In 2006, the Conservative government under Stephen Harper passed a law providing for fixed election dates. As per the CEA, once an election is held, the following election will be set for the third Monday in October, four calendar years in the future. Only two of five elections held since the law was enacted have been on fixed dates (2015 and 2019). All provinces also have fixed-date laws; Nova Scotia only made this change in 2021. It is crucial to point out that the fixed-date law does not alter the role of the governor general in elections. As section 56.1 (1) of the CEA notes, "Nothing in this section affects the powers of the Governor General, including the power to dissolve Parliament at the Governor General's discretion." As such, the prime minister's ability to call an election at any time remains intact.

This then leads to the second circumstance under which a federal election can be held. A prime minister can ask the governor general to call an election at any time the prime minister chooses. For most of the elections in Canadian history, this is how they occurred. When a government has more than half the seats in the House of Common, or a majority government, the prime minister has tremendous latitude over when to call an election. A prime minister might call an election early, sometimes called a "snap election," when they feel public opinion is in their favour. This was seen as the reasons for the 1997 and 2021 elections. However, both Prime Ministers Jean Chrétien and Justin Trudeau did not see their seat totals rise as a result of this cynical use of these powers. Indeed, snap elections have always been controversial because the governing party was seen to be trying to capitalize on electoral circumstances. With fixed dates, the governing party seems to be also breaking the spirit of the law. However, the ability of the prime minister or a premier to request an election has been upheld several times in Canada, most recently in New Brunswick (Bowden 2021). The interest group Democracy Watch asked the New Brunswick Court of Queen's Bench whether Premier Blaine Higgs violated the province's fixed-date election requirements when he called the 2020 election.[2] The court ruled against Democracy Watch, stating that the provincial legislation (similar to the federal legislation) explicitly does not change the power of the lieutenant-governor. Democracy Watch has appealed the decision. However, others suggest that fixed election dates are inconsistent with a parliamentary form of government (Desserud 2005), in which the executive must retain the confidence of the legislature.

The third circumstance is related to the convention of responsible government as central to Canadian government. According to Aucoin and colleagues (2004, 22), responsible government "entails one rule – government is responsible to and must always have the confidence of the majority of elected members of the House of Commons." In the context of calling an election, it means that if the government loses confidence, the prime minister must inform the governor general that they can no longer command the confidence of the House. In most cases, the prime minister will advise the governor general to call a general election; the governor general then dissolves Parliament and instructs the chief electoral officer to issue the writs.[3] This has occurred six times in Canadian history, most recently in 2011, when Stephen Harper's government lost the confidence of the House. However, it remains the discretion of the governor general to take the advice of the prime minister. If they decline, the government must resign, so that a new government can be formed from within the House of Commons. Recently this occurred in British Columbia following the 2017 provincial election (Shaw and Zussman 2018). The incumbent Liberal government under Premier Christy Clark lost a confidence vote on the Speech from the Throne. Clark asked for a dissolution of the legislature and an election. Lieutenant-Governor Judith Guichon declined and asked NDP leader John Horgan to form government. The NDP governed with support of the Greens until 2020. Something similar occurred federally in 1926, in what is known as the "King-Byng affair." In this situation, Liberal prime minister William Lyon Mackenzie King did not lose a vote of non-confidence mainly because he asked the governor general, Lord Byng, to dissolve Parliament and call an election *before* the scheduled confidence vote. Lord Byng refused King and invited Conservative leader Arthur Meighen to form the government. With the support of the Progressive Party, Meighen would have the ability to maintain the confidence of the House. However, Meighen's Conservative government lost confidence after five days. He was forced to ask for an election, and Byng acquiesced. It is worth pointing out here that this election call circumstance is intimately tied to minority governments. When a government does not hold the majority of seats in the legislature, it is difficult (but not impossible) for a government to maintain confidence. Some prime ministers with minority governments will enter formalized alliances with other parties to ensure confidence. These are called confidence-and-supply agreements. This is what occurred in the aforementioned situation in BC, but also in 2022 with the Liberal government and the NDP (Prime Minister of Canada 2022). More commonly, however, prime ministers with minority governments will work with opposition parties on a case-by-case basis to maintain confidence. That said, because of the convention of responsible government, minority governments are electorally precarious, with most such governments lasting less than two years. All of this means that Canada can, at times, have frequent elections. Between 2000 and 2021, eight federal elections were held, compared to six in the United States, where fixed dates are constitutionalized.

It should be clear from this discussion that elections and campaigns in Canada are complex events involving numerous rules, processes, and actors. The goal of this book is to clarify this process. As mentioned, we've organized the text around two key themes: evolution and democracy. The way that federal elections have operated in light of these two themes has not been static. In celebration of the 100th anniversary of the creation of Elections Canada, the electoral management body revised their excellent book *A History of the Vote in Canada* (2020), where they note:

> Canada has always been an electoral democracy. As a nation, we haven't had to fight for the right to vote. There has never been any revolutionary bloodshed nor a Berlin Wall to tear down. Yet, electoral democracy as we know and understand it today is very different from what it was 150 or even 50 years

ago. Things we take for granted – both in the sense that, for us, they are necessary features of democracy and in the sense that we expect them to unfold as a matter of course – were not always so.

We concur with this sentiment. As Canada approaches its 45th federal election, this book provides an excellent opportunity to reflect on the multitude of processes that have guided the functioning of elections and campaigns but also the people and the players who have participated in these processes.

NOTES

1 Those looking for analysis on provincial elections should consider reading: *Big Worlds: Politics and Elections in the Canadian Provinces and Territories* by Jared Wesley; *Fighting for Votes: Parties, the Media and Voters in the 2011 Ontario Election* by Cross et al.; and the short reviews of provincial elections published in the *Canadian Political Science Review.* Those interested in municipal elections should consider work produced using the Canadian Municipal Election Study (CMES) dataset.
2 *Democracy Watch v. New Brunswick (Attorney General)*, 2021 NBQB 233 (CanLII), https://canlii.ca/t/jkw6h.
3 The phrase "dropping the writ" is commonly used to describe the calling of an election by the prime minister. However, the phrase is problematic. Elections Canada states that a writ is "a formal written order instructing the returning officer in each electoral district to hold an election to elect a member of Parliament. The writ: (1) specifies the day by which the names of candidates must be entered into nomination; (2) sets a polling date; and (3) sets a date on which the writ, with the name of the successful candidate noted on the back, is to be returned to the Chief Electoral Officer." This means that there are as many writs as there are electoral districts. Moreover, the prime minister has no role.

REFERENCES

Aucoin, Peter, Jennifer Smith, and Geoff Dinsdale. 2004. "Responsible Government: Clarifying Essentials, Dispelling Myths and Exploring Change." Ottawa: Canadian Centre for Management Development. https://publications.gc.ca/collections/Collection/SC94-107-2004E.pdf.

Blais, André, Elisabeth Gidengil, Richard Nadeau, and Neil Nevitte. 2002. *Anatomy of a Liberal Victory.* Toronto: University of Toronto Press.

Bowden, J. W. J. 2021. "The Courts Uphold the Correct Interpretation of Fixed-Date Election Laws for the Fifth Time Since 2009." *Parliamentum* (blog). December 29. https://parliamentum.org/2021/12/29 /the-courts-uphold-the-correct-interpretation-of-fixed-date-election-laws-for-the-fifth-time-since-2009/.

Carty, R. Kenneth. 2002. "The Politics of Tecumseh Corners: Canadian Political Parties as Franchise Organizations." *Canadian Journal of Political Science/Revue Canadienne de Science Politique* 35 (4): 723–45. https://doi.org/10.1017/S0008423902778402.

Carty, R. Kenneth, William Cross, and Lisa Young. 2001. *Rebuilding Canadian Party Politics.* Vancouver: UBC Press.

Clarke, Harold D., Jane Jenson, Lawrence LeDuc, and Jon H. Pammett. 2019. *Absent Mandate: Interpreting Change in Canadian Politics.* Toronto: University of Toronto Press.

Courtney, John C. 2004. *Elections.* Vancouver: UBC Press.

Cross, William. 2004. *Political Parties.* Vancouver: UBC Press.

———. 2018. "Understanding Power-Sharing within Political Parties: Stratarchy as Mutual Interdependence between the Party in the Centre and the Party on the Ground." *Government and Opposition* 53 (2): 205–30. https://doi.org/10.1017/gov.2016.22.

Crandall, Erin, and Andrea Lawlor. 2018. "Third Party Policy and Electoral Participation after Harper v. Canada: A Triumph of Egalitarianism." In *Policy Change, Courts, and the Canadian Constitution*, edited by Emmett Macfarlane. Toronto: University of Toronto Press.

Dawood, Yasmin. 2012. "Electoral Fairness and the Law of Democracy: A Structural Rights Approach to Judicial Review." *University of Toronto Law Journal* 62: 499–561. https://doi.org/10.3138/utlj.62.4.499.

Department of Justice. 2021. "Charterpedia – Section 3 – Democratic Rights." January 25. https://www.justice.gc.ca/eng/csj-sjc/rfc-dlc/ccrf-ccdl/check/art3.html.

Desserud, Don. 2005. "Fixed-Date Elections: Improvement or New Problems?" *Electoral Insight (2004 General Election)* 7 (1): 48–53.

Eldersveld, Samuel James. 1964. *Political Parties; a Behavioral Analysis*. Rand McNally Political Science Series. Chicago: Rand McNally.

Elections Canada. 2020. *A History of the Vote in Canada*. 3rd ed. https://www.elections.ca/content.aspx?section=res&dir=his&document=index&lang=e.

Flanagan, Thomas. 2010. "Campaign Strategy: Triage and the Concentration of Resources." In *Election*, edited by Heather MacIvor. Toronto: Emond Montgomery Toronto.

Fournier, Patrick, Fred Cutler, and Stuart Soroka. 2019. "Who Responds to Election Campaigns? The Two-Moderator Model Revisited." In *Duty and Choice: The Evolution of the Study of Voting and Voters*, edited by Peter John Loewen and Daniel Rubenson, 129–68. Toronto: University of Toronto Press.

Friedman, Uri. 2016. "American Elections: How Long Is Too Long?" *The Atlantic*. October 5. https://www.theatlantic.com/international/archive/2016/10/us-election-longest-world/501680/.

Giasson, Thierry, and Alex Marland, eds. 2020. *Inside the Campaign: Managing Elections in Canada*. Vancouver: UBC Press.

Gidengil, Elisabeth. 2022. "Voting Behaviour in Canada: The State of the Discipline." *Canadian Journal of Political* Science 55 (4): 916–38. https://doi.org/10.1017/S0008423922000531.

Gidengil, Elisabeth, Andre Blais, Neil Nevitte, and Richard Nadeau. 2002. "Priming and Campaign Context: Evidence from Recent Canadian Elections." In *Do Political Campaigns Matter? Campaign Effects in Elections and Referendums*, edited by David M. Farrell and Rhudiger Schmitt-Beck, 76–90. London: Routledge.

Gidengil, Elisabeth, Neil Nevitte, André Blais, Joanna Everitt, and Patrick Fournier. 2012. *Dominance and Decline: Making Sense of Recent Canadian Elections*. Toronto: University of Toronto Press.

Johnston, Richard. 2020. "Political Participation in Canada." *The Canadian Encyclopedia*, December 14. https://www.thecanadianencyclopedia.ca/en/article/political-participation.

Johnston, Richard, Andre Blais, André, Henry E Brady, and Jean Crête. 1992. *Letting the People Decide: Dynamics of a Canadian Election*. Montreal-Kingston: McGill-Queen's University Press.

Katz, Richard S. 1997. *Democracy and Elections* [Oxford Political Theory]. New York: Oxford University Press.

MacIvor, Heather. 2013. *Canadian Politics and Government in the Charter Era*. Don Mills, Ontario: Oxford University Press.

Marland, Alex, and Thierry Giasson, eds. 2015. *Canadian Election Analysis 2015: Communication, Strategy, and Democracy*. Vancouver: UBC Press/Samara. https://www.ubcpress.ca/asset/1712/election-analysis2015-final-v3-web-copy.pdf.

——, eds. 2022. *Inside the Local Campaign: Constituency Elections in Canada*. Vancouver: UBC Press.

Medvic, Stephen K. 2021. *Campaigns and Elections: Players and Processes*. Milton: Taylor and Francis. https://doi.org/10.4324/9781003125099.

Nevitte, Neil., André Blais, Richard Nadeau, and Elisabeth Gidengil. 1999. *Unsteady State: The 1997 Canadian Federal Election*. Toronto: Oxford University Press.

O'Neill, Brenda. 2009. "Democracy in Action, Political Participation and Citizens' Power." In *Studying Politics: An Introduction to Political Science*, edited by Rand Dyck, 282–315. Toronto: Nelson Education Ltd.

Pammett, Jon H., and Christopher Dornan. 2016. *The Canadian Federal Election of 2015*. Toronto: Dundurn.
———, eds. 2020. *The Canadian Federal Election of 2019*. Montreal-Kingston: McGill-Queen's University Press.
———, eds. 2022. *The Canadian Federal Election of 2021*. Montreal-Kingston: McGill-Queen's University Press.
Pelley, Lauren. 2018. "This Toronto Man Lives Here, Works Here, Shops Here, and Pays Taxes Here – So Why Can't He Vote Here?" CBC News. July 15. https://www.cbc.ca/news/canada/toronto/pr-voting -toronto-1.4742557.
Prime Minister of Canada. 2022. "Delivering for Canadians Now, A Supply and Confidence Agreement." Prime Minister of Canada. March 22. https://pm.gc.ca/en/news/news-releases/2022/03/22/delivering -canadians-now.
Pruysers, Scott, Anthony Sayers, and Lucas Czarnecki. 2020. "Nationalization and Regionalization in the Canadian Party System, 1867–2015." *Canadian Journal of Political Science* 53 (1): 151–69. https://doi .org/10.1017/S0008423919000957.
Rose, Jonathan. 2016. "The Pre-Eminence of Advertising in Canadian Elections." *Jonathan Rose* (blog). July 8. https://jonathanrose.ca/canadian-politics/electionads/.
Safire, William. 2008. *Safire's Political Dictionary*. New York: Oxford University Press.
Shaw, Rob, and Richard Zussman. 2018. *A Matter of Confidence: The Inside Story of the Political Battle for BC*. Victoria: Heritage House Publishing.
Small, Tamara A. 2022a. "Policing Partisan Self-Interest? The Charter and Election Law in Canada." In *Constitutional Crossroads: Reflections on Charter Rights, Reconciliation, and Change*, edited by Kate Puddister and Emmett Macfarlane, 143–59. Vancouver: UBC Press.
———. 2022b. "Did Digital Kill the Television Star? Political Advertising in Canadian Elections." *Canadian Political Science Association. Remote Conference*, May 31–June 3.
Small, Tamara A., Alex Marland, and Thierry Giasson. 2014. "The Triangulation of Canadian Political Communication." In *Political Communication in Canada: Meet the Press and Tweet the Rest*, 3–23. Vancouver: UBC Press.
Statistics Canada. 2022. "Reasons for Not Voting in the Federal Election, September 20, 2021." *The Daily*. February 16. https://www150.statcan.gc.ca/n1/daily-quotidien/220216/dq220216d-eng.htm.
Taras, David. 1990. *The Newsmakers: The Media's Influence on Canadian Politics*. Scarborough: Nelson Canada.
Waddell, Christopher, and Christopher Dornan. 2006. "The Media and the Campaign." In *The Canadian Federal Election of 2006*, edited by Chris Dornan and Jon H. Pammett, 220–52. Toronto: Dundurn.
Young, Lisa. 2016. "Money, Politics and the Canadian Party System." In *Canadian Parties in Transition: Recent Trends and New Paths for Research*, 4th ed., edited by A. Brian Tanguay and Alain-G. Gagnon, 28–43. Toronto: University of Toronto Press.
Young, Lisa, and Joanna Everitt. 2004. *Advocacy Groups*. Vancouver: UBC Press.

PART ONE

The Institutional Setting

CHAPTER TWO

Canadian Election Administration in Transition

Keith Archer

INTRODUCTION

Elections in Canada at the federal, provincial, and territorial levels of government are administered by a set of institutional arrangements that differ in important respects from their counterparts in other democracies, such as the United States or the United Kingdom. Furthermore, there are some striking similarities in the way elections are organized and administered at the federal and provincial/territorial levels, even though the written constitution is largely silent on election administrative matters. Notwithstanding these similarities, there are key differences among the federal, provincial, and territorial levels of governments in Canada in the legislative frameworks in place that provide the structure, authority, and detailed rules and regulations for elections. In short, in Canada, it is the federal government that determines the rules under which federal elections are conducted, and provincial and territorial governments that do so for elections under their jurisdiction.

This chapter sets out to make the following arguments. First, Canada has a distinctive model for administering elections that has both strengths and weaknesses. Second, virtually all aspects of Canada's election administration have changed over time. Some of the changes, like introducing regulations in electoral financing in the 1970s and thereafter, have been highly salient and public, whereas other changes – such as changing the structure of the election office or appointing election officials – have passed with less notice. Furthermore, Canadian election agencies are currently in a period of profound and unprecedented change, in which many of the basic procedures for organizing elections and for casting and counting ballots, are being reconsidered. This is an exciting time for election administrators in Canada. Third, in conferring authority and trust in those elected to office, election agencies in turn rely on the trust of voters and other political stakeholders. We reflect on the importance of trust in elections. At the outset, it should be acknowledged that I write from my vantage point as both an emeritus professor of political science and also from my experience as chief electoral officer of British Columbia from 2011 to 2018. Both of these positions inform my understanding of election administration in Canada.

DEFINITION: THE CANADIAN MODEL OF ELECTION ADMINISTRATION

At the time of Confederation in 1867, Canadian election administration was "federalized," in that the federal government was responsible for administering federal elections and provincial governments did so for provincial elections. Despite this, in elections conducted shortly after Confederation, the federal government used provincial electoral laws on matters such as voter eligibility to determine who could vote in a federal election (see Elections Canada 2021). Variation in eligibility requirements among the provinces meant that Canadians in some provinces were denied the franchise based on characteristics that in other provinces would allow them to vote. And, of course, the franchise was highly restrictive in the first 50 years of Confederation, in which voting was limited to males 21 years of age and older, usually with property requirements, and often with racial or ethnic exclusions as well.[1] Elections during this period were organized and run by the government of the day, with many examples of governments introducing provisions for partisan advantage (Elections Canada 2021).

A major change to election administration in Canada occurred in 1920, with the passage of the *Dominion Elections Act*, a precursor to the current *Canada Elections Act* (Elections Canada 2021). This major federal legislation removed any remaining prohibitions on the right of women to vote, removed all property requirements from voting, and created a new independent federal officer – the chief electoral officer, who was charged with overseeing the administration of elections. In the subsequent decades, the provinces would follow suit, creating their own independent chief electoral officer of the legislature to administer elections (Boda and Archer 2023).

To understand the unique role of the chief electoral officer (CEO) in Canada, it is useful to compare election administrative bodies in several countries. In the Canadian model, the CEO is expected to be a nonpartisan and independent officer of the legislature.[2] Canada has 14 chief electoral officers, one for federal elections and one for each of the 10 provinces and the three territories. Although different jurisdictions use different approaches to appoint CEOs, each method is intended to ensure that input from multiple parties is considered in the process. For example, in British Columbia, where I served as chief electoral officer, the legislature appoints a bipartisan or multipartisan committee, and the committee must make a unanimous recommendation to the legislative assembly for a nomination to proceed. In Alberta there is also the creation of a multiparty committee, although a nomination can proceed to the legislative assembly based on a majority vote of the committee.

At the federal level, the appointment of the CEO proceeds through a vetting process established by the government of the day, with the provision that opposition parties are briefed on the recommended appointment and have opportunities for input into the selection. In each instance, the principle is that the appointment should be generally acceptable to all parties. As a second provision on the independence of the CEO, in all jurisdictions in Canada, the CEO, and in many instances the deputy or assistant CEOs, are not allowed to vote. This provision is intended to emphasize the principle that the CEO has no personal stake in the outcome of the election.

In addition to the appointment of the CEO, it is useful to understand the role and scope of the position and how it differs from other jurisdictions. The CEO in each jurisdiction in Canada exercises their authority by maintaining an ongoing office, known officially as the office of the chief electoral officer but generally operating under the name Elections Canada, Elections British Columbia, Elections Ontario, and so on. These offices are staffed with full-time, permanent public servants, often organized under two broad domains – electoral operations and electoral finance. The staff in electoral operations are responsible for delivering scheduled and unscheduled electoral events – general elections, by-elections, referendums, and plebiscites. For each electoral event, the offices recruit, train, and deploy hundreds or many thousands of temporary workers– to establish field offices, set up polling places, administer and count votes, and report the results.

In contrast, the staff in electoral finance are engaged in the registration of political parties and candidates; training of party officials and candidates in election financing laws and requirements; monitoring of election advertising by political parties, candidates, and third-party advertisers; and receiving and reviewing election-related and annual financial disclosure reports by political parties, as well as election-related disclosure reports by candidates and third-party advertisers. The number of permanent staff in election offices varies considerably among jurisdictions, from as few as three or four staff in Elections Nunavut or Elections PEI to about 80 in Elections BC, several hundred in Elections Ontario, and nearly a thousand in Elections Canada. Canadian election administration is relatively centralized within a federal structure. There are separate agencies for administering election matters at the federal and provincial/territorial levels, but within each level, the agency is a one-stop shop, administering matters consistently across the jurisdiction.

A brief review of some other democracies helps highlight the unique features of the Canadian model. In the United States, responsibility for administering voter registration and voting in national elections is assigned to the states (Boda and Archer 2023, 110). There is no equivalent of Elections Canada (which administers voting to all Canadians in federal elections) in the United States. Instead, the election agency for the state of Michigan administers the ballots for federal elections for voters from Michigan, the agency for Texas does so for voters from Texas, and so on. National elections are synchronized with state elections, so that on election day in the US, one is voting for members to national office, such as president, senator, and House of Representatives, and also for state and local offices, such as governor, the state House of Representatives, and even for local offices such as county sheriff or judge. Furthermore, each state may vary in the provision of resources, and thus in election machinery, from one district or one county to another. Therefore, in some states, people who live in more affluent areas may have more resources devoted to election administration than voters in less affluent areas, leading to differences in, for example, lineups and wait times for voting.

In the US, elections are run through the offices of the secretary of state for each state, who is a member of the statewide administration. Therefore, if the governor of the state is a Republican, the secretary of state also will be Republican. Rather than having a principle of nonpartisanship as in Canada, the US uses a system of partisan election administration. Recently, political strategists have discussed the idea of contesting party nominations for secretary of state, to elect people with stronger partisan beliefs to these positions, with the idea of electing a person who may be more likely to support the overturning of an election if they do not agree with the outcome. Whereas the US does not have a unified agency for administering the vote in elections, it does have a national agency, the Federal Electoral Commission (FEC), that is responsible for overseeing electoral finance. The FEC is a bipartisan commission, with equal numbers of Republican and Democratic members, although many analysts suggest its bipartisanship has led it to be less active and successful than one might expect (see, for example, Skahan 2018).

Election administration in the United Kingdom also has a decidedly local character. The UK has a unitary form of government, rather than federal as in Canada and the US, and therefore there are no equivalents of provincial or state governments. Instead, the major level of government below the national government are the local governments, known as local councils. Although there is a national agency for elections, called the Electoral Commission, its role is solely advisory – it can make recommendations on electoral matters, but has no responsibility for administering ballots. Instead, national elections in the UK are run by local councils, although unlike the US these elections are not synchronized with local elections.

As in the US, the relative affluence of local councils can affect the funds available for administering voting, and thus inequalities in voting opportunities may arise. In addition, as noted, the advisory role of the Electoral Commission can impact the implementation of change and modernization initiatives, since the Commission does not have the authority to implement its recommendations independent of successfully advocating for legislative change or by providing resources that local councils choose to adopt.

Election agencies are the face of democracy for many citizens. They play an important role in determining whether there are administrative barriers to voting. The right to vote is the centrepiece of democratic government. The election agency can strengthen democracy by focusing on two seemingly contradictory functions – making voting easy for everyone entitled to vote, but also preventing everyone not entitled to vote from doing so.

THE EVOLVING CHARACTER OF CANADIAN ELECTION ADMINISTRATION

Some elements of Canadian election administration look remarkably like the features in place 100 years ago or more. For example, for many voters, the act of voting involves presenting themselves at their assigned poll location on election day, where they will identify themselves to two election officials – named the deputy returning officer and poll clerk – who will then either write their name and address in a poll book or place a line through their name (thereby "striking them off"). Following this procedure they will be handed a simple paper ballot with the names (and party affiliation) of the candidates in their electoral district, using a pencil they will place an X in the box next to the name of their chosen candidate, fold the paper ballot, and return it to the deputy returning officer, who then removes the numbered "counterfoil," following which the voter deposits their ballot into the secure ballot box. At the close of voting on election day, these two election officials then count all ballots in their ballot box and report the results to the returning officer for their constituency.

While these features of Canadian elections at the federal and provincial/territorial levels have been consistent over time, many of them are currently in the process of being substantially changed. Thus, in the following review, we discuss changing administrative practices (and in some cases, changing legislation) in the following areas: voter registration, the appointment of election officials, administering the vote, and electoral financing and advertising.

Voter Registration[3]

One of the responsibilities of an election agency is to provide ballots only to people who are eligible to vote. In addition, the agency must have procedures to ensure that any elector can vote only once. To ensure that elections are conducted efficiently, election agencies normally separate the functions of confirming a voter's eligibility from the functions related to issuing a ballot. To do so, a voters' list is created, which includes the name and residential address of all those who are eligible and registered to vote in the election. For the first 100+ years of Confederation, Elections Canada (and its predecessors) created a new voters' list for each election by conducting door-to-door enumeration of all households in the country (see Courtney 2005). Most provincial and territorial election agencies did likewise. However, by the 1930s, British Columbia adopted a "permanent voter register," an ongoing list of eligible voters in the province that was retained and updated between elections. In the 1980s, Elections Canada likewise established the National Register of Electors (NRoE), an ongoing list of eligible voters that it maintains today largely through data-sharing agreements with several federal and provincial agencies, such as provincial driver's licence registries, provincial and territorial election agencies, vital statistics agencies, and others. As Elections Canada adopted the continuous voter registration procedure and agreed to share its data with provincial and territorial election agencies, the latter tended to adopt this method and stopped door-to-door enumeration in 1997 (for an example of a recent change to a permanent voter register, see Elections Saskatchewan 2013).

Voter registration, like voting itself, is an optional procedure in Canada. Although some jurisdictions, most famously Australia, require eligible voter registration and voting (failure to do so can result in being fined), in Canada eligible voters can choose whether they want to be registered and can choose to vote or to abstain from voting. Despite the voluntary nature of voter registration, most jurisdictions have very high rates of registration among eligible voters, with more than 90% of eligible voters registered.[4] Furthermore, most jurisdictions in Canada provide the opportunity to register at the polling place and then provide a ballot.

The change in Canada from using door-to-door enumeration for the creation of a voters' list has led to a considerable increase in the ongoing costs, while at the same time improving the overall quality of the voters' list. Although it is difficult to estimate the exact cost of maintaining a permanent list of electors in a jurisdiction, my experience in British Columbia was that roughly between 1/4 and 1/5 of the permanent staff were focused almost exclusively on maintaining the register. There is an inevitable duplication of effort between the federal and provincial/territorial agencies in having to each maintain a list of the same electors. There have been, and continue to be, ongoing discussions among Canadian election officials to implement ways to make their data sharing as efficient as possible.

There are several ongoing challenges with the voter registration system in Canada. First, since Canada lacks a system of national registration for all residents, and since the country does not have a universal, government-issued identification card, election agencies must continue to devote considerable resources to developing and maintaining a voter register. There is a fine balance between making voting easy and accessible and ensuring electoral integrity, in which elections are decided by eligible voters casting one and only one ballot.

The requirements to vote in most jurisdictions in Canada are that one is a Canadian citizen, is 18 years of age or older, and has fulfilled the residency requirement in the jurisdiction, such as having lived in the jurisdiction for six months. To be included on the voter register, one must attest to the fact that they meet the eligibility requirements – that is, typically when a person registers to vote they do not have to produce documentary evidence of their age, citizenship, or length of residency. Instead, they must attest that they meet the requirements, with the provision that false attestations are punishable by fines and/or imprisonment.

A second ongoing challenge with voter registration is the lag time that exists between a person first becoming eligible to vote and their inclusion as a newly eligible voter on a register of electors. Survey data have shown that although rates of voter registration overall are high at the federal level and in many provinces, those rates are not universally high among all age groups. For example, whereas 94% of eligible voters were registered at the close of polls on election day in BC for the 2017 general election, for those aged 18 to 24, only 68% of eligible voters were registered (Elections BC 2018). Many election management bodies have been seeking ways to increase voter registration among younger groups, and some – such as Elections Canada, Elections Ontario, and Elections Nova Scotia – have recently been provided legislative authority to develop a provisional register of electors for those soon-to-become eligible. Although it is too early to know whether these efforts will increase rates of registration and voting for younger electors, they are a step in the right direction.

Administering the Vote

Although the actual act of voting can look remarkably similar when comparing elections today with those a hundred years ago, in fact some of the changes recently introduced and/or currently under discussion and development are transforming the act of voting in Canada. The basic features of administering the vote are the following: each jurisdiction is divided into separate constituencies (or electoral districts), and each constituency elects one representative to the legislature. Each constituency is overseen by one returning officer and their assistant, the election clerk. Each constituency is divided into separate polling divisions, and the size of each is often set in legislation (often numbering about 300 electors). Every elector, therefore, is assigned to a polling division in their constituency.

Two election-day poll workers – the deputy returning officer and the poll clerk – are assigned to each poll. They are responsible for handling the ballot box for the poll and for administering the ballots for that poll. Their duties include checking voters' identification, striking voters from the poll book (sometimes called the voting book), issuing ballots, initialling issued ballots, removing the counterfoil of completed ballots, and observing voters depositing their ballot in the box. These two officials continue this work from the time the polls open until they close, about 11 or 12 hours. Both officials must be present when ballots are being issued. If one needs a bathroom break, the poll closes temporarily. At the close of polls, and following a long shift, these two officials are responsible for counting the ballots, reconciling the voting book, and reporting the results in the poll to the returning office. They are also responsible for packing voting materials into the ballot box and delivering the ballot box to the returning office.

There are several related changes that are transforming the voting process currently in place or under development in various jurisdictions. Perhaps the most striking change is the increased use of advance voting as a way to make voting more convenient. As recently as 2000, advance voting was a rarely used and exceptional voting opportunity in all jurisdictions in Canada, and doing so typically required a voter to make a special request to the returning officer to receive an advance ballot. In a typical general election, 2–3% of ballots would be cast through advance voting. Over the past generation, advance voting has become a more widely available voting alternative, with a corresponding increase in the number of days of advance voting.

In the most recent election in British Columbia in 2020, for example, more people cast a ballot in advance than did so in their assigned polling place on election day, a trend that is occurring in all jurisdictions. Election agencies establish advance voting polls at far fewer locations than election day polls, and generally every eligible voter can cast their ballot at any advance poll in the constituency. The popularity of advance polls has served to undermine the logic of the use of polling divisions, since the number of people attending their assigned poll on election day has declined so sharply. For example, assume a polling division has 300 registered voters. If voter turnout is 75% (which it generally was from Confederation to the mid-1980s), and if 95% of those who voted did so at their assigned voting place on election day, then one would expect (300 x .75 x .95) about 214 people to vote at each poll on election day. If, however, voter turnout is about 55%, and only half of those voting do so at their assigned poll on election day (the rest doing so either at an advance poll or otherwise), then the expected turnout at each poll (300 x .55 x .5) is about 83 people. The dramatic decrease of work at the election day polls, with the continuing high cost of maintaining these polls, has generated much interest in changing voting practices.

So, too, has the increased availability and use of technology in the voting place. A key ingredient in the current modernizing process is the use of electronic poll books (or e-poll books), which allow election workers to strike off voters from the voters' list in real time. Without the use of e-poll books, election officials are faced with the labour-intensive task of manually striking off people who voted in an advance poll from the voting books used in advance polls on subsequent days, and from the voting books used on election day, to prevent people from casting multiple votes. The use of e-poll books resolves this challenge by providing all poll workers a real-time version of the voting book. E-poll books are currently in use in some jurisdictions, such as Ontario, New Brunswick, and BC, and are under development in many others. The use of e-poll books essentially eliminates the logic of having polling divisions and suggests the voters can be issued ballots at any voting place in their constituency.

A second technology that can radically change voting administration is the ballot tabulator. As noted, the current process in many jurisdictions is to have the deputy returning officer and poll clerk count all ballots at the end of the voting period on election day, extending an already long workday. A ballot tabulator is an optical scanner that reads ballots and records the results, while preserving the original ballots in the event there is a subsequent need for a recount. Ballot tabulators have been shown to be highly accurate, and of course they produce results instantaneously.

The combination of e-poll books and ballot tabulators has enabled a rethinking of staff deployment at elections. Instead of assigning voters to particular polls and assigning staff to oversee only the voters at their polls, one can envision a process in which some staff are assigned the task of confirming eligibility of voters, others strike off and issue ballots, and others oversee the depositing of the completed ballots into a tabulator. These positions are interchangeable and can be increased or decreased depending on how busy the voting place is at different periods of the day. Furthermore, this model of voting administration can eliminate the need to differentiate between advance and general voting, instead simply having a three-, four-, or five-day voting period rather than separate advance and election days. Many of these changes already have been introduced in provincial elections in New Brunswick, some have been introduced in Ontario and BC, and there is active development in this regard in many other jurisdictions (for a description of the new voting model, see Neufeld 2015).

One could extend this "vote anywhere" model beyond the current application of voting anywhere in one's constituency to voting anywhere in the jurisdiction. British Columbia, for example, has permitted voters to vote outside their electoral district since the 1990s, through absentee voting procedures. As it has been administered, voters can show up at any voting location and request a ballot for their electoral district. If they live outside the electoral district that they are attending, they are issued a blank, or write-in, ballot on which they vote either for a candidate or a party. The ballot is placed in a secrecy envelope inside a certification envelope. After election day, the certification envelopes are sent to their appropriate returning office, where the information on the certification envelope is reviewed to determine whether the person has already voted. If they have not, and the information is correct, then the certification envelope is opened and the secrecy envelope is removed and placed in a ballot box for counting.

These are subsequently opened and counted during the "final count" procedure in BC. By introducing a third piece of technology, a ballot printer, into polling locations, and combining it with e-poll books and ballot tabulators, one could simplify the procedures used in BC to implement a process whereby each voter could attend any voting place in the jurisdiction (for example, anywhere in the province or the country), provide their identification, receive a ballot for their constituency, and cast the ballot where they vote. Although this vote-anywhere model may still be one or two election cycles away in some jurisdictions, it represents the direction of change in election administration (see, for example, Elections BC 2020a; Elections Manitoba 2020; Elections Saskatchewan 2017).

Appointment of Election Officials

In elections occurring in the early years following Confederation, the administration work was viewed as an extension of, or as a reward for, partisan political work. There was plenty of paid election work to be handed out by political parties. Elections in Canada are conducted with the support of many thousands, and at the federal level, many tens of thousands, of temporary employees. To the extent that political parties control the appointment process for election administration officials, paid election work could provide an important incentive for parties to encourage their supporters to volunteer on party activities and be rewarded with such administrative duties.

Over time, and particularly since the 1970s, the authority for the appointment of election workers shifted from the government and political parties to the independent election agencies. With few exceptions, it is now the office of the chief electoral officer in each jurisdiction that is responsible for filling all administrative positions in the election agency, both permanent and temporary. Not all governments gave up this authority early or easily. As recently as 2008, the then-chief electoral officer of Alberta published a set of recommendations for legislative change, among which was the proposal that the CEO be provided the authority to appoint returning officers and election clerks (Elections Alberta 2008). A second illustration came to my attention when I attended a visitors' program for the 2014 provincial election in Quebec, where I was surprised to find that at each polling station there were three officials, one each from the three parties with the most seats in the legislature. Political parties retained the right to appoint these election officials as recently as 2014. As the chief electoral officers and their permanent staff increasingly oversee regular staffing decisions, however, we have seen a greater professionalization of election administration, including more information sharing among the various offices.

Election Financing and Advertising

Given the discussion of party financing in Chapter 3 and third-party advertising in Chapter 9, I will provide a very high-level discussion of political financing changes. For the first century after Confederation, election financing in Canada was largely unregulated (see Jansen 2006). There were no limits on who could contribute to a candidate, a party leader, or a political party, nor were there limits on how much money a party or candidate could spend on an election campaign. Because of this situation, political parties developed a relatively efficient system of raising funds by focusing their efforts on getting funds not from individual voters but instead from organizations, either businesses or labour unions.

That situation changed substantially with the passage of the *Election Expenses Act* in 1974, which produced a major shift in party financing in Canada. As the regulatory framework for political and election financing has expanded, so too has the role of election management bodies in administering and overseeing compliance. Election agencies have developed training programs for the chief financial agents of political parties and of candidates to disclose financing by political parties on an annual basis, as well as election financing by political parties, candidates, and third parties in the period following an election, typically several months after the end of the election period. Initially the reporting documents were paper forms, which were completed and made available for public viewing at the election management bodies' offices. Transparency increased when the election agencies began to scan and upload financial reports onto their websites.

For election financing, the transparency tended to be "after the fact," as parties and candidates would report on their contributions and expenditures months after the conclusion of an election, so that voters would not know at the time of voting who contributed to a party or candidate, how much they contributed, and how much money was spent. Today, election agencies are moving toward implementing a system of disclosure that more closely approximates real-time disclosure, where parties report on their contributions shortly after receiving them (Elections BC 2016). For example, in Ontario, financial contributions must be disclosed to Elections Ontario within 15 days of a party depositing the contribution into its banking system, and Elections Ontario must publicly disclose the contribution within two days of receiving this information (Elections Ontario 2023). Similarly, in 2018 BC introduced disclosure requirements by political parties within one month of receiving the contribution. Thus, in at least some jurisdictions, there has been interest among parliamentarians in moving toward real-time disclosure.[5]

Election management bodies likewise oversee compliance with election financing requirements, and more generally with election laws. There are two models of compliance review in Canada. At the federal level and in Manitoba, a separate office called the Commissioner of Elections is responsible for conducting investigations of possible infractions of a jurisdiction's election act, including having the authority either to assess administrative penalties or to refer the matter to the police or Crown prosecutorial service for further investigation and possible criminal charges. The approach used in other jurisdictions is that the responsibility for compliance review rests with the CEO, who can either investigate and invoke administrative penalties or refer the matter to the police and/or Crown prosecution.

An area of particular interest in compliance review is with respect to election advertising. In some jurisdictions there are limits on the funds that can be spent on political advertising, and in other jurisdictions, advertising limits are a subset within the general election spending limits; there also are, in most jurisdictions, specific limits on third-party advertising (see Chapters 3 and 9). Legislation on political advertising in many jurisdictions was written before the widespread use of social media, and in many respects, social media is transforming the way Canadians communicate with one another, including communicating about politics (see Chapter 11).

One way social media has changed political communication is by dramatically extending the reach of political messaging without spending large sums of money. Restrictions on political advertising tend to be based on financial restrictions, with the assumption that advertisers are purchasing paid ads in newspapers, electronic media such as radio and television, or out-of-home advertising such as billboards or on bus shelters. Today, one can reach a broad audience that bypasses all of these venues – by posting material on social media. Where there is a cost to produce the material, it will be subject to similar limits as exist for traditional media outlets. However, where the cost of producing the social media material is minimal, it effectively skirts the legislation's intent. Research by Small (2018, 274) has shown that, despite the potentially low dissemination costs of advertising on social media, third-party advertisers have nonetheless dramatically increased spending on social media advertising in recent elections, with web-based advertising comprising 23% of third-party advertising in 2015.

A second way social media is dramatically changing election advertising is through mis/disinformation. Misinformation is the spread of factually incorrect information without the knowledge that the information is incorrect. Disinformation is the spread of factually incorrect information while knowing that the information is incorrect, often with the intention of changing people's behaviour. Recent analysis by Communications Security Establishment Canada has indicated that both Canadian and non-Canadian based actors engaged in disinformation campaigns during recent elections in Canada (Canadian Centre for Cyber Security 2021; see also Elections BC 2020b). One of the most pressing challenges for election management bodies is to oversee compliance with election advertising regulations in a complex political communications environment.

Challenges associated with administering free and fair elections also arise with respect to attempts by foreign governments (or non-governmental entities) to influence Canadian elections. The full extent of these efforts, and the ability of election management bodies to oversee them, have yet to be revealed. The federal government in March 2023 appointed David Johnston, former governor general, as independent special rapporteur to examine foreign interference in federal elections. In his first report in May 2023, Johnson confirmed evidence of foreign interference and also indicated that in his view, an independent public inquiry into foreign electoral interference was not necessary since the need to review so much confidential information would limit the advantages of such an investigation (Johnston 2023). However, parliamentarians did not agree with the latter conclusion, passing a motion for him to step down, which he did in June 2023. In September 2023, the federal government established a public inquiry headed by Commissioner Justice Marie-Josée Hogue, a judge of the Quebec Court of Appeal. The Commission has announced it will hold public hearings in winter and fall of 2024. As per her mandate, the Commissioner submitted an interim report on May 3, 2024, entitled *Public Inquiry into Foreign Interference in Federal Electoral Processes and Democratic Institutions*.[6]

DEMOCRATIC IMPLICATIONS OF ELECTION ADMINISTRATION

All election management bodies in Canada have mission statements articulating the values of the organization. At Elections Canada, which is typical in this regard, the mission statement articulates six values: knowledgeable and professional workforce, transparency, responsiveness, cohesiveness and consistency, trustworthiness, and stewardship and accountability.[7] These values underlie the processes put in place by the organization, consistent with legislative requirements. While the election management body is responsible for conducting electoral events and overseeing electoral financing according to its values, it also does so within the context of the legislative framework for elections. In many cases, the legislative framework takes a highly prescriptive approach to articulating processes and procedures to be followed in elections and in referendums and plebiscites. For example, legislation often specifies the number of days of advance voting and the hours for which advance and general voting places are open. It also prescribes special voting opportunities, how to cast a ballot, specific forms of ballots, limitations in voting, the voter registration process, the location of returning offices, and the like.

Ultimately, the role of the election agency is to conduct a free and fair general election and to advise the clerk of the legislature on who has been elected to each legislative seat. The election agency also conducts referendums and plebiscites using processes, and in timeframes, set by the government of the day. The goal of this arrangement is that electoral processes provide legitimacy to those elected to office or to the outcomes of public consultations through referendums and plebiscites.

This legitimacy is premised on the election agency itself being perceived as fair and impartial. Fortunately for Canadian election management bodies, and for Canadian politics more generally, these principles have usually prevailed. Canadian election management bodies are held in high regard, and normally there is a high level of respect for them and for the officials that staff these organizations. An exception to this general sentiment occurred in the period following the 2011 federal election, when the government of the day introduced what it called the *Fair Elections Act*, an important aspect of which was to reduce the authority of the federal CEO and, through this, the power of Elections Canada. The friction between the government of the day and Elections Canada, however, did not extend beyond the term of the 41st parliament, and with the election of a new government in 2015, the more traditional non-adversarial relationship was restored.

The recent elections in the United States and Brazil, however, reveal the damage that can be done to a political system when respect for the independence of the election management body is absent. For example, in the lead-up to the 2020 presidential election in the United States, then-president Donald Trump asserted that it was inevitable that he would be re-elected to a second term as president. "The only way we can lose is if they cheat," he remarked in advance of the election (see, for example, Leonnig and Rucker 2021; Woodward and Costa 2021).

Following his defeat in the November vote, Trump refused to concede the presidency, instead repeating false claims that the election had been rigged and stolen, attempting to pressure election officials to change official election results, attempting to convince house speakers in several states to convene special sessions to overturn the election results, and attempting to appoint a false slate of electors to the Electoral College (US House of Representatives 2022). Ultimately, he called for protesters to come to Washington, DC, to interfere with the count of Electoral College votes in Congress, which led to an armed insurrection at the Capitol. These efforts were intended not only to prevent Trump's legitimate defeat at the polls, but to deny legitimacy to the rightfully elected president, Joe Biden.

In the presidential election that Brazil held two years later in October 2022, then-president Jair Bolsonaro, using Trump's playbook to a tee, essentially repeated the same tactics, arguing in advance of the election that he could not lose fairly (which he did), calling the election administrators corrupt, refusing to concede defeat, and encouraging his supporters to riot at the capital (which they did) (see Darcy 2023).

An obvious question is whether the recent challenges to election outcomes in places like the United States and Brazil are short term and unique to those jurisdictions or whether they portend similar challenges elsewhere in the future, including in Canada. Some recent changes in the US are consistent with changes that have taken place in Canada. For example, the recent COVID pandemic led to greater American use of vote by mail and an increase in advance voting, both of which occurred in Canada as well. There is also widespread use of vote tabulators in the US and a growing interest in their use in Canada. Interestingly, however, the Trump campaign launched over 60 legal challenges to the election outcome, many based on the use of election technology, and all of which were rejected by the courts.

What has changed recently in the US, however, is the increasing segmentation and partisanship of news media, in which voters receive one-sided and distorted "news," including what could at times be characterized as misinformation or even disinformation through social media. As there is less agreement on what constitutes the truth, there are greater opportunities for political actors to manufacture dissent to serve their purposes. Hence, it is imperative that election management bodies define themselves as the arbiters of truthful information on election-related matters.

Election management bodies are expected to contribute to the peaceful transition of power, one of the hallmarks of a successful democracy and one of the enduring benefits of democratic governance. Conferring power and authority on one individual or group, and removing it from another, has been an ongoing challenge. History, as well as contemporary politics, is rife with examples of non-peaceful transfers of power – where political leadership is decided by the use of guns rather than by pencils and ballot papers. Canadians have the good fortune of living in a democracy where we've experienced peaceful transitions of power regularly from Confederation in 1867 to the present. Recent circumstances abroad have demonstrated that this outcome is not inevitable, though, and should be cherished and protected. Our independent election management bodies have played a central role in bolstering the legitimacy of those elected to govern by providing free and fair elections, and the future health of our democracy depends on them continuing in these efforts. By being clear on the values they bring to their work, such as accountability, transparency, and responsiveness, and ensuring those values are given real expression in their operating procedures, election management bodies may help ensure Canada's place as a leading electoral democracy.

NOTES

1 For an excellent description of the limitations and extension of the franchise, see Elections Canada (2021).
2 In the corporate title of chief electoral officer in many jurisdictions (such as Elections BC) is the descriptor "an Independent Officer of the Legislature."
3 For a comprehensive discussion of voter registration, see the Administration and Cost of Elections website on this topic. https://aceproject.org/ace-en/topics/vr/default
4 For instance, for the 2017 general election in BC, an estimated 94.4% of eligible voters were registered at the close of voting on election day (Elections BC 2018).
5 All election management bodies maintain databases of financial disclosure by political parties, candidates, and in some instances third-party advertisers. For federal financial disclosure data, see, https://www.elections.ca/content.aspx?section=fin&&document=index&lang=e. For an example of near real-time financial disclosure, see the Elections BC website: https://contributions.electionsbc.gov.bc.ca/pcs/Welcome.aspx
6 Information on the Commission and its mandate can be found at https://foreigninterferencecommission.ca/. The report can be found at https://foreigninterferencecommission.ca/fileadmin/user_upload/Foreign_Interference_Commission_-_Initial_Report__May_2024__-_Digital.pdf. In the nearly 200-page interim report, the Commissioner identified some initial areas of improvement in the communications involving the security establishment, but notably concluded that although there is evidence of intended interference in Canadian elections, she did not find evidence of "bad faith" among Canadian officials. The work of the Commission continues, with the expectation of a final report by December 31, 2024.
7 Elections Canada, *Our Mission, Mandate, and Values*, available at https://www.elections.ca/content.aspx?section=abo&dir=mis&document=index&lang=e.

REFERENCES

Boda, Michael, and Keith Archer. 2023. "Elections: Why Such Differences." In *Canada and the United States: Differences That Count*, 5th ed., edited by David Thomas and Christopher Sands. Toronto: University of Toronto Press.
Canadian Centre for Cyber Security. 2021. Cyber Threats to Canada's Democratic Process: July 2021 Update. https://www.cyber.gc.ca/en/guidance/cyber-threats-canadas-democratic-process-july-2021-update.
Courtney, John. 2005. *Elections*. Vancouver: UBC Press.
Darcy, Oliver. 2023. "Déjà Coup: How Election Lies Sparked the Violent Attack on Brazil's Government." CNN. January 9. https://www.cnn.com/2023/01/09/media/brazil-government-reliable-sources/index.html.
Elections Alberta. 2008. Report on the March 3, 2008 Provincial General Election of the Twenty-seventh Legislative Assembly. Edmonton: Elections Alberta. https://www.elections.ab.ca/uploads/2008PGErpt.pdf.

Elections BC. 2016. Discussion Paper: Disclosure of Political Contributions. Victoria: Elections BC. https://elections.bc.ca/docs/2016-Disclosure-of-Political-Contributions_Discussion-Paper.pdf.

———. 2018. Report of the Chief Electoral Officer on the 2017 General Election. Victoria: Elections BC. https://elections.bc.ca/docs/rpt/2017-election-report/voter-registration.html#outcomes.

———. 2020a. Modern Elections for Modern Times: 2019–20 Annual Report and 2020-2023 Service Plan. Victoria: Elections BC.

———. 2020b. Digital Communications, Disinformation and Democracy: Recommendations for Legislative Change. May. Victoria: Elections BC. https://elections.bc.ca/docs/rpt/2020-CEO-Recommendations.pdf.

Elections Canada. 2021. *A History of the Vote in Canada*. 3rd ed. Ottawa: Elections Canada.

Elections Manitoba. 2020. 2019 Annual Report of the Chief Electoral Officer. Winnipeg: Elections Manitoba. https://www.electionsmanitoba.ca/downloads/2019_Annual_Report.pdf.

Elections Ontario. 2023. Election Finances: CFO Handbook for Political Parties 2023. Toronto: Elections Ontario. https://www.elections.on.ca/content/dam/NGW/sitecontent/Compliance%20Documentation /English/Political%20Parties/CFO%20Handbook%20for%20Political%20Parties.pdf.

Elections Saskatchewan. 2013. Towards a Permanent Register of Voters in Saskatchewan. Regina: Elections Saskatchewan. https://cdn.elections.sk.ca/upload/Permanent-Register-of-Voters-Report-Oct-30 -revised-v2.0.pdf.

———. 2017. Report of the Chief Electoral Officer on the 2016 Election: Volume 2 Administrative Review. Regina: Elections Saskatchewan. https://cdn.elections.sk.ca/upload/ESK-Administrative-Review-Volume -II-low-res.pdf.

Jansen, Harold. 2006. "Political Party Financing in Canada." *The Canadian Encyclopedia*. Updated 2020. https://www.thecanadianencyclopedia.ca/en/article/party-financing.

Johnston, David. 2023. First Report of the Independent Special Rapporteur on Foreign Interference. https://www.canada.ca/content/dam/di-id/documents/rpt/rapporteur/Independent-Special -Rapporteur%20-Report-eng.pdf.

Leonnig, Carol, and Philip Rucker, 2021. *I Alone Can Fix It: Donald J. Trump's Catastrophic Final Year*. New York: Penguin Random House.

Neufeld, Harry, 2015. "Changing the Canadian Voting Services Model." *Journal of Parliamentary and Political Law – Special Issue: The Informed Citizens' Guide to Elections: Electioneering Based on the Rule of Law*. Toronto: Carswell.

Skahan, Kelly Ann. 2018. "Ineffective by Design: A Critique of Campaign Finance Law Enforcement in the United States, Australia and the United Kingdom." *Washington International Law Journal* 27 (2). https://digitalcommons.law.uw.edu/wilj/vol27/iss2/8/.

Small, Tamara A. 2018. "Digital Third Parties: Understanding the Technological Challenge to Canada's Third Party Advertising Regime." *Canadian Public Administration* 61 (2): 266–83. https://doi.org /10.1111/capa.12263.

US House of Representatives. 2022. *Report on the Activities of the Select Committee to Investigate the January 6th Attack on the United States Capitol of the House of Representatives during the One Hundred Seventeenth Congress*. Washington, DC: House of Representatives.

Woodward, Robert, and Robert Costa. 2021. *Peril*. New York: Simon and Shuster.

CHAPTER THREE

Party and Election Finance Laws

Lisa Young

INTRODUCTION

Money is an essential element in election campaigns. Political parties and candidates need money to develop, record, and broadcast messages that try to win voters' support, to run campaign offices, and to get out the vote, among other items. It is possible to hold elections without any rules about money. People running for office might spend their own money or ask for money from friends. And they would spend as much as they could during the campaign in the hope that it would help them win. While it is possible to run elections this way, it is not difficult to identify a series of objections to this approach to democratic competition. It favours the wealthy and the well-connected; it leaves voters wondering if their elected officials owe favours to their anonymous donors; it just does not seem very fair. In response to these very concerns, Canadian governments have, over the past 50 years, created a rigorous legal framework that governs almost every aspect of the money used to fight election campaigns. These rules affect how campaigns are run, how parties are organized, and sometimes even who wins the election.

DEFINING "PARTY AND ELECTION FINANCE"

Although party and election finance legislation focuses mainly on the flow of money to political parties and candidates and their use of that money during campaigns, it requires a framework that defines to whom the rules apply. The first aspect of party and election finance law is a set of rules that define "regulated political entities," which include registered political parties, candidates for election, electoral district associations, and third parties.

Canada has had political parties since its first election in 1867, but they were not recognized in law until decades later. In 1966, a House of Commons committee, known as the Barbeau Committee, recommended the creation of rules to ensure citizens had access to information about the finances of Canadian political parties and to improve the fairness of political competition. They recognized that these objectives could not be realized until political parties were recognized as legal entities. The Barbeau Committee recommended that every national party that planned to run candidates in the next election should be required to register with a national registry. Parliament acted on this recommendation in 1970, establishing a definition of a "registered political party" that was then subject to rules about its internal finances. To remain registered as a party, an organization had to comply with reporting rules and either hold 12 seats in the House of Commons at dissolution or run candidates in at least 50 constituencies (Courtney 1978).

As the scope of legislation governing money in politics has grown, so too has the number of political actors defined by the law. The *Canada Elections Act* (CEA) now defines registered political parties, candidates, third-party advertisers (as discussed in Chapter 9), leadership contestants, and nomination contestants. These definitions are important, as they determine not only to whom the rules apply, but also who is eligible for various benefits, like offering a tax credit to donors or a reimbursement of election expenses. Beyond defining the organizations and individuals who are subject to the law, party and election finance legislation sets out rules about three different aspects of money in politics:

1 Money flowing *to* regulated political entities
    - Limits on who can make contributions and how large these can be (source and size of contributions)
    - Rules governing loans to registered political entities
    - Rules governing the tax treatment of contributions
    - Formulae governing provision of public funds (via reimbursements or other means)
2 How regulated political entities can use their funds
    - Limits on how much they can spend during the campaign period
3 Transparency and accountability
    - Requirements to report on financial matters, including disclosing names and amounts of contributions
    - Requirements for accountability in financial organization, including appointment of an official agent responsible for all financial matters

Some of the rules listed above apply only during the campaign period. For example, there are no rules that govern what a candidate or a political party can spend outside the campaign period, but there are rules about spending during the campaign (and, more recently, during a period just prior to the campaign of a fixed-date general election). Many of these rules, however, apply outside of the election campaign period. For example, limits on who can give money to political entities and requirements that their donation be made public apply year round. These rules are still considered part of party and election finance because they affect the resources available to parties and candidates to fight the election campaign.

The restrictions and requirements that comprise party and election finance shape election campaigns in many ways. Most significantly, they regulate the fundraising activities parties carry out at both the national and local level year round; this in turn affects how much money the parties and their candidates have available to spend during the campaign. When the rules guarantee that candidates or parties will have a portion of their election expenses reimbursed from public dollars, it gives them the confidence that they will have enough money to cover a higher level of expenditure than they would otherwise be able to sustain. The rules also determine how much money candidates and parties can spend during the campaign.

The availability of money in turn affects the kind of campaigns that are run. Where candidates and parties have ample money and spending limits are lenient, they are unconstrained in their ability to communicate their message to voters in multiple ways – through advertisements on radio, television, newspapers, social media, and more. In contrast, where parties and candidates do not have ample resources or face stringent spending limits, they are less able to communicate their message broadly and must budget their spending carefully. In this case, it is likely that fewer voters will be reached.[1] These factors do not determine the outcome of elections; they do, however, have the potential to shape the competitive dynamic. Where there are strict spending limits in place and generous public subsidies to reimburse election expenses, we can expect campaigns to be more competitive. Parties or candidates would have an equitable opportunity to share their messages with voters.[2]

These rules also affect the ways that parties and candidates connect to civil society. If contributions from unions and corporations are permitted, we would expect left-of-centre parties to receive significant contributions from unions and right-of-centre parties to receive significant contributions from businesses. This might make these parties more responsive to these interests as they develop their policy platforms and when they govern. Rules that make parties heavily dependent on public funds might make these parties less responsive to civil society, as they would be less grounded in it (Katz and Mair 1995). Parties that rely on contributions from individuals might be highly responsive to those donors.

THE EVOLUTION OF PARTY AND ELECTION FINANCING IN CANADA

The rules governing campaign and election finance in Canada have evolved significantly over the past five decades. In this section, I discuss two broad, and related, trends in the regulation of political finance for federal parties and elections. The first trend is the significant expansion in the scope of regulation, from virtually none prior to 1974 to a foundational regime from 1974 to 2003 and a substantially more extensive regime from 2004 to the present. The second trend is a shift in the underlying philosophy of the regulatory regime, from egalitarianism to egalitarian-populist. Taking these two trends into account, I identify two distinct regulatory regimes: the foundational regime, established in 1974, which is best described as "egalitarian," and a second regime, established in 2004, which is best described as "egalitarian-populist."

Until 1974, there were relatively few rules governing money in federal elections in Canada, and those that did exist were only loosely enforced (Stanbury 1991). As mentioned, prior to 1970, political parties were not recognized in Canadian law, and rules governing political finance were relatively lax and focused on candidates rather than parties. The *Dominion Elections Act* of 1874 established the "doctrine of agency" for candidates (meaning that all the candidate's financial transactions had to be done by their official agent) and required the agent to report on the candidate's election expenses to the returning officer. Additional requirements were later added, including an amendment in 1920 to require disclosure of the names of all those who had contributed to the campaign. These were, however, unaudited statements, and compliance was relatively low.

The Foundational Regime: Egalitarian Model

Several factors led to significant change in 1974. In 1963, the province of Quebec passed legislation that limited how much parties and candidates could spend and also offered candidates partial reimbursements of their election expenses from public funds (Mowray and Pelletier 2002). The Quebec legislation prompted the Liberal government of Lester B. Pearson to establish a parliamentary committee to examine the financing of federal candidates and political parties. The Barbeau Committee issued its report in 1966. In subsequent years, Parliament followed the recommendations and passed legislation that established a framework for the regulation of money in federal politics, including the *Election Expenses Act* in 1974. Among the significant changes recommended by the Committee was the recognition of political parties in law.

The 1970 and 1974 amendments together established the first legislative regime for political finance at the national level in Canada. Its core elements were:

1 Transparency, by requiring political parties and candidates to publicly disclose the names of donors and the amounts they gave
2 Limits on the amount that candidates and registered parties can spend during election campaigns (expenditure limits)
3 Public funding in the form of partial reimbursement of election expenses for candidates and registered parties during campaigns
4 Public funding in the form of the political contribution tax credit, which provides a generous tax credit to individual donors, effectively subsidizing small contributions from individuals

The elements covered by the first regime are indicated in dark shading on Table 3.1. This first regime did not include any limits on the size or source of contributions. This means that individuals or organizations (including corporations and unions) could contribute an unlimited amount. Because of disclosure rules, however, those donations would be on the public record.

With the exception of the transparency requirements, the other elements of this foundational regime reflected a concern with fairness, or what legal scholar Colin Feasby (1999, 18) described as "a rough political equality." A key objective of the 1974 *Election Expenses Act* was to place candidates and political parties on a roughly equal political footing, to "level the playing field" for political competition. The limits on how much candidates and parties could spend was the primary means of achieving this, bolstered by the public funding offered through reimbursement of election expenses and the political contribution tax credit. Taken as a whole (and reinforced in subsequent court decisions about various aspects of election law), this foundational model reflected what Feasby (1999, 18) termed the "egalitarian model" of election finance law in Canada.

Limits on election expenses were central to the egalitarian model. When first introduced in 1974, they included limits for both political parties and candidates. For parties, the limit was calculated at a rate of $0.30 per eligible elector in the ridings where the party had a candidate. For candidates, the rate was set at $1/eligible elector in the district for the first 15,000 electors, and then at $0.50 for

Table 3.1. Summary of Regimes

Legislative Element	Candidates	National Political Parties	Electoral District Associations of Parties	Nomination Contestants	Leadership Contestants
Registration	1974	1974	2004	2004	2004
Agency	1974	1974	2004	2004	2004
Expenditures					
Disclosure	1974	1974	2004	2004	2004
Limit on amount	1974	1974	–	2004	–
Contributions					
Disclosure of source	1974	1974	2004	2004	2004
Limit on source	2004	2004	2004	2004	2004
Limit on size	2004	2004	2004	2004	2004

Note: Where a year is listed, it indicates the presence of statutory provisions of the entity in the *Canada Elections Act* as of that year.

the next 10,000, and $0.25 for all remaining electors (Stanbury 1991, 36). The formula for calculating parties' expense limits has stayed the same, with the per-elector amount increased over time to $0.73 in 2022. The formula for candidates' spending limits has changed and is currently based on the number of eligible electors in the electoral district, but it is increased for districts where there are fewer electors than the national average and also for sparsely populated electoral districts.

The egalitarian model's concern about political equality focused on making competition between parties and between candidates fairer. It was not concerned with broader political equality, as it implicitly accepted that those organizations and individuals who had sufficient financial means to make contributions should be able to do so without any restrictions. The only nod in the direction of this alternative conception of political equality was to encourage relatively small contributions from individuals through the political contribution tax credit, which subsidized these donations through a generous tax benefit (a 75% credit for donations up to $100 at the time).

The egalitarian model was founded on a belief that transparency was sufficient to manage potential issues of undue donor influence over political decision makers. When it undertook a comprehensive examination of party and election finance in Canada, the Royal Commission on Electoral Reform and Party Finance (RCERPF; Lortie Commission) concluded that "Canadian organizations with a stake in the political future of the country should not be prevented from supporting parties and candidates who share their policies and values, provided the public has full opportunity to be informed about these financial activities" (RCERPF 1991, 450).

Between 1974 and 2003, changes to election finance law were relatively minor, with the exception of a series of efforts to regulate spending by "third parties" (individuals or organizations other than political parties intervening in election campaigns). This is discussed in more detail in Chapter 9.

Second Regime: The Egalitarian-Populist Model

The second regime was established in legislation in 2004 and further consolidated in 2006 and subsequently. It maintained the foundational elements of the first regime but vastly expanded the scope of regulated activity, as shown in Table 3.1. Changes to election finance law often come in the wake of scandal (Scarrow 2004), and the reforms introduced in 2003 fall into this pattern. The Liberal government was caught up in the "sponsorship scandal" when evidence emerged that it had broken rules in its allocation of contracts to Liberal-friendly advertising agencies in the province of Quebec. Faced with political fallout from this scandal, the Jean Chrétien government introduced a suite of reforms focused on ethics, including significant changes to the CEA's provisions governing party and election finance.

In an effort to mitigate the political damage from the scandal, the government integrated key elements of Quebec's approach to election finance into these reforms. Quebec had adopted an approach referred to as *financement populaire* in 1977, banning union and corporate contributions and offering generous public subsidies to parties. This approach was familiar and popular among Quebec politicians, many of whom favoured its use at the federal level (Young and Jansen 2011).

While the first regime focused on levelling the playing field between competitors through spending limits and targeted public funding, the second regime made individuals the only legal source of money in politics by pushing out organizations such as corporations and unions. It also tried to equalize the impact individuals could exert by placing a maximum limit on donation amounts. By removing organizations, the law made people the only legitimate source of money in politics (other than public dollars), and so this regime can be thought of as "populist" political finance, layered onto the foundation of the egalitarian model. The term "populist" is used to refer to movements of "the people" in opposition to one or more elites. Here, it is being used to signify that only members of the electorate – "the people" – are eligible to contribute to candidates and parties, taking organizations out of the picture. The key elements of the second regime maintained those of the first regime and added:

1 A ban on contributions from any source other than individuals[3] and a limit on the maximum amount that could be contributed
2 Extension of the framework to cover electoral district associations, nomination contests, and leadership contests

The legislation passed in 2003 also included significant public subsidies for political parties, delivered on a quarterly basis. This quarterly allowance paid parties $1.50 annually for each vote they won in the most recent election. Between 2004 and 2009, this public funding made up anywhere from 1/3 to 1/2 of the total income for the major political parties and well over half the income of the Green Party and Bloc Québécois (Jansen and Young 2011, 90). Opposition parties on the right, however, objected to these public subsidies, and when the Conservative Party of Canada formed a majority government in 2011, it phased out the quarterly allowance.[4] The 2003 changes also made existing public funding more generous (through reimbursing a larger proportion of election expenses and increasing the amount of donations eligible for the most generous tax credit from $100 to $200); this aspect did not change in 2011.

THE SHIFT TO INDIVIDUAL CONTRIBUTORS

The defining characteristic of this new egalitarian-populist regime is the principle that the only source of private money for parties and candidates should be relatively small contributions from individuals. This involved both a ban on contributions from organizations and a limit on the maximum allowable size of contributions from individuals.

Prior to banning contributions from organizations, the Liberal and Progressive Conservative parties counted on relatively large contributions from corporations to help them fund their campaigns, and the New Democratic Party relied on large contributions from unions. Corporate donors tended to be large corporations in federally regulated industries (including banking, telecommunications, and transportation). The largest single contribution on record was to the Liberal Party from the Canadian Imperial Bank of Commerce, at just over $150,000. The largest contributions (sometimes over $500,000 collectively) came from union organizations, notably the Canadian Labour Congress, to the New Democratic Party, with which they were formally affiliated.

When it introduced these reforms in 2003, the Chrétien government set the maximum allowable amount for a contribution from an individual at $5,000. In 2006, the newly elected Stephen Harper government introduced further reforms, reducing this amount to $1,500. Without this subsequent change, it would be difficult to think of the shift to individual financing as truly populist, as it permitted relatively affluent donors to play a significant role in funding parties.

The decision to restrict who could contribute and how much they could contribute at the federal level set off a sea of changes in the Canadian provinces. Table 3.2 provides a summary of the provincial rules governing political contributions as of 2003, when the federal legislation was passed. It shows that over those two decades, six provinces joined the federal government, Quebec, and Manitoba in banning corporate and union contributions, leaving only Saskatchewan and Newfoundland permitting donations from these sources. In terms of the maximum allowable contribution, the same pattern prevailed. In every province except Manitoba, Saskatchewan, and Newfoundland, the maximum allowable size of a contribution decreased substantially. Taken as a whole, this signals a remarkable shift in the norms governing political finance in Canada.

Thinking back to the idea that parties are shaped by who gives them money, the shift away from corporate and union contributions had significant impacts on political parties. The ban on union contributions weakened, but did not necessarily mute, the influence of organized labour within the NDP; shared ideological commitments and interpersonal networks sustained the relationship (Jansen and Young 2009). Although relationships between corporations and the Liberal and PC parties could also be sustained through interpersonal relationships, the absence of an institutionalized tie arguably made business a less important constituency for these parties once the financial relationship ended.

The loss of corporate and union contributions made political parties and candidates reliant on money from just two sources: public funding and contributions from individuals. At first, state funding took on a significant role, particularly for the national offices of political parties. When they introduced the changes to the CEA, the governing Liberals had calculated the amount for the quarterly allowance to effectively replace corporate contributions.[5] They had not considered the incentive for parties to raise more money from individual donors in order to outspend their rivals. The newly formed Conservative Party of Canada was able to draw on the considerable fundraising experience of the old Progressive Conservative Party and the grassroots ethos of the former Reform/Canadian Alliance Party, and it became a fundraising "juggernaut," forcing the other parties to engage seriously in the challenge of raising money from individual donors (Jansen and Young 2011). Once the quarterly allowance was removed, individual donors became essential to parties' financial well-being.

This gives donors, collectively, considerable potential influence over parties. A survey of donors found that most donate for "political" reasons: because they support a party's values and policies,

Table 3.2. Summary of Restrictions on Size and Source of Contributions, 2003 and 2022

Jurisdiction	2003	2022	Direction of Change: Size	Direction of Change: Source
Canada	None. *Limits adopted effective 2004 ($5,000 maximum, individuals only)*	$1,675 maximum; individuals only	Restricted	Restricted
Newfoundland and Labrador	None	None	None	None
Prince Edward Island	None	$3,150 maximum; individuals only	Restricted	Restricted
Nova Scotia	None	$5,000 maximum; individuals only	Restricted	Restricted
New Brunswick	$6,000 maximum; no restriction on source	$3,000 maximum; individuals only	Restricted	Restricted
Quebec	$3,000 maximum; individuals only	$100 maximum; individuals only	Restricted	None
Ontario	$7,500 maximum; no restriction on source	$3,300 maximum; individuals only	Restricted	Restricted
Manitoba	$3,000 maximum; individuals only	$5,000 maximum; individuals only	Expanded	None
Saskatchewan	None	None	None	None
Alberta	$15,000 maximum; $30,000 maximum during campaigns. No restrictions on source	$4,000 maximum; individuals only	Restricted	Restricted
British Columbia	None	$1,309 maximum; individuals only	Restricted	Restricted

Source: Adapted from Elections Canada (2003). Note that in 2003 many jurisdictions prohibited contributions from outside the jurisdiction. This is not captured in the summary.

want a good representative in Ottawa, or think the party's leader will be a good prime minister, for example. Relatively few placed emphasis on the donation as a transaction, such as helping their career success or "being seen" at a party event (Garnett et al. 2023). This means that donors' views on contentious issues are important to parties, and there is some evidence that donors' views may be systematically different than those of party supporters (Cross et al. 2022, 153).

Donors are also demographically unrepresentative of the electorate. Research has shown that donors are more likely to live in wealthier neighbourhoods (Carmichael and Howe 2014) and be white (Besco and Tolley 2022) and male (Tolley, Besco, and Sevi 2022). Cross et al. (2022, 146) report that donors are more likely to work in the private sector, earn over $90,000, and consider religion to be important in their lives. Taken as a whole, this means that parties are attuned to the views of this group of people, who are unrepresentative of voters or even their party's supporters.

EXTENSION OF THE REGULATORY FRAMEWORK

The second defining characteristic of the framework was a substantial expansion of the individuals and organizations covered by legislation. Much of this was made necessary by the restrictions on the size and source of contributions. It is meaningless to say that corporations cannot give money to a candidate but can give money to a person running to *become* a candidate in a party's nomination, or to ban union contributions to registered political parties but to permit them for individuals running to be party leader.

The 2003 legislation amending the CEA brought virtually all financial activity of registered political parties into the scope of the legislation. Prior to this, parties set the rules governing their nomination and leadership contests, and their electoral district associations (EDAs) were largely unregulated. In essence, parties were treated as private organizations largely beyond the reach of state regulation. The 2003 reforms changed this. By extending the requirement to register, the legislation formalized the existence of electoral district associations; by requiring these EDAs to disclose the contributions they received and the money they spent or transferred, the legislation closed a significant loophole in the transparency requirements for political parties (Coletto and Eagles 2011). The legislation also transformed nomination contests from the private affairs of political parties to a publicly regulated contest with restrictions not only on the size and source of donations to candidates running for the nomination, but also on how much candidates could spend in pursuit of the nomination. Leadership contests were also regulated, but without a publicly imposed spending limit.

As a consequence of these regulatory regime expansions, we now know more about who makes financial donations to nomination contestants and leadership contestants. Because individuals running for a party nomination must now report their income and expenditures to Elections Canada, we have publicly available information about how many contestants run for a party's nomination and how much they spend.[6] We also know more about how electoral district associations use the money they collect (see, for example, Currie-Wood 2020).

IMPLICATIONS FOR DEMOCRACY

"Free and fair" elections are essential to democracy. Rules governing the flow of money to political parties and candidates and restricting the ways they can use that money are an important part of ensuring that these contests are fair. Of course, not everyone agrees on a definition for "fairness" in this context.

Some might argue that "fairness" demands that parties be able to raise as much money as possible from their supporters and then spend it as they see fit. In an important 1976 decision in *Buckley v. Valeo*, the US Supreme Court ruled that in the context of elections, "money is speech"; the court went on to rule that restrictions on how much a candidate or party could spend in an election would be an unconstitutional restriction on freedom of speech. This has meant that American candidates can spend unlimited amounts of money on their campaigns, creating an insatiable demand for money in politics. The two presidential candidates in 2020, for example, spent almost $6 billion between them, while congressional candidates collectively spent over $8 billion.

An alternative view holds that fairness demands a "level playing field" for parties and candidates, with spending limits doing the levelling. This is intended to ensure that the ability to raise and spend money does not give one party an advantage over others. Canadian parties were limited to spending $30 million each in the 2021 federal campaign. Even with these limits in place, there are variations in parties' ability to spend. Figure 3.1 shows that in the 2021 federal election, the three larger national parties spent between 80% and 94% of their allowable limit, while other parties spent far less, suggesting that the playing field is levelled for the larger parties but still inaccessible to smaller ones.[7] Spending less does not necessarily translate into a worse electoral outcome. Figure 3.1 also shows that the BQ spent only $2 for each vote it won, while the NDP spent almost $8.

There are risks to democracy if the rules governing political finance are too restrictive. If the rules leave candidates and parties without enough money to communicate with voters through advertising, signs, and other means, the campaign will suffer. As Ian Brodie argues in Chapter 7, a robust campaign featuring parties and candidates communicating their competing perspectives to voters is beneficial to democracy. It allows voters to make an informed choice when they vote and may even encourage turnout. A political finance regime that stood in the way of this kind of effective communication would be harmful to democracy. Given current spending limits, there is little reason to be concerned that Canadian parties and candidates cannot communicate with voters.

Democracy is enhanced when citizens believe that the rules governing elections help protect the integrity of government; if citizens perceive the role of money in politics to be "legalized bribery," their confidence in government will necessarily decline. The role of election finance rules in this respect is to balance parties' and candidates' need for money to communicate their message to the public, on the one hand, against a public perception that money is a corrupting factor. Laws that require parties and candidates to disclose the identity of their donors and the amounts given are intended to ensure that these transactions are public and subject to scrutiny. Laws that restrict the size and source of donations go even further, as it is difficult to imagine a donor exercising undue influence by giving a thousand dollars.

Political equality is a core value of democracy, reflected in the idea that each person has one vote with equal weight. When parties and candidates rely on contributions from individuals, those donors are able to amplify their voices in the political arena. As discussed earlier, donors are not representative of the broader electorate in demographic terms and may be more polarized in their opinions than the general public. While reliance on relatively small contributions from individuals avoids issues of undue influence and connects parties to society, it also amplifies the voices of those with the means to contribute. Conacher (2023) argues that to achieve true political equality among citizens, Canada should set the maximum amount for a contribution to a party or candidate at $75 annually, a level that would be affordable for most Canadians. This would likely force parties and candidates to seek out a broader base of supporters and perhaps lessen parties' responsiveness to more affluent Canadians able to contribute larger amounts. Another possible corrective to inequality is to turn to the state to fund parties and candidates. When designed to reflect voters' preferences, public funding arrangements can provide parties with money that allows them to run effective campaigns without being beholden to corporate or union interests or affluent subsets of the electorate. But even this approach raises democratic concerns, as there is a risk that parties may become absorbed by the state, with their ties to civil society weakened. This makes them less accountable to the public and thus weakens the power

Figure 3.1. Parties' Spending as Percentage of Limit and per Vote Won, 2021 Federal Election

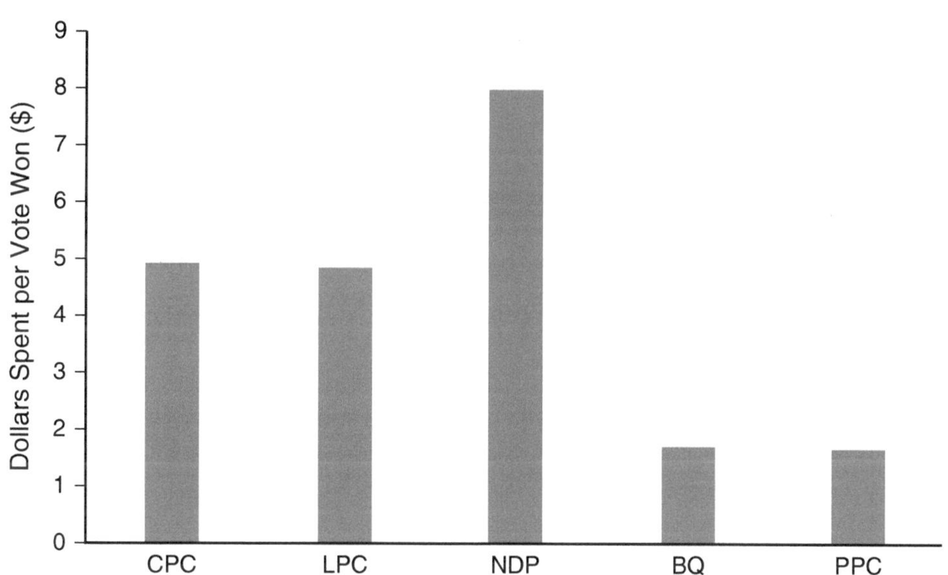

Source: Calculated from Elections Canada data.

of the electorate within the democratic system (Katz and Mair 1995). The competing objectives of ensuring there is sufficient money available for campaigns to flourish, on the one hand, and avoiding the potentially undemocratic pitfalls of various sources of money, on the other, is a central democratic challenge for the regulation of public finance. The Canadian approach, which tries to reduce the cost of political contributions through a generous tax credit, reflects an effort to achieve this balance.

Canada has been an international leader in regulating party and election financing, with more extensive regulation than is found in many other democracies. The extent of regulation reflects an effort, however imperfect, to achieve fairness among political contestants and ensure public confidence in the integrity of the political system.

NOTES

1 While it is difficult to isolate the impact of spending on voter information, Baek (2009) finds that "campaign finance systems that allow more money (and electioneering communication) to enter election campaigns are associated with higher levels of voter turnout."
2 There is a rich American literature looking at the impact of campaign spending on vote share. In the Canadian context, the presence of spending limits makes it difficult to isolate any impact of spending on outcomes. In an analysis of candidate spending at the local level, Milligan and Rekkas (2008) conclude that spending appears to increase incumbents' vote shares, and also that higher spending limits "lead to less close elections, fewer candidates, and lower voter turnout." Put another way, it appears that tighter spending limits increase competitiveness, encourage candidates to run, and increase voter turnout.
3 The legislation introduced in 2003 permitted contributions of up to $1,000 from organizations to candidates; this exception was removed in 2006.
4 For a discussion of the Harper government's attempt to remove the subsidies in 2008, see Jansen and Young (2011).
5 The quarterly allowance was calculated at a rate of $1.25 annually for each vote a party won in the most recent federal election.
6 This database can be found on the Elections Canada website at https://www.elections.ca/WPAPPS/WPR /EN/NC.
7 The national limit for each party is set based on the number of candidates it is running, so the limit for the Bloc Québécois, which ran candidates only in the province of Quebec, was much smaller than the limit for the three major parties, which ran candidates in all the districts across the country. Even with a much lower limit, the BQ spent only 31% of what it was legally allowed to spend.

REFERENCES

Baek, Mijeong. 2009. "A Comparative Analysis of Political Communication Systems and Voter Turnout." *American Journal of Political Science* 53 (2): 376–93. https://doi.org/10.1111/j.1540-5907.2009.00376.x.
Besco, Randy, and Erin Tolley. 2022. "Ethnic Group Differences in Donations to Electoral Candidates." *Journal of Ethnic and Migration Studies* 48 (5): 1072–94. https://doi.org/10.1080/1369183X.2020.1804339.
Carmichael, Brianna, and Paul Howe. 2014. "Political Donations and Democratic Equality in Canada." *Canadian Parliamentary Review* 37 (1): 16–20. http://www.revparl.ca/37/1/37n1e_14_printversion.pdf.
Coletto, David, and Munro Eagles. 2011. "The Impact of Election Finance Reforms on Local Party Organization." In *Money, Politics and Democracy: Canada's Party Finance Reforms*, edited by Lisa Young and Harold J. Jansen, 104–29. Vancouver: UBC Press.

Conacher, Duff. 2023. "Truly Equal? An Analysis of Whether Canada's Political Finance System Fulfills the Egalitarian Model." PhD thesis, University of Ottawa.

Courtney, J.C. 1978. "Recognition of Canadian Political Parties in Parliament and in Law." *Canadian Journal of Political Science / Revue Canadienne de Science Politique* 11 (1): 33–60. https://doi.org/10.1017/S0008423900038750.

Cross, William P., Scott Pruysers, and Rob Currie-Wood. 2022. *The Political Party in Canada*. Vancouver: UBC Press.

Currie-Wood, R. 2020. "The National Growth of a Regional Party: Evidence of Linkages between Constituency Associations in the Conservative Party of Canada." *Canadian Journal of Political Science* 53 (3): 618–37. https://doi:10.1017/S0008423920000360.

Elections Canada. 2003. "Compendium of Election Administration in Canada: A Comparative Overview." https://www.elections.ca/res/loi/com/arc/com2003/compoverview2003_e.pdf.

Feasby, Colin. 1999. "*Libman v. Quebec (A.G.)* and the Administration of the Process of Democracy under the Charter: The Emerging Egalitarian Model." *McGill Law Journal* 44 (1): 5.

Garnett, H., S. Pruysers, L. Young, and W. Cross. 2023. "Lifeblood of the Party: Motivations for Political Donation in Canada." *American Review of Canadian Studies* 52 (4): 442–45. https://doi.org/10.1080/02722011.2022.2147756.

Jansen, Harold J., and Young, Lisa. 2009. "Solidarity Forever? The NDP, Organized Labour, and the Changing Face of Party Finance in Canada." *Canadian Journal of Political Science / Revue Canadienne de Science Politique* 42 (3): 657–78. https://doi.org/10.1017/S0008423909990412.

———. 2011. "Cartels, Syndicates and Coalitions: Canada's Political Parties After the 2004 Reforms." In *Money, Politics and Democracy: Canada's Party Finance Reforms*, edited by Lisa Young and Harold J. Jansen, 82–103. Vancouver: UBC Press.

Katz, R.S., and P. Mair. 1995. "Changing Models of Party Organization and Party Democracy: The Emergence of the Cartel Party." *Party Politics* 1(1), 5–28. https://doi.org/10.1177/1354068895001001001.

Milligan, K. and Rekkas, M. 2008. "Campaign Spending Limits, Incumbent Spending, and Election Outcomes." *Canadian Journal of Economics / Revue canadienne d'économique*, 41 (4): 1351–74. https://doi.org/10.1111/j.1540-5982.2008.00507.x.

Mowray, Tim and Alain Pelletier. 2002. "Election Financing in Canada." *Electoral Insight*. May. https://www.elections.ca/content.aspx?section=res&dir=eim/issue5&document=p2&lang=e.

Royal Commission on Electoral Reform and Party Financing (Canada). 1991. *Reforming Electoral Democracy*. Ottawa: Minister of Supply and Services.

Scarrow, Susan E. 2004. "Explaining Political Finance Reforms: Competition and Context." *Party Politics* 10 (6), 653–75. https://doi.org/10.1177/1354068804046912.

Stanbury, W.T. 1991. *Money in Politics: Financing Federal Parties and Candidates in Canada*. Toronto: Dundurn Press.

Tolley, E., R. Besco, and S. Sevi. 2022. "Who Controls the Purse Strings? A Longitudinal Study of Gender and Donations in Canadian Politics." *Politics & Gender* 18 (1): 244–72. https://doi.org/10.1017/S1743923X20000276.

Young, Lisa, and Harold J. Jansen. 2011. "Reforming Party and Election Finance in Canada." In *Money, Politics and Democracy: Canada's Party Finance Reforms*, edited by Lisa Young and Harold J. Jansen, 1–18. Vancouver: UBC Press.

CHAPTER FOUR

The Perennial Debate over Canada's Electoral System

Harold J. Jansen

INTRODUCTION

Appearances can be deceiving. An outside observer looking at the current uniformity in electoral systems used in Canadian national, provincial, and territorial elections might conclude that there is a consensus on the best way to elect representatives to the country's legislatures. This apparent consensus belies a history of experimentation with different electoral systems, dissatisfaction with the outcomes produced by the electoral system, and regular attempts to reform it at the provincial and national levels. This chapter will look at the role the electoral system plays in shaping elections, examine the way Canada's electoral system has evolved, and discuss the concepts of democracy implied in the current electoral system and its alternatives.

In the introduction to this book, Small and Koop define elections as "a mechanism where the expressed preferences of individuals are aggregated into a decision regarding who will govern." The electoral system is central to this mechanism. Electoral systems are the rules that govern how citizens express their preferences as votes for who will govern and how those votes are in turn translated or converted into seats (Shugart and Taagepera 2017). Although it is possible to combine the components of electoral systems into an almost infinite variety of conceivable outcomes, it is common to divide electoral systems into three main types. The most common category is proportional representation (PR) systems, where the share of the seats each party gets is closely related to its share of the votes. Prominent examples of countries that use these systems are Indonesia, Brazil, Colombia, and Spain. Majority/plurality systems are systems that usually (though not always) use single-member districts and award the seat to the candidate with the most votes (and sometimes require a majority of the vote). This category is only slightly less popular than PR systems and is used in India, the United States, the United Kingdom, and Nigeria. The third category are countries that use mixed systems, combining plurality/majority representatives with others elected through proportional representation. Over the years, these have become increasingly common and are used in countries such as Germany, Japan, Italy, and New Zealand.

The choice between these different types of electoral systems is not neutral. Different systems translate vote shares into seat shares differently, which Maurice Duverger (1959) referred to as the "mechanical effect" of electoral systems. Different systems also create different opportunities and incentives for political actors, such as voters and parties, often described as the "psychological effect." For voters, different ballot structures change the way voters express their preferences as votes. Some systems require voters to cast a vote for a candidate, while others require them to cast their vote for a party list; still others allow separate votes for candidates and party lists. In a case where a voter can only cast a single vote for a candidate, they may have to choose between casting their vote based on the candidate they like best or on the basis of the party they prefer. A two-vote system might lead to voters supporting different candidates since they can separately indicate a preference for their preferred party. Ballot structure may also differ. A categorical ballot – that is, one that requires voters to choose one and only one of the alternatives, typically by marking it with an "X" – might encourage voters to cast their votes differently than they would under an ordinal ballot – one that asks voters to rank candidates in order of preference. The first is an all-or-nothing choice; the second allows the voter to provide more information with their vote. Under an ordinal ballot, a voter might choose to rank a candidate as their first choice even if they do not think that candidate is likely to be successful, knowing that their ballot will likely transfer to their second choice should their most preferred candidate be unsuccessful. Under a categorical ballot, the same voter might very well choose to place their "X" by their second-most-preferred candidate's name to prevent an even less desired candidate from being successful, a phenomenon known as strategic voting (Blais 2002; Merolla and Stephenson 2007; Daoust and Bol 2018).

Political parties are also affected by the incentives of the electoral system as different electoral systems might translate votes into seats differently. Shugart and Taagepera identify the different fates of the Canadian and German Green parties as an example. In 2008, Canada's Greens earned 6.8% of the national vote but no seats in the House of Commons; a decade earlier, Germany's Green Party's 6.7% of the vote translated into 47 of the 669 seats in the Bundestag and the Greens helped form the government and had cabinet positions (Shugart and Taagepera 2017, 3). These divergent outcomes create vastly different incentives for smaller parties to form and to persevere. Similarly, they may create different incentives for voters to continue supporting small parties or to abandon them for fear that they are just wasting their votes (Duverger 1959). Because political parties and candidates are typically motivated by a desire to form government, the electoral system plays a significant role in determining electoral outcomes. Understanding Canada's electoral system is therefore critical to understanding elections in Canada.

DEFINING CANADA'S ELECTORAL SYSTEM

Canada uses a majority/plurality system, specifically the single-member plurality (SMP) electoral system, often known as "first-past-the-post." Under this system, Canada is divided up into electoral districts, each of which elects a single member of Parliament (MP). The division of the country into seats occurs every 10 years after the results of the census are released, a process known as redistribution. The first stage of redistribution in Canada – technically known as reapportionment – divides seats between the provinces. The representation formula used to determine how many seats each province has in the House of Commons has changed many times over Canada's history, most recently in 2022. After an initial allocation of seats to each province (after giving each of the three territories a seat) strictly according to their population, the formula then implements a few special provisions that increase the representation of smaller provinces and protect provinces from losing seats through redistribution (Elections Canada 2023).

The most recent redistribution occurred in 2022; House of Commons seats increased to 343, with Alberta, BC, and Ontario receiving new seats. The impact of those special clauses is that the distribution of seats in the House of Commons deviates significantly from representation by population. For several decades, the provinces of Ontario, Alberta, and British Columbia have been relatively underrepresented in the House of Commons, while Saskatchewan, Manitoba, New Brunswick, Nova Scotia, Prince Edward Island, and Newfoundland and Labrador have been relatively overrepresented. Despite the additional seats given in the most recent redistribution, the average MP in the three underrepresented provinces represents 121,208 people, while the average MP in the six overrepresented provinces represents 83,829 people (calculated from Federal Electoral Districts Redistribution 2022).

The second part of redistribution is the division of each province into single-member districts, a process called redistricting (see Kelly Saunders' discussion of this in Chapter 5). While there remain considerable disparities between provinces based on population, within provinces there has been a tendency toward greater equality in district size, based on population, with some deviation to account for "community of interest" (Courtney 2001, 223). The process of redistribution thus produces a set of single-member districts every 10 years.

If the first half of "single-member plurality" refers to the number of members elected in a district, the "plurality" part of the definition refers to the rules that determine which candidate receives the seat. Plurality means that the seat is awarded to the candidate(s) with the most votes, not necessarily a majority of the vote. The plurality rule is typically used with categorical ballots. In single-member districts, voters can indicate that they vote for one candidate and the candidate with the most votes wins the one seat. In the case of multi-member districts, voters can cast votes for as many candidates as the number of representatives who will be elected, and the candidates with the most votes are the ones who win. In a four-member district, for example, voters can cast votes for up to four candidates and the four candidates who receive the most votes will represent that district in the legislative assembly.

THE EVOLUTION OF CANADA'S SINGLE-MEMBER PLURALITY SYSTEM

Although Canada uses single-member districts in federal, provincial, and territorial elections, this has not always been the case. Federal elections have made limited use of dual-member districts (each district represented by two members) in cities like Ottawa, Victoria, and Halifax, the latter of which had a dual-member district as recently as the 1965 federal election. Many provinces have made use of multi-member districts. New Brunswick, for example, had districts of varying sizes between one and five members until 1974. At the largest extreme, in provincial elections in Manitoba, the city of Winnipeg was a single 10-member district between 1920 and 1949.

As with single-member districts, although the plurality rule is now used across Canada in federal, provincial, and territorial elections, there has been some limited use of different formulas in three Canadian provinces in the period between 1920 and 1955. Massicotte (2008) identifies this as the first wave of electoral reform in Canada. In Manitoba, from 1920 through 1953, the city of Winnipeg elected its members of the Legislative Assembly (MLAs) to the Manitoba legislature using the single transferable vote (STV). STV is a system that asks voters to rank the candidates in order of preference through an ordinal ballot and uses a series of transfers of surplus votes (votes above what a candidate needs to be elected) or votes cast for candidates who are eliminated through the count process because they have the fewest votes of the remaining candidates. Through the successive distributions of the next preferences indicated on the ballots of these transferred ballots, we ultimately end up with the required number of candidates elected. The same system was also used in Alberta to elect MLAs from the multi-member districts in Edmonton and Calgary to its provincial legislature between 1926 and 1955. Although STV does not require political parties to be involved, as votes are cast for individual candidates, it does tend to produce a relatively proportional outcome, where the seat share awarded to a party is approximately the share of first preferences cast for candidates running for that party (Lijphart 1994). Moreover, in both provinces, the districts outside of the major cities used the alternative vote (AV) system to elect MLAs to the provincial legislatures from 1926 to 1955 in Alberta and between 1927 and 1953 in Manitoba. Like STV, AV uses an ordinal or preferential ballot, but it does so in single-member districts. If no candidate has a majority of the vote, the candidate with the lowest number of votes is eliminated and the ballots are redistributed based on the next preferences indicated on them. Candidates are eliminated in successive counts until someone has earned a majority of the vote. This same electoral system was used provincewide in both the 1952 and 1953 provincial elections in British Columbia (Jansen 2004).

Since the mid-1950s, therefore, Canadian federal, provincial, and territorial elections have all been conducted under the plurality rule and for the last few decades exclusively in single-member districts. As discussed earlier in this chapter, electoral systems are not neutral in their effects. There are winners and losers, and the impact of the SMP system on the political system more generally provides fodder for the recurring debate over the electoral system.

THE DEBATE OVER CANADA'S SINGLE-MEMBER PLURALITY SYSTEM

At the heart of the impact of the SMP system and the debate over its appropriateness for Canada is the fact that it does not accurately translate party votes shares into seat shares. For instance, in the 2021 federal election, the Liberals won 47.3% of the seats despite earning only 32.6% of the vote. Vote shares under SMP systems will translate into seat shares differently depending on many factors, including the distribution of votes among a party's competitors and the way votes are distributed geographically.

This inconsistent translation of votes into seats drives contemporary debates about electoral reform in Canada. If the first wave of electoral reform in Canada produced the provincial experiments with preferential voting in Alberta and Manitoba, the impact of the discrepancies between vote shares and seat shares produced a second wave of calls for electoral reform in the late 1970s and early 1980s, as well as a third wave in the 2000s (Massicotte 2008). As Massicotte argues, the discussion in the 1970s and 1980s centred on the impact of the electoral system on regional representation. Cairns' (1968) foundational analysis pointed out the ways in which the electoral system shaped the major parties along regional lines; in some provinces, a party might translate a high percentage of the vote into winning almost every seat in that province, while that same party might win no seats in a province despite winning a significant proportion of the vote (15 to 20%). At the time Cairns was writing, the Liberals won almost all the seats in Quebec and did relatively poorly in western Canada, while the reverse was true for the Progressive Conservatives (PCs). The parties' seat shares masked the fact that there were significant pools of popular vote for the Liberals in the west and for the PCs in Quebec. Cairns also identified that smaller parties with regionally concentrated support – typically parties of regional protest – tended to be rewarded much more generously by the electoral system than parties whose appeal was diffuse and national but not concentrated sufficiently to elect many members of Parliament.

Cairns (1968) argued that these distortions affected perceptions of the parties, but also shaped their behaviour as they responded to the incentives created by the electoral system. Cairns pointed out that it encouraged party campaign strategy to target particular regions. He further asserted that regionally skewed government caucuses combined with the dominance of the parliamentary party in policy formation to lead parties to develop policy without considering the input of all parts of the country. The net impact of all these effects was to exacerbate regionalism and to weaken the potential of political parties to be nationalizing agents.

In the context of the significant regional skewing in parliamentary representation and intergovernmental conflict over the constitution, energy policy, and healthy policy in the 1970s and 1980s, it is not surprising that arguments around electoral reform would centre on this issue. A typical example of electoral reform proposals in this period is William Irvine's (1979) *Does Canada Need a New Electoral System?*, which suggested a mixed-member electoral system that would use a combination of MPs elected under SMP and others elected using party lists allocated to produce overall proportional results. The centrepiece of Irvine's argument is that this system would ensure better representation of the major parties in every part of Canada. In the second wave of electoral reform, however, proposals such as Irvine's largely remained in the arena of academics and think tanks and did not generate much in the way of concrete political action. Furthermore, discussions of the constitution and federalism rather than the electoral system dominated discussions of political reform throughout the 1970s and 1980s. The debate over how best to accommodate regional interests and concerns largely shifted to a debate over Senate reform.

Concern over the impact of the single-member electoral system remained, however. The third wave of electoral reform in Canada emerged in the 1990s and to some extent continues today. Although regional considerations never completely abate in Canada, the focus of the third and most recent wave has tended to be on governmental legitimacy (Massicotte 2008). Much of the debate in this wave has been over the direct mechanical effects of the electoral system. One of the key tendencies of the SMP system is that it almost always over-rewards the party with the largest number of seats with even more seats than it is entitled to based on its share of the vote. Table 4.1 breaks down federal election outcomes since the end of World War II. In every one of these elections, the party with the most seats (and which formed the government) earned more seats than it "deserved"

Table 4.1. Federal Election Outcomes, 1945–2021

Outcome	Elections
Minority government with earned-seat plurality (largest party in seats had largest share of vote)	1945, 1962, 1963, 1965, 1972, 2004, 2006, 2008
Minority government with spurious seat plurality (largest party in seats did not have largest share of vote)	1957, 1979, 2019, 2021
Earned majority (largest party had majority of seats and majority of votes)	1958, 1984
Manufactured majority (largest party had majority of seats but only a plurality of votes)	1949, 1953, 1968, 1974, 1980, 1988, 1993, 1997, 2000, 2011, 2015
Spurious majority (largest party had majority of seats but not a plurality of the vote)	n/a

based on its share of the vote. Of the 25 elections listed in Table 4.1, in only two cases did a party win a majority government with a majority of the vote, known as an "earned majority." The other 11 majority governments were formed through what are often referred to as "manufactured majorities," where a plurality of the vote is translated into a majority of the seats.

This tendency of the SMP system to manufacture majority governments is central to the debate over the merits of Canada's electoral system as opposed to potential alternatives. Notably, in nearly half of the elections in Table 4.1, no party formed a majority government, even with the assistance of the seat boost provided by the SMP system. These minority governments are typically the result of a low share of the popular vote for the largest party but are also partly dependent on the distribution of the vote among the other parties. Johnston (2000) noted a tendency over time for governments to be formed on a diminishing share of the popular vote. The best fit line in Figure 4.1 extends Johnston's observation in 2000 over the last two decades and confirms his analysis. If this tendency continues, majority governments – even manufactured ones – will be increasingly infrequent.

Sometimes SMP can produce anomalous results where a party can win a majority of the seats without having won the most votes, a situation that is sometimes described as a spurious majority, or a "wrong-winner" election. For example, in the 1896 federal election, the Liberals won a majority government with 45% of the vote, even though the Conservatives won 49% of the vote. Although there have been no recent instances of this in federal elections, there have been several cases of spurious majority elections among Canada's provinces, including in British Columbia (1996), Saskatchewan (1986), Quebec (1998), New Brunswick (1974 and 2006), and in Newfoundland and Labrador (1989). More common at the federal level are minority governments where the party with the most seats (and forming government) did not win the most votes. As seen in Table 4.1, this has occurred four times since World War II and twice quite recently (2019 and 2021). These have occurred at the provincial level as well (see Shugart 2008); a recent example is the New Brunswick election in 2018.

The reason behind these anomalies is the vote distribution. Some parties receive too many votes in places where they do not need them and not enough votes in the places where they might contribute to winning seats. In the 2021 federal election, for example, the Conservatives won 33.7% of the vote compared to the Liberals' 32.6%. However, the Liberals won 160 seats and the Conservatives

Figure 4.1. Vote Share of Most Popular Party, 1945–2021

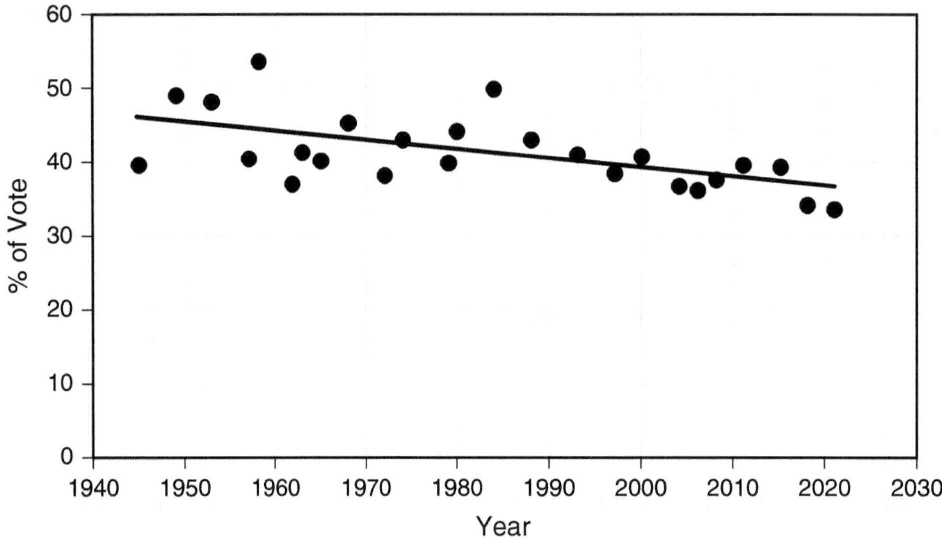

won 119. Because this did not result in a majority government for the Liberals, we can call this a "plurality reversal" (Shugart 2008, 23) instead of a spurious majority. Conservative candidates were more likely to win their seats with overwhelming vote shares, particularly in western Canada. Winning Conservative candidates had an average margin of victory over the second-place finisher in their district of 26.7%. Of the 119 victorious Conservative candidates, 27 won their seats by a margin of victory of 40% or more. By contrast, the average margin for successful Liberal candidates was 17.1%, and only eight of their 160 seats were won by large margins of over 40%. Of the 40 seats in the 2021 election where the margin of victory between first place and second place was less than 5%, the Liberals won 25 and the Conservatives won 11. The Liberal votes more efficiently translated into seats, while more Conservative votes were arguably "wasted" by being cast in areas where the Conservatives were winning by large margins or in districts where the Conservatives had little or no chance to be successful.

If one party receives a larger share of the seats than their share of the votes, this obviously means that other parties are receiving fewer seats than we might expect based on their share of the vote. One commonly observed impact of the SMP electoral system is lopsided majorities, where the opposition is so small that it is difficult for them to scrutinize the actions of the government party. The most famous example is the 1987 provincial election in New Brunswick, which saw the Liberal party win every seat in the provincial legislature, leaving no opposition. Defining the point at which an opposition is too small is somewhat arbitrary. Cairns defined it as a situation where the opposition parties hold fewer than 1/3 of the seats in Parliament. Cairns identified four cases between 1921 and 1965 where the opposition was reduced to "numerical ineffectiveness" (1968, 57); to that, we can add the 1984 federal election, which also met Cairns' criterion. Shugart (2008, 26) establishes a threshold of no opposition party with at least 1/8 of the seats. By Shugart's definition, no recent Canadian federal election has produced a lopsided majority, but he identifies seven provinces that have experienced these recently. Updating his analysis, only Ontario and Manitoba have not had even one lopsided majority since 1970. Furthermore, Alberta and Prince Edward Island have produced multiple lopsided majorities since 1970; however, neither province has produced such an outcome since 2008.

A key characteristic of the third wave of electoral reform is that the debate over electoral systems moved from being a largely academic debate to something seriously considered in several provinces and eventually by the federal government. As attention shifted to these questions of democratic legitimacy, these tendencies of the electoral system helped to trigger electoral reform movements. Shugart (2008, 13) defines the wrong-winner problem and lopsided majorities as examples of systemic failure in the electoral system, which he defines as *the incapacity of the electoral system to deliver the normatively expected connection between the vote and the formation of executive authority*" (emphasis in original). The experiences of Canada's provinces in the 2000s reflect this observation. After several anomalous results, five provinces undertook electoral reform processes.

In 1996, British Columbia experienced a wrong-winner election in which the NDP formed a majority government even though more people voted Liberal. The next provincial election in 2001 produced a lopsided majority in which the Liberals won 77 of the 79 seats in the legislature. The Liberal government established the Citizens' Assembly on Electoral Reform, composed of a group of citizens from across the province who learned about electoral systems, held public hearings, discussed and debated the alternatives, and then recommended an electoral system that was put to a referendum vote. Through the process, the Citizens' Assembly recommended that the province adopt the single transferable vote. The government established a requirement that 60% of the valid votes were needed to pass the referendum and that there would need to be a majority of the vote in favour in at least 60% of the province's electoral districts. The referendum easily met the latter threshold, with 77 of the 79 districts voting in support of the reform, but it fell just short of the first threshold, with only 57.7% of the voters supporting the initiative. In response to the close outcome, the government announced a second referendum in 2009 that also provided voters with a map of what the electoral districts would be like under an STV system. This time, the results were reversed, with a majority of voters in 77 of the province's 85 electoral district and 60.9% of all voters voting in favour of the status quo. This marked an end to the electoral reform process in British Columbia.

Similarly, Quebec underwent an electoral reform process after a wrong-winner election in 1998. Unlike British Columbia, Quebec opted for a more traditional approach to electoral reform, with the provincial government appointing a commission to develop a recommendation. Ultimately, opposition within the government caucus prevented any progress, stalling the reform process. A similar fate happened to the promised electoral reform after the 2018 election. The Coalition Avenir Québec (CAQ) promised to implement a mixed-member proportional (MMP) electoral system if elected, a promise that Premier François Legault repeated after the CAQ won a majority government (Bowden 2019). The government introduced a bill to replace the SMP system with a more proportional mixed-member system, contingent on approval in a provincial referendum. The government backtracked on that promise and proceeded with neither a referendum nor electoral reform. The 2022 provincial election saw the CAQ win a large, manufactured majority government of 90 of 125 seats with 41% of the vote. The four main opposition parties each received between

13% and 15.4% of the vote but won widely different numbers of seats – 0, 3, 11, and 21. The results intensified calls for electoral reform, but the government remained recalcitrant.

Prince Edward Island also experienced anomalous results in the form of overwhelming majorities. After the 2003 election produced a tiny opposition, the government announced the appointment of a commission to study the electoral system. The one-person commission recommended the adoption of an MMP system. In a referendum in 2005, nearly 93% of voters rejected the MMP proposal. An unusual 2016 plebiscite vote used a preferential vote; none of the five options on the ballot received a majority on the first count; MMP won on the final count. Pointing to the low voter turnout, the government held a referendum in conjunction with the 2019 election. Here, 51.74% of voters opted to maintain the SMP system, but a majority of voters in 14 of the 27 electoral districts voted to adopt MMP.

Like Prince Edward Island, New Brunswick has also experienced an overwhelming majority. In 2003, the provincial government appointed the Commission on Legislative Democracy to review the electoral system, among other matters. The Commission proposed an MMP system and recommended that it be put to a referendum. Premier Bernard Lord planned to hold a referendum in conjunction with upcoming 2008 municipal elections in the province, but the PC government called an early election in 2006, losing to the Liberals in a wrong-winner election (Lewis 2018). The Liberals had little interest in electoral reform and cancelled the planned referendum once in power.

Ontario also seriously considered electoral reform in this wave, but it stands as an unusual case in that it had not experienced anomalous results in the immediate run-up to the electoral reform process. Absent specific electoral problems, this seems to have been motivated by a desire to appear to enhance democratic legitimacy. In November 2004, the provincial government established its own Citizens' Assembly, modelled after the one in BC. The Ontario assembly recommended an MMP system, which went to a provincial referendum in 2007. Voters decisively chose to retain the single-member plurality system, with only 36.8% having voted in favour of MMP.

Although none of these provincial efforts resulted in reform, they represent a sustained and intensive period of reflection on and debate over the single-member plurality electoral system in Canada. Through most of this period, there was little in the way of substantive action or debate over the electoral system among federal politicians, although there continued to be considerable interest in the topic among political scientists (see, for example, Milner 1999 and 2004). That seemed likely to change during the lead-up to the 2015 election, when the Liberals pledged that the 2015 election would be "the last federal election conducted under the first-past-the-post voting system." In their platform, the Liberals promised to convene an all-party committee to study alternatives to the SMP system and to introduce legislation to change the electoral system within 18 months of being elected (Liberal Party of Canada 2015, 27). Although this commitment did not name a preferred alternative, the Liberals had indicated support for the alternative vote in the 2012 party convention (Liberal Party of Canada 2023). In the same election, the NDP promised to implement an MMP system if elected (New Democratic Party of Canada 2015).

The NDP commitment to electoral reform was not surprising or new. In all but the 2011 election, the NDP had received fewer seats than it would seem to be entitled to based on its popular vote (see Figure 4.2). Of the three largest parties, the NDP has most consistently discussed or promoted electoral reform. That said, the NDP has not leveraged their support during Liberal minority

Figure 4.2. New Democratic Party Vote Share and Seat Share, 1962–2021

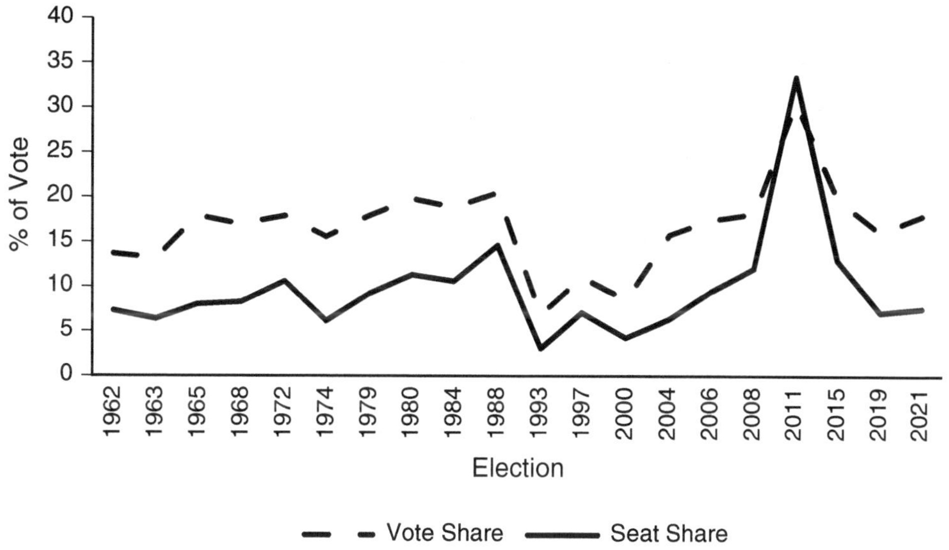

governments to advance the electoral reform agenda. Furthermore, despite the NDP having had majority governments in several provinces, none of them had initiated electoral reform. The Liberal commitment to electoral reform was more surprising, because the Liberals have almost always been beneficiaries of SMP. In 16 of the 21 elections between 1945 and 2011 (inclusive), the Liberals had earned more seats than they deserved. In only three of those 21 elections were they reduced to below 90% of the seats they would have deserved based on vote share. One of those three elections was the Liberal party's disappointing result in 2011, where they earned the third most seats in the House of Commons. Although this was seen as a pressing problem, along with the concern that the Liberals and New Democrats were splitting a centre-left vote, it is hard to point to a long record of disappointing results as motivating the Liberal interest in electoral reform. Instead, this would appear to be like the situation in Ontario, where electoral reform is part of a broader emphasis on democratic revival.

After the Liberals won the 2015 election with a majority government, they had to face the challenge of implementing their promise. prime minister Justin Trudeau tasked Maryam Monsef, minister of democratic institutions, with the electoral reform process. The government established the parliamentary Special Committee on Electoral Reform in 2016; the Committee held hearings throughout the year and delivered its report in December. In its report, the Committee recommended that the government hold a national referendum, choosing between the current electoral system and some form of proportional representation (House of Commons 2016).

Subsequent events revealed that the Committee's recommendations were pretty much dead on arrival. On January 10, 2017, the prime minister shuffled his cabinet and appointed Karina Gould as a new Minister for Democratic Institutions. Justin Trudeau's mandate letter to her on February 1, 2017, could not have been clearer: "Changing the electoral system will not be in your mandate." Although the letter argued that a clear consensus had not emerged and that a referendum was thus not in Canada's interest, it was hard not to see a degree of political self-interest in the decision to abandon electoral reform. By 2015, the Liberals had returned to their traditional position as beneficiaries of the electoral system. An interest in a different electoral system no longer aligned with improving the party's electoral prospects. This marked the end of this brief foray into electoral reform at the national level.

DEMOCRATIC IMPLICATIONS OF SMP IN CANADA

Despite the apparent failure of electoral reform in Canada so far, the underlying debate remains. At its heart, this debate is between two different visions of democracy: a proportional vision and a majoritarian vision (Powell 2000). Reformers are motivated by the proportional vision of democracy, which emphasizes fidelity in translating vote shares into seat shares. Consequently, they tend to advocate for systems that produce this result. For example, Fair Vote Canada, the leading pressure group advocating for electoral reform in Canada, explicitly describes its mission as campaigning for "proportional representation as the most fundamental and urgent change needed in Canadian politics" (Fair Vote Canada 2023). Although electoral reform advocates are typically united by their disdain for the SMP system, they often differ – sometimes vigorously – over the best alternative system (Pilon 2007). Typically, the most preferred options in the Canadian context are systems such as MMP or the STV, which produce relatively proportional outcomes but still maintain electoral districts. As discussed earlier in this chapter, provincial reform efforts have usually settled on an MMP system, except for British Columbia, which voted on an STV system. Both systems, however, produce a more accurate translation of vote shares into seat shares. Given the rarity of a party winning a majority of the vote in Canada, this type of democracy would almost certainly see an end to single-party majority governments. We would likely see minority or coalition governments, requiring bargaining between parties to form government and establish policy. As described by Powell (2000), this vision of democracy is one that prioritizes the proportional influence of political parties based on their vote shares and outcomes that tend to represent the position of the median voter through a process of compromise between parties that work together to control the government.

In contrast to this is the majoritarian vision implied in the SMP system. Unlike the proportional vision, the majoritarian vision of democracy produces an outcome that provides control of the government to a single party, which voters can then hold accountable for government performance. Under the coalition governments typically produced by PR systems, accountability is more complicated. Policy decisions can be the result of compromise between partners in the coalition government, making it more difficult to hold any one party or leader accountable for government actions. Similarly, a party's election manifesto – the reason why some voters may have supported that party – may not survive the negotiations with coalition partners (Goodyear-Grant 2017). The complicated politics of coalition governments make this type of accountability more difficult. In the majoritarian vision, by contrast, it is easy to know which party is responsible for government decisions, since there is only one party in power.

Although Canada's use of the SMP system would suggest that it has settled on a majoritarian model, the challenge facing this vision in Canada is that the country's party system does not resemble the kind of party system that produces consistent single-party majority governments. As Powell notes, the majoritarian vision of elections rests on decisive elections where there is "unambiguous control over policy making for the election winner" (Powell 2000, 176). As discussed earlier in this chapter, Canada's electoral system fares relatively poorly in that respect, often failing to produce majority governments. The long-term trend of a decreasing vote share for the largest party suggests that this problem may persist and even worsen, as the essential prerequisite for a majoritarian vision centred on accountability may not be present in Canada. Over time, persistent minority governments may lead to the development of coalition arrangements between Canadian political parties, leading to the kind of governments seen more typically in PR systems.

Similarly, the geographic distribution of the vote that awards minority governments to the party with the second highest number of votes in Canada (such as in the 2019 and 2021 elections) also impedes accountability. Between 2015 and 2019, the Liberals saw their vote share decrease significantly, to the point where they were the second most popular party in Canada. As discussed earlier, the Liberals' efficiency in converting their votes to seats meant that they still earned the most seats and formed the government, a feat they repeated in 2021. Whereas voters should be able to hold a government accountable by voting against it and having it replaced, in practice Canada's electoral system does this only inconsistently.

It is likely that there will be more calls for electoral reform in Canada. Although Canada's history with electoral reform has only involved provincial or federal governments amending electoral law, the last two decades have seen the rise of commissions that entrust the responsibility of suggesting electoral reform to panels of experts or, increasingly, to citizens' assemblies. The attraction of passing the responsibility for electoral reform from politicians to citizens is partly motivated by frustration on the part of reformers with politicians who seem more motivated by partisan self-preservation than choosing an electoral system that addresses what they perceive as Canada's needs (Pilon 2007), but also by democratic expectations that citizens should have a say in how they choose their representatives (Thompson 2008). Similarly, the widespread use of referendums in the provinces to ratify the recommendations of commissions or citizens' assemblies is indicative of this democratic expectation.

Whatever the potential benefits for involving citizens in the process of electoral reform design and ratification, it is not clear that this will provide greater clarity around the models of democracy that underlie reform proposals. Although pollsters often find majority support for electoral reform among the public (Coletto and Czop 2015; Angus Reid Institute 2019), there often is not a clear consensus on the preferred alternative. Furthermore, electoral reform is often not highly salient or urgent to most Canadians (Coletto and Czop 2015). Underlying Canadians' attitudes toward the electoral system are contradictory hopes and expectations. For example, Coletto and Czop (2015, 9) found that Canadians prize a system that accurately translates votes into seats, but also a system that "makes it easy to get rid of governments that are out of sync with the population." A system that produces minority or coalition government was the lowest ranked goal on the list. Canadians seem to want the proportional seat shares from the proportional vision of democracy with the accountable single-party majorities from the majoritarian vision.

This mismatch between the expectations that the SMP system can produce governments that voters can hold accountable and the reality of how it operates in the context of an increasingly fragmented system that produces anomalous results because of the geographic distribution of party support means that the debate over Canada's electoral system will likely continue for some time. The experience of the 2000s in Canada demonstrates that electoral reform is difficult to achieve, often foundering on the problems of partisan self-interest or lack of salience and poor understanding among voters. Dissatisfaction with the electoral system will likely remain a feature of the Canadian political system for years to come.

REFERENCES

Angus Reid Institute. 2019. "Electoral Reform Revival? Support for Changing Voting System Skyrockets Post Election." https://angusreid.org/wp-content/uploads/2019/11/Electoral-Reform.pdf.

Blais, André. 2002. "Why Is There So Little Strategic Voting in Canadian Plurality Rule Elections?" *Political Studies* 50 (3): 445–54. https://doi.org/10.1111/1467-9248.00378.

Bowden, James. 2019 "Quebec Poised to Adopt Proportional Representation System." *Policy Options*. April. https://policyoptions.irpp.org/fr/magazines/avril-2019/quebec-poised-to-adopt-proportional-electoral-system/.

Cairns, Alan C. 1968. "The Electoral System and the Party System in Canada, 1921–1965." *Canadian Journal of Political Science* 1(1): 55–80. https://doi.org/10.1017/S0008423900035228.

Coletto, David, and Maciej Czop. 2015. "Canadian Electoral Reform: Public Opinion on Possible Alternatives." Ottawa: Abacus Data. https://assets.nationbuilder.com/broadbent/pages/7733/attachments/original/1592500692/Canadian_Electoral_Reform_-_Report.pdf?1592500692.

Courtney, John C. 2001. *Commissioned Ridings: Designing Canada's Electoral Districts*. Montreal: McGill-Queen's University Press.

Daoust, Jean-François, and Damien Bol. 2018. "Polarization, Partisan Preferences and Strategic Voting." *Government and Opposition* 55 (4): 578–94. https://doi.org/10.1017/gov.2018.42.

Duverger, Maurice. 1959. *Political Parties: Their Organization and Activity in the Modern State*. 2nd ed. Translated by Barbara North and Robert North. London: Methuen.

Elections Canada. 2023. "The Representation Formula." https://www.elections.ca/content.aspx?section=res&dir=cir/red/form&document=index&lang=e.

Fair Vote Canada. 2023. "Vision, Mission, and Core Values." https://www.fairvote.ca/wp-content/uploads/2023/06/FVC-Vision-Mission-Values.pdf.

Federal Electoral Districts Redistribution. 2022. "House of Commons Seat Allocation by Province, 2022 to 2032." https://redecoupage-redistribution-2022.ca/red/allo/index_e.aspx.

Goodyear-Grant. Elizabeth. 2017. "Voter Choice and Accountability: A Case for Caution about Electoral Reform." In *Should We Change How We Vote? Evaluating Canada's Electoral System*, edited by Andrew Potter, Daniel Weinstock, and Peter Loewen, 49–62. Montreal: McGill-Queen's University Press.

House of Commons. 2016. *Strengthening Democracy in Canada: Principles, Process and Public Engagement for Electoral Reform*. https://www.ourcommons.ca/DocumentViewer/en/42-1/ERRE/report-3.

Irvine, William. 1979. *Does Canada Need a New Electoral System?* Kingston: Institute of Intergovernmental Relations, Queen's University.

Jansen, Harold J. 2004. "The Political Consequences of the Alternative Vote: Lessons from Western Canada." *Canadian Journal of Political Science* 37 (3): 647–69. https://doi.org/10.1017/S0008423904030227.

Johnston, Richard. 2000. "Canadian Elections at the Millennium." *Choices* 6 (6): 4–36. https://irpp.org/wp-content/uploads/2000/09/vol6no6.pdf.

Lewis, J.P. 2018. "Definitely Maybe: A Recent History of Electoral Reform in New Brunswick." *Journal of New Brunswick Studies* 9: 27–39.

Liberal Party of Canada. 2015. *Real Change: A New Plan for a Strong Middle Class*. https://www.poltext.org/sites/poltext.org/files/plateformesV2/Canada/CAN_PL_2015_LIB_en.pdf.

———. 2023. "Ottawa 2012 – Liberal Biennial Convention Priority Policy Resolutions." https://liberal.ca/legacy-uploads/wp-content/uploads/2013/01/Ottawa-2012_Adopted-Policy-Resolutions.pdf.

Lijphart, Arend. 1994. *Electoral Systems and Party Systems: A Study of Twenty-Seven Democracies, 1945–1990*. Oxford: Oxford University Press.

Massicotte, Louis. 2008. "Electoral Reform in Canada." In *To Keep or To Change First Past the Post? The Politics of Electoral Reform*, edited by André Blais, 112–39. Oxford: Oxford University Press.

Merolla, Jennifer L., and Laura B. Stephenson. 2007. "Strategic Voting in Canada: A Cross Time Analysis." *Electoral Studies* 26 (2): 235–46. https://doi.org/10.1016/j.electstud.2006.02.003.

Milner, Henry, ed. 1999. *Making Every Vote Count: Reassessing Canada's Electoral System*. Peterborough: Broadview.

———. 2004. *Steps Towards Making Every Vote Count: Electoral System Reform in Canada and its Provinces*. Peterborough: Broadview.

New Democratic Party of Canada. 2015. *Building the Country of Our Dreams: Tom Mulcair's Plan to Bring Change to Ottawa*. https://www.poltext.org/sites/poltext.org/files/plateformesV2/Canada/CAN_PL_2015_NDP_en.pdf.

Pilon, Dennis. 2007. *The Politics of Voting: Reforming Canada's Electoral System*. Toronto: Edmond Montgomery.

Powell, G. Bingham. 2000. *Elections as Instruments of Democracy: Majoritarian and Proportional Visions*. New Haven: Yale University Press.

Shugart, Matthew Søberg. 2008. "Inherent and Contingent Factors in Reform Initiation in Plurality Systems." In *To Keep or To Change First Past the Post? The Politics of Electoral Reform*, edited by André Blais, 7–60. Oxford: Oxford University Press.

Shugart, Matthew S., and Rein Taagepera. 2017. *Votes from Seats: Logical Models of Electoral Systems*. Cambridge: Cambridge University Press.

Thompson, Dennis F. 2008. "Who Should Govern Who Governs? The Role of Citizens in Reforming the Electoral System." In *Designing Deliberative Democracy: The British Columbia Citizens' Assembly*, edited by Mark E. Warren and Hilary Pearse, 20–49. Cambridge: Cambridge University Press.

CHAPTER FIVE

Drawing Boundaries: Electoral Redistribution in Canada

Kelly Saunders

INTRODUCTION

As noted in the introduction to this volume, elections in Canada are about more than the casting of votes on election day and the determination of political party winners and losers in the quest for power. They are much bigger, and broader, events at the heart of Canadian governance and democracy than a narrow focus on votes and results would suggest. Elections do not "just happen," but instead depend on and are shaped by the processes, structures, and contexts within which they occur (Hyson 2000, 174). This chapter examines one of the key administrative and legal structures that impacts elections in Canadian politics: the redistribution of federal electoral districts.[1] Redistribution[2] involves the processes that (1) establish the total number of seats in the House of Commons, (2) allocate electoral districts to the individual provinces, and (3) determine electoral boundaries within each of the provinces. Given that these processes impact both the overall size of the House of Commons as well as the individual electoral districts within each province, there are both interprovincial and intraprovincial dimensions to redistribution in Canada.

The democratic significance of redistribution cannot be overstated. In Canada, federal elections depend on the creation of electoral districts, since it is through these territorially defined units that votes are translated into representation in the House of Commons. Moreover, in a first-past-the-post electoral system, in which a minority of votes typically produces a majority government, the placement of electoral boundaries can have a profound effect not only on the size of the governing and opposition parties in Parliament, but also on which party forms government (Archer 1993). At the same time, redistribution calls to mind important questions regarding the nature of representation in liberal democracies, as well as often contested and competing issues of voter equality, communities of interest, and effective representation among voters, politicians, and decision makers involved in redistribution exercises.

We can consider the democratic implications of electoral redistribution through the three lenses of fairness, equality, and representation: the procedural fairness of redistribution processes (and whether this fairness has increased or decreased over time); the impact of these processes and outcomes on voter equality; and their effect on citizen representation (Courtney 2004). In line with the theme of this book, this chapter begins with a definition of redistribution and a description of how the process is currently undertaken in Canada. This will be followed by discussion of how federal redistribution has evolved since the country's first decennial census in 1861. Lastly, questions related to the democratic implications of redistribution will be explored. In examining these issues, I will draw on my own experiences as a commissioner for the Electoral Boundaries Commission for the Province of Manitoba in 2012 and 2022.[3] As we shall see, despite the emergence of nonpartisan and independent commissions, the drawing of electoral boundaries every 10 years in this country remains a "contentious and challenging exercise involving the delicate balancing of often contradictory representational goals" (Bélanger and Eagles 2001, 451).

DEFINING REDISTRIBUTION

When Canadians think about elections, chances are that redistribution, and the configuration of electoral districts within and across the provinces, are not items that immediately come to mind. Yet when we consider the fundamental reason for elections in a representative democracy – to choose political representatives whom we as citizens wish to exercise political authority on our behalf in national legislatures – the processes within which we engage in this selection exercise are profoundly important. This is notably so given that representation in Canada is geographically based, with each province broken up into territorially defined units. Citizens within each of these territorial units, or electoral districts, elect politicians to represent them in the federal House of Commons. The way that these electoral districts are defined and distributed, along with the rules, processes, and actors that undertake these exercises, therefore have strategic consequences. It is no wonder, then, that John Courtney (2001, 5) has described redistribution as a foundational "institutional building block" of representational democracy. The drawing of electoral boundaries takes on added significance in a federal country such as Canada, where issues related to subnational minority rights, communities of interest, and the considerations and bargains that have shaped our history continue to resonate.

The rules, guidelines, and processes that govern redistribution as it is presently conducted in Canada are laid out in our constitution, legislation, and court rulings. The most fundamental consideration here as it directly relates to redistribution are sections 51 and 52 of the *Constitution Act, 1867*. Section 51 stipulates that the number of members in the federal House of Commons, and the representation of the provinces therein, are to be readjusted upon the completion of each decennial national census – in other words, that the redistribution of seats in the Canadian House of Commons is to occur every 10 years. Section 52 states that "[t]he Number of Members of the House of Commons may be from Time to Time increased by the Parliament of Canada, provided the proportionate Representation of the Provinces prescribed by this Act is not thereby disturbed." Section 52 not only grants authority to Parliament to oversee redistribution, it also enshrines the principle of representation by population (or "proportionate representation") in the constitution.

Following the completion of the national census, the federal redistribution process begins with the calculation of what is referred to as the "electoral quotient" by the chief electoral

Figure 5.1. The Representation Formula

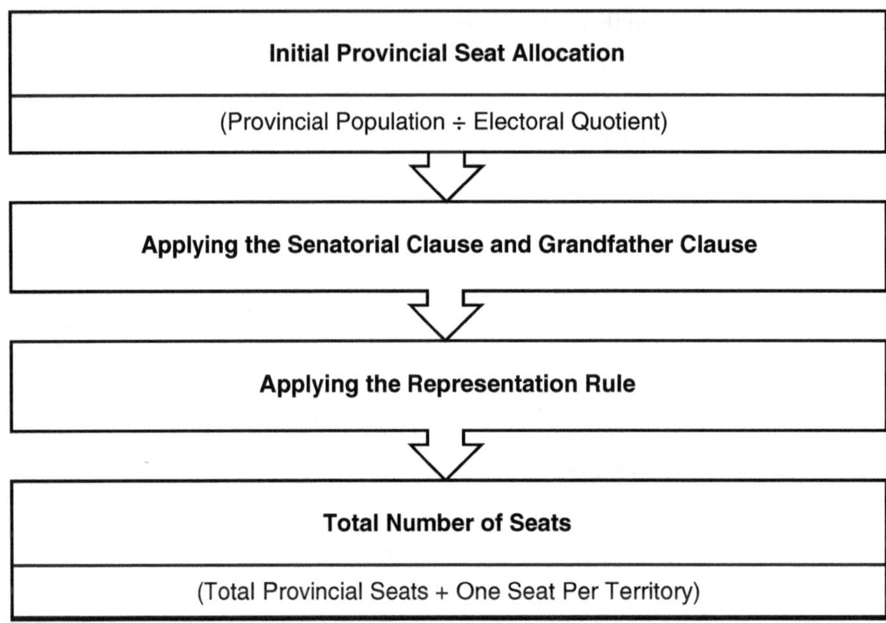

Source: Adapted from Elections Canada. "The Representation Formula." https://www.elections.ca
/content.aspx?section=res&dir=cir/red/form&document=index&lang=e.

officer of Canada, based on a mathematical formula contained in section 51(1) of the constitution (see Figure 5.1). Under the current formula, which was revised in 2022, the electoral quotient is determined by taking the previous quotient from the last decennial redistribution and multiplying this figure by the provincial average population growth rate over the last 10 years (Canada 2022a). More simply, this means multiplying the average population size of each electoral district 10 years ago by the average growth in population today. The population of each province is then divided by the electoral quotient to determine its share of electoral districts in the House of Commons.

The calculation of the electoral quotient leads to the initial allocation of federal seats. Next comes the special, or add-on, clauses that reflect the fact that redistribution in Canada is as much a political enterprise as it is a neutral, mathematical process. These special clauses are:

- The senatorial clause – the guarantee that no province will have fewer seats in the House of Commons than in the Senate
- The grandfather clause – the commitment that no province can have fewer seats than it had in the 43rd Parliament, elected in 2019
- The representation rule – the provision that, if a province was overrepresented in the House of Commons at the completion of the last redistribution process, and if that province was now underrepresented based on the application of the current formula, it will be given extra seats so that its share of seats is proportional to its share of the population

The second stage of the redistribution process involves the determination of boundaries of each electoral district, along with the names assigned to each district, within each province by independent boundaries commissions. The *Electoral Boundaries Readjustment Act* (EBRA) stipulates that following each decennial census, a three-person electoral boundaries commission (EBC) is to be established for each province. EBCs are chaired by a judge chosen by the province's chief justice, along with two other members selected by the Speaker of the House of Commons, both of whom must be residents of the province for which they have been named and who are not members of Parliament.

In preparing their proposals on electoral boundaries in their respective provinces, EBCs are guided by the following: the principle of proportionate representation contained in section 52 of the *Constitution Act, 1867,* the provisions contained in the EBRA, as well as relevant jurisprudence. While the EBRA grants EBCs considerable leeway in formulating their proposals, it does lay down some key guidelines that are to govern their deliberations. Section 15(1)(a) of the EBRA requires that the population of each electoral district correspond as "reasonably possible" to the province's electoral quota (determined by dividing a province's population by its number of seats).[4] This is followed by section 15(1)(b), which calls on EBCs to consider the following factors in determining "reasonable" electoral boundaries: any "community of interest or community of identity in or the historical pattern of an electoral district in the province" and "a manageable geographic size for districts in sparsely populated, rural or northern regions of the province" (Canada 1985).

However, the EBRA also contains two important caveats to section 15(1)(a). Section 15(2) permits a commission to deviate from the provincial quota by as much as +/– 25% in cases where it considers it "necessary or desirable" to do so and to extend this deviation even further in "extraordinary" circumstances. The discretion afforded to EBCs in how these various factors are to be interpreted, prioritized, and applied in each province has resulted in a wide divergence in fundamental principles of redistricting across the country, which in turn has "frustrated the principle of the political equality of all citizens" (Pal 2015, 231) – a point that will be explored further in this chapter.

Commissions are required to publish their proposals and hold public hearings in their respective provinces. Hearings provide an opportunity for the public to express their views on the recommended boundary changes and district names and to provide feedback to EBCs. EBCs then submit their reports, which are tabled in Parliament and referred to the Standing Committee on Procedure and House Affairs. While MPs are welcome to participate in the public consultation process, they can also provide any objections they may have to any proposed changes at the committee stage. Objections filed with the Standing Committee are forwarded to the respective EBC for consideration. It is important to note that EBCs are not bound by law to accept or implement any objections raised by MPs – commissions have final say over the drawing of electoral districts and boundary names in their respective provinces. Final reports are then submitted to the Speaker of the House of Commons and come into effect in the next general election.

THE EVOLUTION OF REDISTRIBUTION IN CANADA

As Andrew Sancton (2010, 1) reminds us, representation by population, or "rep by pop" as it is commonly referred to, constituted a founding principle of Confederation, as evidenced by the reference to "proportionate representation" in section 52 of the original *British North America (BNA) Act*. Rep by pop was also reflected in the country's first House of Commons, whereby each of the four provinces that came together to form the Dominion were allocated seats based on the results of the 1861 census. To protect the principle of rep by pop in the face of what was expected to be rapid population growth in the new country, the fathers of Confederation realized that they needed a formula and a process for the assignment of federal seats in the House of Commons. The original formula used to calculate the electoral quotient contained in section 51 of the *BNA Act* was based on the 65 seats that had been assigned to Quebec in 1867, the same number it had in the pre-1867 assembly (Ward 1987, 89).[5] The electoral quotient was arrived at by dividing the population of Quebec by 65; this figure was then divided into the population of each province to determine its share of seats in the House. In recognition of the fact that the formula would need to be adjusted on occasion as the country's population grew, section 51 delegated authority for redistribution to Parliament – a constitutional power that would come to haunt the country in the following years.

As originally drafted, sections 51 and 52 appeared inherently contradictory. Section 52 enshrined the principle of rep by pop, which inferred that provinces would gain or lose seats as their populations shifted. Section 51, however, included a provision known as the "one-twentieth" rule, which declared that no province could lose seats unless its share of the national population altered by +/− 5% of the total Canadian population (Marleau and Montpetit 2000). This rule, along with the fact that section 51 placed politicians in charge of redistribution, meant that it did not take long for the principle of rep by pop to be seriously undermined.[6] Indeed, John Courtney (2004) points out that from Confederation onward, the number of districts awarded to a province has never strictly conformed to its share of the Canadian population. By the time Manitoba, British Columbia, and PEI entered Confederation, rep by pop had already been "thrown to the winds" by the overrepresentation of federal seats that each province demanded in exchange for their entry into the federation (Ward 1950, 23). With these distortions baked into the system, and Parliament given exclusive purview in the process, it is no wonder that partisan gerrymandering remained "a driving force" behind the drawing of electoral districts in Canada during these years, with redistribution consisting of carefully orchestrated events that benefited whatever Conservative or Liberal government was in power at the time (Canada 1991; Courtney 2004).

Senatorial Floor Clause 1915

Discrepancies between the number of electoral districts a province should have based on its population and the actual number it was able to secure due to political bargaining would be further exacerbated in 1915 by an amendment to section 51, known as the "senatorial floor" clause. Given the ineffectiveness of the Senate as a regionally representative body, pressure began to build after 1867 among some of the smaller provinces for special representational protections in the House of Commons. One such province, Prince Edward Island, would prove successful in getting the *BNA Act* amended in the form of section 51(A), which guaranteed a province the same minimum number of seats in the House of Commons as it had in the Senate. In terms of rep by pop, this amendment would prove to be the "thin end of the wedge" over time, as MPs from provinces with relatively declining populations sought to expand on this precedent and devalue the importance of population in redistribution exercises (Williams 2013, 187).

While section 51(A) was constitutionally entrenched, the formula for the federal allocation of seats and the conventions for how redistribution was to occur were subject to Parliamentary discretion, provided it adhered to the loosely worded requirement in section 52 of "proportionate representation." Hence, in the nine decennial redistribution exercises undertaken between 1872 and 1952, successive governments enacted a variety of different formulas and rules to guide redistribution, notably to deal with differentiated rates of population growth across the country and the political fallout that ensued.[7]

The *Electoral Boundaries Readjustment Act* (1964)

The considerable scope given to the governing party of the day under section 51 to shape the redistribution process as it saw fit, and the blatantly partisan and self-serving gerrymandering exercises that this often resulted in (notably during majority governments), led to mounting demands for reform. In 1964, the Lester B. Pearson Liberal government responded with the *Electoral Boundaries Readjustment Act* (EBRA). The EBRA represented nothing short of a "revolution" in the ways in which redistribution was to henceforth occur in the country (Behrman 2011, 277).[8] The EBRA sought to address what were seen as the two biggest shortcomings of redistribution in Canada: the overtly partisan nature of the exercise and the frequently marked discrepancies in both the geographic size and population of constituencies across the country (Courtney 2001).

To this end, a key plank of the new statute was the establishment of an independent and impartial process for the reapportionment of electoral seats in the House of Commons. Along with mandating the creation of independent electoral boundaries commissions for each province following the completion of each decennial census, the EBRA also stipulated that the population of each electoral district correspond as nearly as possible to the province's electoral quota (determined by dividing a province's population by its number of seats) and that no constituency's population should vary by more than 25% above or below this number. However, commissions were allowed to deviate from the provincial quota under "special conditions"; these included geographic considerations such as sparsity, density, or relative growth rate of population; accessibility, size, and shape of a region; as well as social and economic factors such as communities of interest.

While the EBRA brought in a new, nonpartisan process and "enshrined the principle of comparable population in federal law for the first time," it did not deal with the fact the provinces continued to experience uneven rates of population growth (Canada 1991, 139). In 1974, Parliament passed the *Representation Act*, containing a new amalgam formula that, among other things, automatically allocated 75 seats to Quebec and mandated that the province receive four more seats every 10 years. Importantly, the *Representation Act* also contained a grandfather clause, guaranteeing that no province would lose any of its existing seats in the national legislature due to declining population. Following the 1981 census, the application of the amalgam formula contained in the *Representation Act* would have seen a significant enlargement of the House of Commons, with the bulk of new seats going to British Columbia and Ontario (Ward 1987; Williams 2013; Sancton 2010). When the EBCs presented their final reports to Parliament, MPs refused to accept the new distribution and demanded a halt to the process, resulting in the 1984 federal election being fought on the out-of-date boundaries established after the 1971 census (Williams 2005).

The *Representation Act, 1985*

The conflict led the new government of Brian Mulroney to enact yet another change to the redistribution formula, along with amendments to the EBRA, in the form of the *Representation Act, 1985.* Now the electoral quotient would be based on the division of the national population by 279 (the number of seats from the 1974 redistribution), which would result in the population standard for each riding in the country. Each province's population would then be divided by this quotient to determine its number of electoral districts. As well, the "279 formula," as it was referred to, maintained the guarantee that no province would ever have fewer MPs than it did in 1974, which meant that any province that lost a seat as result of the 279 formula would receive a replacement grandfather or "bonus" seat. EBCs were also given greater discretion in their decision making by enabling them, in extraordinary circumstances, to deviate from the previously established +/− 25% electoral quota for each district based on such factors as community of interest or community of identity; historical patterns; and the maintenance of manageable districts in sparsely populated, rural, or northern regions of the province.

While designed to placate interprovincial tensions and bring greater fairness and equity to the redistribution process, the 1985 amendments did the opposite. By ensuring fixed levels of representation for the provinces experiencing declining populations while limiting the number of new seats available to the fastest-growing provinces, the Act only served to increase the amount of malapportionment in the House of Commons. With few constitutional limitations on Parliament in deciding how provincial seats are assigned, these amendments not only represented a clear move away from the principle of rep by pop but also "opened the door to an increased politicization of the redistribution formula" in Canada (Williams 2013, 202).

As could be expected, in the face of the changes brought in by the revised *Representation Act* and the greater latitude given to commissions to move away from considerations of rep by pop, a hailstorm of new protests from MPs ensued. In the redistribution that followed, parliamentarians raised dozens of objections to commission recommendations from all the provinces except Nova Scotia, PEI, and Manitoba (Sancton 1990).[9]

Yet more partisan wrangling would come in the decades that followed the passage of the *Representation Act, 1985.* In the 1994 redistribution, Parliament voted to suspend the process for two years after receiving reports from the provincial EBCs. Opposition was particularly intense amongst rural and northern MPs, who objected to what they saw as a general transfer of seats to urban areas in the country (Eagles and Carty 1999). Maintaining that the suspension was a political manoeuvre to prevent a redistribution from occurring before the next federal election, the Progressive Conservative majority in the Senate refused to pass the bill. A compromise was reached between the two chambers that saw the process eventually resume, but the controversy revealed the differing understandings of redistribution by MPs and commissions, as well as "the importance of place relative to equality of voting power in Canadian redistribution legislation" (Jenkins 1998, 517). Specifically, MPs expressed concerns over EBCs' apparent prioritization of the electoral quota and voter equality over matters related to communities of interest, effective representation, and the challenges of servicing rural and urban constituencies.

The courts also opened up "legal space" for discretionary freedom by federal boundaries commissions during this period (Bickerton and Graham 2020, 33). The Supreme Court of Canada's ruling in *Reference re. Provincial Electoral Boundaries (Sask)*, 1991, known as *Carter*, stands as the most relevant ruling on redistribution in Canada. In *Carter*, a group of urban citizens in Saskatchewan launched a challenge against a proposed redistribution of seats in the provincial legislature that would have allotted different population levels for northern, rural, and urban ridings. The court determined that the redistribution was acceptable because section 3 of the Charter guarantees "effective representation" and "relative parity of voting power," not "absolute equality of ruling power" (Sancton 2010, 9). The court added that the right to vote comprises many factors, of which equity is only one. While relative parity of voting power is a "prime condition of effective representation," it maintained that "factors like geography, community history, community interests and minority representation" also need to be considered in order to ensure that "our legislative assemblies effectively represent the diversity of our social mosaic" (Bickerton and Graham 2020, 37). With these ambiguities, the court failed to offer firm guidance for reconciling voter equality with other principles such as cultural or group identity (Courtney 2001).

From the Harper Conservatives to the Trudeau Liberals

Given that one of the principal effects of the 279 formula was to artificially increase the share of representation of Quebec and Atlantic Canada in the House of Commons, it not only led to ever-increasing interprovincial malapportionment, it did so in a way that notably hurt the Conservative Party.[10] Unsurprisingly, not long after taking office, the Harper government fulfilled a campaign promise to introduce a bill revising the 279 formula. The new bill aimed to increase the number of MPs in the fastest-growing provinces (BC and Alberta, which were Conservative strongholds, along with Ontario) while keeping the grandfather floor guarantees of no fewer seats than 1974 levels. Given that Quebec's percentage of seats would fall from 24% under the 279 formula to 23% in the new formula, the bill was met with considerable opposition from Quebec MPs; Ontario also argued that the bill represented a further debasement of rep by pop since they would remain underrepresented in the House of Commons even with the new formula in place. In the end, the bill failed to pass, as did a second attempt by the Conservatives in 2010.

Their majority win in 2011 gave the Harper Conservatives the votes they needed to pass Bill C-20, the *Fair Representation Act*, the following year. The Act's revised formula for the calculation of the electoral quotient resulted in new seats for Ontario, Alberta, and BC, as well as a grandfather clause guaranteeing that no province's seat count would drop below the number it had prior to the *Representation Act, 1985*. The *Fair Representation Act* also introduced a new representation rule to federal redistribution, ensuring a traditional level of representation for Quebec of 23% (Williams 2013, 201).

In the intervening years, Canada would continue to travel down the path of deviation from rep by pop. With the completion of the decennial census in 2021 and the application of the redistribution formula, it was revealed that Quebec would drop from 78 to 77 seats in the House of Commons. Following a motion introduced by the Bloc Québécois calling for government action to protect Quebec's representation, Parliament quickly passed Bill C-14, *An Act to Amend the Constitution Act, 1867 (Electoral Representation)*, alternately known as the *Preserving Provincial Representation in the House of Commons Act*, in June 2022. The new Act amended the grandfather clause contained in section 51(1) of the *Constitution Act, 1867*, to the effect that no province can be allocated a number of seats less than it previously had in the 43rd Parliament or in 2019 (Canada 2022b).

DEMOCRATIC IMPLICATIONS OF REDISTRIBUTION IN CANADA

As this chapter has revealed, electoral redistribution in Canada is not a straightforward task; rather, it involves normative choices regarding the manner in which seats in the House of Commons are allocated to provinces, the criteria used to delineate electoral boundaries within the provinces, and the ways in which these criteria are defined, prioritized, and applied by decision makers (Hyson 2000). In a larger sense, redistribution processes can directly impact the quality of representation in Canada; as such, they "raise fundamental issues about the nature of Canadian democracy" (Roach 1991, 3). Russell Williams (2005, 99) argues that Canada's system of representation has traditionally been guided by two separate yet contradictory principles. The first of these, which he identifies as "voter equality," has been the dominant theory in the assignment of electoral districts in representative democracies. The idea behind the equality principle, he asserts, is relatively simple: if each adult citizen is to have the right to vote, then in the interests of democracy and equality, those votes should be roughly equivalent in value. This means that in a representative system of single-member districts, each district should have roughly the same number of people to ensure that some votes are not more valuable than others. By way of example, imagine a voter casting a ballot in an electoral district comprising 100 voters compared to a voter living in a district of 1,000 voters. Voter A would have 10 times the influence on electoral outcomes in their riding compared to Voter B (along with increased access to their elected representative), a situation that strikes at the heart of fairness and equality in a democratic system.

Canada has historically embraced the concept of voter equality. It is contained in the principle of parliamentary democracy, which entails the election of political representatives by individual voters residing in demarcated territorial districts. Voter equality was also included in the country's founding constitution, in the form of section 52 and the reference to "proportionate representation." Section 3 of the *Charter of Rights and Freedoms*, which guarantees citizens the right to vote in an election of members to the House of Commons, represents further evidence of the importance of voter equality in Canada. The right to vote is linked to the idea of voter equality and proportionate representation, for, as Munroe Eagles (1991) points out, if all votes are not accorded equal weight in the electoral process, the right to vote can be seriously impaired.[11]

Yet, from the start, Canada – unlike the United States, which adheres to strict population standards in its redistricting exercises – adopted a more flexible approach that allows for population disparities and the balancing of voter equality with other considerations. This less-rigorous model reflects the second principle of representation highlighted by Williams (2013, 100), what he calls the "pluralist approach." This approach seeks to shelter regions and provinces in Canada experiencing population declines, protect historic levels of representation for small provinces, and ensure that the geographic sizes of rural and northern ridings do not become so cumbersome as to impede effective representation. The pluralist approach also allows for the consideration of "communities of interest" and "communities of identity" in redistribution, principles of group representation that contrast with the United States' emphasis on individual rights (Forest 2012, 323). The roots of the pluralist approach can be found in federalism, which, along with parliamentary democracy and citizen's rights, constitute what Katherine Swinton (1992, 21) identifies as the three pillars of Canadian constitutionalism. There is a tension, however, between these principles: while parliamentary democracy and citizen's rights emphasize the "equality of individuals as a principle of representation – encapsulated in the phrase 'rep by pop' – federalism is preoccupied with the representation of regions." When population is unevenly distributed in a country, determining the appropriate representational weight that should be afforded to the regions becomes especially problematic. These questions take on added complexity in Canada, where representation attaches not only to individual citizens and territorial subunits but also to discrete, rights-bearing national groups (Spitzer 2018).

Given these realities, it is understandable why Parliament has historically "defended the pluralist approach and its justifications for deviations from strict adherence to the equality principle" (Williams 2013, 100). We find evidence of this preference for pluralism over voter equality in the special clauses, grandfathered seats, and representation rules that have been enshrined in the constitution over the years, along with the varying array of legislated formulas and principles. Particularly popular in this regard has been the defence of "communities of interest" in redistricting exercises. First introduced in 1964 with the passage of the EBRA, boundaries commissions are required to consider communities of interest or identity in the drawing of electoral boundaries within the provinces. Yet what this term actually means – does it refer to geographic communities? Ethnic, religious, or linguistic communities? Common economic interests? – along with how it should be evaluated and prioritized against other criteria, such as voter equality, is not made clear in the legislation. Thus, while "community of interest" was seen at one time as a necessary counterweight to the unchecked application of population equality, it remains "one of the least clearly defined and most subjective of the criteria of electoral districting; and it is not always easy to apply or respect" (Courtney 2001, 204). Indeed, the imprecise nature of the term led one scholar to dismiss it as "a factor so hopelessly indeterminate as to be worthless as a guiding principle in distribution" (Johnson 1994, 226).

While the EBRA calls on EBCs to correspond as "reasonably possible" to the province's electoral quota in the course of their work, how this should be balanced with communities of interest remains at the discretion of individual commissions. At the same time, the EBRA permits variations in population in each of the electoral districts by as much as +/− 25%, or even more in the case of "extraordinary circumstances" (which is also not defined in the legislation). Together, these factors have afforded boundaries commissions considerable scope in determining what principles should govern their individual approaches to redistribution.[12] Some argue that this has led to the introduction of differing standards across the provinces, depending on the predisposition of commissioners and the persuasive abilities of MPs within each province (Courtney 1988). Michael Pal (2015, 248) maintains that having representatives within the same legislative body elected according to different rules "violates the equality of voters under federal electoral law and section 3 of the Charter," resulting in a fractured right to vote in Canada.

Matthew Mendelsohn (2010, 1) acknowledges that achieving perfect rep by pop in Canada may not be feasible, and that voter equality must sometimes be measured against other principles. However, he worries about the impact on racialized peoples and newcomers to Canada, given that these voters are more likely to be concentrated in populous urban ridings in the country, and contends that "the violations of rep-by-pop principle in Canada now go beyond what is considered acceptable under international democratic norms." Similar concerns were raised by the Royal Commission on Electoral Reform and Party Financing (also known as the Lortie Commission). In its 1991 final report, the Commission recommended the prioritization of voter equality in redistribution processes, clarification of communities of interest, and a maximum deviation from provincial quotas of no more than 15%.[13] These recommendations have yet to be implemented.

The right to vote and participate in elections is a cornerstone of representative democracy; indeed, this right is enshrined in section 3 of the *Charter of Rights and Freedoms*. The creation of electoral districts is an essential aspect of this right, given that ridings are the basic mechanism through which the votes of Canadians are translated into representation in the House of Commons. Related to the right to vote is representation by population, the principle that each vote should be afforded equal weight in the country. However, uneven population growth across the provinces, along with the historical considerations and trade-offs that shaped the founding of Canada, have rendered the strict application of rep by pop impractical. How to balance the competing principles of voter equality/rep by pop with pluralism remains an open question, and one that has dogged redistribution exercises for decades. Given these considerations, it is not surprising that the processes through which electoral boundaries are drawn in Canada – and the rules, principles, and considerations that shape these processes – remain points of contention, conflict, and confusion.

While the move toward independent and nonpartisan electoral boundaries commissions with the passage of the *Electoral Boundaries Readjustment Act* in 1964 removed some of the more overt gerrymandering that had previously existed, Parliament retains constitutional authority over redistribution in Canada. As we have seen, MPs and governing parties have not been above using this authority to routinely alter the methods through which federal seats are allocated to the provinces and to introduce numerous measures to protect less-populated regions and for other political considerations. Indeed, we saw this happen most recently in June 2022 with the passage of legislation to ensure that Quebec's proportion of seats in the House did not drop below current levels. While the role of Parliament in influencing redistribution has resulted in a degree of entrenched malapportionment and a move away from rep by pop and voter equality, the extensive scope given to EBCs has led to a lack of uniformity in how redistribution is carried out across the country. How individual commissions interpret such concepts as communities of interest and identity, effective representation, and the geographic manageability of sparsely populated, rural, and northern regions within a province, along with differing perspectives between commissioners and MPs regarding the place of equality in the representational process, has exacerbated the issue at various points throughout our history (Archer 1993). For some critics, this has resulted in not only the steady erosion of representation by population as a founding principle of Confederation, but a fracturing of the democratic franchise in Canada.

NOTES

1 The provinces also engage in redistribution exercises every 10 years, undertaken by nonpartisan commissions established under provincial law in each province. This chapter focuses on redistribution at the federal level.

2 The periodic adjustment of geographically defined electoral districts is referred to as "redistricting" or "apportionment" in the United States, but in Canada the legal and administrative term that is primarily used is "redistribution." See Benjamin Forest (2012) and Michael Pal (2015).

3 The arguments presented in this chapter, along with all errors, are solely my own, and do not necessarily reflect the views of my fellow commissioners.

4 The electoral quotient and the provincial quotas, while they sound similar, refer to two separate things. The electoral quotient is essentially the average population size of all electoral districts in the country, while the provincial quota is the average population size of districts within a particular province. In Manitoba's case, our population based on the 2021 census was 1,342,153. Divided by the province's 14 seats, this means that the provincial quota for each electoral district in Manitoba is 95,868. In 2022 the national quotient, or the average size of each electoral district in Canada, was calculated to be 121,891. See the representation formula – Federal Electoral Districts Redistribution (https://redecoupage-redistribution-2022.ca/red/form/index_e.aspx).

5 According to Courtney (2001, 23), this plan was designed to appeal to Quebec by guaranteeing the province the same number of seats that it had in the previous Assembly of the United Canadas.

6 See Andrew Sancton (2010) for an excellent overview of this.

7 Canada 1991, 137. The one-twentieth clause in section 51 of the *Constitution Act, 1867* was repealed in 1946 and replaced with a new formula, which saw Quebec's seats increase from 65 to 73 and the House of Commons to 255. See Ward (1950), 51–57.

8 As John Courtney describes, the Pearson government was influenced by the decisions of Manitoba and Quebec a few years earlier to move toward independent electoral boundaries commissions in provincial redistributions. See Courtney (2001), Chapter 3.

9 Quoted in Sancton (1990), 449. The BC courts were also pulled into the fight on redistribution when the EBC for British Columbia decided to decrease the City of Vancouver's seat count in the House of Commons. The constitutionality of the *Representation Act* was challenged on several grounds, including Parliament's ability to unilaterally amend the redistribution formula without provincial consent. On appeal, the court ruled the Act to be *intra vires* ("within the powers") and maintained that "perfect mathematical representation" has never been prescribed by the constitution.

10 See Williams (2013) for an excellent discussion of the challenges inherent in the 279 formula and the Harper government's efforts to overhaul the redistribution formula during its tenure.

11 As discussed earlier, the interpretation of section 3 was brought before the Supreme Court in regard to the Saskatchewan government's attempts to impose a quota for urban and rural constituencies in a provincial redistribution exercise. In its 1991 ruling, *Reference re. Provincial Electoral Boundaries (Sask),* the court rejected the "one person, one vote" approach of the US Supreme Court in favour of "effective representation."

12 In Manitoba, for example, the 2012 and 2022 Federal Electoral Boundaries Commissions (2022) chose to adopt a population range of +/− 10%.

13 The former chief electoral officer for Canada, Jean-Pierre Kingsley, recommended similar changes to the EBRA in his 2005 report to Parliament. He did not, however, take issue with the "extraordinary circumstances" clause, noting that it has only been used sparingly by boundaries commissions. See Elections Canada 2005.

REFERENCES

Archer, Keith. 1993. "Conflict and Confusion in Drawing Constituency Boundaries: The Case of Alberta." *Canadian Public Policy* 19 (2): 177–93. https://doi.org/10.2307/3551681.

Behrman, Robert W. 2011. "Equal or Effective Representation: Redistricting Jurisprudence in Canada and the United States." *American Journal of Legal History* 51 (2): 277–304. https://doi.org/10.1093/ajlh/51.2.277.

Bélanger, Paul, and Munroe Eagles. 2001. "The Compactness of Federal Electoral Districts in Canada in the 1980s and 1990s: An Exploratory Analysis." *Canadian Geographer* 45 (4): 450–60. https://doi.org /10.1111/j.1541-0064.2001.tb01495.x.

Bickerton, James, and Glenn Graham. 2020. "Electoral Parity or Protecting Minorities? Path Dependency and Consociational Districting in Nova Scotia." *Canadian Political Science Review* 14 (1): 32–54. https:// doi.org/10.24124/c677/20201748.

Canada. 1985. *Electoral Boundaries Readjustment Act, 1985.* https://laws-lois.justice.gc.ca/eng/acts/e-3 /page-1.html#h-213536.

———. 1991. *Royal Commission on Electoral Reform and Party Financing, Reforming Electoral Democracy: Volume 1.* Ottawa: Minister of Supply and Services Canada.

———. 2022a. Federal Electoral Districts Redistribution 2022, "The Representation Formula." https:// redecoupage-redistribution-2022.ca/red/form/index_e.aspx.

———. 2022b. *An Act to Amend the Constitution Act, 1867 (Electoral Representation).* https://laws-lois .justice.gc.ca/eng/acts/C-36.71/page-1.html.

Courtney, John C. 1988. "Parliament and Representation: The Unfinished Agenda of Electoral Redistributions." *Canadian Journal of Political Science* 21 (4) (December): 675–90.

———. 2001. *Commissioned Ridings: Designing Canada's Electoral Districts.* Montreal: McGill-Queen's University Press.

———. 2004. *Elections.* Vancouver: UBC Press.

Eagles, Munroe. 1991. "Enhancing Relative Vote Equality in Canada: The Role of Electors in Boundary Adjustment." In *Drawing the Map: Equality and Efficacy of The Vote in Canadian Electoral Boundary Reform*, edited by David Small, 175–220. Toronto: Dundurn Press.

Eagles, Munroe, and R. Kenneth Carty. 1999. "MPs and Electoral Redistribution Controversies in Canada, 1993-96." *Journal of Legislative Studies* 5 (2): 74–95. https://doi.org/10.1080/13572339908420592.

Elections Canada. 2005. *Enhancing the Values of Redistribution: Recommendations from the Chief Electoral Officer of Canada Following the Representation Order of 2003.* Ottawa: Elections Canada.

Federal Electoral Boundaries Commission for the Province of Manitoba. 2022. Report of the Federal Electoral Boundaries Commission for the Province of Manitoba.

Forest, Benjamin. 2012. "Electoral Redistricting and Minority Political Representation in Canada and the United States." *Canadian Geographer* 56 (3): 318–38. https://doi.org/10.1111/j.1541-0064.2012.00437.x.

Hyson, Stewart. 2000. "Electoral Boundary Redistribution by Independent Commission in New Brunswick, 1990–94." *Canadian Public Administration* 42 (3): 174–97. https://doi.org/10.1111/j.1754-7121.2000.tb01566.x.

Jenkins, Richard W. 1998. "Untangling the Politics of Electoral Boundaries in Canada, 1993–1997." *American Review of Canadian Studies* 28 (4): 517–38. https://doi.org/10.1080/02722019809481616.

Johnson, David. 1994. "Canadian Electoral Boundaries and the Courts: Practices, Principles and Problems." *McGill Law Journal* 39 (March): 224–47.

Marleau, Robert, and Camille Montpetit, eds. 2000. *The House of Commons and Its Members.* Ottawa: Parliament of Canada.

Mendelsohn, Matthew. 2010. "Some Are More Equal Than Others: Canadian Political Representation in Comparative Perspective." *Mowat Centre for Policy Innovation: Mowat Note* (March). https:// mowatcentre.munkschool.utoronto.ca/wp-content/uploads/publications/3_some_are_more_equal _than_others.pdf.

Pal, Michael. 2015. "The Fractured Right to Vote: Democracy, Discretion, and Designing Electoral Districts." *McGill Law Journal* 61 (2): 231–74. https://doi.org/10.7202/1037248ar.

Roach, Kent. 1991. "One Person, One Vote? Canadian Constitutional Standards for Electoral Distribution and Districting." In *Drawing the Map: Equality and Efficacy of The Vote in Canadian Electoral Boundary Reform*, *Vol. 11*, edited by David Small, 3–91. Ottawa: Royal Commission on Electoral Reform and Party Financing.

Sancton, Andrew. 1990. "Eroding Representation by Population in the Canadian House of Commons: *The Representation Act, 1985.*" *Canadian Journal of Political Science* 23 (3): 441–57. https://doi.org/10.1017/S0008423900012701.

———. 2010. "The Principle of Representation by Population in Canadian Federal Politics." *Mowat Centre for Policy Innovation Paper* (March). https://mowatcentre.munkschool.utoronto.ca/wp-content/uploads/publications/2_the_principle_of_representation.pdf.

Spitzer, Aaron John. 2018. "Reconciling Shared Rule: Liberal Group Theory, Electoral-Districting Law and 'National Group' Representation in Canada." *Canadian Journal of Political Science* 51 (2): 447–66. https://doi.org/10.1017/S0008423918000033.

Swinton, Katherine. 1992. "Federalism, Representation and Rights." In *Drawing Boundaries: Legislatures, Courts and Electoral Values*, edited by John C. Courtney, Peter MacKinnon, and David E. Smith, 17–39. Saskatoon: Fifth House Publishers.

Ward, Norman. 1950. *The Canadian House of Commons: Representation.* Toronto: University of Toronto Press.

———. 1987. *Dawson's The Government of Canada.* 6th ed. Toronto: University of Toronto Press.

Williams, Russell Alan. 2005. "Canada's System of Representation in Crisis: The '279 Formula' and Federal Electoral Redistributions." *American Review of Canadian Studies* 35 (1): 99–134. https://doi.org/10.1080/02722010509481251.

———. 2013. "Parties, Politics and Redistribution: The Constitutional and Practical Challenges of Politicized Apportionment." In *Parties, Elections and the Future of Canadian Politics*, edited by Amanda Bittner and Royce Koop, 185–210. Vancouver: UBC Press.

CHAPTER SIX

Elections and Democracy

Holly Ann Garnett

INTRODUCTION

The study of election quality and electoral manipulation has been a staple of political science research for decades. Initially, scholars and practitioners predominately focused on issues in emerging democracies like vote buying, intimidation, or post-election protests (Elklit and Svensson 1997). In Canada, as in other established democracies, however, the issue of election quality was seen as less of a concern. Compared with newer democracies, Canadian elections were agreed to be "clean" of malpractice and of high quality, with few, if any, disputes, and these were easily resolved. This began to change, at least for our neighbours to the south, most notably following the 2000 American presidential election when concerns about ballot design (most famously the Florida "butterfly ballot," which caused confusion among some voters and vote counters) and tabulating machines led to questions about who had actually won the presidential contest. In the wake of these events, a field of work on "election sciences" emerged in the United States. Scholars began to study how the patchwork of electoral management bodies and administrative practices in the United States affected the fairness of elections and voter participation.

Yet Canadians were less alarmed: Elections Canada and their provincial counterparts were widely respected and had excellent capacity to deliver clean elections year after year (Garnett and Leibel 2022). Likewise, when debates over cybersecurity and electronic ballot counting took over the news in the United States, Canadians were not alarmed: ballots were cast and counted on paper, by hand, with no marking devices, machines, or hanging chads required (Laronde 2012). When foreign interference and manipulation came to the forefront in 2016, Canadians braced themselves for impact, but discovered, in their first truly cyber-elections, that Canada was not targeted in the same way that the United States or the United Kingdom had experienced attacks (Garnett and Pal 2022).

In many ways, Canada has remained immune from the serious challenges to electoral integrity faced in other established democracies. And recent data suggest that according to some measures,

Canada has the highest-rated elections in North America and rates among the top countries worldwide for the quality of our elections. But rather than falling into complacency, it is also necessary to consider the challenges Canada does face in terms of electoral integrity, in addition to the major strengths that has put Canada among the examples of high-quality elections around the globe. This chapter therefore considers the question: How does Canada compare to the rest of the world in terms of electoral integrity? What are we doing well, and what challenges remain? It concludes with considerations for future agendas for both public debate and scholarly research on electoral integrity in Canada.

DEFINITION: WHAT IS ELECTORAL INTEGRITY?

Political scientists have long studied elections as they relate to democratic quality. Much of this work considers topics such as the manipulation of elections by authoritarian leaders into "democracy with adjectives" or electoral dictatorships (Schedler 2002; Birch 2011; Collier and Levitsky 1997), the role of election observers and international organizations in democracy promotion (Kelley 2012; Hyde 2011), and the violence, protests, or intimidation that may be used by a variety of actors to circumvent democratic processes (Hafner-Burton, Hyde, and Jablonski 2014).

More recently, a field of research on electoral integrity has expanded this work to other contexts and issues. Using a normative definition, electoral integrity is the adherence to international norms and standards, such as those agreed upon by the United Nations or regional organizations like the Council of Europe or Organization of American States. Norris (2014) argues that electoral integrity can be measured across all countries and contexts, and compared internationally. She also highlights that elections comprise a cycle of activities that include the campaign and election day, but also the pre-electoral activities of defining laws and educating voters, as well as the post-election responses by key stakeholders. Finally, Norris contributes to this debate by stressing that electoral integrity can be under threat in both established and new democracies alike.

Recent research has expanded this field of study further to consider the role of democratic theory, or the evaluation of elections based on how they fulfill the ideals of democratic life (Beetham et al. 2008). It has also addressed the new issues that challenge the quality of elections: the role of social media and new technologies (Garnett and James 2020), the influence of the COVID-19 pandemic on electoral activities (James and Alihodzic 2020), and eroding trust and widening conspiratorial thinking about elections (Garnett 2019b; Norris, Garnett, and Grömping 2019; Berlinski et al. 2021). This expansion also includes the type of data sources relied upon for these studies. This contemporary body of electoral integrity research not only draws on a variety of data sources (such as expert surveys, comparative case studies, and public opinion and experimental research), but also engages in new approaches (such as normative, legal, and sociological ones).

EVOLUTION: CANADA IN COMPARATIVE PERSPECTIVE

Turning to the Canadian context: How does Canada compare to other countries in terms of electoral integrity? One source of comparative data is the Perceptions of Electoral Integrity (PEI) Index,

Figure 6.1. The 11-Stage Electoral Cycle

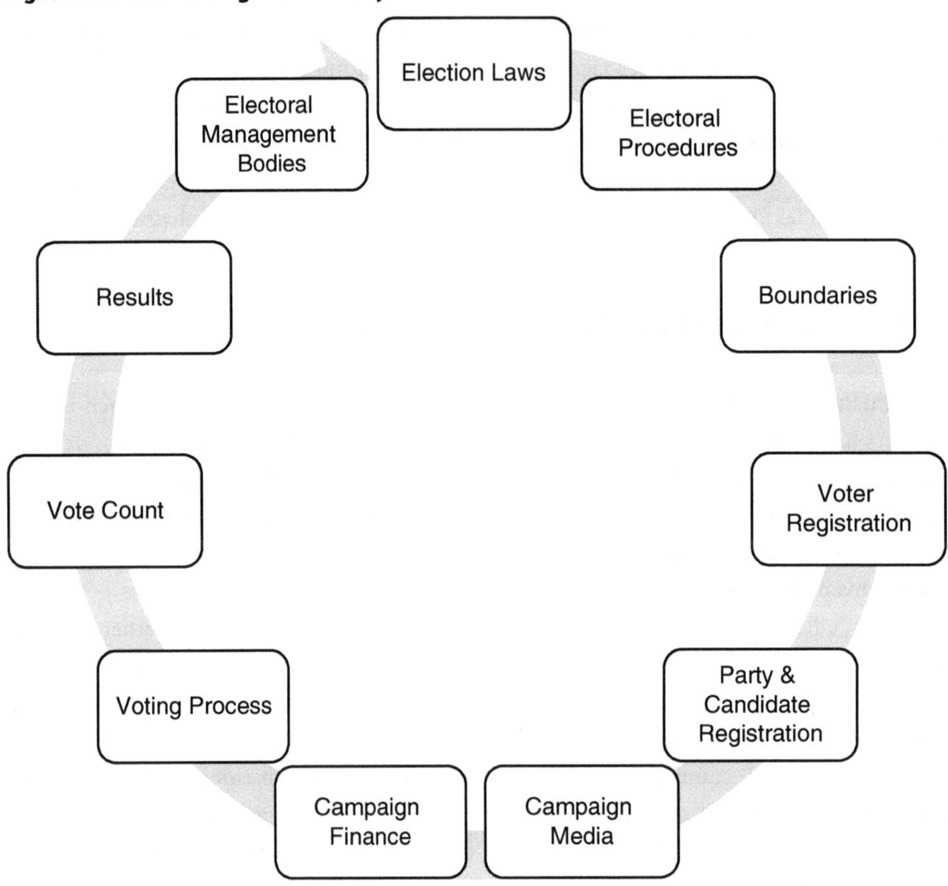

an expert survey covering an 11-stage electoral cycle, that has been conducted on national-level legislative and presidential elections since 2012 (Garnett, James, and MacGregor 2022). For each stage of the electoral cycle, experts are asked to evaluate elections according to a series of questions, providing their opinions on the quality and conduct of the election. Figure 6.1 depicts the 11-stage electoral cycle; see Appendix A for the listing of variables that make up this category. The benefit of these data is that they break down the concept of electoral integrity into multiple indicators, allowing for analysis of each stage of the electoral cycle. The PEI Index has covered three Canadian elections thus far: 2015, 2019, and 2021.

Figure 6.2 depicts the indices for each of the 11 stages of the electoral cycle in addition to the overall PEI Index for each of these elections, as compared to the worldwide average. It presents a picture of the major strengths of Canadian elections (electoral management and campaign finance) and the major challenges remaining to electoral integrity (electoral system and emerging technologies), which are now discussed in turn. The researchers find that overall, Canada's PEI Index is among the highest in each of the years studied (generally within the top 10 countries for overall scores). When country averages between 2012 and 2021 are classified on a scale of "very low" to "very high," Canada is consistently among those elections classified as "very high" electoral

Figure 6.2. Perceptions of Electoral Integrity Index – Canada Compared to Global Means

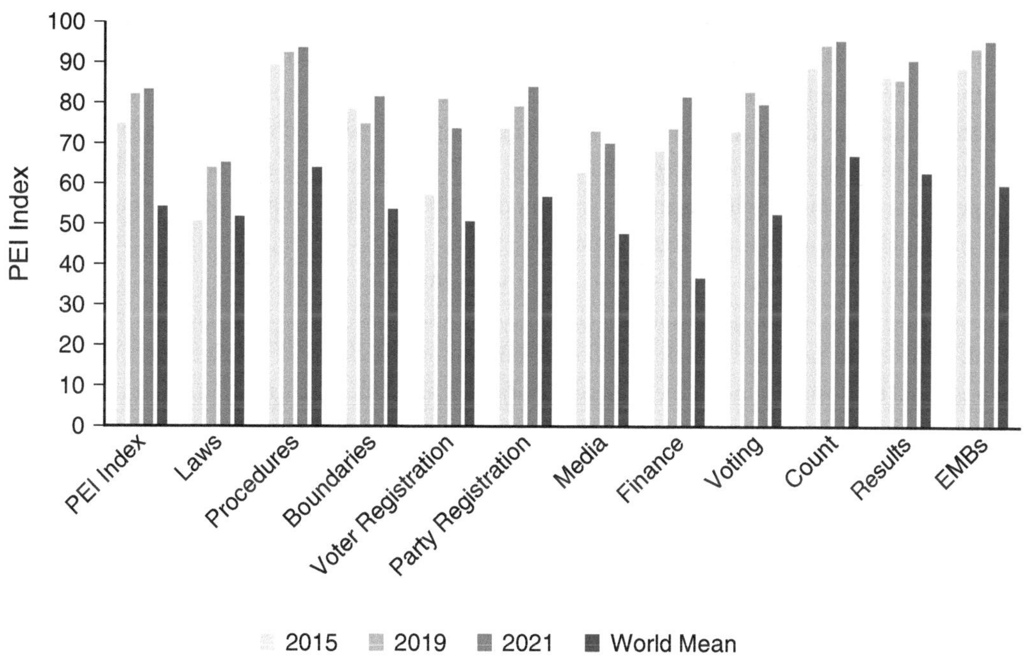

Note: World mean calculated as mean of country means for all elections studied (Garnett, James, and MacGregor 2022).

integrity, scoring similarly to countries like the Netherlands and Germany. With an average score of about 80, it is well above comparator countries like the United States and the United Kingdom, which both have scores in the 60s and are classified as "high" (but not "very high").

Major Strengths

ELECTORAL MANAGEMENT

Among the top-performing aspects of Canada's electoral system are the election procedures, vote count, and election management bodies (EMBs). Each of these aspects predominantly consider the administrative aspects of elections, which are mostly handled by Canada's federal EMB, Elections Canada (see Chapter 3).

The study of electoral management concerns the technical aspects of the administration of elections, from registering voters to setting up polling places to counting the ballots (James et al. 2019; Wall et al. 2006). These tasks fall under the purview of one or more EMBs (Garnett 2022). Around the world, there are a surprising number of variations in models of electoral management. Their formal or legal independence concerns their distance from the executive branch of government, with an independent or agency model (as is Elections Canada) often seen as the "gold standard" of electoral management models (van Ham and Garnett 2019). However, other countries, including a great deal of European countries, have governmental models, where elections are run out of a government department or ministry.

Additionally, EMBs can be divided according to their level of centralization – on a spectrum from national elections run entirely by a centralized body (as is the case of Elections Canada, though of course other bodies are also involved [Garnett 2022]), or highly decentralized models as we find in the United States. The American example is perhaps one of the most extreme in its levels of decentralization, since each state and even county runs national elections according to their own administrative rules and procedures (James 2014). For example, voter registration could take place online in one state but require paper forms in another. Voters could require photo identification in one, but no identification is required in another.

Finally, we may compare systems of electoral management according to their capacity – be that the personnel (numbers or qualifications) they employ, resources (financial or material) at their disposal, or access to new technologies and other innovations in electoral management. While firm figures about the costs of running elections comparatively are difficult to ascertain, other measures of capacity have found Canada to be among those countries with high EMB capacity (Garnett 2019a).

The characteristics of Canada's system of electoral management body, Elections Canada – a centralized and well-resourced EMB that follows the independent agency model – contribute to high expert perceptions of many its aspects covered in the PEI Index. The independent model, operating at arm's length from the governing leader, contributes to perceptions of fairness.[1] Centralization may assist in the dissemination of widely known (and consistent) information about electoral procedures[2] and resources supporting the concrete activities affecting the overall performance of the EMB.

It is unsurprising that these areas concerning electoral management are among the highest rated of the stages of the electoral cycle. Canada's electoral management system has been widely praised by both scholars and practitioners, paralleled by the Canadian population's high level of trust in their EMB and its activities – Canadian Election Study data have shown repeatedly that most Canadians trust or highly trust elections (Garnett and Leibel 2022). This is not to say that there are never irregularities or technical mishaps, such as complaints about long lines during the COVID-19 pandemic (Harell and Stephenson 2022)[3] and lack of access in First Nations communities.[4] A notable controversy in recent years around electoral management concerned the restriction of the role of the chief electoral officer in providing civic education, as proposed in the 2014 *Fair Elections Act* (Government of Canada 2014). This development in Canadian election law was widely disputed by several electoral experts and academics in Canada.[5] But despite these challenges, electoral management remains one of the greatest strengths of Canada's elections, contributing to a reputation for high-quality elections when compared to other countries around the world.

CAMPAIGN FINANCE

When comparing Canada with worldwide averages, one stage of the electoral cycle is particularly striking for its comparative strength: campaign finance. Canada's PEI on this aspect is the highest around the globe when ranked by mean score (75), placing just above Norway and Luxembourg, and substantially higher than the United States (with an average score of only 47).

Elsewhere around the world, issues of money and politics are seen as one of the most pressing challenges and consistent areas of weakness in electoral integrity (Tokaji 2018; Scarrow 2007; Norris, Abel van Es, and Fennis 2015). Concerns about political financing globally include the

Figure 6.3. Campaign Finance Sub-Index Components

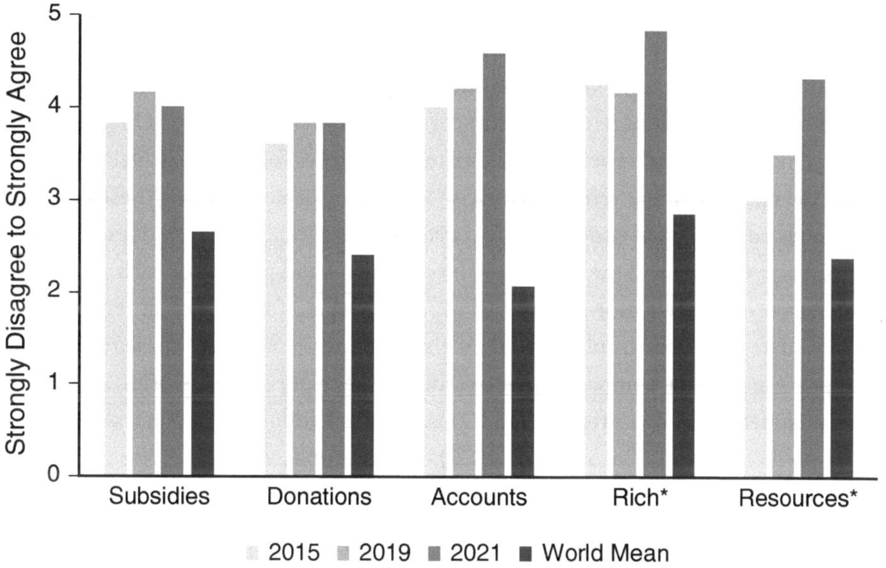

Note: * denotes reverse coding, so higher numbers mean better electoral integrity.

inordinate role of large donors (be they individual or corporate) in influencing who wins elections; the shaping of policy based on the interests of who is financing political parties and politicians; political polarization that may result from extreme fundraising messaging; the inability of small parties or candidates, especially from equity-seeking groups, to have their message disseminated or to win office; and a lack of transparency and reporting of funding sources and expenses.

Campaign finance includes key aspects of this issue of political financing, all for which Canada scores remarkably well (Figure 6.3). Components include equitable access to funds through donations and public subsidies,[6] as well as a lack of use of state resources for campaigning[7] and transparent records of donations and expenses.[8] Lisa Young, in Chapter 3, provides a detailed discussion of the evolution of party financing in Canada, while Pauline Beange covers campaign finance regarding third parties in Chapter 9.

Regarding the equity of access to funding, we turn first to public subsidies. In some countries, political parties and candidates are provided public financing, as they are seen as playing an important educative and organizational function in elections (van Biezen 2004). This may come in the form of direct funding, tax rebates for donations, or even in-kind allocations like media time. In Canada today, public subsidies for political parties and candidates exist through a system of rebates and tax receipts for donors (Young and Jansen 2011; Young 2004). These forms of financing require the parties and candidates to provide "up-front" costs, with rebates coming after the campaign.

The other major source of financing is donations, which raises the issue of equitable voice through political donation.[9] In Canada, limits on spending and donations also contribute to equality among candidates, as a limit adjusted for the riding and year prevents any single candidate from spending more than a common ceiling of funds on their campaign. While a per-vote subsidy, given directly to parties, was in place between 2004 and 2015, it was subsequently phased out. However, some public discussion remains as to whether this allows voters to "donate with their vote," allowing for further inclusivity in the donation process.

Finally, questions about political financing consider the implementation of these regulations and their enforcement through transparent accounting of donations and expenses.[10] On its website, Elections Canada publishes financial reports of candidates and parties following each election to a remarkable level of detail. While there remain some issues in terms of ease of using these data, the completeness of the records published provides a great deal of transparency as to the donors financing political campaigns in Canada and the funds used by candidates and parties for each campaign.

In sum, the inclusion of the two aforementioned aspects – regulations aimed at levelling the playing field for candidates and donors, plus the enforcement/implementation of these regulations through transparency – means that campaign finance is one of the major success stories of electoral integrity in Canada. Nonetheless, there remain questions about the influence of donors and fundraising in Canada's political system (Garnett et al. 2022) – for example, whether access to funding influences who decides to run for office (Tolley, Besco, and Sevi 2020). Recent debate has also suggested that reliance on citizen donors may encourage parties and candidates to appeal to the extreme ends of the ideological spectrum, leading to greater polarization (Raj 2022).

Key Challenges

THE ELECTORAL SYSTEM

When considering the weaknesses of electoral integrity in Canadian elections, the first place to look is election laws – the sub-index that includes fairness to smaller parties[11] and fairness to non-governing parties.[12] For election laws, Canada had its lowest scores in all three elections covered by the PEI Index (Figure 6.2). While not particularly lower than the global means, they are nonetheless below other sub-indices for Canada.

This speaks to one of the most ongoing and contentious debates regarding electoral integrity in Canada: the issue of electoral system reform. Scholars and practitioners have long debated the merits of shifting to a more proportional system that would aim to address some key issues in Canadian elections (which is further covered in Chapter 4 of this volume) (Barnes and Robertson 2009; Pilon 1999 and 2007; Massicotte 2001). Scholars and practitioners have noted that the existing single-member plurality system in Canada tends to advantage larger or regional parties, to the detriment of smaller parties who may have diffuse electoral support across the country but not enough support to garner a seat in any riding. It has also been linked to feelings that an individual voter's ballot is "wasted" when the winner takes all in the riding and can lead voters to feel pushed to strategic voting, also contributing to dissatisfaction with electoral politics (Milner 1999).

But even *consideration* of a change of electoral system in Canada has been fraught with challenges. The experience of the provinces, and most recently the short-lived federal debate following the 2015 election, suggests that this potential challenge to electoral integrity is unlikely to change in the near future (see, for example Garnett [2014]; Stephenson and Tanguay [2009]; Pilon [2010]). On the part of the policymakers, it has become clear that politicians are not keen to disrupt the system that put them in power, and for citizens, electoral reform has failed to garner the type of support needed to push policymakers to act (Katz 2004).

This leads us to a broad conclusion about the challenges of electoral integrity in Canada: they tend to be institutional rather than overt manipulation like ballot-box stuffing or vote rigging. Issues like the electoral system remain challenges because these sorts of "big-picture" challenges to electoral integrity are more difficult to communicate and thus fall behind in debate.

EMERGING TECHNOLOGIES

Finally, we turn to new challenges, unimaginable in 2012 when the PEI was first piloted, that have come to the forefront as major challenges for electoral integrity in Canada. Most notable among these are the challenges associated with new technologies in the electoral process. Research in this area has noted two major threats: cybersecurity of election technology and the information environment with the ubiquity of social media (Garnett and James 2020; Garnett and Pal 2022).

While some may argue that Canada's elections are technology-free, since ballots at the federal level are cast and counted on paper, there remain several technologies employed by election administrators for the management of elections, including online and registration databases. But perhaps more concerning than the use of technology for recordkeeping among election managers is the potential for cyberattacks on political parties' records, which likewise contain large amounts of personal data on voters. But unlike government institutions, parties' capacity for online security may be lower due to limited finances and a volunteer-based workforce (Esselment 2022).

In a series of questions asked alongside the PEI survey in 2018 and 2019 (Figure 6.4), experts in Canada are more concerned about potential cyber-threats than elsewhere.[13] This heightened concern in 2019 could be related to the ubiquity of technology in the electoral process (albeit not in balloting) or fear spilling over from the American elections.

The second cyber-threat is related to the discourse and information that is circulated online during elections, including both official information on the voting process (for example, how and where to vote) and the information that is disseminated by political parties, candidates, and other interest groups (whether official third parties or, to the other extreme, foreign influencers such as Russian troll farms [Akman 2019]). To start with, the good news for Canadian elections, as Figure 6.4 shows, is that Canada scored higher than worldwide means for the questions regarding journalism,[14] media monitors,[15] and the accuracy of news about the election.[16] The role of journalists in Canadian elections is discussed further in Chapter 10.

However, we see that for other information and technology challenges, Canada is facing similar challenges to their counterparts around the globe. One area where Canada only met (but did not exceed) global averages at the mean is the prevalence of hate speech.[17] While negative and fierce campaigning is hardly new, the anonymity provided online can foster an environment where hate speech is more prevalent (Tenove, Tworek, and McKelvey 2018; Tenove and Tworek 2021). This has especially impacted racialized and female candidates, who are subject to attacks online and, subsequently also, offline.[18] Like other countries, Canada has also faced the challenge of mis- and disinformation online (or "fake news"), with information either blatantly false or misleading promulgated by a variety of actors in order to advance their agendas (McKay and Tenove 2020).[19] It

Figure 6.4. Elections, Technology, and Information

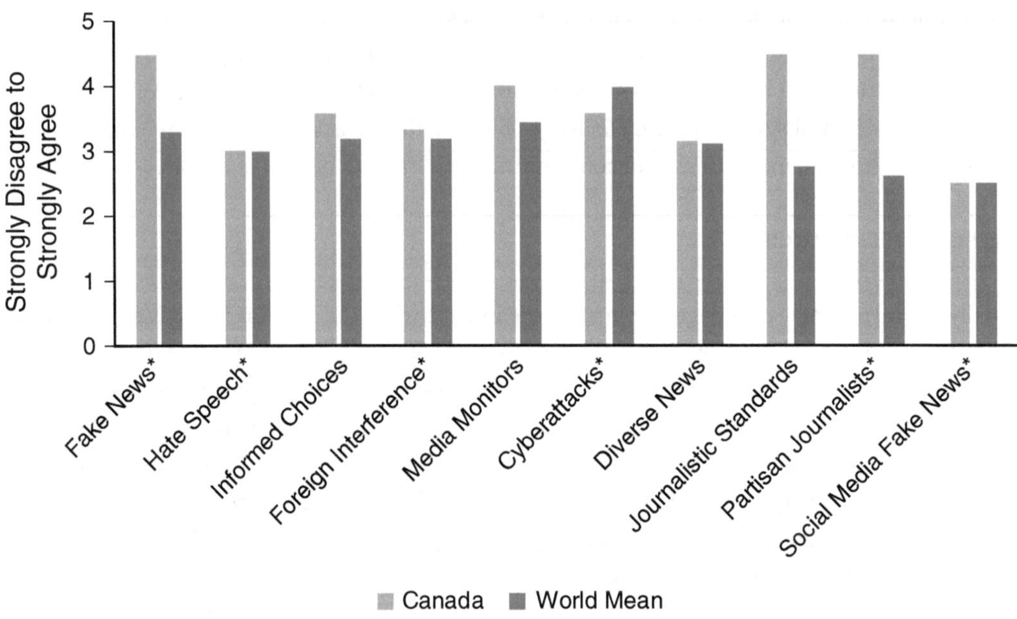

Note: Mean of all elections while this battery of questions was being asked (2018–2019). See Appendix A for question wording. * denotes questions that were reverse coded, so higher numbers denote higher electoral integrity.

is noteworthy that when experts are asked about social media specifically, Canada performs much more poorly than the indicators that concern the traditional news, broadly speaking. The shift from traditional to social media sources (and consequently with voters getting information from less reliable sources) could prove dangerous to the health of Canadian democracy. This may push voters to the extreme ends of the ideological spectrum, as voters hear different messaging through their personal news feeds, leading to more and more extreme messaging and disrupting the democratic process founded on common deliberation.

IMPLICATIONS FOR DEMOCRACY

This chapter has demonstrated that Canada's elections rate quite well for electoral integrity cross-nationally. Canada's electoral institutions present some of the greatest challenges and greatest strengths of the system. Longstanding systems of electoral management serve to strengthen the integrity of the administration of elections. But at the same time, established electoral systems exclude smaller parties from breaking in and perhaps create some measure of dissatisfaction among Canadians.

Common emerging threats to electoral integrity around the planet are also mixed in their applicability to Canada. While political financing is one of the leading challenges worldwide, Canada's system of contributions, expenses, and transparency has made it one of the clear examples of campaign finance regulation gone well (albeit, like any issue, with some remaining challenges). On the contrary, however, the emerging threats of cyber-challenges to elections, an issue that has come to the forefront of electoral integrity debates globally, have become apparent in the Canadian context as well, particularly concerns about cyberattacks and disinformation online.

What are the implications of these strengths and weaknesses of electoral integrity for Canadian democracy? They demonstrate that no country, even the most established, longstanding democracies, is immune to challenges to electoral integrity – be that from long-established and persistently "sticky" institutions or from emerging issues, unheard of in the early days of Canada's democracy, like the new technological developments. While elections in Canada may rank high when compared internationally, recent developments of potential cases of "democratic backsliding" abound worldwide, as evidenced by the rise of anti-democratic leaders like Hungary's Orbán or Brazil's Bolsonaro, extreme rhetoric, and even attempts to overturn election results in longstanding democracies, as evidenced by the January 6 insurrection in the United States. These examples should caution us to remain vigilant in protecting electoral integrity in Canada.

APPENDIX A: PEI DATASET QUESTIONS

	Sections	Performance Indicators	Direction
PRE-ELECTION	1. Electoral laws	1-1 Electoral laws were unfair to smaller parties	N
		1-2 Electoral laws favoured the governing party or parties	N
		1-3 Election laws restricted citizens' rights	N
	2. Electoral procedures	2-1 Elections were well managed	P
		2-2 Information about voting procedures was widely available	P
		2-3 Election officials were fair	P
		2-4 Elections were conducted in accordance with the law	P
	3. Boundaries	3-1 Boundaries discriminated against some parties	N
		3-2 Boundaries favoured incumbents	N
		3-3 Boundaries were impartial	P
	4. Voter registration	4-1 Some citizens were not listed in the register	N
		4-2 The electoral register was inaccurate	N
		4-3 Some ineligible electors were registered	N
	5. Party registration	5-1 Some opposition candidates were prevented from running	N
		5-2 Women had equal opportunities to run for office	P
		5-3 Ethnic and national minorities had equal opportunities to run for office	P
		5-4 Only top party leaders selected candidates	N
		5-5 Some parties/candidates were restricted from holding campaign rallies	N
CAMPAIGN	6. Campaign media	6-1 Newspapers provided balanced election news	P
		6-2 TV news favoured the governing party	N
		6-3 Parties/candidates had fair access to political broadcasts and advertising	P
		6-4 Journalists provided fair coverage of the elections	P
		6-5 Social media were used to expose electoral fraud	P
	7. Campaign finance	7-1 Parties/candidates had equitable access to public subsidies	P
		7-2 Parties/candidates had equitable access to political donations	P
		7-3 Parties/candidates publish transparent financial accounts	P
		7-4 Rich people buy elections	N
		7-5 Some state resources were improperly used for campaigning	N

(Continued)

	Sections	Performance Indicators	Direction
ELECTION DAY	8. Voting process	8-1 Some voters were threatened with violence at the polls	N
		8-2 Some fraudulent votes were cast	N
		8-3 The process of voting was easy	P
		8-4 Voters were offered a genuine choice at the ballot box	P
		8-5 Postal ballots were available	P
		8-6 Special voting facilities were available for the disabled	P
		8-7 National citizens living abroad could vote	P
		8-8 Some form of internet voting was available	P
POST-ELECTION	9. Vote count	9-1 Ballot boxes were secure	P
		9-2 The results were announced without undue delay	P
		9-3 Votes were counted fairly	P
		9-4 International election monitors were restricted	N
		9-5 Domestic election monitors were restricted	N
	10. Results	10-1 Parties/candidates challenged the results	N
		10-2 The election led to peaceful protests	N
		10-3 The election triggered violent protests	N
		10-4 Any disputes were resolved through legal channels	P
	11. Electoral authorities	11-1 The election authorities were impartial	P
		11-2 The authorities distributed information to citizens	P
		11-3 The authorities allowed public scrutiny of their performance	P
		11-4 The election authorities performed well	P

2018–2019 Rotating Battery*

Variable	Question	Direction
fakenews	Much news was fake	N
hatespeech	Campaign media spread hate speech	N
informedchoices	Campaign media allowed informed voting choices	P
foreigninterference	Foreign interests interfered in the campaign	N
mediamonitors	Media watch groups monitored campaign news	P
cyberattacks	Cyberattacks on official voting records occurred during the election	N
diversenews	Campaign news generally reflected the diversity of views and interests in society	P
journalisticstandards	Campaign news generally maintained high journalistic standards	P
partisanjournalists	Journalists were often highly partisan in their campaign reporting	N
fakesocial	Social media often contained fake news	N

Source: www.electoralintegrityproject.com.
Note: The direction of the original items: P = positive, N = negative. In this chapter, data are reverse coded when negative, so higher numbers denote better-quality elections.
* Each year, a set of questions are developed for the PEI Rotating Battery. In 2018 and 2019, the questions listed in the table above were included in this additional battery of questions, in addition to the core PEI questions.

NOTES

1 "Election officials were fair"; "The election authorities were impartial."
2 "Information about voting procedures was widely available."
3 See, for example, https://www.cbc.ca/news/politics/elections-canada-website-lineups-1.6182570.

4 See, for example, https://www.aptnnews.ca/national-news/elections-canada-apologizes-to-3-first-nation-communities-in-ontario/.

5 See https://www.utoronto.ca/news/fair-elections-act-and-open-letter.

6 "Parties/candidates had equitable access to public subsidies"; "Parties/candidates had equitable access to political donations."

7 "Some state resources were improperly used for campaigning"

8 "Parties/candidates publish transparent financial accounts."

9 "Rich people buy elections."

10 "Parties/candidates publish transparent financial accounts."

11 "Electoral laws were unfair to smaller parties."

12 "Electoral laws favoured the governing party or parties."

13 "Cyberattacks on official voting records occurred during the election."

14 "Campaign news generally maintained high journalistic standards"; "Journalists were often highly partisan in their campaign reporting."

15 "Media watch groups monitored campaign news."

16 "Much news was fake."

17 "Campaign media spread hate speech."

18 See https://www.cbc.ca/news/politics/mps-staff-online-hate-security-measures-1.5347221 or https://globalnews.ca/news/9131146/quebec-election-crown-prosecutors-threats-consequences/.

19 "Social media often contained fake news."

REFERENCES

Akman, Peter. 2019. "How Russian Troll Farms Could Impact Canada's Federal Election." CTV News, September 20. https://www.ctvnews.ca/w5/how-russian-troll-farms-could-impact-canada-s-federal-election-1.4600619.

Barnes, Andre, and James R. Robertson. 2009. *Electoral Reform Initiatives in Canadian Provinces*. Ottawa: Library of Parliament, Law and Government Division. http://www2.parl.gc.ca/Content/LOP/Research Publications/prb0417-e.htm#British2.

Beetham, David, Edzia Carvalho, Todd Landman, and Stuart Weir. 2008. *Assessing the Quality of Democracy: A Practical Guide*. Stockholm: International IDEA.

Berlinski, Nicolas, Margaret Doyle, Andrew M. Guess, Gabrielle Levy, Benjamin Lyons, Jacob M. Montgomery, Brendan Nyhan, and Jason Reifler. 2021. "The Effects of Unsubstantiated Claims of Voter Fraud on Confidence in Elections." *Journal of Experimental Political Science* 10 (1): 1–16. https://doi.org/10.1017/XPS.2021.18.

Birch, Sarah. 2011. *Electoral Malpractice*. Oxford: Oxford University Press.

Collier, David, and Steven Levitsky. 1997. "Democracy with Adjectives: Conceptual Innovation in Comparative Research." *World Politics* 49 (3): 430–51. https://doi.org/10.1353/wp.1997.0009.

Elklit, Jørgen, and Palle Svensson. 1997. "What Makes Elections Free and Fair?" *Journal of Democracy* 8 (3): 32–46. https://doi.org/10.1353/jod.1997.0041.

Esselment, Anna Lennox. 2022. "Digital Campaign Threats: Party Responses in an Age of Disinformation." *Cyber-Threats to Canadian Democracy*, edited by Holly Ann Garnet and Michael Pal, 151–73. https://doi.org/10.1515/9780228012795-008.

Garnett, Holly Ann. 2014. "Lessons Learned: Referendum Resource Officers and the 2007 Ontario Referendum on Electoral Reform." *Canadian Political Science Review* 8 (1): 63–84. https://doi.org/10.24124/c677/2014387.

———. 2019a. "Evaluating Electoral Management Body Capacity." *International Political Science Review* 40 (3): 335–53. https://doi.org/10.1177/0192512119832924.

———. 2019b. "On the Front Lines of Democracy: Perceptions of Electoral Officials and Democratic Elections." *Democratization* 26 (8): 1399–1418. https://doi.org/10.1080/13510347.2019.1641797.

———. 2022. "Who Runs Elections? A Cross-National Analysis of Electoral Management throughout the Electoral Cycle." *Commonwealth & Comparative Politics* 60 (2): 146–68. https://doi.org/10.1080/14662043.2022.2047482.

Garnett, Holly Ann, and Toby S. James. 2020. "Cyber Elections in the Digital Age: Threats and Opportunities of Technology for Electoral Integrity." *Election Law Journal: Rules, Politics, and Policy*: 111–26. https://doi.org/10.1089/elj.2020.0633.

Garnett, Holly Ann, Toby S. James, and Madison MacGregor. 2022. "Perceptions of Electoral Integrity (PEI-8.0)." Harvard Dataverse.

Garnett, Holly Ann, and Edward Leibel. 2022. "Public Perceptions of Electoral Management in Canada." *Journal of Election Administration Research & Practice* 1 (1): 32–52. https://electioncenter.org/files-journal/documents/JEARP-volume01-issue-01-public-perceptions-of-electoral-management-in-canada.pdf.

Garnett, Holly Ann, and Michael Pal, eds. 2022. *Cyber-Threats to Canadian Democracy*. Montreal: McGill-Queen's University Press.

Garnett, Holly Ann, Scott Pruysers, Lisa Young, and William P. Cross. 2022. "Lifeblood of the Party: Motivations for Political Donations in Canada." *American Review of Canadian Studies* 52 (4): 422–45. https://doi.org/10.1080/02722011.2022.2147756.

Government of Canada. 2014. *Fair Elections Act*.

Hafner-Burton, Emilie M., Susan D. Hyde, and Ryan S. Jablonski. 2014. "When Do Governments Resort to Election Violence?" *British Journal of Political Science* 44 (1): 149–79. https://doi.org/10.1017/S0007123412000671.

Harell, Allison, and Laura B. Stephenson. 2022. *Elections during a Health Crisis: Voter Involvement and Satisfaction across Pandemic Elections in Canada*. IRPP Report.

Hyde, Susan D. 2011. *Pseudo-Democrat's Dilemma: Why Election Monitoring Became an International Norm*. Ithaca: Cornell University Press.

James, Toby. 2014. "Centralising Electoral Management and Electoral Integrity: Lessons from Britain." Annual Political Studies Association International Conference, Manchester, UK.

James, Toby S., and Sead Alihodzic. 2020. "When Is It Democratic to Postpone an Election? Elections during Natural Disasters, COVID-19 and Emergency Situations." *Election Law Journal* 19 (3): 344–62. https://doi.org/10.1089/elj.2020.0642.

James, Toby S., Holly Ann Garnett, Leontine Loeber, and Caroline van Ham. 2019. "Electoral Management and the Organisational Determinants of Electoral Integrity: Introduction." *International Political Science Review* 40 (3): 295–312. https://doi.org/10.1177/0192512119828206.

Katz, Richard S. 2004. "Problems in Electoral Reform: Why the Decision to Change Electoral Systems Is Not Simple." In *Steps Towards Making Every Vote Count: Electoral System Reform in Canada and Its Provinces*, edited by Henry Milner, 85–102. Peterborough: Broadview Press.

Kelley, Judith. 2012. *Monitoring Democracy: When International Election Observation Works, and Why It Often Fails*. Princeton: Princeton University Press.

Laronde, Paul. 2012. *Technologies in the Voting Process: An Overview of Emerging Trends and Initiatives*. Ottawa: Elections Canada.

Massicotte, Louis. 2001. "Changing the Canadian Electoral System." *IRPP Choices* 7 (1). https://irpp.org/wp-content/uploads/2015/08/vol7no1.pdf.

McKay, Spencer, and Chris Tenove. 2020. "Disinformation as a Threat to Deliberative Democracy." *Political Research Quarterly* 74 (3): 703–17. https://doi.org/10.1177/1065912920938143.

Milner, Henry. 1999. "The Case for Proportional Representation in Canada." In *Making Every Vote Count*, edited by Henry Milner, 37–50. Peterborough: Broadview Press.

Norris, Pippa. 2014. *Why Electoral Integrity Matters*. Cambridge: Cambridge University Press.

Norris, Pippa, Andrea Abel van Es, and Lisa Fennis. 2015. "Checkbook Elections." Money, Politics and Transparency Project.

Norris, Pippa, Holly Ann Garnett, and Max Grömping. 2019. "The Paranoid Style of American Elections: Explaining Perceptions of Electoral Integrity in an Age of Populism." *Journal of Elections, Public Opinion and Parties* 30 (1): 1–21. https://doi.org/10.1080/17457289.2019.1593181.

Pilon, Dennis. 1999. "The History of Voting System Reform in Canada." In *Making Every Vote Count: Reassessing Canada's Electoral System*, edited by Henry Milner, 111–22. Peterborough: Broadview Press.

———. 2007. *The Politics of Voting: Reforming Canada's Electoral System*. Toronto: Emond Montgomery Publications Limited.

———. 2010. "The 2005 and 2009 Referenda on Voting System Change in British Columbia." *Canadian Political Science Review* 4 (2–3): 73–89. https://doi.org/10.24124/c677/2010251.

Raj, Althia. 2022. "Want to Make Canada's Political Parties More Accountable? Pay Them." *Toronto Star*, April 14. https://www.thestar.com/politics/political-opinion/2022/04/13/want-to-make-canadas -political-parties-more-accountable-pay-them.html.

Scarrow, Susan. 2007. "Political Finance in Comparative Perspective." *Annual Review of Political Science* 10: 193–210. https://doi.org/10.1146/annurev.polisci.10.080505.100115.

Schedler, Andreas. 2002. "The Menu of Manipulation." *Journal of Democracy* 13 (2): 36–50. https://doi .org/10.1353/jod.2002.0031.

Stephenson, Laura, and Brian Tanguay. 2009. "Ontario's Referendum on Proportional Representation: Why Citizens Said No." *IRPP Choices* 15 (10). https://irpp.org/research-studies/ontarios-referendum -on-proportional-representation/.

Tenove, Chris, and Heidi Tworek. 2021. "Stopping the Hostile Online Attacks Hurled at Candidates." *Policy Options*, September 13. https://policyoptions.irpp.org/magazines/septembe-2021/stopping -the-hostile-online-attacks-hurled-at-candidates/.

Tenove, Chris, Heidi Tworek, and Fenwick McKelvey. 2018. "Poisoning Democracy: How Canada Can Address Harmful Speech Online." *Public Policy Forum*, November 8. https://ppforum.ca/publications /poisoning-democracy-what-can-be-done-about-harmful-speech-online/.

Tokaji, Daniel P. 2018. "Campaign Finance Regulation in North America: An Institutional Perspective." *Election Law Journal: Rules, Politics, and Policy* 17 (3): 188–208. https://doi.org/10.1089/elj.2018.0512.

Tolley, Erin, Randy Besco, and Semra Sevi. 2020. "Who Controls the Purse Strings? A Longitudinal Study of Gender and Donations in Canadian Politics." *Politics & Gender* 18 (1): 244–72. https://doi .org/10.1017/S1743923X20000276.

van Biezen, Ingrid. 2004. "Political Parties as Public Utilities." *Party Politics* 10 (6): 701–22. https://doi .org/10.1177/1354068804046914.

van Ham, Carolien, and Holly Ann Garnett. 2019. "Building Impartial Electoral Management? Institutional Design, Independence and Electoral Integrity." *International Political Science Review* 40 (3): 313–34. https://doi.org/10.1177/0192512119834573.

Wall, Alan, Andrew Ellis, Ayman Ayoub, Carl W. Dundas, Joram Rukambe, and Sara Staino. 2006. *Electoral Management Design, The International IDEA Handbook Series*. Stockholm: International Institute for Democracy and Electoral Assistance.

Young, Lisa. 2004. "Regulating Campaign Finance in Canada: Strengths and Weaknesses." *Election Law Journal* 3 (4): 444–62. https://doi.org/10.1089/1533129041492259.

Young, Lisa, and Harold J. Jansen. 2011. *Money, Politics, and Democracy: Canada's Party Finance Reforms*. Vancouver: UBC Press.

PART TWO

The Players

CHAPTER SEVEN

The National Campaign

Ian Brodie

INTRODUCTION

A Canadian general election is a major event. Just over 17 million people voted in the 2021 election. Twenty-two political parties offered up 1,919 candidates. The four major parties – the Conservatives, the Liberals, the NDP, and the Bloc Québécois – each received more than a million votes. Two minor parties – the People's Party and the Green Party – received hundreds of thousands of votes. Two more – the Free Party and Maverick – received tens of thousands of votes. All eight of these parties ran candidates in multiple ridings (Officer of the Chief Elections Officer 2022). Not all of them were campaigning to form a government; parties compete for different reasons (Flanagan 2014). Regardless of its ambitions, any party that runs more than a handful of candidates in a handful of ridings during a federal election needs a national campaign in addition to the riding-level campaigns that each candidate runs.

DEFINING NATIONAL CAMPAIGNS

The national campaign does three major things. First, it keeps the party's leader in the public eye during the election. The biggest parties are trying to make their leader the prime minister, the "alpha" who will control the machinery of government after the votes are counted (Flanagan 2014, 3). Voters want to know about these party leaders, what kind of people they are, what they stand for, and how they might govern if given the chance. Every national campaign, regardless of its ambition, features its leader as its primary face to the public and must show off that leader from coast to coast with public events and debates. Second, the national campaign runs national advertising, voter outreach, and media campaigns to pitch its case to voters. These help to keep the party's leader in the public eye but also help local candidates and their campaigns. Finally, the national campaign supports and oversees the party's local campaigns and candidates with specialized help: print and online materials for the local campaign, advice on dealing with voters and journalists, data systems

Table 7.1. Political Party Election Expenses and Reimbursements, 2021 Canadian General Election

Registered Political Party	Expenses ($)	Reimbursements ($)	Spending Limit ($)
Bloc Québécois	2,244,701	1,122,350	7,162,417
Conservative Party	28,342,380	14,171,190	30,043,902
Green Party	1,218,917	614,889	22,659,866
Liberal Party	27,010,581	13,505,290	30,127,505
New Democratic Party	24,190,208	12,095,432	30,127,505
People's Party	1,414,037	707,018	27,957,508

Source: Office of the Chief Electoral Officer 2021a and 2021b.

for tracking voters, and training on the latest campaign tactics. If a party has enough money, the national campaign might send money to support local campaigns as well. If the party's legal structure permits, the national campaign may have an overt role in picking the party's local candidates. All three efforts help the party achieve its goals for the election, whatever they might be.

A national campaign is always short of two things: time and money. Canadian federal elections are short – as short as 36 days. Since jet airplanes became available to the parties, the leaders of the major parties have been expected to visit every province and sometimes the territories. They visit all of Canada's major cities and every "target" riding that their party is making a special effort to win. These leaders must attend at least two televised debates, and leaders usually need a day or two to prep for each one. These leaders will be asked to speak on dozens of election issues and to thousands of voters. But in a 36-day campaign, there is never enough time to visit every part of the country that deserves to be visited, to deal with every issue facing the country, or to speak to every voter. Before the era of air travel, the major party leaders could not travel as extensively but were still expected to visit more ridings than it was possible to reach. National campaigns are always short of time.

A national campaign can make up for some of these time problems by spending money. Leasing a dedicated campaign airplane lets a party move its leader quickly from one place to another, making better use of time. Leasing two airplanes lets staff deliver staging and AV equipment to a city before the leader's airplane arrives, making even better use of the leader's time (BBC News 2019). Money also buys advertising. With enough money, a campaign can quickly send millions of pieces of mail and hire the services of a professional phone bank to contact thousands of voters directly. But a national campaign never has enough money to use all the tools they would like to contact all the voters they would like to reach.

For the last five decades, federal law has capped the amount of money a national campaign can spend during a federal general election. The major national parties ran their 2021 campaigns under a cap of about $30 million (see Table 7.1). Before spending caps were imposed, a national campaign could spend as much money as the party could raise. Spending caps force even a well-funded party to make decisions about which voters they will try to reach and which they will simply ignore. Every dollar spent on one aspect of a campaign comes at the expense of another aspect of the campaign (Brodie 2020). Spending caps force every party to ignore millions of voters. Because time and money are in short supply, the national campaign team must work from a campaign plan to make the best use of these resources. In other words, a national campaign must prioritize.

EVOLUTION OF NATIONAL CAMPAIGNS

Before the Campaign: Prioritizing and Planning

A national campaign works from a plan, and that plan usually takes shape long before a campaign begins. The plan starts with the party's objective for a particular election. Is it aiming to form government after the election or is it enough to win a certain number of seats? For a smaller party, maybe it is enough to highlight an issue that its members care about. Once the campaign's objective is clear, the rest of the national campaign's plan follows. Canadian elections are settled by more than 300 riding-level results. Since no party plans to win every seat, each party must prioritize a list of seats where it will focus its efforts – its "target seats." Tom Flanagan, a political scientist and an experienced campaign manager for right-of-centre parties, calls this prioritization the "triage." When he ran campaigns, he focused his resources on ridings where his party won or lost by ten points in the previous election (Flanagan 2014). Parties with few resources or declining popularity may focus on a tighter list of target ridings, perhaps aiming simply to re-elect incumbents facing difficult re-election campaigns or to work in ridings where their priority issues resonate.

Once a national campaign has a list of target ridings, it begins to develop an idea of the kinds of voters it needs to have onside to win those ridings and the considerations that would motivate those voters to support the party's candidates. Identifying and understanding the kinds of voters that are "accessible" to a party – that is, open to the possibility of supporting a party – was once a matter for relatively crude politics. In the early twentieth century, support for Canadian political parties typically fell along religious lines, with Roman Catholic and Protestant voters supporting different parties depending on where they lived (Johnston 2017). Neighbourhoods or entire towns were known as Liberal or Conservative strongholds, and campaigns had to rely on networks of local leaders to understand what issues were motivating their voters. With the emergence of telephone polling in the 1950s and 1960s, more precise individual-level information became available. Traditional polling probably reached its zenith as a campaign technique in the 1990s, when the cost of telephone calling dropped and most people still answered when their land lines rang. Over the past two decades, traditional polling has become less dependable as telephone habits have changed. Parties therefore increasingly rely on broader types of market intelligence to track the views of voters (Turcotte and Grenier 2020). Traditional opinion polling and "focus groups" – structured, in-person conversations with carefully recruited voters in key cities – are still helpful, but insights from social media platforms, consumer behaviour research, and door-to-door canvassing are also powerful ways to identify accessible voters and what motivates them. As smartphones have become ubiquitous and data analytics have become more accessible, analyses of voting groups by national campaigns have become increasingly fine-grained.

With a list of target seats, accessible voters, and the considerations that motivate those accessible voters, the team can identify a set of communications tactics it will use to win over that electorate.

These tactics might include a collection of policy promises the party can credibly offer to attract the attention of its target voters. This set of policies is sometimes referred to as a "platform" and will reflect input from the party's parliamentary caucus and sometimes the input of rank-and-file party members. Or it might include a set of values the party will try to embody (sometimes referred to as a "vision"). Some accessible voters might feel the economy is doing poorly and be looking to support a party that promises a change in economic policy. Others might notice that rising crime makes them feel unsafe and be looking for better approaches to criminal law enforcement. Still others might feel that an identity that is important to them is better recognized by one party over the others. Hundreds or thousands of these considerations go into constructing the target universe of voters that a national campaign needs to win over in order to achieve its campaign objectives.

The national campaign team then needs "channels" to bring its platform, vision, or values to the attention of target voters. These channels have evolved with the technology available to national campaigns.[1] Handbills, advertisements in local newspapers, and "whistle-stop" tours by party leaders delivering speeches from the back of a train were once the only channels available. Eventually radio, television, and advertising in newspapers with more than merely local distribution became available. National campaign teams spent time and money trying to get traditional TV, radio, or print media to cover their leader and the party's policies or values. A national campaign team relied on an advertising agency and an ad-buying firm to craft advertising spots and decide where to place them for maximum impact. With the sharp decline in the audience for traditional media, these efforts have become less important. Today, campaign channels might be paid advertisements placed on social media, TV, or other traditional channels, or they might be telephone or text messages that connect with voters directly. The channels might also be "earned" placements the team does not pay for directly, such as its volunteers' efforts to persuade and mobilize voters in person or through social media accounts. Parties develop "captive" social media channels and influencers long before a campaign begins and may acquire others during a campaign period. The move to digital campaigning through online platforms means the executives of the major social media platforms cooperate closely with campaign teams to determine when and how to reach the millions of voters who follow friends and family on Facebook, Instagram, or any of the other platforms operating in Canada.

A national campaign's planning efforts should be focused and relentless. Given the shortage of time and money, every effort should focus on voters in target ridings. Within those ridings, campaigns must focus on getting their dependable supporters to the polls and converting "accessible" voters into supporters. As Flanagan argues of national campaigns, "Keep your core supporters loyal, ignore hard-core opponents, and concentrate our resources to appeal to soft supporters who need to be reassured and to soft opponents who can be won over" (Flanagan 2014, 6).

Each party's national campaign team usually starts to emerge a year or two before an election is called. Canadian political parties are organized around their party leaders, and in each party the leader usually hand selects the national campaign director or manager. The national campaign director must have the leader's trust. Many of the director's most difficult jobs entail telling the leader news that he or she doesn't want to hear – that things are going poorly, or the leader's pet issue is a loser when it comes to attracting accessible voters in target ridings. The national campaign director must also be trusted by other senior figures in the party. He or she will work with the party's national governing authorities to recruit and vet candidates, raise and spend money before the election is called, and make other preparations for the campaign. The director must also work with the party's permanent staff to prepare both national and local campaign teams. The party's leader will want the director to keep the parliamentary caucus up to date on national campaign preparations and get input from astute caucus members on the campaign plan and its priorities. Since the rest of the director's most difficult jobs entail telling senior party figures news they don't want to hear – that a particular candidate has become a liability and has to be dropped, that an issue they care about is not going to be tackled by the national campaign, or that the riding the party holds in the House of Commons is no longer a target riding and won't be getting a visit from the leader – he or she must earn the trust of those senior figures. National campaign directors who win are forgiven for every mistake they made and lauded for delivering victory. Directors who lose are reviled even for decisions they got right and for things that were beyond their control.

Once selected, a national campaign director shapes the national campaign team and its plan. The national campaign needs a tour group to plan the leader's election travel, select destinations, organize events, ensure the leader's security, accommodate news media and social media coverage, and make sure the leader's work is serving the overall campaign plan. The tour group includes planners and organizers at the national campaign headquarters, as well as advance teams, media handlers, drivers, pilots and airplane crew, and dozens of others who travel with the leader. The national campaign also needs a messaging, strategy, or scripting group to plan, day to day, what the national campaign, the leader and, ideally, the party's local candidates are saying to accessible voters in target ridings. This team monitors polling and market research every day to ensure the campaign messaging is still hitting its target audiences. The national campaign will have one or more groups devoted to producing video, audio, digital, and print materials that support the messaging, and a team that feeds these materials into the communications channels – social media platforms, telephone banks, news reporters, supportive communities, and social groups – that are available. There might be a separate team to manage issues that crop up during the national campaign or to respond to attacks from the other parties. And every national campaign should have a team of organizers to support local candidates, local campaign organizers, and local party activists. The heads of all these groups and teams – the senior team – should not only be competent at their tasks, but they should include a variety of viewpoints, have personal connections to all the regions with target ridings, and possess a record of showing good judgment while under pressure.

The national campaign director might want to be involved in recruiting candidates in the target ridings. A party's leader and its caucus members all meet potential candidates in their travels and want to have a say in who runs under the party banner. If the party's structures permit it and the leader agrees, would-be candidates might need a "green light" from the national campaign director, or a group named by the director, before they can run for a party nomination. The parties have different internal rules on this point. In some circumstances, the national campaign can intervene to ensure a certain number of women, Indigenous, or racialized candidates run. In others, the local members in a given riding pick the candidate. National campaigns once tried to ensure their local candidates did not have a history of making controversial public comments or being involved in controversial movements. In the digital age, every part of a potential candidate's life is on the public record, so it is no longer possible to have perfectly "clean" candidates. Every candidate has said or done something that could be portrayed in an embarrassing light, so national campaign teams look for candidates who are self-aware enough to see which comments or acts are embarrassing. In the digital era, a candidate must be resilient in the face of personal attacks, either because they can side-step embarrassing aspects of their past, explain them away adroitly, or because the controversial background contributes to the national campaign's sense of authenticity. In ridings the party has little hope of winning, candidate recruiting can face the opposite problem – namely, just finding someone to put their name on the ballot beside the party's name. The closer a riding gets to the top of a party's target riding list, the more interest there is in getting the nod to be that party's candidate.

Media reporting about the covert involvement of foreign governments in Canada's democratic process has drawn attention to the relatively open way that Canada's political parties nominate their candidates. One official review that drew on Canadian intelligence reporting noted that foreign governments might take advantage of the grassroots political process to ensure supportive politicians are elected to Parliament (Johnston 2023). As further reviews unfold, local party organizations will likely come under closer scrutiny by national campaign teams and others in an effort to preserve the integrity of Canadian democracy.

The national campaign usually also runs campaign colleges or training schools for candidates and their local campaigns, partly because local campaigns need certain skills and knowledge, but mostly because a party must campaign as a team and a campaign college is a good way to build the team's spirit.

The legislative cap on campaign spending makes budgeting for a national campaign simple but difficult. As mentioned, a national party that runs candidates in every riding will have a national spending cap of around $30 million. Leasing an airplane or two and moving the leader around Canada for 36 days will take up $5 to $7 million of that cap. The salaries and consulting fees of the national campaign team should be known in advance and contracts for services like polling or market intelligence, social media consulting, advertising advice, and field organization will also ideally be negotiated in advance. Any TV advertising the national campaign wants to do will have to be paid for on the first business day after the election is called.

National campaigns earn a reimbursement of 50 cents on each dollar spent during the campaign period (and 90 cents for accessibility expenses) from Elections Canada when the party files its election spending reports with that agency. A political party planning to mount a full national campaign therefore needs to have $15 million in cash on hand and be able to borrow an additional $15 million from the country's banks when the campaign begins. Its national campaign team will then be able to spend $30 million and earn a $15 million rebate to repay the banks once the campaign is over. Now that corporate donations to political parties are illegal, the banks must extend these loans on commercial terms.

Before the election is called, the national campaign, its parliamentary caucus, and the party's permanent organization work in parallel to improve its organization, raise money, and burnish its profile in ridings the party holds and in ones it hopes to win. The party's elected officers and staff have considerable sway over how the party operates. Once an election is called, all hands are expected to report for election duty, taking on whatever responsibilities the campaign director assigns.

The Campaign Period

Once the writs of election are issued, the campaign period begins and the national campaign goes public. National campaign teams staff up to their full complement. They take possession of their campaign plane. They start buying advertising on digital platforms, TV networks, radio stations, and local billboards. The national campaign director takes charge of all party resources, including the money it has raised for the campaign. The party's national governing authority steps into the background; its members may join the national campaign team under the director or lend their talents to organizing in a target riding. Party staff move over from their regular jobs to roles on the national campaign team. An election campaign is the big show for a national political party, and until election day no party function or operation is as important as working on the election campaign.

The national teams work around the clock to deliver on the campaign plan. Before the campaign period begins, they typically plan each day of the campaign period around the leader and the leader's "tour" of the country. The leader is the principal or "lead" spokesperson for the national campaign, and what they do and say can be communicated to voters either by paid amplification (advertising), by volunteer effort (online or in person work by party supporters), or by "earned" media (professional reporting by legacy or new media news reporting). Leader's tours used to invite professional reporters from news organizations that could afford to do so – major TV and radio networks, wire services, sometimes print outlets – onto their airplanes. With the disintegration of traditional news reporting services, and even with heavy public subsidies to try to keep traditional news reporting services afloat, fewer and fewer national reporters join the tour. A leader's tour is now more likely to be covered by local reporters who turn up at events in their towns. To compensate, parties make their own arrangements to bring news from the leader's tour to target voters with online tools or by providing footage of the events free to news organizations.

Each day of the campaign involves two types of message "tracks." The proactive "message of the day" focuses on a policy plank from the platform for policy-oriented campaigns or a value that the national campaign wants to highlight for target voters. Regardless of the message, the national campaign will try to turn the policy or value into a live, dynamic visual image that conveys the policy or value to busy voters. This might involve creating a contrived event at a location that reinforces the policy or value being highlighted – a leader loading a pizza into the oven of a small pizzeria could illustrate a policy promise aimed at independent business operators, or a leader laughing with small children at a daycare centre might give credence to a promise aimed at families with young children. Campaigns built around values work the same way, with a contrived event at a location that reinforces the value that the national campaign wants voters to associate with its political positions. A leader looking concerned about suburban development in a protected greenbelt around a city reinforces the value of environmentalism. A leader discussing business challenges with women entrepreneurs at a woman-run business reinforces the value of professional feminism. Taking target practice at a hunting lodge reinforces the values of tradition and rural identity.

It was once thought important to schedule "message of the day" events early in the morning, to try to set the agenda for the day's media coverage before other issues crowded in. But since the audience for traditional news outlets has almost disappeared, a message of the day event can now take place at any time. With the multiplicity of online news sources, a national campaign can run several messages in a day, each tailored to a different segment of the voting public.

A second type of message track is the "response" or "issues management" track. A national campaign must respond to the messages of the other national campaigns, to highlight their shortcomings and mobilize voters who are opposed to policies the other campaigns advance or values they stand for. A national campaign also tries to smear other campaigns with "oppo" events that highlight the scandals, corruption, and hypocrisy of the other teams. Some of these responses draw on opposition research conducted before the campaign period begins. Sometimes a national campaign gets lucky and seizes on revelations researched by other actors.

For example, during the 2019 election campaign, news reporters came into possession of photographic evidence that Liberal leader Justin Trudeau had developed a habit of dressing in blackface while he was a professional teacher (Kambhampaty, Carlisle, and Chan 2019). NDP leader Jagmeet Singh, the only racialized leader of a major political party, held a news conference to respond to the revelations. The news conference was a moment of high drama since the photos were so stunning. Singh could have used the occasion to attack the Liberal leader for hypocrisy – Trudeau had spent years highlighting a supposed personal commitment to embracing the racial diversity of Canada. Instead, he soft-pedalled his attack on the Liberal leader and emphasized his solidarity with racialized voters. The NDP's national campaign director felt his response was the "finest moment" of the NDP campaign in that election (McGrath and McGrane 2020, 145). The NDP response did little to rescue its poor campaign, however. The party lost 15 of its 39 seats and dropped from 19.7% to 16% of the popular vote on election day.

The highest profile stretches of a 36-day election campaign are the first few days, when news outlets are trying to set the "framing" of their campaign stories, and the closing days of the campaign, when voters who pay only fleeting attention to politics decide whether to bother showing up to the polls at all. In the last few days of a campaign period, most news organizations focus their coverage on "horserace" reporting. They highlight who is winning and who has a chance of catching up, who has had a "good" campaign and who has put in a "poor" performance. New issues and new attacks get washed out of the coverage.

But the closing days of an election campaign are an opportunity for a well-run national campaign to speak to the concerns of the busy voters who only tune into elections as they wrap up. These voters are not influenced by horserace reporting but are looking for a reason to bother with the hassle of casting a vote. The best tactics to reach these voters in the closing days of an election focus on fear. The objective is to scare busy voters into casting a negative vote – that is, to endure the hassle of voting to stop someone else from winning. Fear is an excellent motivation for human actions, and there are lots of reasons to fear someone becoming prime minister. So national campaigns comb the policy promises and speeches of their opponents to find anything that will cause pain to a specific group of voters. Threats of "extremism" and hidden agendas are ideal closing messages to persuade marginal voters to figure out the location of their polling station, carve out time to get there during the inconvenient hours that polling stations are open, remember to bring photo ID, and find a candidate who can stop the extremists from winning. Political reporters sometimes frame these messages as Hail Mary passes tossed in the closing minutes of the election's equivalent of the fourth quarter. But if they are reinforced with advertising and plausible proof points, these messages can garner enough votes to move a few seats and influence the outcome. If Canada ever adopted mandatory voting, these closing pitches would likely be even more important since low-motivation voters will be forced to cast a vote.

Once an election is called, caucus members return to their ridings, either to run for re-election or to support the candidates they hope will replace them in Parliament. They cannot use their parliamentary resources, paid for by public monies, in their election campaigns. Caucus members with a good public profile might be assigned to a "secondary tour," travelling to ridings the leader cannot reach to draw attention to rookie candidates and rally local volunteers. An MP who raises more money than can be spent in the local re-election effort is expected to send that money to a target riding that can make use of the funds (Currie-Wood 2020). Incumbent MPs and senators may also be asked to provide advice and support to rookie candidates who are running for the first time.

National campaigns face a third shortage once a campaign begins – the shortage of "normies" on the team. National campaign teams are staffed by political professionals with a long history of working on a party's behalf. They might work on Parliament Hill for an MP or in the leader's office, or they might work in the party's off-Hill offices. If not, they probably once worked either on the Hill or in the party offices. Regardless, a national campaign team is made up of people who are the very opposite of "normal" voters. Unlike normies, campaign team members are committed partisans who live in a political world, get their news from specialized sources, and have strong views about election campaigns, leaders, candidates, and issues. Some are motivated by their ideas about a particular issue, and some are motivated by their ambition to be "important" in the political world.

But if the challenge of a national campaign team is to communicate with thousands or millions of accessible voters and have those voters pay attention for a moment or two, then a national campaign must overcome its own views from inside the political world to find people who think like "normies." Normal voters live in the workaday world where election campaigns are background noise. They spend limited time following politics. They have few ideas about campaigns, leaders, candidates, and issues. Normies are not motivated by the ideas or issues or ambition that motivate campaign team members. If normies tune into the esoteric, highly abstract language that national campaign teams use to discuss the leaders, candidates, and issues that matter to *them*, normies only hear gibberish. Consciously or unconsciously, national campaign teams gradually seal themselves off from the real world of ordinary voters. They need to draw on individuals who can relate to and connect with those real voters outside the political bubble. The longer a campaign goes on, the harder it is to find team members who think like normies.

For a small, issue-oriented party, living in a world of ideas that is focused on a narrow set of issues might help motivate an election campaign team. But for a party that wants to elect MPs or turn their leader into a prime minister, the political groupthink of a national campaign team can be fatal.

Polling and market intelligence can help prepare a national campaign to deal with normies, but in the cut and thrust of a campaign, issues and scandals crop up so quickly that the national team has to make decisions before polling is available. There are never enough people that have the technical qualifications to work on a national campaign and who can, at the same time, see the campaign through the eyes of the "normies."

THE DEMOCRATIC IMPLICATIONS OF NATIONAL CAMPAIGNS

In democratic countries, politics is a team sport. After all, a country where only one person matters is a dictatorship. So, parties are a vital part of the political landscape of almost every democratic country. A party's national campaign is simply the arm of a political party that contests the general election.

But a national campaign has deeper democratic functions as well. Each national campaign presents voters with an option: an agenda for governing the country or some other important expression about the country's future. The competition between national campaigns gives an election its structure and infuses it with meaning. Different voters have different levels of knowledge and interest in politics. A national campaign team must work constantly to understand how different voters see politics, to see which issues they think matter, and to communicate with them in terms that connect to them as they live. A good national campaign team turns the high-level objectives of its party leader, its caucus, its candidates, and its supporters into a program that voters will notice and support. It helps voters to understand what is at stake in an election and to see why their votes matter. It also helps the party leaders see what kind of mandate they have received when the votes are counted.

Whereas it was once common to hear complaints that the major parties were all the same and that elections presented voters with a choice between Tweedledum and Tweedledee (Brodie and Jenson 2007), over time the parties have sharpened their differences in an effort to draw the support of increasingly demanding voters. When Canadian political allegiances fell largely along sectarian, Catholic-Protestant lines, the major parties had to broaden their election appeal on other issues to avoid alienating voters on "their" side of the religious divide (see, for example, Johnston 2017). These "brokerage" parties ran bland campaigns (Patten 2016). Today, the national campaign teams work hard to distinguish themselves from each other on issues that matter to voters. As voter turnout declines, national campaigns must work ever harder to give voters a reason to show up at the polls and cast a ballot. These are vital functions that only national campaigns can perform for voters, even if it means we now hear more complaints about political polarization than about the parties being hard to tell apart.

A national campaign also influences which candidates run under a party's banner. When a national campaign team decides that a candidate cannot run under its banner (Chapter 8), it is setting the boundaries for what it sees as acceptable or important in Canada's politics. If the national party prioritizes gender or racial equality when recruiting candidates, that has an impact on the composition of Canada's political elites (see Chapters 16 to 18). If it prioritizes grassroots input, it helps keep Canadian politics in tune with public opinion. Further attention to the covert interference of foreign governments in Canadian elections (see Major 2023) will bring increased scrutiny to the selection of local candidates and may serve to further centralize national campaign influence over the selection of local candidates.

NOTE

1 See Flanagan 2014, especially Chapter 5: The Technology of Persuasion.

REFERENCES

BBC News. 2019. "Trudeau Defends the Number of Planes Used by His Campaign." BBC.com. October 3. https://www.bbc.com/news/world-us-canada-49901452.

Brodie, Ian. 2020. *Testimony. Select Special Democratic Accountability Committee. Nov. 5, 2020.* Transcript No. 30-2-11. Edmonton: Legislative Assembly of Alberta, DA159.

Brodie, Janine, and Jane Jenson. 2007. "Piercing the Smokescreen: Brokerage Parties and Class Politics." In *Canadian Parties in in Transition*, 3rd ed., edited by Alain-G. Gagnon and A. Brian Tanguay, 33–54. Peterborough: Broadview Press.

Currie-Wood, Rob. 2020. "The National Growth of a Regional Party: Evidence of Linkages between Constituency Associations in the Conservative Party of Canada." *Canadian Journal of Political Science* 53 (3): 618–37. https://doi.org/10.1017/S0008423920000360.

Flanagan, Tom. 2014. *Winning Power: Canadian Campaigning in the Twenty-First Century.* Montreal/Kingston: McGill-Queen's University Press.

Johnston, David. 2023. *First Report: Independent Special Rapporteur on Foreign Interference.* https://www.canada.ca/content/dam/di-id/documents/rpt/rapporteur/Independent-Special-Rapporteur%20-Report-eng.pdf

Johnston, Richard. 2017. *The Canadian Party System: An Analytic History.* Vancouver: UBC Press.

Kambhampaty, Anna Purna, Madeleine Carlisle and Melissa Chan. 2019. "Justin Trudeau Wore Brownface at 2001 'Arabian Nights' Party While He Taught at a Private School." *Time.* September 19.

Major, Darren. 2023. "Do Political Parties Need Stronger Rules for Local Nomination Elections?" CBC News. March 5. https://www.cbc.ca/news/politics/political-parties-local-nomination-election-interference-1.6767922.

McGrath, Anne, and David McGrane. 2020. "National Campaign Directors." In *Inside the Campaign: Managing Elections in Canada*, edited by Alex Marland and Theirry Giasson, 135–46. Vancouver: UBC Press.

Office of the Chief Electoral Officer. 2021a. *Final Election Expenses Limits for Registered Political Parties – 44th General Election – September 20, 2021.* https://www.elections.ca/content.aspx?section=ele&dir=pas%2f44ge%2fpollim&document=index&lang=e.

———. 2021b. *Total Paid Election and Accessibility Expenses and Reimbursements, by Registered Political Party – 2019 General Election.* Ottawa: Elections Canada.

———. 2022. "Elections Canada." *Forty-fourth General Election 2021 Official Voting Results.* April 7. https://elections.ca/res/rep/off/ovr2021app/53/table9E.html.

Patten, Steve. 2016. "The Evolution of the Canadian Party System. From Brokerage to Marketing-Oriented Politics." In *Canadian Parties in Transition: Recent Trends and New Paths for Research*, 4th ed., edited by Alain-G. Gagnon and A. Brian Tanguay, 3–27. Toronto: University of Toronto Press.

Turcotte, André, and Éric Grenier. 2020. "Pollsters." In *Inside the Campaign: Managing Elections in Canada*, edited by Alex Marland and Thierry Giasson, 99–108. Vancouver: UBC Press.

CHAPTER EIGHT

The Constituency Campaign

Royce Koop and Anthony M. Sayers

INTRODUCTION

Constituency campaigns are a crucial aspect of Canadian elections. Despite this, they are often unremarked upon in the heat of Canadian election campaigns. Media coverage focuses on party leaders, following them across the country while they make promises and hold press conferences and photo ops (see Chapter 10). But this obscures the fact that to win, parties must clinch more constituency races then their opponent. The quality of the organizations that contest those races at the grassroots are therefore of utmost importance.

The central challenge facing Canada's political parties, Carty (2002b) argues, is one of linking what is essentially an American society to European-style governing institutions. On the one hand, Canada's is a vast, diverse, complex, segmented, mobile, continually growing, and changing society. In linking society to state, Canadian parties must grapple with all this within the confines of a first-past-the-post (FPTP) (see Chapter 4) electoral system that provides one elected member of Parliament (MP) to represent each disparate corner of the country.

Canada is an immigrant-heavy society with high levels of internal migration and complex patterns of overlapping local, provincial, and regional political cultures. Further, the nature of Canadian geography means that the population is necessarily separated from one another and can live quite different lives in different parts of the country. The superimposition of single-member electoral districts onto this vast, complex, and segmented society challenges political parties to build electoral platforms that make sense across a wide variety of local conditions. Parties' mixed success in doing so is seen in comparatively high levels of electoral volatility, with Canada experiencing the highest levels of sustained MP turnover of any established democracy (Matland and Studlar 2004). This volatility results in great variation in the strength of local party organizations and their capacity to run campaigns. It also encourages fierce competition and the ready adoption of technologies that might provide an electoral edge. These are the societal and institutional settings that give rise to both the development of constituency campaigns in Canadian elections and to the dual local-national character of these campaigns.

To remain competitive, district campaigns must respond to the societal characteristics of the local constituency – which, due to immigration into and movement within the country, may change markedly over time – while adapting to changing technologies that reshape political communication. Understanding these shifts is crucial to understanding constituency campaigns as well as their place in the overall structure of Canadian parties. But it is important not to overstate the extent of change. Success or failure depends on sensitivity to local conditions. Many of the goals of local campaigns remain the same, even if the technologies in use continue to change.

We explore constituency campaigns by first providing a rigorous definition and working through their characteristics and their places within Canadian parties' overall structures both between and during election campaigns. We then turn to identifying the key ways in which constituency campaigns have evolved over time, as well as ways in which these structures have remained remarkably resilient. We conclude by exploring the democratic implications of constituency campaigns and revisiting some of the themes that emerge from our analysis.

DEFINING CONSTITUENCY CAMPAIGNS IN CANADA

Katz and Mair (1993) argue that political party organizations can be understood as consisting of three "faces" that have certain powers and competencies. The party in public office consists of the leader and elected members; the party in central office includes the president and other party functionaries; and the party on the ground refers to members and activists in the constituencies. This framework applies well to Canadian parties. The societal and institutional characteristics of Canada give rise to a distinct type of party organization characterized by power at both the national and local levels of the party. This is what Carty (2002a) refers to as the *franchise party model*, which in Canada is characterized by a trade-off between national (as discussed in the previous chapter) and local. Under the terms of the party's "franchise bargain," party leaders have the right to determine party policy but give up detailed control of most local campaigns while members on the ground hold the right to nominate candidates and shape local campaigns but have little say in party policy. In these parties, the party in public office and the party at the grassroots are empowered at the expense of a relatively weak party in central office.

Constituency campaigns are therefore preceded by nomination contests – where local members come together to select a candidate – that are organized by the party's constituency organizations with rules developed by the national party (Cross et al. 2022). The nature of these nomination races differs in response to several factors. In a seat where the party has a strong chance of winning, the nomination race will likely be very competitive. Nominations also differ between the parties. NDP nomination races, for example, tend to favour candidates with long histories in the party. In contrast, Liberal and Conservative races have tended to be more open to "local notable" candidates with little partisan experience but who enjoy local name recognition and support. The strategic calculations of party members, nomination candidates, and local campaigners are shaped by these differences (Sayers 1999).

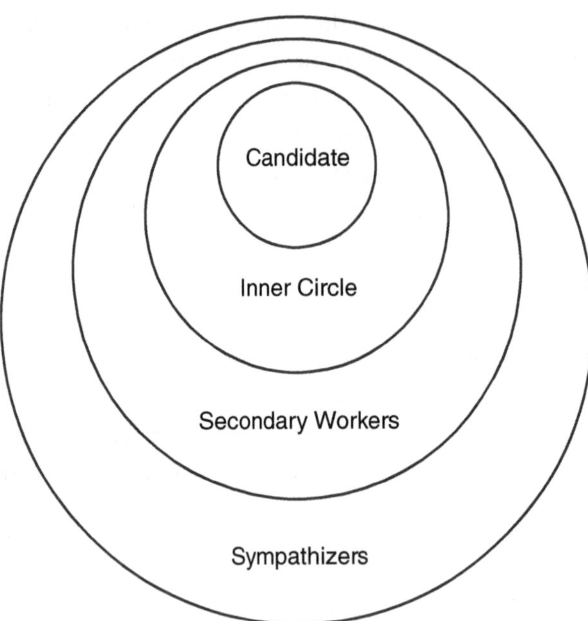

Figure 8.1. Staff of Constituency Campaigns

Nominations are the purview of local party members, but there are limits to this power. Party leaders have the power to block and appoint candidates. They can "parachute" preferred candidates into constituencies in order to allow star candidates or members of traditionally underrepresented groups to bypass the local nomination process (Koop and Bittner 2011). This exercise of power, however, can have the effect of alienating local party members and so is used sparingly. In contrast, there is widespread use of various tools by the central party to screen potential candidates for past peccadillos or social media indiscretions, lest these command media attention in the middle of an election campaign (see Brodie's discussion of these processes in Chapter 7). Local party officials, particularly the electoral district association (EDA) president, act as gatekeepers, shaping nomination outcomes (Albaugh 2022). EDAs are increasingly turning to formal candidate search processes, in part to enhance the diversity of the party's candidate pool (Cross et al. 2022). As Hameed and Tolley note in Chapter 17, diversity at this stage is crucial for the representativeness of Parliament.

Constituency campaigns have several different actors performing important roles. Sayers (1999) views constituency campaigns as a series of concentric circles emanating out from the candidate, with each successive circle carrying out less specialized roles within the campaign. Figure 8.1 illustrates this model of constituency campaigns.

The first of these concentric circles is the insiders that surround and advise the candidates and who perform specialized, indispensable tasks for the campaign. The most important such figure is the campaign manager. These officials may be recruited by the candidate from outside partisan politics based on their prior professional or personal relationship, or they may be selected based on a long record of running constituency campaigns. In some cases, the central party may provide an experienced manager in seats the party has identified as priorities, such as when the party has a good chance of winning a close race. Depending on how well-resourced the campaign is, the manager might be paid.

Koop and Sayers (2022) argue that there are three key challenges facing campaign managers: managing downward, managing upward, and managing outward. Managing downward refers to managing the staff and volunteers who populate local campaigns and carry out key functions during the campaign, such as canvassing, calling voters, delivering signs, and get-out-the-vote activities. Managing upward refers to managing the candidate: scheduling the candidate's appearances, advising them on how to address issues and themes, and encouraging or discouraging certain activities. Finally, managing outward refers to interactions between the local and national campaigns, and the campaign manager is the key local actor engaging with the national campaign.

The other figures in the candidate's inner circle similarly perform specialized, indispensable tasks. This can include the campaign's official agent, who oversees the finances and financial reporting for the campaign, and other leadership positions such as people who supervise volunteers, schedule canvassing throughout the campaign, organize get-out-the-vote activities, or deliver and collect signs. Well-resourced campaigns allow the campaign manager to delegate key tasks to these intermediaries, whereas campaigns without resources may see campaign managers performing all these tasks themselves.

The next circle consists of secondary workers – the volunteers who perform the on-the-ground grunt work of the campaign. Volunteers, Wilson (2022, 218) rightly argues, are "the lifeblood of a campaign." Volunteers for constituency campaigns are there for a variety of reasons: some are committed partisans or ideologues who help no matter who the candidate is, whereas others are primarily motivated to help out the candidate and may in fact have little experience in local campaigning. For some volunteers, campaigning is a social activity, and they look forward to working with their friends and veterans of previous campaigns (Koop 2011).

Both the number and the commitment of these volunteers differ by campaign. Some campaigns drown in volunteers, and the campaign manager or designate struggles to assign tasks and stay organized. But others suffer from a chronic shortage of volunteers, and so the candidate or members of the inner circle must perform time-intensive tasks that would ideally be delegated to others. Volunteers also differ in their commitment and thus in the time and intensity of their participation in the campaign. Some volunteers appear at the campaign office regularly in the morning and work hard for the entirety of the campaign; others show up haphazardly and primarily hang around the campaign office drinking coffee and visiting with other volunteers.

The final circle consists of campaign sympathizers, people who might show up a handful of times to help but who cannot be counted on consistently. If a candidate or party successfully generates interest or there is a perception that they are on the cusp of winning, then sympathizers may be drawn to such campaigns (Sayers 1999). It is this diversity in both the number and commitment of campaign volunteers that lends constituency campaigns their sometimes-chaotic character and that poses enormous logistical challenges to campaign managers, for whom running these spectacles may result in premature aging. The task of recruiting and organizing volunteers is crucial and so usually falls to the campaign manager, although a more junior campaign official can also be assigned to the role (Wilson 2022).

EVOLUTION OF CONSTITUENCY CAMPAIGNS

Have constituency campaigns changed over time? While it would be reasonable to expect such evolution, the crucial features of Canadian society and elective institutions – a diverse, rapidly changing, segmented, and far-flung country combined with the FPTP electoral system – have not changed, so neither have the core functions of constituency campaigns. The perpetual goal of constituency campaigning involves transmitting local concerns to the party and shaping the party message to constituency realities. At the same time, changes in communication technology offer new ways of meeting these challenges. Given the competitiveness and local volatility of Canadian elections, the parties have eagerly embraced these technologies to gain a competitive advantage over their opponents. The result is that constituency campaigns have evolved in some crucial ways while also maintaining their traditional functions.

Traditional Functions of Constituency Campaigns

There are four traditional tasks constituency campaigns carry out. The first and most important function of constituency campaigns is the local canvass. Robbins-Kanter (2022a, 227) defines the canvass as follows:

> direct, unmediated, personal contact between voters and campaign workers or candidates. It entails both door knocking and telephone contact. A canvasser seeks to ascertain voters' political leanings, likelihood of voting for the canvasser's party, and willingness to offer other forms of support, such as accepting lawn signs.

The classic picture of the canvass is of the candidate and volunteers – whether it's shining, snowing, or raining – making their way down streets knocking on doors, dropping off literature, and collecting information about those who live at the address. While canvassing by phone is possible, campaign managers tend to view the in-person canvass as the gold standard, and political scientists have borne out that wisdom in noting that face-to-face mobilization can boost turnout whereas contact over the phone fails to do so (Gerber and Green 2000). The key is to boost turnout among supporters, making the reliable mapping of partisans the overwhelming goal of this effort. All the other critical functions of the local campaign – particularly get-out-the-vote (GOTV) activities and signs – are made possible by this activity.

The nature of the canvass varies in several ways based on the wider context of the campaign (see Robbins-Kanter 2022a). Canvassing in far-flung rural seats, for example, differs greatly from the challenges of canvassing in dense, built-up urban seats, where candidates may be spotted sneaking into apartment lobbies behind tenants so they can knock on all the doors inside. In well-staffed constituency campaigns, canvassing can resemble a well-oiled machine as the team engages in what Wilson (2022, 219) identifies as "leap-frogging": a team of volunteers knock on several doors at a time and the candidate jogs from house to house when people answer to shake hands and answer questions. But when a campaign is weak, the candidate may be spotted out alone knocking on doors. While candidates may wish to stop and chat or even try to persuade undecided voters, campaign managers must remind them that the point of the canvass is to identify supporters, and persuasion is a poor use of their time.

The second function of local campaigns is the distribution and maintenance of campaign signs. The goal of signs is to boost recognition of the local candidate and campaign, and even create a sense of momentum for the process. During Canadian campaigns, signs sprout up across the country, with candidates and their volunteers claiming both public land such as prime locations along busy roads and, when they have permission, the lawns of residents (Maurice and Small 2022). The position of sign chairperson is a common one in local campaigns, and campaigns often have a crew of local volunteers who oversee the planting of signs on public land, repairing and maintaining signs when they are assailed by vandals or the weather, and delivering lawn signs when they are requested.

Large signs on public land may have excellent visibility, but campaign workers prioritize lawn signs since they are a marker of support (Maurice and Small 2022). While the electoral importance of signs is contested by political scientists, campaign workers are convinced they are a crucial aspect of local campaigns, and they measure their success in part through the number of signs they can erect throughout the constituency (Wilson 2022).

Just like the national party, the third function of local campaigns is to generate financial contributions to support the campaign. Constituency campaigns in Canadian elections are quite expensive: Cross and colleagues (2020, 6) report that the average candidate in the 2015 federal election spent roughly $66,000 during the campaign. It has long been recognized both in Canada and elsewhere that local campaign spending is related to increased local vote shares (Carty and Eagles 2005), and the source of campaign funds – whether they originate from the national party or the local community – shapes the nature and emphasis of the local campaign (Cross et al. 2020).

Constituency campaigns are funded from a variety of sources: from the local EDA, which raises money to support the campaign; from the central party, because of transfers from other EDAs; and from limited contributions candidates can make toward their own campaigns. Fundraising for constituency campaigns is often focused on the candidates, especially if the party is running a well-known local personality (see Crandall and Blois 2022). As we will see, access to funds creates new possibilities for constituency campaigns to carry out their other functions more easily along with the need to manage a large and challenging base of volunteers.

Campaign activities culminate in GOTV, in which campaign volunteers work to ensure that as many identified supporters as possible make it out to vote for their candidate. The canvass conducted during the campaign is crucial to a reliable list of supporters to turn to for GOTV purposes. GOTV now begins prior to election day, as campaigns are eager to persuade supporters to vote in advance polls; doing so ensures less work on election day. Certainly, campaign volunteers and anyone working on the campaign is encouraged to vote in advance polls so they can more fully focus on GOTV activities on election day.

Election day sees campaigns come to life, with some volunteers staffing the phones to remind supporters to GOTV while others may knock on supporters' doors or leave a door hanger to provide the reminder. These volunteers can provide supporters with information about what poll they should visit to cast their ballots. A well-functioning constituency campaign will have volunteers with a fleet of vehicles ready to pick up any supporters, especially the most reliable voters of all, seniors, who need a ride to the polls. Other volunteers will act as scrutineers. If the local campaign can afford to do so, the campaign manager will hand out gift cards for Tim Hortons or other drive-thru restaurants so volunteers can grab a bite to eat without missing a beat in their GOTV activities.

All four of these activities – the local canvass, signs, fundraising, and GOTV – are connected in some way. Executing all four well creates the best possible conditions for local victory. Failure at any one task ripples across the entire campaign.

Data-Driven Constituency Campaigning

If constituency campaigns are doing a great deal of what they've always done, what has changed? Data-driven campaigning – the use of large datasets to provide parties with an electoral advantage – is often examined with reference to national campaigns and their use of new political marketing techniques (Dommett et al. 2023; Marland and Wagner 2020). But there is some limited evidence that constituency campaigns are also using these techniques. Belfry Munroe and Munroe (2018 and 2022) demonstrate that significant amounts of data on local voters is available to constituency campaigns, and many campaigns are taking advantage of this to update old campaign strategies and develop new activities. It is now a regular occurrence for the national campaign to transfer data about local voters and residents to the constituency organizers to aid those campaigns. Data are embedded in new campaign platforms that allow campaign managers and volunteers to carry out their roles more effectively.

The availability of data and new platforms has meant that parties can update and improve the ways in which they canvass. It is now routine for volunteers to upload canvassing apps to their smartphones that provide information about households before they knock on any doors, including whether the resident has previously supported or opposed the party in the past. Canvassers use this information to greet residents and, if the information is incorrect, it is immediately updated. If the resident is willing to vote for the candidate or host a sign, or needs a ride to the polls, all this information can be instantly uploaded on the app and made available to the campaign manager so that other volunteers can act on this. In this case, new information technology effectively updates the ancient activities of constituency campaigns.

The parties' data management platforms also have the capability of inferring voters' preferences through predictive analysis based on their other characteristics. This allows constituency campaigns to tailor their outreach activities by targeting voters who are likely to be (but not known to be) party supporters. In the 2021 campaign, for example, Belfry Munroe and Munroe (2022) noted that one constituency campaign tried to call residents designated by predictive analysis as Tier 1 (Liberal) or Tier 2 (Likely Liberal), on the view that doing so was a far better use of volunteers' time than calling unlikely Liberals or likely supporters of the other parties.

In addition, the fact that these apps and data are provided by the national campaign means that officials from the national campaign both have access to updated data and can monitor local campaign officials. If, for example, campaigns are not knocking on enough doors, they can expect to receive a call from the national office instructing them to get a move on.

Similarly, data and platforms like the Liberal Party's Liberalist can be used to inform GOTV operations (see Belfry Munroe and Munroe 2022). If a constituency candidate was not successful in their canvassing operation, then data provided by the central party on past supporters can make up for that even if it is dated and thus imperfect, as the local campaign can then try to turn identified supporters out to vote on election day. In this case, data can be used to make up for other deficiencies in the constituency campaign.

That said, Belfry Munroe and Munroe (2022) caution about the significance of data-driven campaigning in the constituencies, noting that many constituencies do not use such techniques. Some are hostile to these new opportunities, seeing them as the national party impinging on local responsibilities.

Use of Capital in Constituency Campaigns

Growing use of technology has shifted local campaigning away from labour-intensive toward capital-intensive activities and required new positions to manage data and analytical programs. Constituency campaigns in Canadian elections have always relied on grassroots armies of local volunteers to carry out the essential campaign tasks, and we know that the number of volunteers participating on a constituency campaign is related to the number of votes those campaigns receive (Carty and Eagles 2005). But constituency campaigns that are flush with cash can sometimes use those funds to reduce the campaign's reliance on volunteers, creating a more sleek and professional constituency campaign by leaning more heavily on these new technologies.

One way that this occurs is in paying the campaign manager or even other figures in the constituency campaigns. Anecdotal evidence suggests that most campaign managers are unpaid volunteers. But paying campaign managers allows for a professional and experienced figure to take the lead on the campaign rather than relying on leadership from an amateur campaigner who may be a friend or associate of the candidate. In well-funded campaigns, other figures in the constituency campaign may also be paid for their work, with campaign managers able to formally delegate tasks to these employees. In these situations, campaign officials are much more accountable for their work, and some of these campaigns may run like well-oiled machines. Koop and Sayers (2022) report on a campaign in the 2021 election where the manager and several other officials were paid: in this campaign, the manager so effectively delegated tasks that he felt guilty about hanging around the campaign office without much to do.

Managing volunteers, particularly secondary and drop-in workers, can be a daunting challenge for any campaign manager or official. As an alternative, some campaigns have sufficient money to replace the efforts of campaign volunteers with the services of professional outsiders. This comes in many forms. Campaigns may hire local entrepreneurs with a pickup truck to deliver, install, and maintain the campaign's signs until election day. Some campaigns will hire local businesses to distribute literature across the constituency or even conduct the canvass on their behalf. Still others will hire businesses with phone banks to conduct a phone canvass (although this is recognized to be less effective than door-to-door canvassing) and to engage in GOTV activities.

In so doing, constituency campaigns can reduce the number of volunteers necessary to staff the campaign and thus the overall complexity of the organization without necessarily sacrificing success on election day. What does change somewhat are the skills required of a campaign manager, who becomes something more like an office manager.

Relationships between the Constituency and National Campaigns

There have also been recent developments in how constituency campaigns relate to and interact with central party campaigns. Carty's franchise theory posits that constituency campaigns are responsible for adapting the broad themes identified by the national campaign to local tastes and concerns. The diversity of Canadian constituencies and the agency of local actors ensure that the possibility of a rigorously disciplined and controlled campaign from sea to shining sea is next to impossible. Instead, mutual interdependence opens the door for a wide range of local campaign behaviours, ranging from very compliant campaigns that march in lockstep with national themes and concerns to campaigns that operate largely independently from the central campaign, focusing instead on local needs and considerations. This very much depends on the nature of the transaction between the central and local parties (Carty 2004), which is largely shaped by the perceived value of the local campaign to the national party and the extent of local resources.

Outside crisis management, national party involvement in local affairs is driven by three imperatives. The first is the need to maintain the impression of a party that has a national reach, long seen as key to winning Canadian elections. This drives national parties to ensure that a base level of resources is provided in districts where it is electorally weak. Intervention may involve providing the candidate, some workers, and modest financial assistance. At the other end of the spectrum are those local campaigns that the national party has an interest in associating with to benefit from the reflected glow of their likely success. These campaigns are usually well-resourced and not in need of much help but can call on assistance if necessary. Some of these local campaigns may play an outsized role in a party's national strategy and thus attract additional attention. Examples include those into which the national party has parachuted a candidate (Koop and Bittner 2011). Between these end points lie those campaigns the central party is most keen to identify and assist – those that might be turned from a losing to a winning effort with the application of the right additional resources.

The final character of any national involvement in local affairs depends on the intersection of national intent, local conditions, and the attitude of activists on the ground to outside assistance. A national campaign may not be too worried if locals in an unwinnable seat resist its help. A weak local campaign may well be open to accepting direct intervention given limited district-level resources. It is the campaigns in the middle – those that might be turned from losing to winning efforts – that absorb a great deal of effort on the part of the national party and in which the attitude of locals to outside involvement (those who might feel sufficiently well-resourced to win) can be key to how collaboration unfolds. The central party may be willing to offer inducements such as additional funds, workers, or intelligence to encourage potentially competitive campaigns to accept its help. For its part, the local campaign may be willing to collaborate or feel no need to accept outside assistance if it believes itself to be more than capable of funding and managing its own effort. This is also true of those high-profile campaigns central to the national effort. They may see themselves as able to resist or set the terms of any national involvement.

Calculations regarding the value of national intervention are particularly important when the competitiveness of a local campaign changes. On one hand, the national party will see these contests as the route to power and be driven to try and help. On the other, constituency campaigns may be more or less interested in external involvement in light of their view of the quality of the national campaign. A strong national campaign may be seen by locals as an opportunity to "coattail" in the hope of improving its electoral chances. External involvement or focusing on national issues may be seen as an advantage. If the national campaign is perceived as poor, resisting outside involvement, or emphasizing local issues to avoid electoral damage, makes sense. This is not so much rebellion as self-defence. "We do not find 'disloyal' local candidates in the Canadian context," Cross and Young (2015, 308), for example, report. "Rather, personalization is expressed through subtle emphases on local issues, an implicit downplaying of the national platform and organizational reliance on the resources and skills of the local candidate."

In his investigation of undisciplined constituency campaign behaviour in Canadian elections, Robbins-Kanter (2022b) finds five distinct behaviours: ignoring party instructions, distributing unvetted material, critiquing the party leadership privately, contradicting the party's position on a policy issue, cooperating with an opposing party, and critiquing party leadership publicly. The frequency of these behaviours is negatively related to the severity of the conflict with the central party: 42% of constituency campaigns reported ignoring the central party's directives, whereas only 5% engaged in public criticism of the party leader. Some campaigns, Robbins-Kanter argues, are insubordinate to the national campaign; others are innovative and creative, and they defy the central party not to rebel, but rather to assert their own approach to local campaigning; still others are incompetent and simply unable to work effectively with the central party. This is to be expected in Canada, where a very high proportion of candidates in any given election are running as stop-gap candidates (Carty et al. 2003).

That all said, the relationships between the constituency and central campaigns can be quite positive, with central campaigns recasting their role in terms of helping constituency campaigns who have local knowledge rather than policing them to hold to some national standard. In interviews of campaign managers in the 2021 election, Koop and Sayers (2022) found that most managers were quite positive about the role of the central campaign. Some local managers were gratified to receive a boost in central party funding that flowed from being identified as a competitive campaign. Some managers appreciated the arrival of national or regional officials able to advise the local campaign on how to improve their operations or streamline processes. While some accounts suggest campaign managers chafe under this apparent impingement on local ways of doing things, the campaign managers interviewed by Koop and Sayers expressed appreciation for the time and effort expended by these officials for the benefit of the local campaign.

Overall, campaign managers expressed satisfaction with their interactions with the central campaign, and this included among the parties that ultimately lost the election. This is consistent with the surprising finding from a recent survey of local EDAs that activists would prefer *more* central party involvement in local affairs (Cross et al. 2022). This suggests that the central parties may be rethinking their approach to managing local campaigns in a more positive manner than was perhaps the case in the past. Structured and perceived as collaboration rather than control, the role of the national party can be positive for both campaigns. This interesting finding fits well within Carty's franchise party model, as the local and national campaigns have adapted to one another over time.

DEMOCRATIC IMPLICATIONS OF CONSTITUENCY CAMPAIGNS

In this section, we address some themes about how constituency campaigns and the parties at the grassroots contribute to the democratic quotient of Canadian political life. The most important democratic contribution of constituency campaigns is ensuring that local needs and preferences in each region of the country are addressed both during and between elections. The temptation for party strategists is to develop a sleek, professional, national campaign that is designed to win elections. But both the nature of Canadian society and the particularities of Canada's FPTP election system require parties to have additional local elements. Constituency campaigns connect national campaigns and Canada's parties to the communities of the nation. They also provide the only opportunity for most Canadians to participate in and contribute to the election of candidates.

Constituencies and the campaigns run in them shape the way in which the complex national geography of political interests is translated into political demands. There is great variation in how this operates from place to place. For example, some constituencies are safe seats for parties, and so the local race does not provide voters with meaningful choices. Canada does not lack such safe seats: Lapointe (2021), for example, finds that roughly 1/3 of constituency races in the 2019 election were won with at least a 25% margin over the next nearest competitor, with 13 candidates scoring a margin in excess of 70%! In these situations, the local nomination race – the choice before the choice – for the locally dominant party may provide residents their main voice into Parliament.

As Harold Jansen notes in Chapter 4, FPTP demands that political interests in Canada be represented via geography, and these interests are both interpreted through and understood via physical space. The operation of constituency campaigns is defined by both the borders of the local seat and the characteristics of that seat: is it small or large, dense or far-flung, diverse or homogenous? The geographically confined understanding of the local riding that informs constituency campaigning goes on to inform the nature of representation and subsequent efforts of re-election: the candidate for Riding X during election campaigns becomes the honourable member for Riding X afterward. The mechanics of FPTP, which focus politics to some extent on the local and the physical, come into conflict with efforts to represent other, non-geographically defined interests such as women, members of visible minority groups, or Indigenous peoples. MPs sometimes engage in *surrogate representation*, working to further the interests of groups and residents they are concerned with but who do not live within the boundaries of their constituencies (Carrière and Koop 2023). Some electoral systems incentivize such behaviour, but Canada's FPTP system decidedly does not. Even if MPs may wish to engage in advocacy of non-geographically defined interests, the imperative of running for election and re-election within an individual seat typically trumps that hope. Constituency campaigns are the practical response of power-seeking politicians to the need to win and retain power in response to the incentives of both the FPTP electoral system and Canadian society.

In this sense, geographically defined constituency campaigns build a peculiar form of democratic responsiveness to local communities and voters. Most models of representation are *sanction models*, in which it is assumed that MPs act as representatives for their constituents because, if they fail to do so, the voters will sanction them by booting them out of public office in the next election. It is in constituency campaigns that candidates introduce themselves to voters and in which they make the commitments and promises that carry through to their representational activities as MPs. The democratic relationship between MPs and their constituents begins in the constituency campaign, is honoured between elections (often in spite of party discipline), and is refined in future re-election contests.

For constituency campaigns to be democratically meaningful, they must have some influence over the outcomes of constituency races. There is a longstanding debate in Canadian politics about whether voters cast their ballots primarily for the local candidate or for the party and leader. Blais and colleagues (2003) demonstrated that roughly 5% of voters in a single election were swayed by the local candidate, whereas more recent research conducted by Sevi and colleagues (2022) shows that local candidates are a decisive consideration for between 5% to 8% of voters outside Quebec. Nevertheless, we know that strong constituency campaigns can significantly help boost candidates' vote shares. Carty and Eagles (2005), for example, demonstrate that both more volunteers and more money spent by constituency campaigns translates into greater vote shares. Constituency campaigns, they argue, "have a significant impact on the outcome on election day" (2005, 134).

CONCLUSION

Canadian elections are shaped by the superimposition of geographically defined electoral districts on a vast and changeable national society. The difficulty of maintaining simultaneous, consistent support in each of the disparate constituencies drives a great deal of observed partisan and electoral politics. National parties struggle to maintain stable organizations across the various regions, provinces, and urban-rural divides that give expression to this social variation. The devolving of critical functions to local party organizations – the franchise bargain – recognizes this challenge. Key among these are the selection of candidates and the management of local campaigns.

Devolution shifts the burden of managing variation to the local level where it is mechanically best handled but does not alter its underlying logic. Local party organizations and candidates must manage great uncertainty. Their electoral fortune – and with it, their capacity to attract funds and workers and quality local candidates – is dependent on highly changeable local conditions. Electoral volatility drives them to seek whatever advantage they can find in the hope of either resisting a swing against them or maximizing their chances of being swept into office as fortunes change.

As a result, while many of the core functions of a local campaign remain much as they have across the last 170 years, the search for marginal electoral gains drives adoption of new technologies that reshape the ways in which these tasks are fulfilled. Prime among these are data collection and political communication. Adoption of these has reshaped traditional roles and created new ones. Their cost, the need for professional management, and the new data and avenues to voters they provide are both opportunities and challenges for local campaigns. Campaigns now know more about voters and can reach them in new ways. However, managing these tasks and technologies is technically and financially costly. At the same time, old stalwarts such as lawn signs remain a key indicator of campaign vitality, and direct contact with voters is the key to electoral success.

REFERENCES

Albaugh, Quinn M. 2022. "Gatekeeping by Central and Local Party Actors: Theory and Evidence from a Field Study of New Brunswick Nominations, 2017–2018." *Canadian Journal of Political Science* 55 (3): 561–82. https://doi.org/10.1017/S0008423922000385.

Belfry Munroe, Kaija, and H.D. Munroe. 2018. "Constituency Campaigning in the Age of Data." *Canadian Journal of Political Science* 51 (1): 135–54. https://doi.org/10.1017/S0008423917001135.

———. 2022. "Local Data-Driven Campaigning." In *Inside the Local Campaign: Constituency Elections in Canada*, edited by Alex Marland and Thierry Giasson, 244–65. Vancouver: UBC Press.

Blais, André, Elisabeth Gidengil, Agnieszka Dobrzynska, Neil Nevitte, and Richard Nadeau. 2003. "Does the Local Candidate Matter? Candidate Effects in the Canadian Election of 2000." *Canadian Journal of Political Science* 36 (3): 657–64. https://doi.org/10.1017/S0008423903778810.

Carrière, Réal, and Royce Koop. 2023. "Indigenous Political Representation in Canada." *Canadian Journal of Political Science* 56 (2): 1–22. https://doi.org/10.1017/S0008423923000173.

Carty, R. Kenneth. 2002a. "The Politics of Tecumseh Corners: Canadian Political Parties as Franchise Organizations." *Canadian Journal of Political Science* 35 (4): 723–45. https://doi.org/10.1017/S0008423902778402.

———. 2002b. "Canada's Nineteenth Century Cadre Parties at the Millennium." In *Political Parties in Advanced Industrial Democracies*, edited by Paul Webb, David Farrell, and Ian Holliday, 345–78. Oxford: Oxford University Press.

———. 2004. "Parties as Franchise Systems: The Stratarchical Organizational Imperative." *Party Politics* 10 (1): 5–24. https://doi.org/10.1177/1354068804039118.

Carty, R. Kenneth, and Munroe Eagles. 2005. *Politics Is Local: National Politics at the Grassroots*. Vancouver: UBC Press.

Carty, R. Kenneth, D. Munroe Eagles, and Anthony Sayers. 2003. "Candidates and Local Campaigns: Are There Just Four Canadian Types?" *Party Politics* 9 (5): 619–36. https://doi.org/10.1177/13540688030095006.

Crandall, Erin, and Kody Blois. 2022. "Local Party Fundraising." In *Inside the Local Campaign: Constituency Elections in Canada*, edited by Alex Marland and Thierry Giasson, 266–81. Vancouver: UBC Press.

Cross, William P., Rob Currie-Wood, and Scott Pruysers. 2020. "Money Talks: Decentralized Personalism and the Sources of Campaign Funding." *Political Geography* 82: 1–11. https://doi.org/10.1016/j.polgeo.2020.102242.

Cross, William P., Scott Pruysers, and Rob Currie-Wood. 2022. *The Political Party in Canada*. Vancouver: UBC Press.

Cross, William P., and Lisa Young. 2015. "Personalization of Campaigns in an SMP System: The Canadian Case." *Electoral Studies* 39 (3): 306–15. https://doi.org/10.1016/j.electstud.2014.04.007.

Dommett, Katharine, Andrew Barclay, and Rachel Gibson. 2023. "Just What Is Data-driven Campaigning? A Systematic Review." *Information, Communication & Society* 27 (1): 1–22. https://doi.org/10.1080/1369118X.2023.2166794.

Gerber, Alan S., and Donald P. Green. 2000. "The Effects of Canvassing, Telephone Calls, and Direct Mail on Voter Turnout: A Field Experiment." *American Political Science Review* 94 (3): 653–63. https://doi.org/10.2307/2585837.

Katz, Richard S., and Peter Mair. 1993. "The Evolution of Party Organizations in Europe: The Three Faces of Party Organization." *American Review of Politics* 14: 593–617. https://doi.org/10.15763/issn.2374-7781.1993.14.0.593-617.

Koop, Royce. 2011. *Grassroots Liberals: Organizing for Local and National Politics*. Vancouver: UBC Press.

Koop, Royce, and Amanda Bittner. 2011. "Parachuted into Parliament Candidate Nomination, Appointed Candidates, and Legislative Roles in Canada." *Journal of Elections, Public Opinion and Parties* 21 (4): 431–52. https://doi.org/10.1080/17457289.2011.609297.

Koop, Royce, and Anthony M. Sayers. 2022. "Campaign Managers in Constituency Campaigns." In *Inside the Local Campaign: Constituency Elections in Canada*, edited by Alex Marland and Thierry Giasson, 190–207. Vancouver: UBC Press.

Lapointe, Mike. 2021. "Top 33 'Safest Seats' in Canada Won by Conservatives in 2019." *The Hill Times*. September 13. https://www.hilltimes.com/story/2021/09/13/top-33-safest-seats-in-canada-won-by -conservatives-in-2019-with-top-13-winning-by-a-70-per-cent-margin-or-more/229603/.

Marland, Alex, and Angelia Wagner. 2020. "Scripted Messengers: How Party Discipline and Branding Turn Election Candidates into Brand Ambassadors." In *Political Branding: More Than Parties, Leaders and Policies*, edited by Christopher Pich and Richard I. Newman, 59–79. London: Routledge. https://doi .org/10.4324/9781003045199-4.

Matland, Richard E., and Donley T. Studlar. 2004. "Determinants of Legislative Turnover: A Cross-national Analysis." *British Journal of Political Science* 34 (1): 87–108. https://doi.org/10.1017/S000712340300036X.

Maurice, Gillian, and Tamara A Small. 2022. "Campaign Signs." In *Inside the Local Campaign: Constituency Elections in Canada*, edited by Alex Marland and Thierry Giasson, 344–61. Vancouver: UBC Press.

Robbins-Kanter, Jacob. 2022a. "Voter Canvassing." In *Inside the Local Campaign: Constituency Elections in Canada*, edited by Alex Marland and Thierry Giasson, 226–44. Vancouver: UBC Press.

———. 2022b. "Undisciplined Constituency Campaign Behaviour in Canadian Federal Elections." *Canadian Journal of Political Science* 55 (2): 444–66. https://doi.org/10.1017/S0008423922000282.

Sayers, Anthony M. 1999. *Parties, Candidates, and Constituency Campaigns in Canadian Elections*. Vancouver: UBC Press.

Sevi, Semra, Marco Mendoza Avina, and Andre Blais. 2022. "Reassessing Local Campaign Effects." *Canadian Journal of Political Science* 55 (2): 480–85. https://doi.org/10.1017/S000842392200004X.

Wilson, Paul. 2022. "Local Campaign Workers." In *Inside the Local Campaign: Constituency Elections in Canada*, edited by Alex Marland and Thierry Giasson, 208–25. Vancouver: UBC Press.

CHAPTER NINE

Third Parties in Canadian Elections: The Wild Card

Pauline E. Beange

INTRODUCTION

This chapter addresses the activities of "third parties" in Canadian general elections and provincial elections. The term "third party" or "tier" in Canadian election law and literature refers to players or actors outside of political parties, their political entities, and candidates, who choose to advertise or act in the period prior to an election announcement or in the election period itself. This use of "third party" should not be confused with "third party" in the Canadian political party literature, which refers to minor or non-mainstream parties that have never become the governing party (Bélanger 2017).

The *Canada Elections Act* addresses third parties. If individuals and organized interests intend to advertise in traditional media or online platforms (including social media) or undertake election-related activities over a threshold amount of money, they must register as third parties with Elections Canada. Third parties may form ad hoc prior to an election or be well-organized groups; some third parties have no members but large email lists that are used to solicit donations; still others are coalitions of actors sharing the same goals. Beange (2012) finds that third parties have been influential actors in several elections and have been the subject of intense study as well as legislative, judicial, and bureaucratic revisions to their activities, with legislation moving continuously toward more regulation. The regulation of third parties is indeed a "wicked" policy problem – not an ordinary yet hard problem, but instead one that is marked by conflicting values, uncertainty about cause and effect, and high variability because of changing political and social factors (Head 2018).

This chapter will first survey the role of organized interests in Canada as representational vehicles. The second section will trace the evolution of third-party actors in Canadian elections. The interaction of federal electoral law changes on third-party activity in the provinces will be examined in the case of Ontario, where the role of third parties in provincial elections is ambiguous. Last, the adaptive responses of organized interests to regulatory changes and the democratic implications of regulatory change will be considered.

DEFINING THIRD PARTIES

While political parties are the primary avenues for representation, organized interest groups also play a significant role. An interest group is "an association of people or organizations with shared concerns that attempts to influence public policy" (Medvic 2021, 147). Other, similar terms are pressure or advocacy groups or groups gathering for "collective action" (Olson 1965; North 1990). Some organize for material benefits such as higher wages or for more favourable business conditions. Others organize for "feel-good" reasons and still others to achieve collective benefits that aim to benefit society. There is, however, a blurry line between these types. Some groups that claim to be acting in the public interest also advocate for specific ideological, partisan views or views that will bring material benefits to members. Others, in their advocacy for policies benefiting their members, may provide positive spillover effects for society as a whole. Therefore, this chapter will use the term *organized interests*. Organized interests that undertake electoral advertising, certain partisan activities, and specific types of electoral surveys prior to or during an election period are *third parties* in Canadian election terminology[1] and must register with Elections Canada, subject to a threshold (Elections Canada 2023a).

The formal institutional context is important in structuring activities by such groups and, by extension, that of third-party activities in Canadian elections. Barber (1984, 117–18) contends that "[s]trong democracy is consonant with – indeed it depends upon – the politics of conflict, the sociology of pluralism, and the separation of private and public realms of action." Following Barber, Beange (2012) examines how formal and informal institutions and campaign finance regulations affect both political parties and organized interests as civil society actors. State–civil society relations in Canada,[2] the UK, and the US are pluralistic. In the pluralist model, organized interests compete to represent a given "interest" or policy to the government or state. Collusion, or the intended or actual circumventing of electoral regulations by electoral actors, is prohibited, although specific legislation varies among jurisdictions. This institutional context contrasts with that of many European democracies, where the system of state–interest group relations is corporatism, a hierarchical and often formal legal arrangement in which the state selects and grants a monopoly to a limited number of players to represent their declared interests. A second, often unacknowledged factor in third-party regulation is the importance of federalism, where legislation is not uniform across the provinces nor does it necessarily align with federal law. Organized interests may see these differences as political opportunities.

There is a critical balance that must be maintained in the regulation of actors and their financing and spending in elections. The tug-of-war is between maintaining rights of free speech and free political expression while also attempting to ensure that third parties and organized interests face the same accountability and transparency required of political parties and candidates. Such freedoms – and activities by organized interests – were articulated and upheld by political norms, practices, codified and uncodified constitutions, and common law in Canada, the UK, and the US – three mature democracies – long before constitutional documents formally specified such rights (Beange 2012).

In the 1982 *Canadian Charter of Rights and Freedoms* (the Charter), section 2(a), specifies "freedom of conscience and religion"; section 2(b) "freedom of thought, belief, opinion and expression, including freedom of the press and other media of communication"; section 2(c) freedom of peaceful assembly; section 2(d) freedom of association. Third parties in Canadian elections operate under these freedoms. The framework to determine whether a law abides by the Charter's section 1 is the *Oakes* framework, which evaluates whether a limit on a Charter right is "reasonable" and "demonstrably justified" (Department of Justice 2023).

The Charter rendered the *Canada Elections Act* (CEA) subject to legal challenges in general and for third parties specifically. Actors and activities in Canadian elections are governed not just by the CEA but by a network of formal rules, including legislation, administrative regulations, and multiple agencies covering political expression via lobbying and the political voices of registered charities. Informal rules, such as changing views of appropriateness or perceptions of corruption – even if no laws are broken – also influence third-party electoral engagement. Aside from Boatright (2011) and Beange (2012), there is relatively little comparative work on how unions, corporations, and other organized interests have responded to the many interventions in third-party regulation by all branches of the Canadian state. This evolving regime has democratic implications: How have third parties responded to this panorama of changes?

EVOLUTION OF THIRD PARTIES IN CANADIAN ELECTIONS

As discussed by Lisa Young in Chapter 3, the Canadian Parliament struck the Barbeau Committee in 1964 to explore matters of political finance in part due to rising party advertising expenses and partly due to heightened activities by organized interests in American elections. The Committee's report recommended that *only political parties and their candidates* be permitted to buy paid media advertising or post public notices or explicitly advocate for a party or candidate *during* an election campaign (Barbeau Committee 1966). This recommendation to "muzzle" partisan speech was a marked departure from Canadian tradition (Beange 2012, 75) and was a harbinger of future restrictions on third parties. Explicit support and naming of a political party or candidate are often deemed "express" or "partisan" advocacy versus "issue" advocacy, which is for or against policy ideas. The Committee's report therefore recommended a ban on "express" advocacy, but not "issue advocacy," by third parties during elections. Overall, the report expressed fear that "too much money" was being spent in Canadian elections but did not attempt to quantify how much money was actually needed for effective mobilization of voters. Parliament incorporated many of the Committee's recommendations in the 1974 *Election Expenses Act*, which prohibited express advocacy by third parties *during* the election period.

The Royal Commission on Electoral Reform and Political Finance (RCERPF) further investigated political finance. Ideas expressed in its reports (1991–1992) have significantly shaped subsequent legislation and court decisions. The Commission chose to focus on one democratic value rather than attempting to balance competing values: "[F]airness may justifiably restrict certain freedoms.... Fairness is thus the *central value* that must inform electoral laws" (RCERPF 1991, Vol. 1: 4, 322; my emphasis).

The Commission recommended that third parties be restricted to spending only $1,000 during an election, arguing that this limit would enable groups to "engage in a significant amount of election activity" and was "the least restrictive way of limiting freedom of expression while promoting the objective of fairness" (RCERPF 1991, Vol. 1: 353, 355). Legislation in 1993 enacted fixed dollar limits (with an inflationary adjustment) for spending by third parties. The fixed limits appear arbitrary, with no specific rationale except that third parties represented a challenge to political parties. By comparison, spending limits for candidates and political parties remained significantly more generous and flexible. The RCERPF articulated what has become known as the egalitarian model of electoral fairness, in which regulation is aimed at "fairness" or a "level playing field" among electoral players, often defined as the equivalent treatment in what various actors can spend.[3]

Several organizations[4] and individuals challenged the spending ceilings for third parties as violations of the freedoms expressed in section 2(b) of the Charter. Some cases ended at the superior court of a province and others were heard at the Supreme Court of Canada.[5] As noted above, limitations on Charter rights must be "reasonable" and "demonstrably justified." The Supreme Court of Canada in 2004, in a 6–3 decision in *Harper v. Canada (Attorney General)*, ruled that third-party spending limits did violate section 2(b) of the Charter but the limits were justified. However, the reasoning of the three dissenting judges in this case and dissenting opinions in other third-party spending cases demonstrate that there is unease among the justices about the democratic legitimacy of third-party spending limits (Beange 2012). Two citations illustrate their view: "the incursion [created by third-party spending limits] essentially denies effective free expression and far surpasses what is required to meet the perceived threat that citizen speech will drown out other political discourse … the draconian nature of the infringement [of Charter freedoms] … overshoots the perceived danger" (*Harper*, 2, 39).

In 2018, Bill C-76, the *Elections Modernization Act* (EMA), was passed in the House of Commons; the law made changes to Canada's entire electoral regime, including third parties. A Charter statement was issued to inform debate on the bill's consistency with the Charter (Department of Justice 2018), with respect to sections 2(b) and 2(d). Both sections are integral to the rights of third parties. With respect to section 2(d), freedom of association is essentially meaningless, it is argued, if an organized interest cannot publicize its interests and spend freely. Key provisions for third parties follow.[6]

First, this law covers more than traditional advertising: it also includes limits on election surveys, addresses political ads on online platforms by political entities and third parties, and requires a digital registry of regulated ads by internet sites or applications that sell advertising space and surpass a threshold of Canadian visitors or users (Elections Canada 2023a). Second, the EMA creates a pre-election period beginning June 30 of a *fixed-election year*; the election period covers the time between the election announcement and election day. Each period has different third-party spending limits at the national and district levels; each period specifies the types of activities and advertising that are permitted or prohibited for third parties. Third, the law defines "partisan" advertising and activities as those designed to "support or oppose a political candidate, including an issue closely associated with a particular candidate or political party" (CEA, section 349). However, the law also specifies that "partisan" does not include "issue" advertising. Elections Canada clarifies that issue advertising is the "transmission of a message to the public that takes a position on an issue with which a candidate or registered party is clearly associated, without identifying the candidate or party in any way. *Issue advertising is regulated only during the election period.* Like other election advertising, it must include a tagline" (Elections Canada 2023b; original emphasis).

Also significant are provisions requiring timely, detailed third-party reporting of contributions and expenditures to Elections Canada prior to, during, and following an election. These provisions address longstanding concerns that voters had previously been unable to access either the sources of money given to third parties or of their spending until well after election day. Sections of the CEA now prohibit any foreign state and non-state actors from contributing funds to registered Canadian third parties.[7] Foreign entities are permitted to spend on issue advertising but are prohibited from spending on partisan or election advertising or election surveys during an election period. Unions and corporations operating in Canada, municipal governments, and provincial/territorial political parties may also advertise during federal elections.

Beyond the legislature and the courts, the bureaucratic arm of the state also shapes the political space available for third parties. The chief electoral officer (CEO), head of Elections Canada, reports to Parliament, not to a federal minister, and is empowered to make recommendations directly to Parliament. CEO recommendations on third-party regulation are influential because of the CEO's stature as an officer of Parliament.[8] The Commissioner of Canada Elections (2024) is responsible for compliance and enforcement of the CEA.

In summary, many factors have contributed to the frequent rule changes in third-party regulations. This part of Canada's election regulation may be the most complex – and wicked – because it involves so many players, moving parts, strategic responses, growth of digital avenues, and potential interference from foreign entities. It is not insignificant that even the chief electoral officer acknowledges the complexity of third-party regulation (Elections Canada 2019).

Third-Party Spending in Practice: The Canadian Experience

Both theoretical and empirical studies of public policy indicate that organized interests will adapt to new legislation and regulations. Following the 2006 ban on union and corporate contributions to federal political parties, several other strategic options opened. These included organized interests (either foreign-funded or domestic) registering as third parties in federal elections; advertising in the pre-election period prior to 2018; shifting venues via donating to provincial political parties and candidates and to municipal candidates for office (where permitted); registering as third parties in provincial and territorial elections;[9] becoming registered charities and spending up to the allowable limit on political activities; and increasing lobbying at all levels of government. It is possible that businesses and unions felt relieved of their perceived obligation to contribute money to federal political parties, and it is just as likely that organized interests welcomed the money that was "freed up" by the ban and was now potentially available to be donated to them.

Table 9.1 shows the increasing number of third-party actors and the tenfold increase in total spending over seven elections. Peak spending occurred in 2019, the only election covered by new legislation requiring third parties to report spending in the 73-day pre-election period. Lawlor and Crandall (2022) analyzed the trends in third-party spending and noted that the number of union-funded third parties peaked in 2015; the number of organized interest group third parties

Table 9.1. Third-Party Actors and Spending in Canadian General Elections, 2004–2021

	2004	2006	2008	2011	2015	2019	2021
Number of actors*	47	66	57	46	104	56; 111**	92
Expenditures ($)	721,079	1,045,985	1,260,483	1,240,270	5,960,255	11,693,429	7,900,000

Source: Data for 2004–2008, Lawlor and Crandall (2011); 2011–2019, Elections Canada (2022a); 2021, author.
Notes: Figures are rounded. Expenditures are in Canadian dollars.
* Number of actors includes registered third parties with non-zero spending.
** In the 2019 election, there were 151 registered third parties; 56 chose to spend in the pre-election period and 111 chose to spend during the election period.

Table 9.2. Top 12 Third-Party Spenders in Canadian General Elections, 2015–2021

	2015		2019		2021	
Spending by Category	Number*	$ Spent	Number*	$ Spent	Number*	$ Spent
Public-sector unions	4	1,045,776	2	633,058	2	669,863
Labour organizations	4	1,397,987	4	1,862,755	3	1,355,171
Private-sector unions	2	731,542	2	2,538,645	1	509,874
Business organizations	0	0	1	311,698	3	794,045
Individually funded groups	2	497,782	3	1,361,210	3	748,521
Total, top 12 spending	12	3,673,087	12	6,707,366	12	4,077,474

Source: Elections Canada (2018, 2022c, 2022d).
Notes: Amounts spent are in Canadian dollars. Category of spender based on major sources of donations; labour organizations are multi-union financed; business organizations are multi-business or individually financed. The figures for 2019 use original submission; amendments usually involve very small amounts. In 2019 and 2021, dollars spent include pre-writ and election-period spending. Complete tables available from author.
* Total number of third parties is the number that chose to spend.

took the lead in 2018 and 2021. No major Canadian corporation has registered as a third party since 2006. The reasons for this withdrawal include, first, that corporations had begun to withdraw from political donations prior to the 2003 partial ban on their contributions to political parties and candidates due to public concern surrounding conflicts of interest and ethics; second, corporations are subject to significant risk if they choose the "wrong" side in a partisan debate. Major corporations have experienced significant boycotts as a result of taking a stand on a political issue (Hsieh and Wu 2017). Unions, either private or public sector, do not face an equivalent risk.

It is important to look at spending, not just the number of actors. As Table 9.2 shows, public-sector labour unions[10] and labour organizations (which are multi-union financed, usually by public-sector unions) dominate the top 12 spenders in all three elections. Spending by business organizations varied from zero in 2015 to $794,045 in 2019. Aside from the top 12 spenders, environmentally oriented third parties figured predominantly. Few individuals register or spend as a third party, and those who do spend only a few thousand dollars.

Reporting for the 2019 and 2021 elections is more detailed because of new requirements in the EMA of 2018. For 2019, 46% of third parties reported partisan spending and 39% in 2021, with

Table 9.3. Spending Limits for Candidates and Third Parties in Two Electoral Districts, 44th General Election, September 20, 2021

Electoral District	Number of Electors in District	Party Candidate Spending Limit ($)		Third-Party Spending Limit ($)	
		In District	Per Elector in District	In District	Per Elector in District
Labrador, NL	20,239	107,803	5.33	4,506	0.22
Edmonton-Wetaskawin, AB	133,800	152,378	1.14	4,506	0.03

Source: Elections Canada (2021, 2022b, 2022c, 2022d).
Notes: Figures are rounded to nearest dollar. Amounts spent are in Canadian dollars.

percentages based on the number of third parties that chose to spend, not as a percentage of total registered third parties. Some organized interests reported very little partisan spending while others reported 100% of their spending as partisan. Third parties spent increasing amounts on election surveys in 2019 and 2021 and have advertised increasingly on online platforms. The latter may not be a trend since societal and political context are critical to decisions on when, where, and how to promote the interests of a registered third party. For example, if an expansion of free trade were an electoral issue, union-funded third parties would likely spend more to defend the interests of union members.

Third-party spending limits at the electoral district level are rarely mentioned yet must be considered in the metaphor of a "level playing field." As Table 9.3 shows, the allowable spending limit in an electoral district is significantly higher for a party candidate than for a third party: the limit for a candidate is calculated based on the number of electors in a district *and* by an inflation factor for each election. The spending limit for a third party in an electoral district is fixed and is adjusted only for inflation. In the 2021 election, the Labrador electoral district had the smallest number of electors; the Edmonton-Wetaskawin district had the largest number. The size differential in electors meant that because of the spending limit, third parties in urban Edmonton-Wetaskawin could spend only three cents per elector while third parties in the rural Labrador district could spend 22 cents per elector. At face value, there is an apparent inequity, but its effect on local vote choice is unknown. Electoral district spending limits may decrease in importance because online advertising reaches beyond electoral boundaries, and as observed in the UK, micro-targeting of voters blurs the line between national and district advertising (United Kingdom 2021).

To summarize, organized interests adapted, in part, to the ban on union and corporate contributions to federal political parties through registering as third-party actors. There has been significant regulatory change regarding third parties at the federal level. In a federal system such as Canada's, the effects of national-level regulatory changes may spill over to the provinces. It is possible that organized interests shifted venues and became more active in provincial elections in response to federal changes.

Evolution of Third Parties' Spending in Practice: The Experience in Ontario

While federal electoral politics is the focus of this book, it is worth reflecting on recent experiences in Ontario. The importance of legislature, bureaucracy, and courts vis-à-vis third parties outlined above is mirrored in Ontario, as is the ability of third-party actors to switch tactics in the pursuit of electoral and policy influence. Moreover, Ontario laws and subsequent court cases likely have implications for third parties federally and in other provinces. Tracking of third-party expenditures began in the 2007 Ontario election. Sixteen third parties spent $1.7 million; in 2011, 19 groups spent $6.1 million and in 2014, 31 groups spent $8.7 million. This dramatic growth and the "cash-for-access" Ontario Liberal Party contributor scandal (Morrow 2016) prompted amendments to the longstanding *Election Finances Act* (EFA), which covers all electoral players, including third parties.

The Ontario legislature passed amendments to the EFA in 2016. Of greatest significance to third parties were the following. First, the legislation banned corporate, union, and foreign contributions to provincial political parties and affiliates, "freeing up" potential money for third parties. Importantly, spending limits for third parties for issue advertising were set at $600,000 provincewide and $24,000 per electoral district, both indexed for inflation, in the six months preceding a fixed-date election; and $100,000 provincewide and $4,000 per electoral district in the election period. This ratio of third-party spending limits to political party and candidate spending limits was more generous than the ratio in the EMA. In 2021, the Ontario Progressive Conservative government under Doug Ford introduced Bill 254, amending the EFA, with many third-party regulations paralleling the federal 2018 EMA legislation. Included were more timely reporting of expenses (generally seen as contributing to a more informed electorate) and a prohibition on intentional acts to circumvent the EFA. Most contentiously, the regulated pre-election period was lengthened from six to twelve months, while the spending limit in this period was unchanged at $600,000. This meant that third parties were regulated longer than political parties by six months in the pre-election period.

Unions fought back vigorously. The Working Families Coalition (WFC), a group of very large public-sector unions, mounted three legal challenges to the changed rules. For the sake of simplicity, these cases will be referred to as WFC 1, WFC 2, and WFC 3. In 2021, WFC 1 challenged Bill 254's extension of the pre-election period to 12 months, arguing that it infringed on the freedoms in section 2(b) of the Charter. An Ontario Superior Court justice, employing the *Oakes* test, struck down the provision lengthening the longer pre-election period, stating that this restriction was more than a "minimal impairment" of the rights to free expression (WFC 1).

The PC government tabled Bill 307, the *Protecting Elections and Defending Democracy Act*, 2021, whose text was very close to the previous legislation but invoked the "notwithstanding" (section 33) clause of the Charter. Use of this provision enables provincial or territorial legislation to stand for up to five years even if it overrides a section of the Charter. This was Ontario's first-ever use of the notwithstanding clause. The WFC, in WFC 2, again challenged the extended pre-election period, this time arguing that the legislation infringed a different Charter right, the section 3 right to vote, which is exempt from the "notwithstanding" clause. The Ontario Superior Court justice this time upheld the legislation (WFC 2).

Table 9.4. Top 12 Third-Party Spenders in Ontario Elections, 2014–2022

Spending by Category*	2014		2018		2022	
	Number	$ Spent	Number	$ Spent	Number	$ Spent
Public-sector unions	7	4,569,960	5	2,223,982	7	3,518,373
Labour organizations	3	3,632,692	1	282,500	1	546,109
Private-sector unions	0	0	1	211,644	1	422,607
Business organizations	1	84,501	3	1,014,494	2	901,699
Municipal government organization	0	0	1	113,296	0	0
Other interest groups**	0	0	0	0	1	301,844
Individually funded groups	1	83,768	1	663,979	0	0
Total, top 12 spending	12	8,370,921	12	4,509,891	12	5,690,632
Total, all third parties***	28	8,610,463	49	5,226,295	63	8,298,796

Source: Elections Ontario 2022. https://finances.elections.on.ca/en/third-party-advertisers.
Notes: Amounts spent are in Canadian dollars. Figures rounded to nearest dollar.
* Category of spender based on major sources of donations.
** Report shows "Third Party's Own Funds"; no contributions reported.
*** Number of registered third parties that spent in the pre-election or election period.

Finally, the Working Families Coalition appealed, and the Ontario Court of Appeal heard the challenge in June 2022 in WFC 3. The Ontario Court of Appeal, in March 2023, struck down the Bill 307 ruling that it did infringe section 3 of the Charter (WFC 3). The court ordered the province's legislature to prepare Charter-compliant legislation within one year. It is difficult to know if this is the end of the story or whether the issue will make its way to the Supreme Court like *Libman* (a case about Quebec third parties) and *Harper*.

Amid this regulatory turmoil, third parties were very active. Table 9.4 shows the number of third-party actors, total spending, and total advertising by the 12 biggest spenders, including spending in the pre-election and election periods. The number of third parties that chose to spend rose from 28 to 49 to 63 in the three elections shown. Spending peaked in 2014 at $8.6 million, likely due to the rising popularity of the Conservatives, whose more cautious public spending policies were anathema to public-sector union interests, sparking "anything but the Conservatives" themed advertising by third parties aligned more with the freer-spending Liberal and New Democratic parties. Third-party spending in total dropped to $5.2 million in 2018 and rose to $8.3 million in 2022. As Table 9.4 indicates, spending by public-sector unions and labour organizations, which are multi-union funded, constituted 95% of total third-party spending in 2014, 48% in 2018, and about 50% in 2022. In the elections shown, only one or two business associations were among the top 12 spenders; spending by business organizations was minimal in 2014, peaked at 19% of total third-party spending in 2014, and fell back to 11% of total third-party spending in 2022. The top 12 spenders took advantage of the lengthened pre-election period, raising their spending from $4.5 million in 2018 to $5.7 million in 2022, while reducing their election-period spending in the same two elections. Not all of the changes in third-party actors or spending in these elections can be attributed to changes in the EFA, though. Organized interests, no matter how well funded, must use their funds strategically and may sit out certain elections if their members' interests are not in play.

DEMOCRATIC IMPLICATIONS

Despite or perhaps because of the cascade of regulatory changes surrounding third parties, the regulation of organized interests in Canadian elections still stands as a wicked policy problem. Organized interest groups, acting as third parties, clearly contribute to representation and are integral to democratic legitimacy but may, if working collaboratively, have outsized influence over political parties and the party in government. Third parties in Canadian elections are the political voice for well-organized interests but only minimally for individuals or small groups that, if they participate, advertise locally. The primary function of a well-funded third party is to represent a defined set of its members' interests rather than the nation's interests, the ideal of Burkean liberal democracy. Acting collaboratively but not collusively, such combinations of large interest groups may minimize the chance of electoral success by the party they oppose, even if the party is strongly supported by the electorate. Age-old suspicions regarding the predominance of wealthy elites shaping third parties does not seem to be sustained by the evidence in this study unless such elites are funding the non-union third parties.

Several observations can be made. The age-old conundrum of whether third-party spending *shapes* a party's policy agenda or *follows* a party's declared platform remains. Second, the presence and power of organized interests, acting as third parties, varies extensively across elections and across Canada's divergent political cultures and economic and demographic structures. Federalism, as a formal institution, influences third-party activities and affords multiple venues where third parties can choose to operate. It is thus imperative that third-party policy analysis casts a wide net in anticipating how electoral players might respond to regulatory changes and court decisions.

Bans on corporate and union donations to federal political parties have been championed and have merit, particularly because they are clear. However, such bans have also, in Canada and Ontario, seemingly pushed money into third-party activity, and such activities are harder to track (Young 2004) and require fine distinctions between "partisan" and "nonpartisan" spending by the enforcement agency. In 2022, Canada's chief electoral officer recommended that, for purposes of transparency and fairness, the Act "should regulate paid issue-based electoral communications – not only issue advertising – that can reasonably be seen as having the purpose of promoting or opposing a party or candidate during the election and pre-election periods. To clarify … a list of factors should be provided in the Act" (Office of the Chief Electoral Officer of Canada 2022, 19). While these recommendations appear reasonable at face value, they continue to push against Charter freedoms. Last, additional amendments of third-party regulation may be subject to diminishing returns: early regulation accomplishes more than later regulation.

Regulatory policy of third parties as electoral players has historically treated unions and businesses as a single category of organized interests, albeit with usually opposing interests. However, the growth of public-sector unions since the 1960s invites a new analytical lens. Marlow and Orzechowski (1996) find that public-sector unions are special interest groups whose members benefit from expanded public spending and services. This orientation supports political parties that advocate for greater state spending and, derivatively, a larger membership for public-sector unions. Canadian labour relations are governed by the Rand formula, in which an employer hires only union members and workers must pay union dues even if they disagree with a union's political leanings. Taken together, public-sector unions have significant resources at their disposal, with minimal accountability to either members or the voting public (Beange 2016).

We should also consider three other political opportunities for organized interests. The first is the possibility of lobbying various levels of government. Statistics published by the Office of the Commissioner of Lobbying of Canada (2022) show rising total numbers of lobbying registrations in the years since 2005, although the numbers have stabilized in recent years. Whether this increase is attributable specifically to the political finance regime changes in 2003 and 2006 cannot be ascertained, but some influence is likely and worthy of investigation. A second opportunity is that an organized interest may choose to register as a charity, then register the charity as a third party. In 2018, amendments to the *Income Tax Act* permitted charities to engage in public policy dialogue and development activities as long as such activities are connected with their purpose and are not directly or indirectly partisan (Canada Revenue Agency 2021). Thus far, only a few have registered as third parties (Lawlor and Crandall 2022). Last, organized interests have become players in municipal elections (City of Toronto 2023), but as Taylor and Vanhooren (2021) point out, there has been little study of funding and advocacy in such municipal processes.

It is difficult to justify that party and candidate spending limits at the national level are adjusted, prior to an election, for inflation *and* for the number of electors while the limit on third-party spending is adjusted only for inflation. A second problem with fixed spending limits, even with an inflationary adjustment, for either third parties or political parties is that political context changes frequently; rising costs (advertising, travel, event management) may exceed the inflation factor by a wide margin and voters are left with less-than-optimal information. Online advertising, once thought to be cheap and a possible boon to third parties, has increasingly become a major expense for advertisers (Small 2018). While early scholarship on political finance pointed to "too much money" in elections, there is no established benchmark for how much a fair and free election *should* cost, especially for a diverse electorate.

The RCERPF (1991, 322) argued that "fairness" should be the central value in electoral law. The ongoing primacy of "fairness" as an ideal continues despite the challenge of making it operational. Fairness, often described by the "level playing field" metaphor, presumes a measure of equilibrium. Yet conditions between elections rarely stay constant. As Kirkpatrick (1981, 340–41) argues, actual institutions, such as elections, "never very closely resemble ideas – being too complex, too varied, too multifunctional, too unpredictable and uncontrollable – they never conform to ideals or analytical constructs."

With this in mind, electoral law in Canada will remain open to further changes. What has been accomplished is more than worthwhile: Canadian elections, comparatively, are widely considered to be "fair and free." Legislators, justices, bureaucratic actors, and the media are to be commended for their efforts at rendering third parties more transparent and accountable. Vigorous oversight of electoral players remains needed. "Misinformation" was found to have occurred in the 2019 election,[11] and in 2023, concerns about foreign interference prompted the government to establish the Public Inquiry into Foreign Interference in Federal Electoral Processes and Democratic Institutions (Foreign Interference Commission 2024). The "virtues" of third parties are that they are remarkably broad in scope, resilient, and adaptable in their representational functions. These virtues nevertheless challenge long-term stability in law and practice; hence the "wicked" characterization of third-party regulatory policy remains. Debate has focused on the normative aspects of spending by electoral players. There is a wide-open field for research into the practical impact of third-party spending on actual electoral outcomes in all Canadian elections.

NOTES

1 UK legislation (2022) uses the term "non-party campaigners"; several types of organized interests are active in US elections (Medvic 2021).

2 Quebec is the only province where state–civil society relations adhere more closely to the corporatist model, in part because of the province's French and Catholic heritage.

3 The principal alternative can be termed the liberal democratic model, or the libertarian model, the latter term often used by those opposed to greater free expression and spending. The liberal democratic model emphasizes that free expression is a meaningless right if an individual or group has little latitude to share its opinions, surveys, and research through spending. Also of note is that money may follow a policy position adopted by a party or organized interest, so that it is not necessarily elite donors with policy intentions attempting to shape electoral discourse.

4 These include *National Citizens' Coalition Inc. v. Attorney-General of Canada* (1984); *Barrette v. Canada (Attorney General)* (1996); *Somerville v. Canada (Attorney General)* (1996); *Libman v.* Quebec (1997); and *Harper v. Canada (Attorney General)* (2004).

5 *National Citizens Coalition v. Canada (AG)* (1984), 32 Alta. LR (2d) 249 (QB); *Somerville v. Canada (Attorney General)* (1996) AJ No. 515, 136 DLR (4th) 205 (CA); [affirming] [1993] AJ No. 504 (QB); *Libman v. Quebec (Attorney General)* (1997) 3 SCR 569; *Harper v. Canada (Attorney General)* (2004), SCJ No. 28, 1 SCR 827 SCC.

6 The *Canada Elections Act,* Part 17, deals with third-party advertising, partisan activities, and election surveys; Part 16 deals with communications, including election advertising, online platforms, and election surveys.

7 Prior to the 2018 *Elections Modernization Act*, foreign entities could provide unlimited monies to third parties outside an election period; even if those funds were not used for advertising expenses, they could be used for activities that could impact Canadian elections (Senate Committee on Legal and Constitutional Affairs 2017). One US-based group boasted its campaign had "moved the needle during the 2015 national election, contributing greatly to the ousting of the Conservative Harper Government" (Krause 2019). BC-based Tides Canada (now MakeWay; see Bennett 2020), which has received funding from US entities in the past, contributed to registered third parties, including the Council of Canadians, Dogwood Initiative, and Équiterre, as recently as 2016 (Rethink Campaigns n.d.). All three were registered third parties in the 2015, 2019, and 2021 elections.

8 The chief electoral officer is one of only nine officers of Parliament (Parliament of Canada 2021).

9 The Alberta government (2021) published the findings of an inquiry into "funding being used by foreign special interest groups to landlock Alberta's natural resources."

10 This number includes public-sector unions – for example, the Canadian Union of Postal Workers and teachers' federations whose members are employed by Ontario school boards (which are technically registered charities) and membership is mandatory.

11 One study finds that there was "widespread misinformation during the 2021 Canadian federal election" but "the overall election was minimally impacted by mis- and disinformation" with "*disinformation* impl[ying] that false or misleading information is intentionally created or shared to mislead or cause harm, whereas *misinformation* also encompasses false information shared accidentally or unintentionally" (Media Ecosystem Observatory 2022, 3, 7).

REFERENCES

Alberta Government. 2021. *Report of the Public Inquiry into Anti-Alberta Energy Campaigns*. https://open .alberta.ca/publications/public-inquiry-into-anti-alberta-energy-campaigns-report.

Barbeau Committee (Committee on Election Expenses). 1966. *Studies in Canadian Party Finance*. Ottawa: Queen's Printer.

Barber, Benjamin. 1984. *Strong Democracy: Participatory Politics for a New Age*. Berkeley: University of California Press.

Beange, Pauline E. 2012. "Canadian Campaign Finance Reform in Comparative Perspective 2000–2011: An Exhausted Paradigm or Just a Cautionary Tale?" PhD thesis, University of Toronto. https://tspace.library .utoronto.ca/handle/1807/32664.

——. 2016. "Fuller and Faster Online Disclosure of Political Donations Should Be at the Heart of Any Reforms to the System." *Policy Options*. May 9. https://policyoptions.irpp.org/magazines/may-2016/party-finance -in-ontario-what-kind-of-change/.

Bélanger, Éric. 2017. "Third Parties in Canada: Variety and Success." In *Canadian Parties in Transition*, 4th ed., edited by Alain-G. Gagnon and A. Brian Tanguay. Toronto: UTP.

Bennett, Nelson. 2020. "Tides Canada Rebrands Following 'Smear Campaign.'" BIV. June 15. https://biv.com /article/2020/06/tides-canada-rebrands-following-smear-campaign.

Boatright, Robert G. 2011. *Interest Groups and Campaign Finance Reform in the United States and Canada*. Ann Arbor: University of Michigan Press.

Canada Revenue Agency. 2021. *Charitable Activities*. https://www.canada.ca/en/revenue-agency/services /charities-giving/charities/operating-a-registered-charity/activities/charitable-activities.html.

City of Toronto. 2023. *List of Certified Candidates & Third Party Advertisers*. https://www.toronto.ca /city-government/elections/candidate-list/.

Commissioner of Canada Elections. 2024. *About Us*. https://www.cef-cce.ca/about-us.

Department of Justice. 2018. *Charter Statement – Bill C-76 An Act to amend the Canada Elections Act and Other Acts and to make certain consequential amendments*.

——. 2023. Section 1 Reasonable Limits. https://www.justice.gc.ca/eng/csj-sjc/rfc-dlc/ccrf-ccdl/check/art1 .html#:~:text=The%20Oakes%20test,Alberta%2C%20%5B1998%5D%201%20S.C.R.

Elections Canada. 2018. *Third Party Election Advertising Reports for the 42nd General Election*. https://www .elections.ca/content.aspx?section=fin&document=index&dir=oth/thi/advert/tp42&lang=e.

——. 2019. *CEO Statement Regarding Third Party Requirements on Issue Advertising*. August 19. https:// www.elections.ca/content.aspx?section=med&document=aug2019&dir=spe&lang=e.

——. 2021. *44th General Election: Official Voting Results (raw data). Table 11: Voting Results by Electoral District*. https://www.elections.ca/content.aspx?section=res&dir=rep/off/44gedata&document=summary&lang=e.

——. 2022a. *Financial Administration – Expenses – Third Party Report – A Comparative Look at Third Party Information from the 2011, 2015 and 2019 Federal General Elections*.

——. 2022b. *Report on the 44th General Election of September 20, 2021*. https://www.elections.ca/res/rep /off/sta_ge44/stat_ge44_e.pdf.

——. 2022c. *Third Party Expenses Limits – 44th General Election – September 20, 2021*. https://www .elections.ca/content.aspx?section=ele&document=index&dir=pas/44ge/thilim&lang=e.

——. 2022d. *Third Party Financial Returns for the 43rd General Election*. https://www.elections.ca/content .aspx?section=fin&document=index&dir=oth/thi/advert/tp43&lang=e.

——. 2022e. *Third Party Financial Returns for the 44th General Election*. https://www.elections.ca/content .aspx?section=fin&dir=oth/thi/advert/tp44&document=index&lang=e.

——. 2023a. *Registry Requirements for Political Ads on Online Platforms*. October 31. https://www .elections.ca/content.aspx?section=pol&dir=regifaq&document=index&lang=e.

——. 2023b. *Questions and Answers for Third Parties*. September 19. https://www.elections.ca/content .aspx?section=pol&dir=thi&document=backgrounder&lang=e.

Elections Ontario. 2022. *Third Party Advertisers*. https://finances.elections.on.ca/en/third-party-advertisers.

Foreign Interference Commission. 2024. Public Inquiry into Foreign Interference in Federal Electoral Processes and Democratic Institutions. https://foreigninterferencecommission.ca/.

Harper v. Canada (Attorney General) (2004). 1 SCR 827, 2004 SCC 33.

Head, Brian. 2018. Understanding "Wicked Policy Problems". *Policy Options*. January 9. https://policyoptions.irpp.org/magazines/january-2018/understanding-wicked-policy-problems/.

Hsieh, Nien-he, and Victor Wu. 2017. *Making Target the Target: Boycotts and Corporate Political Activity*. Cambridge: Harvard Business Education Publishing. https://hbsp.harvard.edu/product/317113-PDF-ENG.

Kirkpatrick, Jeane J. 1981. "Democratic Elections, Democratic Government and Democratic Theory." In *Democracy at the Polls: A Comparative Study of Competitive National Elections*, edited by David Butler, Howard R. Penniman, and Austin Ranney. Washington: American Enterprise Institute.

Krause, Vivian. 2019. "Obama Wasn't the Only One Interfering in the Canadian Election." *National Post*. October 22. https://nationalpost.com/opinion/vivian-krause-obama-wasnt-the-only-american-interfering-in-the-canadian-election/wcm/4ea60288-6257-4ef8-8390-f0c26799f6e5.

Lawlor, Andrea, and Erin Crandall. 2011. "Understanding Third-Party Advertising: An Analysis of the 2004, 2006 and 2008 Canadian Elections." *Canadian Public Administration* 54 (4): 509–29. https://doi.org/10.1111/j.1754-7121.2011.00190.x.

———. 2022. "The Political Changes and Challenges to Third Party Election Advertising in Canada." *Journal of Elections, Public Opinion and Parties* 32 (2): 449–62. https://doi.org/10.1080/17457289.2020.1824185.

Marlow, Michael L., and William Orzechowski. 1996. "Public Sector Unions and Public Spending. *Public Choice* 89: 1–16. https://doi.org/10.1007/BF00114274.

Media Ecosystem Observatory. 2022. "Mis- and Disinformation During the 2021 Canadian Federal Election." https://www.mediaecosystemobservatory.com/reports/misinformation-and-disinformation-2021-federal-election.

Medvic, Stephen K. 2021. *Campaigns and Elections: Players and Processes*. 4th ed. Routledge.

Morrow, Adrian. 2016. "An Inside Look at Cash-for-Access Ontario Liberal Fundraisers." *Globe and Mail*. July 6. https://www.theglobeandmail.com/news/national/investigation-reveals-likely-guests-for-ontario-liberal-cash-for-access-fundraisers/article30783097/.

North, Douglass C. 1990. *Institutions, Institutional Change and Economic Performance*. Cambridge: Cambridge University Press.

Office of the Chief Electoral Officer of Canada. 2022. *Meeting New Challenges Recommendations from the Chief Electoral Officer of Canada following the 43rd and 44th General Elections*. https://www.elections.ca/res/rep/off/rec_2022/rec2022_e.pdf.

Office of the Commissioner of Lobbying of Canada. 2022. *Reports and Publications*. https://lobbycanada.gc.ca/en/reports-and-publications/.

Olson, Mancur. 1965. *The Logic of Collective Action: Public Goods and the Theory of Groups*. Cambridge: Harvard University Press.

Parliament of Canada. 2021. *Appointment of Officers of Parliament*. Publication No. 2009-21-E https://lop.parl.ca/sites/PublicWebsite/default/en_CA/ResearchPublications/200921E.

Rethink Campaigns. n.d. *The Tar Sands Campaign: >400 Payments via Tides to 100 Organizations in Canada, USA & Europe*. https://fairquestions.typepad.com/rethink_campaigns/tar-sands-campaign-400-payments.html.

Royal Commission on Electoral Reform and Party Financing. (RCERPF). 1991. *Reforming Electoral Democracy*. Vols. 1–4. Ottawa: Queen's Printer.

Senate Committee on Legal and Constitutional Affairs. 2017. *Controlling Foreign Influence in Canadian Elections*. The Honourable Bob Runciman, Chair. The Honourable George Baker, PC, Deputy Chair. https://sencanada.ca/content/sen/committee/421/LCJC/reports/Election_Report_FINAL_e.pdf.

Small, Tamara A. 2018. "Digital Third Parties: Understanding the Technological Challenge to Canada's Third Party Advertising Regime." *Canadian Public Administration* 61 (2): 266–83. https://doi.org/10.1111/capa.12263.

Taylor, Zack, and Shanaya Vanhooren. 2021. "Local Election Campaign Finance Regimes in Canada: Toward a Research Agenda." *Canadian Public Administration* 64 (1): 99–121. https://doi.org/10.1111/capa.12400.

United Kingdom. 2021. Committee on Standards in Public Life. *Regulating Election Finance: A Review by the Committee on Standards in Public Life*. Chapter 8. https://assets.publishing.service.gov.uk/government/uploads/system/uploads/attachment_data/file/999636/CSPL_Regulating_Election_Finance_Review_Final_Web.pdf.

United Kingdom Electoral Commission. 2022. *Guidance: Non-Party Campaigner*. https://www.electoralcommission.org.uk/i-am-a/campaigner/non-party-campaigner.

Working Families Ontario v. Ontario. 2021 ONSC 4076 [WFC 1].

Working Families Coalition (Canada) Inc. v. Ontario. 2021 ONSC 7697 [WFC 2].

Working Families Coalition (Canada) Inc. v. Ontario. 2023 ONCA 139 [WFC 3].

Young, Lisa. 2004. "Regulating Campaign Finance in Canada: Strengths and Weaknesses." *Election Law Journal* 3 (3): 444–62. https://doi.org/10.1089/1533129041492259.

CHAPTER TEN

The Canadian News Media and Election Campaigns

Brooks DeCillia

INTRODUCTION

The sweeping 1997 documentary series *Dawn of the Eye* spotlights politicians' efforts to use electronic news media to mould and manipulate public opinion. Part four, "The Electronic Battalions," features the hand-wringing of several prominent Canadian broadcast journalists worried about being co-opted by the Progressive Conservative spin machine that propelled Brian Mulroney to a second majority government in 1988. One journalist, in fact, concedes that Canadian reporters had surrendered much of their autonomy to set the news agenda because they had "been totally caught up by what the parties wanted us to see" (Starowicz 1997). Overall, the series laments the failure of journalists to resist the manipulation of spin and photo op–focused political campaigns of the emerging electronic age.

The documentary's critical history of broadcast news paints a sharp contrast between the television air war campaign of 1988 and the more traditional campaigns of the past, which featured Canadian politicians vying for a seat in the House of Commons, meeting citizens *unmediated* in village squares and town halls to win votes with their skilled rhetoric and campaign pledges. In 1988, the Progressive Conservatives (PCs) upended the analogue campaigns of the past (Nolan 1981), importing the image-driven strategy of Ronald Reagan with its focus on optics and soundbites over substance. The 1988 federal election, according to a longtime political correspondent, marked the "Americanization" of Canadian campaigns, whereby the PCs "slavishly imitated" the successful media image control tactics pioneered by Reagan and his political advisors (Starowicz 1997). Longtime Tory strategist Allan Gregg, who handled communication and polling for the PCs in 1988, concedes the party pandered to the spectacle of television news. Prime Minister Brian Mulroney did not travel to different parts of the country during that campaign to convince people in that region to vote for his party but because the location offered the best backdrop to coax news organizations to cover the party's preferred political communication. The governing PCs, as one frustrated Parliament Hill reporter recalled, "would create the issue. They would create the event.

They would pretend that something real was happening. And we as journalists would pretend it was news and we would deliver almost scripted" (Starowicz 1997). The 1988 federal campaign left journalists wanting to reassert their ideally imagined role as honest – independent – storytellers in a democracy. Scholarly accounts of the news coverage of subsequent campaigns suggest that all the hand-wringing in 1988 by Canadian journalists did not, in turn, improve the news media's campaign coverage in the coming decades (Adams 2020; Brin and MacDonald 2020; Lawlor 2017; Popplewell 2022; Taras 2012; Taras and Waddell 2012; Waddell 2012 and 2020).

This chapter outlines the essential normative role imagined for the news media in Canadian election campaigns. Canadians continue to rely on media – traditional news media and increasingly social media – as sources of political information, although only four in ten (40%) of Canadians say they trust the news media (Brin and Charlton 2023). This chapter begins by sketching the idealized function of the news media in our democratic political system. The second part of the chapter traces the evolution of the Canadian news media's role in campaigns from partisan hacks to critical muckrakers. Finally, this chapter considers the potential democratic implications of the Canadian news media's reporting on political campaigns by evaluating the power of the Canadian news media to influence voters and elections. Ultimately, the coming pages explore the news media's potential power to shape public opinion. As Todd Gitlin ([1980] 2003, 9) explains, the news media are "a significant social force in the forming and delimiting of public assumptions, attitudes, and moods," making campaign news coverage a potentially influential force in shaping our politics and democracy.

DEFINITION: NORMATIVE NOTIONS OF THE NEWS MEDIA

The *Canadian Charter of Rights and Freedoms* guarantees the "freedom of thought, belief, opinion, and expression, including freedom of the press and other media of communication." Political theorists and legal scholars[1] consistently highlight the fundamental importance of free speech and a free press in Canada's democracy. The Supreme Court summed up this thinking well:

> Indeed, a democracy cannot exist without that freedom to express new ideas and to put forward opinions about the function of public institutions. The concept of a free and uninhibited speech permeates all truly democratic societies and institutions. The vital importance of the concept cannot be overemphasized. (*Edmonton Journal v. Alberta (Attorney General)* 1989)

Underpinning this is the assumption that news media provide citizens with information so that they can "make an informed assessment of the issues which may significantly affect their lives and well-being" (*Canadian Broadcasting Corporation v. New Brunswick (Attorney General)* 1996). As a result, journalists frequently get imagined as neutral actors merely holding a supposedly impartial or objective mirror to the world, reflecting "back the reality of everyday life, as it really is" (Taras 1990, 5).

On the other hand, more critical accounts of the media contend that journalism produces coverage that strictly adheres to dominant capitalist ideology, helping to *manufacture consent* (Herman and Chomsky [1988] 2002), cheerleading for big corporations (Goodman and Goodman 2006), and sometimes even act as an *attack dog* instead of a watchdog when political actors stray too far from political consensus (Cammaerts, DeCillia, and Magalhães 2017). Generally, it is argued that media are (1) too cozy with official and elite sources; (2) rigid adherents to conventional thinking; (3) constrained by outdated norms and practices; (4) fixated on daily events at the expense of more thematic coverage; and (5) too focused on conflict and cynical accounts of politics.[2]

It is, however, fair to think of journalists as important actors (or an institution) in the political system with agency and constraints imposed by the Canadian political, economic, legal, and cultural structure. Yet, at the same time, Canadian journalists possess the agency and resources to expand the range of voices in our public discourse, hold decision makers to account, and produce investigative, insightful, and meaningful coverage of public policy and politics. Unquestionably, scholarly assessments of the news media's place in Canada's democratic system tend to be bifurcated by questions of *what ought to be* and *what is* the case.

In the minds of most Canadian journalists, the idealized function or role of the news media flows from liberalism, whereby journalists are *watchdogs* and *truth speakers* who serve democracy by keeping citizens informed (Taylor and DeCillia 2021; Ward 2015). In this monitorial role – a fourth estate akin to the three other branches of Canada's government – journalists act as observant storytellers, illuminating and educating the public (Christians et al. 2009). The state and political elites need to be kept in check by journalists:

> Tenacious reporters expose lies as falsities, cutting exaggerated boasts down to size. They insist elected representatives make good on their electoral pledges and spend taxpayers' money wisely. In this watchdog role, the media constitute what's often referred to as a 'fourth estate': a check on executive power. (Carruthers 2011, 9)

But news coverage of politics has not always been so decidedly fair, balanced, or neutral. In fact, the first newspapers in Canada began as government gazettes – and for much of Canada's history, the news had a decidedly partisan and even propagandist bent.

EVOLUTION OF NEWS COVERAGE OF CANADIAN ELECTION CAMPAIGNS

Despite former US president Donald Trump bragging that he invented the term "fake news" (Schaub 2017), fakery in politics is not new. For instance, the "penny press" of the early 1800s in the US was notorious for fabricating news. In early Canada, many politicians were in the perpetual business of founding and financing newspapers to promote their political agendas (Taras 1990).[3] The current *Globe and Mail* newspaper combines a liberal paper (*The Globe*) and a conservative newspaper founded by John A. Macdonald (*The Mail*, later *The Mail and Empire*). Stewart (1980, 14) describes newspapers as "party organs designed to pump propaganda into the national bloodstream."

In this era, reporters were more stenographers of politicians than independent storytellers. One journalist recalls in his memoir being sent by his conservative newspaper to both cover Prime

Minister Arthur Meighen's 1921 trip to London and to act as the first minister's aide (Westell and Cumming 1982). The symbiosis between politicians and the press even extended to Quebec premier Maurice Duplessis frequently slipping reporters five- or ten-dollar bills at his campaign events or news conferences in exchange for positive stories (Taras 1990). During the 1949 campaign, journalist Peter Dempson (1968), writing for a conservative newspaper, recalls receiving advice to attack a Liberal leader and hype a Conservative leader. The political model of journalism eventually gave way to the objective paradigm, undermined by commercial pressures, the professionalization of journalism, and technological advances. While the heyday of Canada's partisan press came between Confederation and World War I, real-world vestiges of the partisan press lived on until the 1960s, and traces of the bias can arguably be detected even today.

The telegraph's invention and wire news services pressured journalists to prioritize facts over partisan coverage. The truncated communication system also demanded simplified and generic reporting that appealed to wider audiences. The telegraph's necessity for brevity entrenched the inverted-pyramid style of storytelling – the who, what, when, where, and sometimes why of news events in descending order of newsworthiness. In the 1920s, preeminent journalist Walter Lippmann led the charge against biased reporting about World War I and the Russian Revolution. Lippmann wanted newsrooms filled with better educated and independent journalists who were "clear and free of irrational … unexamined … and unacknowledged prejudgments" (as quoted in Schudson 1978, 154). This became reality when a confluence of forces – increased urbanization, education, mass consumerism, and technological advancements – transformed North American news coverage after the end of World War II. Newspaper owners increasingly positioned their newspapers as nonpartisan to boost circulation and attract more advertising revenue. The goal was "to make newspapers unprovocative, impartial, standardized and 'public service' in their approach" (Kesterton 1967, 83). Additionally, public service broadcasting, with its commitment to neutrality and impartiality, took root in Canada in this period. The CBC's 1941 guidelines required the public broadcaster to ensure that its "[d]omestic political news must be treated with the absolute impartiality" (Troyer 1980, 91).

Pioneering news sociologist Gaye Tuchman (1972, 660) called objectivity a "strategic ritual" that protects journalists from the risks of their craft. Opinions, in this vein, get attributed to sources and not the reporters themselves. On the other hand, some contend that news bosses use objectivity as an "industrial discipline" to control journalists (Schudson 2011, 75). Despite the debate, objectivity remains – for many – a "cornerstone of the professional ideology of journalists in liberal democracies" (Lichtenberg 1996, 225). Similar principles frequently top the journalistic standards and practices of most mainstream Canadian news organizations. CBC News' (2024) journalistic standards and practices underscore that Canadians expect the public broadcaster "to provide a wide range of information and context so that they can make decisions during election and referendum campaigns" while ensuring that the news service gives "all candidates, parties and issues equitable treatment."

Amid the 1960s and 1970s social upheaval that questioned and challenged so many norms, objectivity came under scrutiny. Pioneering journalists expanded the definition of journalism with their more subjective, interpretive, analytical, and literary style. This third paradigm – critical journalism – pushed the boundaries of mainstream journalism, questioning objectivity and truth.

Canadian journalists in this era moved from "being the handmaidens of politicians to being their harshest critics" (Taras 1990, 54). Modern political journalism prizes conflict and the horserace and overemphasizes the negative (Cappella and Hall-Jamieson 1997; Patterson 1996; Sabato 1991). The Vietnam War and the Watergate scandal triggered a profound repositioning of news organizations from objective to critical in both the US and Canada. "The working hypothesis almost universally shared among correspondents," opined investigative journalist Edward Jay Epstein (1973, 215), "is that politicians are suspect; their public image probably false, their public statements disingenuous, their moral pronouncements hypocritical, their motives self-serving, and their promises ephemeral." Of course, this cynicism was implanted into campaign coverage as the relationship between politicians and the press turned decidedly adversarial in the 1970s.

In a critical assessment, Meyer (2002, xiv, 57) argues that this new critical news media form transformed traditional party democracy into a "media democracy," whereby "the rules of the media logic recast the constitutive factors" of politics and democracy.

> From the "spin-doctoring" that follows every televised debate to the timing and stagecraft of press conferences, political elites devote considerable effort towards influencing not only *what* information gets on the air but *how* it is presented. (Nelson, Oxley, and Clawson 1997, 224; italics in original)

As discussed in Chapter 11, Canadian political parties, on the other hand, have dramatically increased their resources and use of marketing media and public relations techniques to help (1) manage their brands, (2) manage issues and controversies, and (3) win votes (Marland 2016; Marland and DeCillia 2020). With the help of sophisticated communication and polling experts, parties pay close attention to news media coverage while also trying to shape it (Taras 1990; Mancini and Swanson 1996).

When it comes to campaigns, political parties carefully plan and choreograph their leaders' tours for elections, strategically crafting the media message like a movie they want to play out on the national stage over the weeks-long drama. The news media's coverage of campaigns also represents a massive undertaking for the journalists and news organizations that cover the democratic events (Brin and MacDonald 2020). The planning for both the political parties and the news media begins months – even a year – in advance. Fixed elections, along with the increasing frequency of minority parliaments, have left most parties on a permanent campaign footing over the last two decades. As this volume's introduction makes plain, the parties use the leaders' tour *not* as an opportunity to meet voters but to perform for the news cameras. The leaders' airplane or bus tour is a gruelling schedule jam packed with events – often 18-hour days, seven days a week. The so-called bubble or cocoon tours, whereby media and public access to the leader are restricted, are highly scripted and risk averse. Political leaders rarely interact with anyone but partisan supporters for fear of a gaffe or so-called bozo eruption, whereby the leader, in an unscripted moment, makes an ill-considered, ill-tempered, or controversial statement or move in reaction to a journalist's question or an interaction with a voter. The crammed schedule is also strategic. It's part of political parties' efforts to control the media narrative. A packed timetable does not give journalists on the plane or bus much time to engage with actual voters, although gaffes, surprises, and external events can still push campaigns off their preferred messaging. In the 2019 election, for example, photos of Prime Minister Justin Trudeau in brownface from 2001 published by *Time* magazine upended an already tight race (Purna Kambhampaty, Carlisle, and Chan 2019). Parties invest considerable resources – complete with intrusive questionnaires about dating apps and sex lives – checking the background of candidates to prevent explosive stories from detonating during campaigns (Marland and DeCillia 2020).

The interpretive turn in journalism also coincided with increasing critique about what journalists covered and how they covered it. Research consistently highlights news coverage dominated by elites, males, and white sources (Clark 2022). Some have argued that the idealized practice of objectivity perpetuates white male dominance in news coverage (Thompson-Bristol and Roberts Forde 2022) and hegemonic interpretations of events, issues, and politicians (Shoemaker and Reese 2014). Undoubtedly, assumptions about race and diversity are baked into Canadian political coverage (Tolley 2016). Similarly, political coverage tends to frame politics as a masculine world that often marginalizes women (Gidengil and Everitt 1999 and 2000).

The news media also faces an information integrity dilemma. Disinformation, hate speech, online harassment, and even death threats are on the rise, testing the resilience and credibility of political reporting (CBC Radio-Canada 2021). Donald Trump made terms like "fake news," "alternative facts," and "post-truth" part of our political vocabulary. The contagion spread outside the US. Only hours after winning the leadership of the Conservative Party, Pierre Poilievre accused a parliamentary correspondent of being "a Liberal heckler" when the journalist interrupted his scrum (Labine 2022). The phenomenon of politicians *chirping at the referee*, to use a hockey metaphor, is not new. Politicians – and their professional communication staff – often question the impartiality of journalists and frequently cast the news media as the bad guys or their opposition.

Moreover, perpetual downsizing – along with growing digital demands and constant deadlines – across the news media industry has dramatically undercut the quality of journalism produced during campaigns (Brin and MacDonald 2020; Taras 2012). The proliferation of misinformation and disinformation has also made Canadian journalists' jobs harder when there are fewer of them to verify and fact-check information (Taylor and DeCillia 2021). Waddell (2012) argues that the sum of increased workload, social media, the obsession with horserace politics and strategy (reporting on who wins and loses each day over substantive issue coverage), and a focus on images and soundbites have resulted in impoverished election campaign coverage. The coming pages attempt to sort out what all this means for Canada's politics and democracy.

DEMOCRATIC IMPLICATIONS OF THE NEWS MEDIA'S COVERAGE OF CANADIAN CAMPAIGNS

Ideally, Canada's news media does three things during political campaigns: (1) informs citizens about the race and the issues at stake; (2) amplifies the voice of voters to the politicians vying to run the country; and (3) holds those politicians to account – asks tough questions and fact-checks their promises and spin. As the previous section makes clear, journalists face several daunting challenges. This section begins by examining the democratic implications of the challenges facing Canadian political coverage and then turns to illuminating how the news media can shape our politics and democracy.

More than seven in ten Canadians worry about disinformation and misinformation (Edelman 2022). The news media faces continued assaults from both the left and right of the ideological spectrum. Branded "fake news" by authoritarian populists and "lapdogs" by critics on the left, the authority of traditional news organizations – or the so-called legacy mainstream news media – has declined in recent years (Lewis and Westlund 2015). Digital technologies have also undermined the gatekeeping function of the Canadian news media, once dominated by a handful of television networks and newspaper chains. However, the proliferating digital media and self-mediating system continues to fill with new players (influencers, bloggers and vloggers, etc.) and platforms (Reddit, Twitter, TikTok, Facebook, Snapchat) that promulgate myriad competing agendas. Additionally, embedded in social media and search engines, algorithms push news consumers to more personalized experiences and content, leaving citizens to navigate and make sense of our "mediatized culture" (Schrøder 2011, 6). Arguably, the speed and abundance of information circulating in our public sphere and the weakening institutionalization of its production further erodes public trust in news and information sources, weakening established modes of news consumption. The sum of this cacophony of communication compounds the post-truth or "epistemic crisis" that marks our current democratic public sphere (Dahlgren 2018, 20).

Canada's political reporters and commentators do not win many fans for their obsession with the "who is winning" and "who is losing" approach to campaign reporting. Undoubtedly, there is an overreliance on the "game frame" or "horserace" coverage at the expense of issue-focused journalism in Canadian political coverage (Sampert and Trimble 2003). This propensity undermines ostensibly normative information, providing a rationale for journalists in a democracy. Admittedly, horserace coverage is easier and cheaper to produce. In addition, a plethora of public polls anchors this type of coverage during campaigns (DeCillia 2023; also see Chapter 13). Yet now, more than ever, when democracy is under threat across the globe (Fisher 2022) and political actors increasingly bend the truth or even lie to exploit feelings of resentment shared by voters, factual, in-depth, issue-focused reporting is needed.

As noted earlier, political coverage frequently underrepresents and stereotypes equity-deserving groups. Considerable research details the Canadian news media's propensity to either ignore altogether (Leavitt et al. 2015) or adopt colonial assumptions about Indigenous people (Cronlund, Anderson, and Robertson 2011). Moreover, stories about Indigenous people tend to get framed by "Eurocentric discourse founded in Canadian colonialism" (Clark 2014, 44). Erin Tolley (2016) shows that Canada's news media frequently portrays racialized politicians more negatively and as less politically viable. Similar concerns persist about the news coverage of female politicians. Decades of political science work highlights how female politicians – and party leaders, in particular – get assessed by a "gender-based double standard" in political news coverage (Sampert and Trimble 2003, 226). "Cultural notions about gender, race, sexuality, age, and class together" continue to "shape the production of, and response, to political rhetoric and news coverage" (Wagner and Everitt 2019, 20). While the visibility of female politicians may have increased in recent decades, Goodyear-Grant's (2013, 186) careful examination of Canadian news found women disproportionately get framed as "sex object, mother, pet, and iron maiden." This problematic news coverage undermines ideals of participatory and inclusive democracy, and this is pronounced during campaigns. Moreover, if these troublesome representations of women, 2SLGBTQ+ and racialized people, and other equity-deserving groups persist in the news media, it is hard to imagine a fully participatory Canadian democracy.

A century ago, Walter Lippmann hinted at the idea of media framing in his description of competing political ideas in the popular press attempting to shape the so-called "pictures in our heads" (Lippmann [1927] 2009, 3). The news media often interpret the *world outside* (framing), triggering the importance of specific issues by covering them so much (agenda-setting) while also suggesting standards (priming) by which to evaluate political problems, events, and actors. Politics campaigns – what politicians say and do – presume that the words and actions of politicians shape the pictures in our heads. In fact, politicians and their communication experts carefully craft their words and images, hoping to win votes not only in campaigns but continuously throughout the permanent campaign (Marland, Lennox Esselment, and Giasson 2017). We must be careful never to assume a linear relationship between political messaging and what voters think and do. As well, considerable studies suggest that most Canadian voters do not pay much attention to politics, often relying on the commonsensical framing of issues and events offered by politicians to form their opinion (Andrew 2007).

News frames frequently "organize everyday reality" (Tuchman 1978, 193) so that news consumers can understand issues and events. For example, in the 2015 campaign, NDP leader Tom Mulcair, hoping to differentiate his party from the Conservatives, highlighted his party's pacifist roots, insisting Canada should not play a military role in the conflict in Syria and Iraq while also accepting more refugees. As part of a counter-framing effort, Prime Minister Stephen Harper, however, criticized the NDP for its rejection of military force to fight what he called the "root cause" of the suffering experienced by the refugees. In this way, framing brings "order to events" and provides a language to "make the world make sense" (Manoff and Schudson 1986, 228). Mulcair and Harper's words offered voters a mental shorthand, per se, that they could use to help make sense of the world and construct their own opinions.

One of the leading thinkers about framing, Entman (2007, 164), suggests that media frames "typically perform four functions: problem definition, causal analysis, moral judgment and remedy promotion." For example, in the wake of the headline-grabbing news – and emotionally disturbing images – of a dead three-year-old Syrian refugee boy washed up on the coast of Turkey in September 2015, Liberal leader Justin Trudeau began his remarks by empathizing with the father of Alan Kurdi and highlighting the magnitude of the refugee crisis (thus defining the problem). Trudeau then criticized Harper's government, saying it had ignored the pleas of the international community to do more for Syrian refugees (causal analysis). The Liberal leader also suggested that the Conservatives lacked compassion (moral judgment) while also pledging to accept 15,000 more Syrian refugees than the 10,000 the ruling Conservatives had promised to bring to Canada (remedy promotion) (Postmedia 2015). The way politicians talk about things (their framing) can spark connections in our brains. Their words – their strategic interpretations – can shape our thinking and provide us with the language to "make the world make sense" (Manoff and Schudson 1986, 228). These frames can also potentially shape our political opinions and preferences (Moscrop 2019; Scheufele 1999).

What politicians say – conveyed to voters through the news media – can in turn shape public opinion. Political scientist John Zaller challenges the idea that voters have just one hard and fast opinion about issues and politicians. According to Zaller (1992), your head is like a bucket; the receptacle usually fills up with information or considerations you hear, see, or read in the media. When asked for an opinion, you reach into the bucket for a sample of considerations (usually those near the top) to take an average of all your considerations to arrive at your opinion. It is not just one news story but the accumulation of news that can influence people's political opinions and preferences over time. In that vein, the news media can make certain issues, events, and political characters more at the top of citizens' minds – to set the agenda – and represent another potentially decisive role for the news media during campaigns.

At the most superficial level, messages emphasized in the news become elevated (or salient) in the Canadian public's mind. Decades of evidence, starting with Maxwell McCombs and Donald Shaw's groundbreaking research, linked the prominence of news media messages and what are considered top issues for the public. News, acting as a stimulus, triggers an increase in the salience or accessibility of specific issues in our minds, heightening "the importance placed on the topics placed in the public agenda" (McCombs and Reynolds 2002, 238). The agenda-setting hypothesis, simply put, suggests that lots of coverage of an issue will make that issue more top of mind for the public. It is also important to note that what gets covered in the media – the prevalence of stories – is acknowledged to be a bidirectional relationship between the news media and politicians.

The news media ecosystem and politics have changed considerably since the Chapel Hill studies found a strong correlation between the prevalence of media messages and public opinion. The research predates our modern digital communication environment. Our current abundant and fractured media landscape threatens – but does not entirely erode – legacy media's historical ability to shape the public agenda (Chaffe and Metzger 2001; Williams and Delli Carpini 2011). Nearly half (49%) of Canadians continue to get their news from television (Brin and Charlton 2023). Undoubtedly, new digital journalistic organizations and social media sites can also shape what the public thinks is important (Fabrizio et al. 2022; Harder, Sevenans, and Van Aelst 2017; Sanders and Ferré 2020).

The priming thesis suggests media messages can also influence the criteria we use to evaluate news, including political campaigns (Iyengar and Kinder 1987; Iyengar, Peters, and Kinder 1982). Priming – an extension of agenda-setting theory – *can* be profound because when the news media puts issues top of the mind, the new stories also often come with values and standards that news consumers (voters) can use to judge political leaders and issues.

CONCLUSION

The health of our political community depends on the narratives people use to make sense of their world and interpret the everyday life we all share. Harvard University political philosopher Michael Sandel (1998, 350) contends that the best political debate is not just about competing policies but also about the quality of the discourse surrounding the "competing interpretations of the character of the community, of its purpose and its ends." The documentary *Dawn of the Eye*, described in this chapter's introduction, highlights the unease journalists felt with the increasing use of spin and photo-op campaign tactics by Canadian political parties to control the news media. Coverage of that campaign also sparked considerable reflection among Canadian journalists about their role – specifically, their lack of autonomy – in the country's democratic process. Then, like now, most Canadian journalists want to serve the public and our democracy well (Taylor and DeCillia 2021). The reporters who cover campaigns aim to produce thoughtful and illuminating coverage. Yet, as this chapter details, journalists are not entirely free to do as they please but are part of a complicated ideological, institutional, and political system that shapes their news coverage of campaigns. Waves of layoffs and cuts have also considerably shrunk Canada's news industry in recent decades. But as this chapter argues, Canadian journalists possess the agency and resources to expand the horizon of their reporting about politics and public policy.

Echoing Sandel, Street (2001) argues that we need to value the new media because it constructs the narrative of our politics. Still, we can also criticize those narratives because they fail to improve and enhance our political discourse. As this chapter clarifies, Canada's news media's imperfections are pervasive. Election coverage may lack diversity, is frequently gendered, and often is cynical horserace/strategy-obsessed accounts of style and image over substance. On top of that, our politicians rely on poll-tested soundbites to win votes. Our entire political communication system may not be democratically ideal. But as this chapter describes, our politics and news media systems continually evolve. The great thing about our democracy and media system is that we can make collective choices. If we don't like the current form of our political campaigns and the news coverage of elections, we can change them.

NOTES

1 This section relies on the excellent media law analysis and historical account in Dean Jobb's book *Media Law in Canada*.
2 These concerns echo Doris A. Graber's editorial note for Michael Schudson's chapter "Why Democracies Need an Unlovable Press" in *Media Power in Politics* (2007).
3 The conceptual framework for this section comes from David Taras' *The Newsmakers: The Media's Influence on Canadian Politics*. Additionally, this section draws several examples from Taras' historical account of Canadian journalism to illustrate the evolution of Canada's news media.

REFERENCES

Adams, P. 2020. "The Media: Challenges of Covering the Campaign." In *The Canadian Federal Election 2019*, edited by J.H. Pammett and C. Dornan, 174–197 Montreal: McGill-Queen's University Press.

Andrew, B.C. 2007. "Media-generated Shortcuts: Do Newspaper Headlines Present Another Roadblock for Low-information Rationality?" *Harvard International Journal of Press/Politics* 12 (2): 24–43. https://doi.org/10.1177/1081180X07299795.

Brin, C., and S. Charlton. 2023. "Canada." In *Reuters Institute Digital News Report 2023*, edited by N. Newman, R. Fletcher, K. Eddy, C. T. Robertson, and R. Kleis Nielsen, 114–15. https://reutersinstitute.politics.ox.ac.uk/sites/default/files/2023-06/Digital_News_Report_2023.pdf.

Brin, C., and R. MacDonald. 2020. "News Editors." In *Inside the Campaign: Managing Elections in Canada*, edited by A. Marland and T. Giasson, 85–97. Vancouver: UBC Press.

Cammaerts, B., B. DeCillia, and J.C. Magalhães. 2017. "Journalistic Transgressions in the Representation of Jeremy Corbyn: From Watchdog to Attackdog." *Journalism* 21 (2): 191–208. https://doi.org/10.1177/1464884917734055.

Canadian Broadcasting Corporation v. New Brunswick (Attorney General) [1996], 3 SCR 480 at 475.

Cappella, J.N., and K. Hall-Jamieson. 1997. *Spiral of Cynicism: The Press and the Public Good.* New York: Oxford University Press.

Carruthers, S.L. 2011. *The Media at War.* 2nd ed. New York: Palgrave Macmillan.

CBC News. 2024. "Journalistic Standards and Practices." https://cbc.radio-canada.ca/en/vision/governance/journalistic-standards-and-practices.

CBC Radio-Canada. 2021. "Canadian Journalists Increasingly under Attack Online, Says Ipsos Survey." November 9. https://cbc.radio-canada.ca/en/media-centre/canadian-journalists-under-attack-says-ipsos-survey.

Chaffe, S.H., and M.J. Metzger. 2001. "The End of Mass Communication?" *Mass Communication and Society* 4 (4): 365–79. https://doi.org/10.1207/S15327825MCS0404_3.

Christians, C.G., T.L. Glasser, D. McQuail, K. Nordenstreng, and R.A. White. 2009. *Normative Theories of the Media: Journalism in Democratic Societies.* Chicago: University of Chicago Press.

Clark, B. 2014. "Framing Canada's Aboriginal Peoples: A Comparative Analysis of Indigenous and Mainstream Television News." *Canadian Journal of Native Studies* 34 (2): 41–64.

———. 2022. *Journalism's Racial Reckoning: The News Media's Pivot to Diversity and Inclusion.* New York: Routledge.

Cronlund Anderson, M., and C.L. Robertson. 2011. *Seeing Red: A History of Natives in Canadian Newspapers.* Winnipeg: University of Winnipeg Press.

Dahlgren, P. 2018. "Media, Knowledge and Trust: The Deepening Epistemic Crisis of Democracy." *Javnost – The Public* 25 (1–2): 20–27. https://doi.org/10.1080/13183222.2018.1418819.

DeCillia, B. 2023. "Standard Error: The Polls in the 2019 Alberta Election and Beyond." In *Blue Storm: The Rise and Fall of Jason Kenney*, edited by D. Bratt, R. Sutherland, and D. Taras, 59–79. Calgary: University of Calgary Press.

Dempson, P. 1968. *Assignment Ottawa: Seventeen Years in the Press Gallery.* Toronto: General Publishing Company.

Edelman. 2022. "Edelman Trust Barometer 2022: Country Report Trust in Canada." https://www.edelman.ca/trust-barometer/2022-edelman-trust-barometer-trust-canada.

Edmonton Journal v. Alberta (Attorney General) [1989] 2 SCR 1326.

Entman, R. 2007. "Framing Bias: Media in the Distribution of Power." *Journal of Communication* 57: 163–73. https://doi.org/doi:10.1111/j.1460-2466.2006.00336.x.

Epstein, E.J. 1973. *News from Nowhere.* New York: Vintage.

Fabrizio, G., T. Gessler, M. Kubli, and S. Mülle. 2022. "Social Media and Political Agenda Setting." *Political Communication* 39 (1): 39–60. 10.1080/10584609.2021.1910390.

Fisher, M. 2022. "How Democracy Is Under Threat Across the Globe." *New York Times.* August 19. www.nytimes.com/2022/08/19/world/democracy-threat.html

Gidengil, E., and J. Everitt. 1999. "Metaphors and Misrepresentation: Gendered Mediation in News Coverage of the 1993 Canadian Leaders' Debates." *Harvard International Journal of Press/Politics* 4 (1): 48–65. https://doi.org/10.1177/1081180X99004001005.

———. 2000. "Filtering the Female: Television News Coverage of the 1993 Canadian Leaders' Debates." *Women & Politics* 21 (4): 105–31. https://doi.org/10.1300/J014v21n04_04.

Gitlin, T. [1980] 2003. *The Whole World Is Watching: Mass Media in the Making and Unmaking of the New Left.* Berkley: University of California Press.

Goodman, A., and D. Goodman. 2006. *Static: Government Liars, Media Cheerleaders, and the People Who Fight Back.* New York: Hyperion.

Goodyear-Grant, E. 2013. *Gendered News: Media Coverage and Electoral Politics in Canada.* Vancouver: UBC Press.

Harder, R., J. Sevenans, and P. Van Aelst. 2017. "Intermedia Agenda Setting in the Social Media Age: How Traditional Players Dominate the News Agenda in Election Times." *International Journal of Press/Politics* 22 (3): 275–93. https://doi.org/10.1177/1940161217704969.

Herman, E., and N. Chomsky. 2002 [1988]. *Manufacturing Consent: The Political Economy of Mass Media*. New York: Pantheon.

Iyengar, S., and D. Kinder. 1987. *News that Matters: Television and Public Opinion*. Chicago: University of Chicago Press.

Iyengar, S., M.D. Peters, and D.R. Kinder. 1982. "Experimental Demonstrations of the Not-so-minimal Political Consequences of Media." *American Political Science Review* 76 (4): 848–58. https://doi.org /10.2307/1962976.

Jobb, D. 2023. *Media Law in Canada*. Toronto: Emond.

Kesterton, W.H. 1967. *A History of Journalism in Canada*. Toronto: McClelland and Stewart.

Labine, J. 2022. "Pierre Poilievre Calls Journalist 'Liberal Heckler' at News Conference." iPolitics. September 13. https://www.ipolitics.ca/news/pierre-poilievre-calls-journalist-liberal-heckler-at-news-conference.

Lawlor, A. 2017. "Media-Party Parallelism: How the Media Covers Party Messaging." In *Permanent Campaigning in Canada*, edited by A. Marland, T. Giasson, and A. Lennox Esselment, 67–86. Vancouver: UBC Press.

Leavitt, P.A., R. Covarrubias, Y.A. Perez, and S.A. Fryberg. 2015. "'Frozen in Time': The Impact of Native American Media Representations on Identity and Self-Understanding." *Journal of Social Issues* 71 (1): 39–53. https://doi.org/10.1111/josi.12095.

Lewis, S.C., and O. Westlund. 2015. "Actors, Actants, Audiences, and Activities in Cross-Media News Work." *Digital Journalism* 3 (1): 19–37. https://doi.org/10.1080/21670811.2014.927986.

Lichtenberg, J. 1996. "In Defence of Objectivity Revisited." In *Mass Media and Society*, edited by J. Curran and M. Gurevitch, 225–42. New York: Arnold.

Lippmann, W. [1927] 2009. *The Phantom Public*. New Brunswick: Transaction Publishers.

Mancini, P., and D.L. Swanson. 1996. "Politics, Media, and Modern Democracy: Introduction." In *Politics, Media, and Modern Democracy: An International Study of Innovations in Electoral Campaigning and Their Consequences*, edited by D.L. Swanson and P. Mancini, 1–26. Westport: Praeger.

Manoff, R.K., and M. Schudson. 1986. *Reading the News: A Pantheon Guide to Popular Culture*. New York: Pantheon Books.

Marland, A. 2016. *Brand Command: Canadian Politics and Democracy in the Age of Mass Control*. Vancouver: UBC Press.

Marland, A., and B. DeCillia. 2020. "Reputation and Brand Management by Political Parties: Party Vetting of Election Candidates in Canada." *Journal of Nonprofit & Public Sector Marketing* 32 (4): 342–63. https:// doi.org/10.1080/10495142.2020.1798857.

Marland, A., A. Lennox Esselment, and T. Giasson. 2017. "Welcome to Non-Stop Campaigning." In *Permanent Campaigning in Canada*, edited by A. Marland, A. Lennox Esselment, and T. Giasson, 3–27. Vancouver: UBC Press.

McCombs, M., and A. Reynolds. 2002. "News Influence on Our Pictures of the World." In *Media Effects: Advances in Theory and Research*, edited by J. Bryant and D. Zillmann, 1–18. New York: Lawrence Erlbaum Associates Publishers.

Meyer, T. 2002. *Media Democracy: How the Media Colonize Politics*. Cambridge: Polity.

Mindich, D.T.Z. 1993. "Edwin M. Stanton, the Inverted Pyramid, and Information Control." *Journalism Monographs* 140: 1-28. https://www.proquest.com/openview/b4159ffed8d26f8e301fa6e349316326 /1?pq-origsite=gscholar&cbl=1818570.

Moscrop, D. 2019. *Too Dumb for Democracy: Why We Make Bad Political Decisions and How We Can Make Better Ones*. Fredericton: Goose Lane.

Nelson, T.E., Z.M. Oxley, and R.A. Clawson. 1997. "Towards a Psychology of Framing Effects." *Political Behaviour* 19 (3): 221–46. https://pdfs.semanticscholar.org/9eed/82c751a8fe8c47896461cf786e475cbd4729.pdf.

Nolan, M. 1981. "Political Communication Methods in Canadian Federal Election Campaign 1867–1925." *Canadian Journal of Communication* 7 (4): 28–46. https://doi.org/10.22230/cjc.1981v7n4a260.

Patterson, T.E. 1996. Bad News, Period. *PS: Political Science and Politics* 29 (1): 17–20. https://doi.org /10.1017/S1049096500043997.

Popplewell, B. 2022. "The Media: The Narratives that Defined the Mainstream Election Coverage." In *The Canadian Federal Election 2021*, edited by J.H. Pammett and C. Dornan, 148–70. Montreal: McGill-Queen's University Press.

Postmedia. 2015. "'Too Easy' to Start Assigning Blame for Syrian Boy's Death, Mulcair Says; Trudeau Slams Handling of Crisis." *National Post*. September 3. https://nationalpost.com/news/politics/too -easy-to-start-assigning-blame-for-syrian-boys-death-mulcair-says-trudeau-slams-handling-of-crisis.

Purna Kambhampaty, A., M. Carlisle, and M. Chan. 2019. "Justin Trudeau Wore Brownface at 2001 'Arabian Nights' Party While He Taught at a Private School." *Time*. September 19. https://time.com/5680759 /justin-trudeau-brownface-photo/.

Sabato, L. 1991. *Feeding Frenzy: How Attack Journalism Has Transformed American Politics*. New York: Free Press.

Sampert, S., and L. Trimble. 2003. "'Wham, Bam, No Thank You Ma'am': Gender and the Game Frame in National Newspaper Coverage of Election 2000." In *Women and Electoral Politics in Canada*, edited by M. Tremblay and L. Trimble, 211–26. Toronto: Oxford University Press.

Sandel, M. 1998. *Democracy's Discontent: American in Search of a Public Philosophy*. Cambridge: Belknap Press/Harvard University Press.

Sanders, S.W., and J.P. Ferré. 2020. "Reader Responses to Religion News: Discussions about Ark Encounter on Reddit." *Journal of Religion, Media and Digital Culture* 9 (1): 107–30. https://doi.org/10.1163/21659214 -bja10008s.

Schaub, M. 2017. "Trump's Claim to Have Come Up with the Term 'Fake News' is Fake News, Merriam-Webster Dictionary Says." *Los Angeles Times*. October 9. https://www.latimes.com/books/jacketcopy /la-et-jc-fake-news-20171009-story.html.

Scheufele, D.A. 1999. "Framing as a Theory of Media Effects." *Journal of Communication* 49 (1): 103–22. https://doi.org/10.1111/j.1460-2466.1999.tb02784.x.

Schrøder, K.C. 2011. "Audiences Are Inherently Cross-media: Audience Studies and the Cross-media Challenge." *Communication Management Quarterly* 18 (6): 5–27. https://www.ceeol.com/search/article-detail?id=547435.

Schudson, M. 1978. *Discovering the News: A Social History of American Newspapers*. New York: Basic Books.

———. 2007. "Why Democracies Need an Unlovable Press." In *Media Power in Politics*, edited by D.A. Graber, 36–47. Washington, DC: CQ Press.

———. 2011. *The Sociology of News*. New York: Norton.

Shoemaker, P.J., and S.D. Reese. 2014. *Mediating the Message in the 21st Century: A Media Sociology Perspective*. New York: Routledge.

Starowicz, M. (Writer). 1997. *Dawn of the Eye* [TV]. Toronto and London: CBC and BBC. https://www .youtube.com/watch?v=u_K7tDfnbbk.

Stewart, W. 1980. "No Virginia, There Is No Lou Grant." In *Canadian Newspapers: The Inside Story* (Vols. 1–14), edited by W. Stewart, 9–37. Edmonton: Hurtig Publishers.

Street, J. 2001. *Mass Media, Politics and Democracy*. New York: Palgrave.

Taras, D. 1990. *The Newsmakers: The Media's Influence on Canadian Politics*. Toronto: Nelson Canada.

———. 2012. "The Past and the Future of Political Communication in Canada: An Introduction." In *How Canadians Communicate IV: Media and Politics*, edited by D. Taras and C. Waddell, 1–25. Athabasca: AU Press.

Taras, D., and C. Waddell. 2012. "The 2011 Federal Election and the Transformation of Canadian Media and Politics." In *How Canadians Communicate IV: Media and Politics*, edited by D. Taras and C. Waddell, 71–107. Athabasca: AU Press.

Taylor, G., and B. DeCillia. 2021. "Canada: A Strong Foundation with an Uncertain Future." In *The Media for Democracy Monitor 2021: How Leading Newsmedia Survive Digital Transformations*, volume 2, edited by J. Trappel and T. Tomaz, 43–84. Goteborg: Nordicom.

Thompson-Bristol, B., and K. Roberts Forde. 2022. "Journalism Has Long Conflated Objectivity with White Perspectives." *Washington Post*. July 14. https://www.washingtonpost.com/made-by-history/2022 /07/14/journalism-has-long-conflated-objectivity-with-white-perspectives/.

Tolley, E. 2016. *Framed: Media and the Coverage of Race in Canadian Politics*. Vancouver: UBC Press.

Troyer, W. 1980. *The Sound and Fury*. Toronto: Wiley.

Tuchman, G. 1972. "Objectivity as Strategic Ritual: An Examination of Newsmen's Notions of Objectivity." *American Journal of Sociology* 77 (4): 660–79. https://doi.org/10.1086/225193.

———. 1978. *Making News*. New York: Free Press.

Waddell, C. 2012. "Berry'd Alive: The Media, Technology, and the Death of Political Coverage." In *How Canadians Communicate IV: Media and Politics*, edited by D. Taras and C. Waddell, 109–28. Athabasca: AU Press.

———. 2020. "Digital Journalism: The Canadian Media's Struggle for Relevance." In *Digital Politics in Canada: Promise and Realities*, edited by T.A. Small and H. Jansen, 159–80. Toronto: University of Toronto Press.

Wagner, A., and J. Everitt, eds. 2019. *Gendered Mediation: Identity and Image Making in Canadian Politics*. Vancouver: UBC Press.

Ward, S.J.A. 2015. *The Invention of Journalism Ethics: The Path to Objectivity and Beyond*. Montreal: McGill-Queen's University Press.

Westell, A., and C. Cumming. 1982. "Canadian Media and the National Imperative." In *Government and the News Media*, edited by D. Nimmo and M. Mansfield, 161–83. Waco: Baylor University Press.

Williams, B.A., and M.X. Delli Carpini. 2011. *After Broadcast News: Media Regimes, Democracy, and the New Information Environment*. New York: Cambridge University Press.

Zaller, J. 1992. *The Nature and Origins of Mass Opinion*. New York: Cambridge University Press.

PART THREE

The Campaign

CHAPTER ELEVEN

Political Communication in Canadian Campaigns: "Go Where the Voters Are"

Andrew J.A. Mattan and Tamara A. Small

INTRODUCTION

In the lead-up to the 2019 federal election, Jagmeet Singh, the leader of the NDP, became a TikTok superstar when he posted a 15-second video expressing who he's "in it [the campaign] for" (Patel 2021). Capitalizing on a meme, by lip-synching to "Choices" by rapper E-40, Singh was able to briefly outline his campaign by pointing "yup" to the individuals and issues he wanted to support (e.g., families in need of medication, the environment, the unhoused, and the average person) and "nope" to who and what he was fighting against (e.g., the pharmaceutical industry, polluters, housing speculators, and the wealthy and powerful). Captured on the back of the NDP campaign tour bus by his then-digital director, the clip garnered 1.3 million views within the first day (Patel 2021).

Singh's innovative use of TikTok provides a useful example of a key aspect of any election campaign: *political communication*. According to Chaffee (1975, 415), political communication is defined as the "role of communication in the political process." As mentioned in the introductory chapter, campaigns are essentially communication events (Medvic 2021). That is, political actors seek to have their ideas, policies, brands, and personnel be more successful than their opponents. Political communication encapsulates the ways in which actors do this; it is the production, transmission, and reception of political messages (Small, Marland, and Giasson 2014). Political messages can be spoken or written words, but also in images, audio, and audiovisual forms; they can also be live or recorded.

This chapter focuses on the evolution and democratic importance of political communication in Canadian federal elections. We argue that the guiding principle of campaign communication is to go where the voters are. While the medium and technologies change, the strategy of parties meeting with people where they congregate is anything but novel. With each innovation, political actors embrace and utilize these new tools in interesting and different ways. However, new tools are used in addition to – rather than in replacement of – their current repertoire, with the ultimate goal of getting their specific political messages across to voters in as many ways as possible. The importance of political communication in campaigns is further highlighted by the extent it is regulated within Canadian electoral politics. While the goal of political communication remains the same, with each new technology comes a new set of democratic potentials and pitfalls. In the final section, we identify and reflect on four concerns that arise from modern campaign communication.

DEFINITION OF POLITICAL COMMUNICATION

Scholars often note that the political communication process involves three main actors: political institutions, the news media, and citizens (McNair 2018; Small, Marland, and Giasson 2014). Given DeCillia's discussion of journalists in Chapter 10, we focus little on the political communication activities that political parties engage in to attract media attention during the campaign such as events, news interviews, and press conferences. However, drawing on Holtz-Bacha and Kaid (2006), a useful distinction can be made between controlled and uncontrolled political communication. In the news media, political actors do not exercise full control over messages transmitted to the public. Despite media management techniques, actors always run the risk of their messages being altered during the media production process. As such, parties give significant attention to controlled forms of political communication in order to inform, mobilize, and ultimately persuade voters. Singh's TikTok is an excellent example of a very new form of controlled political communication. However, as will be discussed, social media is just the latest way to communicate with voters. Canadian parties engage in many forms of controlled political communication, such as lawn signs, brochures, party platforms, and political advertisements.

The difference between paid and unpaid forms of controlled political communication is another crucial distinction. The term *political advertising* is regularly used to refer to paid forms of political communication, where political actors purchase the opportunity to communicate with the public (Holtz-Bacha and Kaid 2006). Consider a television ad: a party will pay for the location, the actors, the editing, and directing of the commercial, plus the cost of buying ad time on televisions stations so people can see it. With advertising, there is a cost for the production and the placement of the message. It is worth pointing out that one factor behind the regulation of election expenses in 1974 was the steep rise in costs associated with the growth in television advertising by political parties during campaigns (Elections Canada 2020; also see Chapter 3).

However, not all controlled political messages are paid. This is mainly a function of the digital technologies in politics. Consider the multitude of X/Twitter, Facebook, and Instagram posts, or videos on YouTube that are made by political actors. Canadian election law does not consider these digital message as advertising because there are no placement costs and often they are free to produce (Elections Canada 2015). Digital politics scholars sometimes refer to unpaid digital messages on the internet as "organic content" (Kruschinski and Bene 2022; Mattan and Small 2022). Again, Jagmeet Singh's TikTok proves illustrative; the video was made at the back of the NDP campaign bus for free, but it had a big impact, being seen by millions of users.

Political communication aims to achieve two very different objectives in an election campaign: one democratic and one strategic. In terms of their democratic role, campaigns play an important educative function. They inform citizens about the important issues and problems of the day and outline each parties' proposed solutions. Ostensibly, the first objective of political communication is to ensure voters have appropriate information to make an effective decision on election day. The second objective of this communication is to influence voters to behave as advertisers desire (Cunningham 1999). At the end of day, parties want voters to vote for them and not their opponents. Indeed, the strategic objective is more crucial to the individual success of parties. Through political advertising and organic political content, parties not only make a case for why their team of candidates is the best to manage the political issues of the day, they also focus on their opponents. This is known as negative campaigning, where political messages focus on "what is wrong with the opponent, either personally or in terms of issue or policy stances" (Kaid 2000, 157). Despite being widely criticized by voters and the media, negative campaigning is commonplace. For better or worse, research shows that negative political messages tend to elicit more attention than positive ones (Daignault, Soroka, and Giasson 2013). The research also shows that while campaign information, such as issue planks and leader characteristics, matter to voters (Cross et al. 2015), the issues debated during an election affect vote choice only in a limited manner (Gidengil et al. 2012).

EVOLUTION OF CANADIAN CAMPAIGN COMMUNICATION

The history of political communication is often divided into stages or phases (for instance, see Blumler and Kavanagh 1999; Norris 2000; Gibson and Rommele 2001). Typically, the first phase of political communication is focused on direct, face-to-face forms, such as canvassing, meetings, and rallies. Technological change has brought about the next phase in the form of broadcasting. This phase begins with radio but is defined by television. The most recent phase is defined by cable television and digital technologies. Political communication is currently highly fragmented, as political actors have so many more venues to communicate with voters. These phases are useful in understanding the evolution of political communication in Canadian campaigns.

The desire to get political messages across to voters has existed in Canada since before Confederation (Nolan 1981). Prior to the growth of the newspaper industry in the 1820s, political communication was limited to the first phase of direct, face-to-face public meetings and canvassing (Koerber 2011). Given the vastness of Canada, electoral campaigns before 1878 were conducted constituency by constituency rather than as national contests. The inability for national party leaders to communicate with the mass electorate is highlighted by historian George M. Wrong, who stated in 1882, "In Britain a political leader can make a speech in the south of England in the morning and repeat it in the capital of Scotland on the same day. In Canada it takes about six days and nights to pass from one end of the country to the other" (cited in Nolan 1981, 28). Political communication during this time also came in the form of electoral posters. The most often cited is John A. Macdonald's "The Old Flag, The Old Policy, and the Old Leader" from the 1891 federal election (Small and Giasson 2020). The poster was created by the Toronto Lithographing Company, likely making it an early form of paid political advertising.[1]

By the mid-nineteenth century and into the first quarter of the twentieth century, the affordability and availability of the printing press, along with growing literacy rates and mass readership, saw political actors harnessing the power of the proliferating newspaper industry (Koerber 2011). As indicated in Chapter 10, political leaders relied heavily on overtly partisan newspapers – in some instances owned or financially supported by politicians – to communicate with the electorate. Although the press became a central mode for such communication, politicians still relied heavily on public meetings, debates, platform speeches, pamphlets and other printed materials, and canvassing. Train travel made campaigns much more structured and concise. With this development came the political picnic: a staged event developed by Macdonald to present himself as an approachable politician to the people, consisting of music, meals, handshakes, and merriment (Nolan 1981). Taking a condensed form of the political picnic on the road and across Canada, Wilfrid Laurier and his staff would perfect the practice of the campaign train whistle-stop (Marland and Delacourt 2020).

A new age of nonpartisan news reporting driven by advertising began during the 1920s (Nolan 1985). Spurring on these developments was the advent of the radio, ushering in a new phase of political communication characterized by broadcasting. Broadcasting follows the one-to-many logic, where a small number of individuals can unidirectionally communicate a limited amount of information to a mass audience (Zittel 2004). As with all new technologies, politicians were initially reluctant to use this new medium (Ward 1999). Even by the 1930s, Conservative Party leader R.B. Bennett and Liberal Party leader Mackenzie King were still using radio in a limited manner, merely adding live-to-air broadcasts to their conventional public meetings, rallies, or speeches (Nolan 1981). Nevertheless, as noted by Axworthy (1991, 183), "politicians go where the voters are," and with radio "a new venue for political communication became possible – the living room." Interestingly, the first novel use of radio occurred at the provincial level of Canadian politics with Alberta Social Credit Party leader William "Bible Bill" Aberhart's weekly radio series of "Mr. Orthodox Anonymous" and "Man from Mars" (Ward 1999). Using the radio for political advertising in a serial format was soon replicated by the federal Conservatives during the 1935 campaign (Ward 1999). In a series of six 10-minute programs, the Bennett Conservatives introduced Mr. Sage, "a cracker barrel philosopher ... who had several unkind things to say about [the Liberal prime minister] Mackenzie King" (Axworthy 1991, 184). In the first couple of episodes, the Conservatives had failed to identify themselves as the program's sponsor, outraging the Liberals (Levine 1993). Upon returning to power, the Liberals abolished dramatized political broadcasts.

In that same campaign, Bennett conducted a series of five radio addresses, coined the "New Deal broadcasts" (Nolan 1985). Emulating the successful "fire-side chats" of US president F.D. Roosevelt, Bennett chummily introduced his scheme for economic recovery right into the living rooms of Canadians via the radio. Unlike radio broadcasts before then, these five speeches were recorded in a studio, took a more conversational form, and were delivered with a quieter, made-for-radio tone (Ward 1999). The speeches, described by Levine (1993, 171) as "sensational," quickly captured the imagination of Canadians and "by the time the last broadcast was aired on January 11, the entire country ... [was] gathered around their ... sets for 'Bennett Parties.'" Thus, although the radio was clearly not going to displace more traditional forms of campaigning, it was finally embraced as a new medium that, when used correctly, held the capacity to simultaneously reach the masses in their homes and was not simply an extension of other forms of political communication (Nolan 1985).

While radio ushered in a new era, the impact of the arrival of television on political communication is often described as revolutionary (Ward 2001). Television brought forth new dimensions to politics, including a predisposition toward the visual, the dramatic, and mass appeal (Taras 1990). Indeed, in Canada's first televised election in 1957, Newman (1973) suggests that how a politician discussed policy became as, if not more, important than the policies themselves. Conservative leader John Diefenbaker is seen as the first Canadian politician to capitalize on the affordance of television. Diefenbaker was a skillful orator and the capacities made available to him by television allowed him to perform for the audience, gesticulating and bellowing his speeches off the cuff. This very much contrasted with his opponent, then–prime minister and Liberal leader Louis St. Laurent, who eschewed television and whose oration was described as akin to reading speeches "like legal briefs" (Newman 1973, 6).

Like radio, there was a slow adoption of television by all political actors. However, by the 1960s and stretching into the 1980s, campaigns became television centred, with leaders' tours organized as televised media events. Pierre Elliot Trudeau also made effective use of television during the 1968 campaign (Ward 1993). In the very first "made-for-TV campaign" (Litt 2016, 322), Trudeau was able to use his charisma, youthful appeal, and fashion sense to create his own brand of political celebritization called "Trudeaumania" (Small and Giasson 2020, 140). It was "Trudeau's ability as a screen actor [that made him successful as a leader] … [and] came across well on TV … [as it] provided the visual action television demanded: interesting gestures, flips off a diving board, slides down banisters, boogying beside a broken campaign bus, [and] a fake fall down a staircase" (Litt 2016, 322).

During this period, television slowly evolved into the main advertising medium of choice. In fact, by the 1990s, television attracted roughly two out of every nine dollars spent on advertising (Maclean-Hunter 1990). This resulted in the use of private advertising agencies and specialists, leading to the professionalization of parties and a decline in the importance of both grassroot support and newspapers (Spencer and Bolan 1991). Smith (1981) suggests that these trends worked to erode party identification and contributed to the instability of political views among Canadians.

Television advertising remains a central component of campaign communication even in the twenty-first century, and parties continue to spend significant portions of their election budgets on it. For instance, in the 2015 election, the Conservatives ran a series of ads claiming that Justin Trudeau was "Just Not Ready" to be prime minister. Polling data showed that the ads, which mocked both Trudeau's competency and his hair, had "definitive impact" on the way people perceived the Liberal leader. The "Just Not Ready" ads are representative of a trend, coinciding with the popularity of television advertising, that is characterized by the predisposition of ads to go negative (Romanow 1999). One of the most infamous examples of negative political advertising gone wrong in Canada was the Conservatives' "Is this a Prime Minister?" ad, which appeared to highlight the facial paralysis of Liberal leader Jean Chrétien in the 1993 election (Haddock and Zanna 1997, 206).[2] The ad proved to be an unmitigated disaster, leading to what some consider to be the most devastating political defeat in Canadian history and demonstrating the power of advertising to affect voters' attitudes, whether positively or adversely (Haddock and Zanna 1997). As demonstrated in these examples, advertising can either be an enormous positive benefit for parties or backfire.

Overall, television and particularly paid advertising has had a destabilizing effect on partisan identification, as viewers have become exposed to a variety of different political outlooks (Spencer and Bolan 1991). This ability to broadcast information to a general audience saw campaigning become a nationalized – rather than localized – event (Lee 1989). The latest form of political communication often connects to the current form of party organization and contemporary relations between political actors, the media, and citizens (Carty et al. 2000). So, the introduction of television during the 1950s both reflected and facilitated the transition from regional to pan-Canadian politics and the proliferation of parties with a brokerage or catch-all appeal during the third-party system (Carty et al. 2000; Carty 2013).

Since its introduction in the 1950s, television has changed: it has gained colour, thousands more channels, and round-the-clock news programming (Mazzoleni 2003). As a result, audiences have never been more fragmented, no longer limited to a handful of channels (Small et al. 2014). To counteract this fragmentation – or at the very least, to home in on the audiences they desire – political actors have turned to the internet to further target advertising, a process sometimes referred to as narrowcasting (Mattan and Small 2022).

The Liberals became the first Canadian political party to establish themselves online, creating a website where information could be shared and feedback collected from potential voters (Kippen 2000). By 1996, most parties had followed suit (Small et al. 2008; Barney 2007). These early websites lacked sophistication and were tangential to campaign communication. Interestingly, Small (2007) notes that it was actually the 2004 election that saw the internet become fully integrated into parties' overall campaign strategy. The early use of Web 1.0 technologies, characterized by their unidirectional sharing of information, was important for political actors to covertly target their messages to specific voters without also sharing that message with other parties, the media, or other voters (Carty et al. 2000). It also made a wide variety of information available to potential voters (Small 2004).

While Web 1.0 technologies were limited to the top-down form of broadcasting information and largely amplified traditional communication at a more targeted audience and at a lower cost (Barney 2007), the 2006 election saw the introduction of Web 2.0 into the political world, which added the capacity for interactivity. Web 2.0 technologies, such as social media, transform users from passive consumers of political information into content generators and amplifiers (Small 2014). Although the 2011 Canadian election is often dubbed Canada's first "Twitter Election," it was actually in 2008 that all five major federal parties had operating accounts on the platform now known as X (Small 2014). Generally, research finds that despite this widespread adoption, political actors are paradoxically taking the social out of social media, using these venues as yet another broadcast tool (Small 2014). However, that is not to suggest their impact is nonexistent, as social media contains the unique capability for political actors to personalize their messages, particularly through visuals, and to bypass the media, thereby controlling the narrative (Mattan 2018).

As with all the technological changes discussed above – be it the newspaper, the radio, television, or the internet – the process is characterized by latency between introduction and political adoption (Epstein 2013) and the supplementation rather than displacement of prior technologies (Small et al. 2014; Small and Giasson 2020). Taras (2012, 1–2) notes "the stark reality today is that every medium is merging with every other medium, every medium is becoming every other medium, and all media are merging on the Internet."

This reflects the third phase of political communication. As mentioned at the outset of this section, this era is marked by parties attempting to harness the capacities of the internet and social media to identify, reach, and convince an increasingly fragmented and individualized populace. Research demonstrates that parties are using the sophistications of social media to narrowcast their messages, creating private conversations between parties and voters, and potentially creating individualized political echo chambers (Mattan and Small 2022). The fragmentation of communication is further compounded by regionalization and the need to include seat-rich Quebec and the French-speaking population in electoral strategies. The mere fact of bilingualism, not to mention the distinct political culture within Quebec, highlights the necessity of political actors to tailor campaign communication on a regional basis in Canada. However, whether regionally targeting voters using social media, broadcasting national ads on television or radio, or canvassing to individual voters door to door, all forms of political communication – regardless of phase – share the common aim of going where the voters are. Mirroring this broader theme, once parties are there, regulations tend to follow.

Regulating Campaign Communication

Earlier, we mentioned the banning of serialized advertising after the Mr. Sage scandal in 1935. To some extent, all jurisdictions in Canada regulate election advertising, especially in terms of spending, to ensure fairness (Boyer 1981; Elections Canada 2017). As indicated in the previous discussions of campaign finance by Young in Chapter 3 and Beange in Chapter 9, the regulation of advertising is consistent with the egalitarian model, which is premised on the notion that political actors should have an equal opportunity to participate in the electoral process. Advertising is tantamount to speech; the more money a party has, the more speech it has.

Parties are subject to limits on what they can spend during a campaign. Advertising has been a regulated expense in the *Canada Elections Act* (CEA) since 1974, though it has only been regulated in the pre-campaign since 2018. Indeed, advertising is the only regulated expense in the pre-campaign. Advertising is generally defined as the transmission of an advertising message to the public, by any means during an election period, that promotes or opposes a registered party or candidate.[3] Expenses include the production and distribution of advertising. Eight months after election day, registered political parties are required to submit their expenses to Elections Canada and, with regard to advertising, they must report the total amount spent in five categories: online, print media, radio, TV, and other.

Another relevant set of rules in the CEA, found in the section titled Political Broadcast, is meant to ensure equity in party advertising. Directed at Canadian broadcasters – that is, television and radio stations as defined by the *Broadcasting Act* (Elections Canada n.d.) – these rules legally obligate broadcasters, such as the CBC, Global News, and CTV, to provide free and paid advertising time to registered political parties during a federal election. The rules require each broadcaster to make available six and a half prime-time hours for purchase at the lowest rate available. Moreover, certain networks must also make six and a half hours of broadcast time freely available.

It is important to remember that registered political parties are more numerous and diverse than the parties we normally think about and that typically win seats in elections. Registered parties also include longstanding minor parties such as the Communist Party as well as newer minor ones like the Maverick Party. In theory, this rule ensures that the ability of all registered political parties to get their message to voters is not impeded by unduly high prices of purchasing broadcasting time, especially during prime-time hours when audience numbers are highest. In practice, however, the law favours larger parties such as the Liberals and Conservatives. The CEA tasks the Broadcasting Arbitrator with allocating time among all registered political parties. The formula used by the Broadcasting Arbitrator takes into consideration each parties' percentage of seats in the House of Commons and percentage of the popular vote at the previous general election. This means the larger parties have higher allocations of broadcasting time. For instance, in the 2021 election, the Liberals were allocated 77 minutes whereas the newly registered True North Party was allocated six minutes. The provision only addresses one part of advertising: distribution. The production or the cost of making radio and television is not addressed, which also makes it more difficult for minor parties to make use of the time compared to larger ones. Finally, it is worth noting that this rule does not cover advertising on new digital technologies such as Facebook or YouTube. This means that larger parties have a greater ability to communicate with voters both off- and online – because they have more resources.

That said, the CEA is not completely silent on digital advertising. One of the significant changes that occurred with the *Elections Modernization Act* in 2018 was regarding the online electoral environment. The rationale for these changes was not only due to the growing importance of digital technologies but also the negative consequences of their use in campaigning. For instance, in the 2016 US presidential election, purveyors of misinformation purchased advertisements on social media meant to confuse and mislead voters. One example was an advertisement suggesting that Pope Francis had endorsed Donald Trump. Many of these problematic ads were created by foreign actors for nefarious or monetary purposes. Canada, like many other jurisdictions, introduced provisions in order to combat misinformation on social media (Small 2020). Rather than regulating what parties or other actors can say online, the rules regulate online platforms.

Starting with the 2019 federal election, online platforms such as, Facebook, X, Google, and the websites of major news organizations are legally obligated to publish a "Registry of Partisan and Election Advertising." Whenever a political actor purchases digital advertising, the platform must include an electronic copy of the message and the name of the person who authorized its publication in its registry. Each registry must then remain on the platform for two years following the election, and the information from the registry must be kept for an additional five years. Finally, the law makes it an offence for online platforms to knowingly sell election advertising to foreign actors. This discussion of regulation of political communication reinforces our argument that as parties go where voters are, the laws governing elections must follow them.

DEMOCRATIC IMPLICATIONS

This chapter has proposed that evolving forms of political communication have both reflected and impacted the dynamics within parties and the relations between political actors, the media, and citizens. In this final section, we identify four concerns of modern campaign communication. First, while all forms of political communication are being used in concert, with each new evolution, there is a noticeable move toward more professionalized parties that are less concerned with local support and more focused on attracting individual voters using political marketing techniques, voter data management, and algorithms (Savigny 2011; Giasson et al. 2012; Hendricks and Schill 2017). With this comes more efficient and precise forms of communication, but this comes at the expense of transparency and privacy (Howard 2006). Carty and colleagues (2000) emphasize that we should be concerned about these private conversations between political actors and citizens.

We also wonder about the ethical considerations surrounding covertly directing messages to specific voters on social media, without having to share that message with other parties, the media, or other voters. Although showing the capacity to increase voter interest, this same narrowcasting shows the potential to isolate citizens within their own partisan bubbles or echo chambers. An echo chamber ensures people only encounter information and opinions that they find agreeable, filtering out those they find objectionable (Small and Jansen 2020). Algorithms, built into social media, only exacerbate this problem by not only filtering out information that users find uninteresting but creating vastly different information experiences from user to user (Mattan and Small 2022). As forewarned by Sunstein (2018, ix), in a "well-functioning democracy, people do not live in echo chambers or information cocoons. They see or hear a wide range of topics and ideas." Thus, we should be concerned about the evolution of political communication to the detriment of politics as a collective experience (Small and Jansen 2020).

Another privacy concern is related to data collection. One benefit of social media for any advertiser is the ability to collect information from users in order to better direct or target messages. Cotter and colleagues (2021, 1), for example, argue that Facebook ads are "driven not by a goal of making *all* users available to advertisers, but of making the '*right*' individuals available" (italics in original). However, the collection of personal data and the lack of transparency in its use by political parties is a concern, since individual privacy may be violated (Judge and Pal 2021). Indeed, Jagmeet Singh has recently paused his use of TikTok due to privacy concerns (Patel 2023). In 2023, the Government of Canada removed and blocked the use of TikTok on devices used by Canadian federal public servants. According to the Treasury Board (2023), the ban is related to "concerns about the legal regime that governs the information collected from mobile devices." TikTok is based out of China. According to Judge and Pal (2021), federal privacy laws and elections have failed to keep up with development in data-driven campaigning. Consistent with our earlier argument, we hope to see future election legislation to address these gaps.

Next, as political communication has become more professionalized, it has also become more strategic. One of the outcomes of this is the tendency to go negative. From Mr. Sage to "Is this a Prime Minister?" to your run-of-the-mill social media attack posts, political communication in Canada has historically been and continues to have a flair for the negative. However, what is less settled is whether this negativity spurs or demobilizes voters. Some research suggests that negative advertising increases voter engagement and knowledge (Kahn Fridkin and Kenney 2004). Other research suggests that negativity turns voters away from the political process (Ansolabehere and Iyengar 2010). What is more agreed upon is that negative campaigning works (Lau and Pomper 2004). As highlighted by Romanow (1999), negative campaigning sits at the crossroads of effective and offensive. But what impact does it have on citizen's general perception of political institutions?

Negativity around political campaigns may indeed contribute to the general loss of trust in political leaders and institutions.

Third, advances in digital technologies have slowly altered the role of media and journalism in Canadian politics. In this third stage of political communication, we have seen a dramatic increase in the ability of political actors to bypass the media. Political actors can use social media and the internet to distribute messages – whether to a mass or targeted audience – without any vetting (Waddell 2020). That is, not only are voters potentially seeing different information, but the media is also unable to play its role as a political watchdog or gatekeeper (Chadwick 2013). This is undoubtedly a benefit to political actors, as they attempt to get their messages across, but it seems to be very problematic for citizens and democracy.

Finally, while political actors going to the places people congregate appears, at least on its face, to be a positive development and potentially something that may counteract democratic malaise – as parties and political actors can be responsive and communicate with voters – we question whether these interactions are actually occurring. Research suggests that political actors are using social media as a broadcast medium, with no evidence of communication or interactions with citizens. Given these concerns, how problematic is it that political leaders are using these apps, when they are known to be collecting, tracking, and selling personal data? Does the use of these digital technologies for political communication purposes give them a sense of credibility that they do not deserve?

CONCLUSION

Beginning the chapter with Singh's novel use of TikTok follows the logic of many modern discussions of political communication. We used this example throughout to highlight an innovative use of social media to communicate with voters. However, rather than emphasizing how it differed, we sought to use this example to demonstrate how the goal of political communication in Canada has largely remained the same: go where the voters are. Each new era sees actors using the newest technologies in interesting ways, but this has occurred in addition to – rather than in replacement of – the mediums of the past. Social media may be the newest political communication tool that Canadian parties have used, but it is not the only one. Parties still make television and radio commercials; they still even send brochures through post. If the overall objective of a political campaign is to convince voters to vote for your candidates, using as many tools as possible only makes sense.

NOTES

1 The poster can be viewed on the McCord Stewart Museum website at https://collections.musee-mccord -stewart.ca/en/objects/details/35183.
2 This ad can be viewed on YouTube at https://www.youtube.com/watch?v=QMjdp3TTTyk.
3 For greater specificity, *Canada Elections Act* refers to advertising in the election period and "election advertising" and "partisan advertising" in the pre-election period. These definitions are found in the section "Interpretation of the Act."

REFERENCES

Ansolabehere, Stephen, and Shanto Iyengar. 2010. *Going Negative: How Political Ads Shrink and Polarize the Electorate*. New York: Simon and Schuster.

Axworthy, Thomas. 1991. "Capital-Intensive Politics: Money, Media and Mores in the United States and Canada." In *Election Broadcasting in Canada*, edited by Federick J. Fletcher, 157–234. Toronto: Dundurn Press Limited.

Barney, Darin. 2007. "The Internet and Political Communication in Canadian Politics: The View from 2004." In *Canadian Parties in Transition*, 3rd ed., edited by Alain-G. Gagnon and A. Brian Tanguay, 371–84. Scarborough: Nelson.

Blumler, Jay G., and Dennis Kavanagh. 1999. "The Third Age of Political Communication: Influences and Features." *Political Communication* 16 (3): 209–30. https://doi.org/10.1080/105846099198596.

Boyer, J. Patrick. 1981. *Political Rights: The Legal Framework of Elections in Canada*. London: Butterworths.

Carty, R. Kenneth. 2013. "Has Brokerage Politics Ended? Canadian Parties in the New Century." In *Parties, Elections, and the Future of Canadian Politics*, edited by Amanda Bittner and Royce Koop, 10–23. Vancouver: UBC Press.

Carty, R. Kenneth, William P. Cross, and Lisa Young. 2000. *Rebuilding Canadian Party Politics*. Vancouver: UBC Press.

Chadwick, Andrew. 2013. *The Hybrid Media System: Politcs and Power*. Oxford: Oxford University Press.

Chaffee, Steven H. 1975. *Political Communication: Issues and Strategies for Research*. Beverly Hills: SAGE Publications.

Cotter, Kelley, Mel Medeiros, Chankyung Pak, and Kjerstin Thorson. 2021. "'Reach the Right People': The Politics of 'Interests' in Facebook's Classification System for Ad Targeting." *Big Data & Society* 8 (1). https://doi.org/10.1177/2053951721996046.

Cross, William, Jonathan Malloy, Tamara A. Small, and Laura Stephenson. 2015. *Fighting for Votes: Parties, the Media and Voters in the 2011 Ontario Election*. Vancouver: UBC Press.

Cunningham, Stanley B. 1999. "The Theory and Use of Political Advertising." In *Television Advertising in Canadian Elections: The Attack Mode, 1993*, edited by Walter I. Romanow, Michel de Repentigny, Stanley B. Cunningham, Walter C. Soderlund, and Kai Hildebrand, 11–25. Waterloo: Wilfrid Laurier University Press.

Daignault, Pénélope, Stuart Soroka, and Thierry Giasson. 2013. "The Perception of Political Advertising during an Election Campaign: A Measure of Cognitive and Emotional Effects." *Canadian Journal of Communication* 38 (2): 167–86. https://doi.org/10.22230/cjc.2013v38n2a2566.

Elections Canada. 2015. "Election Advertising on the Internet (Written Opinions, Guidelines and Interpretation Notes: 2015-04)." Ottawa: Elections Canada. https://www.elections.ca/content.aspx?section=res&dir=gui/app/2015-04&document=index&lang=e.

——. 2017. "Compendium of Election Administration in Canada." August 30. Ottawa: Elections Canada. https://www.elections.ca/res/loi/com/compendium/june2017_e.pdf.

——. 2020. "Discussion Paper 1: The Regulation of Political Communications under the Canada Elections Act." Elections Canada. July 8. https://www.elections.ca/content.aspx?section=res&dir=cons/dis/compol/dis1&document=index&lang=e.

——. n.d. "Broadcasting Arbitrator." https://www.elections.ca/content.aspx?section=abo&document=index&dir=bra&lang=e.

Epstein, Ben. 2013. *From the Fireside Chats to the First Political Tweet: The Origin and Diffusion of Political Communication Innovations from the Radio to the Internet*. Chicago: APSA 2013 Annual Meeting Paper.

Giasson, Thierry, Jennifer Lees-Marshment, and Alex Marland. 2012. "Challenges to Democracy." In *Political Marketing in Canada*, edited by Alex Marland, Thierry Giasson, and Jennifer Lees-Marshment, 241–55. Vancouver: UBC Press.

Gibson, Rachel, and Andrea Römmele. 2001. "Changing Campaign Communications: A Party-Centered Theory of Professionalized Campaigning." *Harvard International Journal of Press/Politics* 6 (4): 31–43. https://doi.org/10.1177/108118001129172323.

Gidengil, Elisabeth, Neil Nevitte, André Blais, Joanna Everitt, and Patrick Fournier. 2012. *Dominance and Decline: Making Sense of Recent Canadian Elections*. Toronto: University of Toronto Press.

Haddock, Geoffrey, and Mark P. Zanna. 1997. "Impact of Negative Advertising on Evaluations of Political Candidates: The 1993 Canadian Federal Election." *Basic and Applied Social Psychology* 19 (2): 205–23. https://doi.org/10.1207/s15324834basp1902_4.

Hendricks, John A., and Dan Shill. 2017. "The Social Media Election of 2016." In *The Social Media Elections of 2016*, edited by Robert E. Denton Jr., 121–50. London: Palgrave Macmillan.

Holtz-Bacha, Christina, and Lynda Lee Kaid. 2006. "Political Advertising in International Comparison." In *The Sage Handbook of Political Advertising*, edited by Lynda Lee Kaid and Christina Holtz-Bacha, 3–14. California: Sage Publications.

Howard, Philip. 2006. *New Media Campaigns and the Managed Citizen*. Cambridge: Cambridge University Press.

Judge, Elizabeth F., and Michael Pal. 2021. "Voter Privacy and Big-Data Elections." *Osgoode Hall Law Journal* 58 (1): 1–56. https://doi.org/10.60082/2817-5069.3631.

Kahn Fridkin, Kim, and Patrick J. Kenney. 2004. *No Holds Barred: Negativity in US Senate Campaigns*. New Jersey: Prentice Hall.

Kaid, Lynda Lee. 2000. "Ethics and Political Advertising." In *Political Communication Ethics: An Oxymoron?*, edited by Robert E. Denton, 147–77. Westport: Praeger.

Kippen, Grant. 2000. *The Use of Information Technologies by a Political Party*. Vancouver: SFU-UBC Centre for the Study of Government Business.

Koerber, Duncan. 2011. "Style over Substance: Newspaper Coverage of Early Election Campaigns in Canada, 1820–1841." *Canadian Journal of Communication* 36 (3): 435–53. https://doi.org/10.22230/cjc.2011v36n3a2444.

Kruschinski, Simon, and Márton Bene. 2022. "In Varietate Concordia?! Political Parties' Digital Political Marketing in the 2019 European Parliament Election Campaign." *European Union Politics* 23 (1): 43–65. https://doi.org/10.1177/14651165211040728.

Lau, Richard R., and Gerald M. Pomper. 2004. *Negative Campaigning: An Analysis of US Senate Elections*. Lanham: Rowman & Littlefield.

Lee, Robert M. 1989. *One Hundred Monkeys: The Triumph of Popular*. Toronto: Macfarlane Walter and Ross.

Levine, Allan. 1996. *Scrum Wars: The Prime Ministers and The Media*. Toronto: Dundurn Press.

Litt, Paul. 2016. *Trudeaumania*. Vancouver: UBC Press.

Maclean-Hunter. 1990. *Advertising Revenues in Canada*. Toronto: Maclean-Hunter Research Bureau.

Marland, Alex, and Susan Delacourt. 2020. "Introduction: Constantly Shopping for Votes." In *Inside the Campaign: Managing Elections in Canada*, edited by Thierry Giasson and Alex Marland, 3–27. Vancouver: UBC Press.

Mattan, Andrew. 2018. *Tweeting Pass the Media: An Analysis of Visual Image Management on Twitter during the 2018 Ontario Provincial Election*. Guelph: Department of Political Science, University of Guelph.

Mattan, Andrew J.A., and Tamara A. Small. 2022. "Regionalized Campaign Communication: Facebook Advertising in the 2021 Federal Election." In *The Canadian Federal Election of 2021*, edited by Jon H. Pammett and Christopher Dornan, 171–91. Montreal-Kingston: McGill-Queen's University Press.

Mazzoleni, Gianpietro. 2003. "Political Communication and Television: Between Old and New Influences". In *Political Communication in a New Era: A Cross-National Perspective*, edited by Philippe J. Maarek and Gadi Wolfsfeld, 32–40. London: Routledge.

McNair, Brian. 2018. *An Introduction to Political Communication*. London: Taylor & Francis.

Medvic, Stephen K. 2021. *Campaigns and Elections: Players and Processes*. Milton: Taylor and Francis. https://doi.org/10.4324/9781003125099.

Newman, Peter C. 1973. *Renegade in Power: The Diefenbaker Years*. Toronto: McClelland and Stewart.

Nolan, Michael. 1981. "Political Communication Methods in Canadian Federal Election Campaign 1867–1925." *Canadian Journal of Communication* 7 (4): 28–46. https://doi.org/10.22230/cjc.1981v7n4a260.

———. 1985. "Canadian Election Broadcasting: Political Practices and Radio Regulation 1919–1939." *Journal of Broadcasting & Electronic Media* 29 (2): 175–88. https://doi.org/10.1080/08838158509386575.

Norris, Pippa. 2000. *A Virtuous Circle: Political Communications in Postindustrial Societies*. New York: Cambridge University Press.

Patel, Raisa. 2021. "Jagmeet Singh Is a TikTok Superstar. Here's What That Means for the Next Election." *Toronto Star (Online)*. July 5. https://www.thestar.com/politics/federal/2021/07/05/jagmeet-singh-is-a-tiktok-superstar-heres-what-that-means-for-the-next-election.html.

———. 2023. "Pierre Poilievre, Jagmeet Singh Take TikTok Hiatus amid Government Ban over Privacy Concerns." *Toronto Star (Online)*. February 27. https://www.thestar.com/politics/federal/2023/02/27/pierre-poilievre-jagmeet-singh-take-tiktok-hiatus-amid-government-ban-over-privacy-concerns.html.

Romanow, Walter. 1999. "Introduction." In *Television Advertising in Canadian Elections: The Attack Mode, 1993*, edited by Walter I. Romanow, Michel de Repentigny, Stanley B. Cunningham, Walter C. Soderlund, and Kai Hildebrand, 1–9. Waterloo: Wilfrid Laurier University Press.

Savigny, Heather. 2011. *The Problem of Political Marketing*. London: Continuum.

Small, Tamara A. 2004. "Parties@canada: The Internet and the 2004 Cyber-Campaign." In *The Canadian General Election of 2004*, edited by Jon H. Pammett and Christopher Dornan, 203–34. Toronto: Dundurn.

———. 2007. "Canadian Cyberparties: Reflections on Internet-Based Campaigning and Party Systems." *Canadian Journal of Political Science* 40 (3): 639–57. https://doi.org/10.1017/S0008423907070734.

———. 2014. "The Not-So Social Network: The Use of Twitter by Canada's Party Leaders." In *Political Communication in Canada: Meet the Press and Tweet the Rest*, edited by Alex Marland, Thierry Giasson, and Tamara A. Small, 92–110. Vancouver: UBC Press.

———. 2020. "Digital Campaigning in the Era of Misinformation." In *The Canadian Federal Election of 2019*, edited by Jon H. Pammett and Christopher Dornan, 198–220. Montreal-Kingston: McGill-Queen's University Press.

Small, Tamara A., and Thierry Giasson. 2020. "Political Parties: Campaigning in the Digital Age." In *Digital Politics in Canada: Promises and Realities*, edited by Tamara A. Small and Harold J. Jansen, 136–58. Toronto: University of Toronto Press.

Small, Tamara A., and Harold J. Jansen. 2020. "Introduction: Twenty Years of Digital Politics in Canada." In *Digital Politics in Canada: Promises and Realities*, edited by Tamara A. Small and Harold J. Jansen, 1–21. Toronto: University of Toronto Press.

Small, Tamara A., Alex Marland, and Thierry Giasson. 2014. "The Triangulation of Canadian Political Communication." In *Political Communication in Canada: Meet the Press and Tweet the Rest*, 3–23. Vancouver: UBC Press.

Small, Tamara A., David Taras, and Dave Danchuk. 2008. "Canada: Party Websites and Online Campaigning during the 2004 and 2006 Federal Election." In *Making a Difference: A Comparative View of the Role of the Internet in Election Politics*, edited by Stephen Ward, Diana Owen, Richard Davis, and David Taras, 113–31. Lanham: Lexington Press.

Smith, A. 1981. "Mass Communications." In *Democracy at the Polls: A Comparative Study of Competitive National Elections*, edited by David Butler, Howard Penniman, and Austin Ranney, 173–95. Washington, DC: American Enterprise Institute for Public Policy Research.

Spencer, David R. and Catherine M. Bolan. 1991. "Election Broadcasting in Canada: A Brief History." In *Election Broadcasting in Canada*, edited by Frederick J. Fletcher, 3–38. Toronto: Dundurn Press Limited.

Sunstein, Cass R. 2018. *#Republic: Divided Democracy in the Age of Social Media*. Princeton: Princeton University Press.

Taras, David. 1990. *The Newsmakers: The Media's Influence on Canadian Politics*. Scarborough: Nelson Canada.

———. 2012. "Introduction." In *How Canadians Communicate IV: Media and Politics*, edited by David Taras and Christopher Waddell, 1–25. Athabasca: Athabasca University Press.

Treasury Board of Canada Secretariat. 2023. "Statement by Minister Fortier Announcing a Ban on the Use of TikTok on Government Mobile Devices." February 27. https://www.canada.ca/en/treasury-board -secretariat/news/2023/02/statement-by-minister-fortier-announcing-a-ban-on-the-use-of-tiktok-on -government-mobile-devices.html.

Waddell, Christopher. 2020. "Digital Journalism: The Canadian Media's Struggle for Relevance." In *Digital Politics in Canada: Promises and Realities* edited by Tamara A. Small and Harold J. Jansen, 159–80. Toronto: University of Toronto Press.

Ward, Ian. 1993. "'Media Intrusion' and the Changing Nature of the Established Parties in Australia and Canada." *Canadian Journal of Political Science* 26 (3): 477–506. https://doi.org/10.1017 /S0008423900003413.

———. 1999. "The Early Use of Radio for Political Communication in Australia and Canada: John Henry Austral, Mr. Sage and the Man From Mars." *Australian Journal of Politics and History* 45 (3): 311–29.

———. 2001. "Trudeaumania and It's Time: The Early Use of TV for Political Communication." *Australian-Canadian Studies* 19 (1): 1–22.

Zittel, Thomas. 2004. "Political Communication and Electronic Democracy: American Exceptionalism or Global Trend?" In *Comparing Political Communication: Theories, Cases, and Challenges*, edited by Frank Esser and Barbara Pfetsch, 231–50. Cambridge: Cambridge University Press.

CHAPTER TWELVE

The Debates: Party Strategies, Media Demands, and the Public Interest

Spencer McKay

INTRODUCTION

Broadcast debates are a prominent feature of election campaigns in many democracies (Anstead 2016). While often referred to as "televised" debates, these events have long been broadcast on radio and are increasingly streamed online. Debates are important because, while some citizens follow campaign coverage quite closely from day to day, many do not. Debates offer busy voters an opportunity to hear representatives of multiple major parties speak on a variety of issues in a relatively short amount of time. As a result, debates are usually the single most-watched event of the campaign, and even voters who do not watch a debate might catch glimpses of what happened as notable moments from the event are often rebroadcast and shared on social media. In some cases, debates appear as turning points for a campaign – changing the fortunes of parties – while in others they mark the "starting point of the *real* campaign," the point at which voters start to pay attention to politics more closely (Leduc 1997, 207).

This chapter focuses on understanding debates as a democratic institution. The value of debates is often called into question because they take place in the context of partisan campaigns. Instead of trying to educate voters or work with their political rivals to address policy issues, participants generally try to mobilize and persuade voters. Even the "rules of the game" for debates – such as who is invited, the scheduling and length of the debate, the format – have traditionally been subject to negotiations between parties and broadcasters. Political parties have historically made competing demands that reflect the terms they expect will be most favourable to their own party leader. These demands may be backed up by the threat that a party leader will not participate in the debate if the broadcasters and other parties do not agree to their terms. Similarly, while broadcasters might portray themselves as "more capable than anyone else to provide impartiality and fairness," they may also insist that their own journalists appear during the debate or that these events must be scheduled so that they do not replace programs that bring in considerable advertising revenue (Amber 1999, 134–35). Broadcasters have the leverage to make such demands because they control much of the infrastructure by which the debates are transmitted to viewers. The events that result often reflect compromises among various private interests, even though an alternative method of organization might better ensure the democratic quality of debates.

One way of assessing the democratic value of election campaigns is to investigate whether they are competitive, whether they reflect norms of political equality, and whether they enable deliberation (Lipsitz 2004). Debates have not always succeeded in these respects, although there have been a variety of attempts to hold them to such standards. One recent attempt to take the organization of the debates out of the hands of party officials and private media outlets is the Leaders' Debates Commission (LDC). Created in 2018, the LDC has certainly not resolved all the problems that accompany debates, but its independence from parties and media outlets suggests that it has the potential to organize debates that serve the public interest.

DEFINING CAMPAIGN DEBATES

A campaign debate is an event – with a formal set of rules – where candidates with opposing positions respond to questions or prompts in order to present their competing ideas to an audience (Carlin 1989). Debates take place in many countries, including Argentina, Germany, Mexico, South Korea, and the United States (McKay 2020). Because such debates occur within the context of a broader election campaign, it is worth distinguishing them from other related events. Debates are not party-organized campaign events with audiences largely made up of supporters. Campaign events allow parties to set the agenda, feature a single party leader, and rarely provide opportunities for follow-up questions. Debates are not press conferences, where leaders set the agenda. Debates are also distinct from media interviews with party leaders. There are some similarities, particularly when media organizations pose the same set of questions to all party leaders, but these interviews do not allow leaders to interact directly with their opponents.

While viewers may tune into debates for a variety of reasons – learning about party positions on policy issues, judging the ability of leaders to communicate competently, evaluating the character of candidates, or cheering on their preferred candidates – many of these goals might be achieved by other means. Citizens might follow the campaign on television, social media, party mailing lists, or by discussing with others. What makes debates unique campaign events is that they involve real-time interaction between multiple party leaders and offer the potential of less scripted, more authentic interaction. Debates provide focal points for election campaigns, drawing the attention of citizens who might not otherwise be engaged and allowing viewers to compare issues, candidates, parties, and platforms (Jamieson and Birdsell 1990; McKinney 2005; McKinney and Carlin 2004). These functions are facilitated, in part, by high levels of media attention, including an initial "debate about the debates," the debate itself, and post-debate coverage (Chadwick 2011; Kaid, McKinney, and Tedesco 2000; McKinney and Carlin 2004). Combined with the fact that watching a two-hour debate is a smaller commitment than trying to closely follow the day-to-day developments of the campaign, it is easy to see why debates attract such large audiences.

The formats of the debates themselves can vary quite widely, depending on how the organizers want to manage interactions between the participants (Bernier and Monière 1991). Some debates are essentially parallel press conferences, in which participants are each given time to respond individually to questions. However, such debates offer participants little to no opportunity to interact with one another. Other debates are built around direct confrontations that give participants unstructured time to interact, enabling back-and-forth exchanges between leaders. In practice, many debates use a mixed approach that pairs direct confrontation with structured questions. For instance, leaders may be given the opportunity to bookend verbal confrontations with uninterrupted opening or closing statements. In other cases, participants may each provide an answer to a question before time is allocated for open debate.

Mixed combinations are relatively common, perhaps because debate organizers anticipate that this will address the shortcomings of both the parallel press conference and direct confrontation approaches. For instance, the parallel press conference seems to largely undermine the unique contribution that debates might make. Rather than encouraging participants to push each other to give more authentic responses, the parallel press conference format might allow participants to give scripted answers that are similar to those heard throughout the campaign (McKinney and Carlin 2004; Coleman and Moss 2016). On the other hand, direct confrontation can lead participants to fight for speaking time, making it difficult for anyone to get their point across.

The rest of this chapter focuses on leaders' debates in Canadian federal elections. While debates between candidates also take place between provincial party leaders and local candidates in many elections, the federal leaders' debates are the most watched and the most studied.[1] Unfortunately, it is not possible to also provide detailed accounts of the substantive issues discussed in each debate or the effect of the debates on the election results. Such accounts exist for many of the debates in question (Attallah and Burton 2001; Barr 1991; Bernier and Monière 1991; Leduc 1994 and 1997; LeDuc and Price 1985; Waddell and Dornan 2006; Turcotte 2016 and 2020). Instead, I focus here primarily on how attempts by relevant players to shape the process of debates themselves may have strengthened demands for debates to serve the interests of citizens.

THE EVOLUTION OF DEBATES IN CANADIAN ELECTIONS

Thirty-eight federal leaders' debates have occurred in Canada between 1968 and 2024. These debates have been organized by a variety of media organizations, government agencies, and political groups. The format has also changed considerably from debate to debate. Much of this variation reflects the outcomes of negotiations between the parties and broadcasters; however, the scope of these negotiations has sometimes been narrowed by growing expectations that the debates will reflect democratic principles. Once debates became an established aspect of campaigns, a set of norms followed. This included the organization of debates in both English and French, as well as a commitment to roughly equal speaking time among participants. In what follows, I divide the evolution of debates into five periods.

Episodic Debates (1968–1980)

In the first period the debates were episodic, as their occurrence in any given election relied on the ability of parties and broadcasters to reach agreement. Canadian leaders' debates take their inspiration from presidential debates in the United States, which emerged alongside the growing accessibility of television. While the first televised presidential debate in the United States took place in 1960, Prime Minister John Diefenbaker refused Liberal leader Lester B. Pearson's challenge to a "televised showdown" in 1962 (Ditchburn 2015). The first televised leaders' debate would take place in 1968, and these would occur only sporadically until 1984.

The 1968 televised leaders' debates were organized by CTV and the CBC. While the networks initially only invited Liberal prime minister Pierre Elliott Trudeau and Progressive Conservative (PC) leader Robert Stanfield, the NDP threatened to protest if leader Tommy Douglas was not included (Ditchburn 2015). The Liberal Party then demanded that all parties with seats in the House of Commons be present and that, given Canada's substantial francophone population, the debate be bilingual.[2] Despite the electoral importance of largely French-speaking Quebec, the PCs and NDP leaders did not speak French and responded that they would require simultaneous translation, which the Liberals begrudgingly conceded (Bernier and Monière 1991). Réal Caouette, leader of the Ralliement créditiste, was invited to participate for the final 45 minutes. This debate was two hours long and did not allow for direct exchanges between leaders. As a result, it has been criticized for essentially being a joint press conference rather than a real debate (Rogers 2010). Trudeau concluded that he "wouldn't want to impose another debate on the Canadian public. I don't think they could stomach the platitudes and general dullness" (Hurst 1988).

There were no debates in the 1972 and 1974 campaigns since the networks were uninterested in leaders' debates without Prime Minister Trudeau, who saw little benefit to accepting debate invitations. This changed in 1979, when Trudeau found himself in a tight race. He pressured PC leader Joe Clark to agree to a debate, and the networks also invited NDP leader Ed Broadbent (LeDuc and Price 1985). A French debate was considered but ultimately did not go ahead because Trudeau refused to accept a format that would accommodate party leaders who could not speak French (Bernier and Monière 1991). There was one English-language debate with opening statements, three 30-minute one-on-one debates, and closing statements. The networks (CBC, CTV, and Global) hoped that the one-on-one confrontations would generate a livelier debate than in 1968, even if not all leaders spoke in relation to all the discussed issues (Bernier and Monière 1991; LeDuc and Price 1985).

There was no debate in the 1980 election campaign. The three English-language networks that organized the 1979 debate were joined by two French-language broadcasters (Radio-Canada and TVA) as part of a *broadcast consortium*. The consortium proposed debates in both English and French, using the same format as 1979. The Liberals refused, claiming they wanted a debate on issues rather than a clash of personalities, and insisted that the involvement of reporters "interferes with true debate" (*Globe and Mail* 1980a and 1980b). The Liberal counter-offer for a series of debates was refused by the broadcasters. While NDP leader Ed Broadbent offered to debate Prime Minister Clark, the broadcast consortium decided not to proceed without Trudeau (*Globe and Mail* 1980b).

Regularization of Debates (1984–1993)

In this period, the debates became regularized as the broadcast consortium solidified its position as the organizer of debates. Additionally, norms about participation, language, and format began to develop. The 1984 election campaign was again marked by considerable "debate about the debates"

(Leduc 1990). In negotiations with the parties, the broadcast consortium stipulated that it would only organize the debates if "all three leaders take part and journalists selected by the networks be allowed to ask questions" (*Globe and Mail* 1984). PC leader Brian Mulroney's eagerness to debate gave him little bargaining power, so the Liberals successfully demanded that the debates be scheduled earlier in the campaign and that there be two debates, one in each official language (Bernier and Monière 1991). The 1984 election campaign is also notable for the bilingual leaders' debate on women's issues that was organized by the National Action Committee (NAC) on the Status of Women. While the NAC had unsuccessfully demanded such a debate in 1979, 1984 was the "election of the gender gap," and Liberal prime minister Turner was under fire for inappropriate physical contact with two women staffers (Thrift 2013). Mulroney and Broadbent agreed to participate, and the NAC indicated that they would proceed with the debate regardless of whether Turner agreed to participate (Lipovenko 1984), which he eventually did.

The 1988 debates were also subject to heated negotiations. The Liberals and the NDP wanted a total of six debates: three in each language, one "general debate, a free-trade debate and a women's issues debate" (Kennedy 1988). The PCs demanded that there would "be only two debates and that they take place early in the campaign" (Bernier and Monière 1991, 186). The resulting compromise was two three-hour debates – one in English and one in French – with one hour of each dedicated to discussion of women's issues (*The Gazette* 1988). While the broadcast consortium had promised a format that would allow for three-way debate, the format ultimately resembled earlier events: one-on-one debates bookended by uninterrupted opening and closing statements (Kennedy 1988).

The 1993 debates were a foregone conclusion. Debates were "[approaching] the point of becoming institutionalized" and refusal to participate was no longer a sure-fire strategy for preventing a debate from happening (Leduc 1994). Prime Minister Kim Campbell was seen to have little to gain by debating as she was already well-known. In contrast, both the Liberals and NDP had new leaders who wanted a chance to introduce themselves to voters. There were also two new parties: the Bloc Québécois (BQ) and the Reform Party. This reignited the question of who ought to participate in the debates. The PCs saw this as an opportunity to scuttle the debates by making demands that appealed to important principles but that were unreasonable in practice (Amber 1999). They objected that Campbell would only participate if "all official parties with 50 or more candidates" were invited too, such as the National Party and the Christian Heritage Party. Opposition parties pointed out that this would lead to 14 or more leaders in the debate, and the consortium objected that more than five parties would be too many (Doyle 1993).

The broadcast consortium clearly wanted the Reform and BQ leaders included, even though leaders had historically been excluded for not speaking the language, as in the case of Reform's Preston Manning, or not running candidates across the country, as was the case for the BQ (and Reform, to a lesser extent). Apart from the PC's gambit, the other parties do not appear to have seriously tried to prevent the Reform or BQ leaders from participating (Leduc 1994). However, the Liberals, NDP, BQ, and Reform parties all agreed to exclude parties that did not hold seats in the House of Commons (*Kitchener-Waterloo Record* 1993). The National Party launched and lost a court case demanding their inclusion (*National Party of Canada v. Canadian Broadcasting Corp.* 1993).

Ultimately, the parties agreed to two debates, one in each official language. While the PCs and Liberals had indicated they would permit Manning to participate using simultaneous translation for the whole debate, the Quebec networks refused because of a belief that "translation would make the debate less appealing to viewers" (Priegert 1993). In the French-language debate, Manning made opening and closing statements and was given a special segment to answer questions in English with simultaneous translation (*Hamilton Spectator* 1993). The 1993 debates were also notable because they allowed citizens from the audience to pose questions for the first time. However, these citizens did not participate until the last 45 minutes of the English debate and the last 30 minutes of the debate in French (Lumb 1994).

Debates as Convention (1997–2011)

The next few election campaigns suggested that perhaps the era of heated disputes about the debates was over. There was now a convention that the debates would take place and the consortium had solidified its place as organizer, although it continued to tinker with the format. This may have been motivated by the fact that debates between 1993 and 2004 involved four or five party leaders in open debate segments and this drew considerable criticism about interruptions, incivility, and a lack of substance (Waddell and Dornan 2006). Nevertheless, the format remained largely the same, with only minor changes in 1997 and 2000. The 2004 debates abandoned questions from citizens in favour of a panel of journalists and reintroduced one-on-one debate segments.

The 2006 election campaign featured four debates, two in English and two in French, due to a longer-than-usual campaign. These debates featured a more rigid format in which leaders answered specific questions and other leaders could only briefly reply to those answers within strict time limits and without interruption by the other leaders (Rogers 2010). Reporters dismissed the format as boring, and BQ leader Gilles Duceppe requested that the second set of debates change the format to permit more direct clashes between candidates (*Ottawa Citizen* 2005).

In 2008, getting new Green Party leader Elizabeth May into the debates was a key priority for the party (Harada 2009). The Green Party had unsuccessfully tried to gain admittance to the debates in previous elections by appealing to the Canadian Radio-television and Telecommunications Commission (CRTC) and, later, the general public (*Sault Star* 2004). This time a former Liberal MP crossed the floor to the Greens before the 2008 election. Despite now having a seat in the House of Commons, all the major parties – except for the Liberals – argued that May should be excluded (Curry 2008). The consortium initially refused to invite May out of fears that the other parties would refuse to participate but eventually bowed to public pressure (MacPherson 2008). While May was ultimately invited to the 2008 debates, she was not invited to return in 2011. This time the Green Party did not have a sitting MP and there was less public outrage since the other parties did not openly oppose her participation. Otherwise, the debates that took place were largely similar in format to 2008.

Debates in Flux (2015)

Debates entered a state of flux in 2015 when Conservative prime minister Stephen Harper refused an invitation from the broadcast consortium. The Conservative Party sought more than two debates, believing that the new Liberal and NDP leaders would struggle with a greater number of events (Turcotte 2016). The Liberals and NDP countered that they would only participate in additional debates if the balance between English- and French-language debates was preserved (Jones 2015). The result was two debates in English (hosted by *Maclean's* magazine and the *Globe and Mail*), two debates in French (hosted by TVA and Radio-Canada), and one bilingual debate (hosted by the Munk Debates). This proliferation of debates was enabled not only by Harper's rebuke to the consortium, but also by technological developments that enabled smaller organizations to affordably livestream debates to viewers online. While there were more opportunities to tune in, audiences were small and probably limited largely to voters who were already following the campaign (Turcotte 2016).

The apparent failure of the 2015 debates motivated reflection on how to organize debates in the future. There was an emerging view that an independent organizer was required for debates to serve the public interest (IRPP 2018; Owen and Griffiths 2011; Rogers 2010). Resurrecting the consortium model appeared to pose its own problems, notably that the details of debates were often negotiated once campaigns were already underway (Turcotte 2016). Karina Gould, then minister of democratic institutions, was tasked in early 2017 with developing options for an independent commission to organize leaders' debates.

A New Convention? (2019 to Present)

In late 2018, Minister Gould announced the creation of the Leaders' Debates Commission (LDC). The LDC was mandated to "organize one leaders' debate in each official language during each general election period" (Government of Canada 2018). However, hopes that the LDC would reduce partisan "debates about the debates" were quickly revealed as overly optimistic. There was concern that the LDC would allow the government of the day to unilaterally set the terms of the debates. Such a fear was reiterated when the Liberal government nominated David Johnston – former governor general and moderator of the 1979 and 1984 debates – as debates commissioner without consulting the other parties (Grenier 2018).

The 2019 election was the first to feature debates organized by the LDC and it was marked by further controversy. The first issue was around the decision of whether to invite Maxime Bernier of the People's Party of Canada (PPC). The LDC had been tasked with inviting leaders by applying a set of participation criteria developed by the government, one of which required significant interpretation on the part of the commissioner. Despite efforts by other parties to encourage his exclusion, Bernier was ultimately invited (Boutilier 2019). The second major controversy was the LDC's decision not to accredit reporters from Rebel Media and the True North Centre, right-wing media outlets, due to their history of political advocacy. A court compelled the LDC to accredit reporters from both organizations on the grounds that the decision was procedurally unfair (Wirth and Chadha 2020). The third issue was whether the LDC fulfilled its mandate of providing "effective, informative, and compelling" debates. The 2019 debates attracted large audiences, although the English-language debate was criticized for its "complicated format, many moderators, and frequent exchanges in which all the leaders spoke at once" (Jeffrey 2020, 35). The French debate was seen as an improvement, although debates organized by *Maclean's* and TVA were widely seen as better than the LDC's offerings. A proposal for a 2019 Munk debate on foreign policy was cancelled due to Prime Minister Trudeau's refusal to participate (Griffiths 2019).

The 2021 campaign provided an opportunity to reassess the LDC. There was now only one competing debate – a French-language debate organized by TVA – and the LDC's Order in Council had been revised to address shortcomings from 2019. The participation criteria were made public in advance and applied with minimal controversy, but media access continued to be a problem as the LDC once again found itself compelled by an injunction to admit applicants it had refused to accredit. Finding an effective format remained a challenge. Just as the rancorous 2004 debates led to overly structured debates in 2005 and 2006, the chaos of 2019 led to a format in 2021 that provided few opportunities for clashes between leaders. A study commissioned by the LDC found that voters learned little about party positions from watching the debate. Moreover, a scandal erupted – particularly among Quebecers – when moderator Shachi Kurl asked the BQ leader about his party's support for laws that she linked to racism and described as "discriminatory."

It is probably too early to draw firm conclusions about the success or failure of the LDC. Many of the challenges faced by the LDC have plagued other debate organizers as well. But broadcasters are private entities that have long lamented that organizing the debates costs them money (Bernier and Monière 1991). In comparison, the LDC is a public body that is explicitly mandated to pursue the public interest. As a result, they are understandably held to a higher standard. The LDC's capacity and mandate to assess its own performance after each election will likely be essential if it is to succeed in making the debates a truly democratic exercise.

IMPLICATIONS FOR DEMOCRACY

Leaders' debates could contribute to democracy in a variety of ways. Many scholars and commentators agree that debates should provide citizens with opportunities to learn about the character and competence of party leaders as well as their policy proposals for problems facing the country (Jamieson and Birdsell 1990). Debates can also draw the attention of citizens and encourage them to reflect on issues or discuss politics with others (Turkenburg 2022). There are also other underappreciated potential benefits to debates. While many aspects of campaigns are marked by inequalities of resources, debates offer a relatively level playing field between invited party leaders. In some instances, they also offer citizens opportunities to participate and perhaps raise important questions that might not be asked otherwise (Jackson-Beeck and Meadow 1979; Carlin et al. 2009).

However, it is not obvious that leaders' debates in Canada, as they have been organized, have consistently been a boon for democracy. Part of the reason may be that the debates have largely been cobbled together as compromises reflecting the interests of parties and media organizations. While some commentators hoped that an independent organization could improve the democratic value of debates by taking them out of the hands of parties and broadcasters (Coyne 1997), the experience of the LDC has raised questions about the ability to put the public interest first. This section summarizes some of the recurring challenges to making the debates a truly democratic exercise and looks at potential solutions.

Participation and the Ideal of Competition

The question of which leaders are invited to participate in the debates is directly relevant to the democratic ideal of competitiveness (Lipsitz 2004). By negotiating with the broadcasters to exclude certain rivals, major parties have tried to lock in their own advantage, to the detriment of challengers. However, data suggest that viewers are generally supportive of a more inclusive approach that invites a broad array of leaders (Leaders' Debates Commission 2020). Debate organizers have sometimes been reluctant to do so, in part because a greater number of participants makes it more challenging to arrive at a format that facilitates intelligible debate.

From 1984 to 2011, when debates were organized by the consortium, it was unclear what criteria were guiding decisions about invitations or if these criteria were consistently applied (IRPP 2018). The Green Party was repeatedly excluded for not holding a seat in Parliament, a criterion that might have originated in the 1968 debate. However, it appears that the consortium also had other criteria, such as "fielding candidates nationwide" and "receiving federal funding" (Campion-Smith 2008), although the BQ was repeatedly invited despite not fielding candidates nationally. The lack of clarity and transparency has motivated various attempts at publicly articulating alternative criteria. In 2007, the Green Party proposed that a leader should be included if their party meets two of the following three criteria: "a party must have an elected MP in the House, run in all or nearly all ridings in Canada and/or have 4 percent of the vote in the previous election" (Leblanc 2011). Others recommended a modified version of the American criteria based on polling results and candidates in a majority of ridings (Rogers 2010). The 2019 campaign left the debates commissioner in the unenviable position of interpreting criteria that were difficult to operationalize. In 2021, the LDC had the power to set its own participation criteria and it made these criteria and decisions public.

The ideal of fair competition is not undermined solely by organizers, but also by the control that major parties might exert over the debates (Lipsitz 2004). Party leaders may strategically use the threat of refusal to demand concessions, such as the exclusion of other party leaders. The refusal of candidates to participate can lead to debates being cancelled, such as in 1972, 1974, 1980, 2015, and 2019 (Leduc and Price 1985; Leduc 1990; Rogers 2010; Griffiths 2019; Turcotte 2016). In a contribution to the 1989 Royal Commission on Electoral Reform and Party Financing, Widdis Barr (1991) argued that party leaders should be required by law to participate because otherwise a single party leader might prevent citizens from receiving the benefits of debates. Similar proposals have been made, although there appears to be little appetite to compel participation in this way (IRPP 2018). The current approach relies on leaders participating because they are concerned that voters will impose political costs if they do not. However, it's not clear whether voters actually punish leaders who fail to show up to debates. If leader behaviour begins to undermine the potential of debates, then it may be necessary to revisit the question of mandatory participation.

Language and Political Equality

Canada is a multilingual society, and the democratic ideal of equality suggests that debates need to accommodate linguistic differences. If members of different linguistic groups have fundamentally different experiences with leaders' debates, we might question whether they embody democratic values. While the first election debate in 1968 was bilingual, it was not until 1984 that the practice of holding separate debates in both English and French became standard. Once implemented, debate organizers struggled with the challenge of how to include leaders who were not bilingual into both debates. Leaders who struggle in one of the two official languages have been subject to considerable criticism for their performances in debates, and this may help explain the increased emphasis on selecting leaders who are fluent in both languages (Riga 2015).

The French-language debates have also been criticized for focusing too much on issues related specifically to Quebec, ignoring national issues and the concerns of more than a million francophones who live outside of the province (Bourgeault-Tassé 2019). The 2021 campaign included two French-language debates and one English-language debate, breaking with the language parity that had been preserved since 1984. Returning to bilingual debates might have potential to address some of these problems, but surveys suggest that viewers prefer to watch a debate in their own language and may be less likely to watch a bilingual debate, especially for viewers who would rely on simultaneous translation (McAndrews et al. 2020). At the same time, the LDC has increasingly made the debates available to a wider audience by expanding translation options, including several Indigenous languages, and offering accessible formats, such as American Sign Language, closed captioning, described video, and Quebec Sign Language (Leaders' Debates Commission 2020).

Format and Deliberation

The quality and format of the debates has often been criticized by academics and the media. A 1984 editorial cartoon mocked the idea that a viewer could have enjoyed the televised debates (Graston 1984). While Rex Murphy (2004) compared debates to professional wrestling, a 2005 headline complained that the "New Format Drains Drama From Debates" (Curry 2005). I focus here on the debate agenda and moderation, two issues relevant to the democratic ideal of deliberation – the expectation that political positions can be publicly justified.

Who should choose the topics and pose the questions at the heart of leaders' debates? While journalists often take on this role, there is a concern that their questions focus too much on political intrigue rather than substantive issues that matter to voters (*Ottawa Citizen* 1988). Occasionally, leaders have been permitted to pose questions to one another, although there is a concern that this merely replicates the partisan posturing of question period (*Ottawa Citizen* 1988). Citizens have regularly been invited to submit questions, and organizers regularly receive thousands of submissions. The process by which these questions are selected is rarely explained to the public. Perhaps a panel of randomly selected citizens could develop the core topics or even develop a set of questions. Having a group, rather than individuals, generate questions might avoid questions that stir controversy, as in the 2021 English-language LDC debate.

Another important issue is how many questions ought to be posed. The LDC's 2021 English-language debate posed 45 questions to the leaders in a two-hour period. This stands in contrast with the consortium's 2008 debate, which only featured eight questions in the same amount of time. While there is no "right" number of questions, debate organizers need to consider the possible trade-offs between covering a range of topics and giving leaders sufficient time to discuss issues that arise during the debate.

Moderators are also important to the success of leaders' debates. For one, they may play an important role in upholding deliberative norms – say, by stopping leaders who are interrupting one another. Additionally, they can play a key role in ensuring that leaders provide justifications for their positions. Large majorities of citizens who viewed the 2019 LDC debates agreed that the moderators could have done more to "push leaders who avoided answering the question" and who "gave factually inaccurate answers" (McAndrews et al. 2020).

What is apparent is that organizing the debates requires weighing many competing considerations. Parties and media organizations often justify their conflicting demands with reference to the public interest. It is unlikely that debates will ever meet the idealized expectations of some critics. Debate organizers have often had to make judgments about how these events can be formatted to achieve their desired outcomes. With a clearer conception of the democratic potential of debates and a growing body of evidence about the effects of format, perhaps future debates can put to rest questions about whether they serve the public interest.

NOTES

1 For a notable exception, focusing on the leaders' debates in the 2011 Ontario election, see Cross et al. (2015, chap. 7).
2 The Social Credit Party's leader, A.B. Patterson, did not receive an invitation. It's not entirely clear why, given Trudeau's demand, although Social Credit won few seats in the 1968 election and merged with the Ralliement créditiste – a party that had earlier split from Social Credit – shortly after. Perhaps this informed the decision to include only one of the two parties (Bernier and Monière 1991; Rogers 2010).

REFERENCES

Amber, Arnold. 1999. "Making the Debates Happen: A Television Producer's Perspective." In *Televised Election Debates: International Perspectives*, edited by Stephen Coleman, 130–56. New York: Springer.

Anstead, Nick. 2016. "A Different Beast? Televised Election Debates in Parliamentary Democracies." *International Journal of Press/Politics* 21 (4): 508–26. https://doi.org/10.1177/1940161216649953.

Attallah, Paul, and Angela Burton. 2001. "Television, the Internet, and the Canadian Federal Election of 2000." In *The Canadian General Election of 2000*, edited by Christopher Dornan and Jon H. Pammett, 215–42. Toronto: Dundurn Press.

Barr, Cathy Widdis. 1991. "The Importance and Potential of Leaders Debates." In *Media and Voters in Canadian Election Campaigns*, edited by Frederick J. Fletcher, 107–56. Research Studies, Vol. 18. Toronto: Dundurn Press.

Bernier, Robert, and Denis Monière. 1991. "The Organization of Televised Leaders Debates in the United States, Europe, Australia, and Canada." In *Media and Voters in Canadian Election Campaigns*, edited by Frederick J. Fletcher, 157–211. Research Studies, Vol. 18. Toronto: Dundurn Press.

Bourgeault-Tassé, Isabelle. 2019. "Francophones hors Québec: ne nous oubliez pas au débat des chefs." *La Presse*. September 25. https://www.lapresse.ca/debats/opinions/2019-09-25/francophones-hors-quebec-ne-nous-oubliez-pas-au-debat-des-chefs.

Boutilier, Alex. 2019. "Bernier Invited to Official Election Debates." TheStar.com. September 16. https://www.thestar.com/politics/federal/2019/09/16/bernier-invited-to-official-election-debates.html.

Campion-Smith, Bruce. 2008. "Greens Claim Spot in TV Debate; Independent from BC Becomes Its First MP and Now Leader Says Party Is in Mainstream." *Toronto Star*. August 31.

Carlin, Diana B., Tammy Vigil, Susan Buehler, and Kelly Mcdonald. 2009. *The Third Agenda in US Presidential Debates: DebateWatch and Viewer Reactions, 1996–2004*. Westport: Praeger.

Carlin, Diana Prentice. 1989. "A Defense of the 'Debate' in Presidential Debates." *Argumentation and Advocacy* 25 (4): 208–13. https://doi.org/10.1080/00028533.1989.11951400.

Chadwick, A. 2011. "Britain's First Live Televised Party Leaders' Debate: From the News Cycle to the Political Information Cycle." *Parliamentary Affairs* 64 (1): 24–44. https://doi.org/10.1093/pa/gsq045.

Coleman, Stephen, and Giles Moss. 2016. "Rethinking Election Debates: What Citizens Are Entitled to Expect." *International Journal of Press/Politics* 21 (1): 3–24. https://doi.org/10.1177/1940161215609732.

Coyne, Andrew. 1997. "Improve Staging of Debates." *The Record.* May 15.

Cross, William P., Jonathan Malloy, Tamara A. Small, and Laura Beth Stephenson. 2015. *Fighting for Votes: Parties, the Media, and Voters in an Ontario Election.* Vancouver: UBC Press.

Curry, Bill. 2005. "New Format Drains Drama from Debates: Tame Television." *Globe and Mail.* December 17.

———. 2008. "Liberals Push to Add Green Party to Debates." *Globe and Mail.* September 4.

Ditchburn, Jennifer. 2015. "Ruffled Feathers, Power Plays: Canada's First TV Debate Was Also a Headache." *Toronto Star.* May 25. https://www.thestar.com/news/canada/2015/05/25/ruffled-feathers-power-plays -canadas-first-tv-debate-was-also-a-headache.html.

Doyle, Patrick. 1993. "Tories Accused of Undermining Leaders' Debates." *Toronto Star.* September 1.

Gazette, The. 1988. "Opposition, Grumbling, Agrees to Debates Oct. 24, 25." October 12.

Government of Canada. 2018. "Order in Council 2018-1322." https://orders-in-council.canada.ca/attachment .php?attach=38858&lang=en.

Globe and Mail. 1980a. "Grits Reject Format, TV Debate up in Air." January 5.

———. 1980b. "Trudeau Refuses to Participate in TV Debate." January 12.

———. 1984. "Liberals Dictate Rules for TV Debate: NDP." July 17.

Graston, Michael. 1984. *I WATCHED THE TELEVISED ELECTION DEBATE AND, QUITE FRANKLY, I WAS IMPRESSED!!* Cartoon. Box 10335. Library and Archives Canada.

Grenier, Éric. 2018. "Ex-Governor General David Johnston Nominated as Canada's First Debates Commissioner." CBC. October 30. https://www.cbc.ca/news/politics/debates-commissioner-johnston-1.4883646.

Griffiths, Rudyard. 2019. "Opinion: Why We Cancelled the Munk Debate – and Why Our Democracy Is in Trouble." *National Post.* September 24. https://nationalpost.com/news/politics/election-2019/opinion -why-we-cancelled-the-munk-debate-and-why-our-democracy-is-in-trouble.

Hamilton Spectator. 1993. "Networks, Parties Agree on Details of Election TV Debates." September 7.

Harada, Susan. 2009. "The Promise of May: The Green Party of Canada's Campaign 2008." In *The Canadian Federal Election of 2008*, edited by Chris Dornan and Jon H. Pammett, 162–93. Toronto: Dundurn Press.

Hurst, Lynda. 1988. "TV Debates Changed Politics Forever." *The Gazette*, October 22.

IRPP. 2018. "Creating an Independent Commission for Federal Leaders' Debates." Montreal: Institute for Research on Public Policy. https://irpp.org/wp-content/uploads/2018/04/Creating-an-Independent -Commission-for-Federal-Leaders-Debates.pdf.

Jackson-Beeck, Marilyn, and Robert G. Meadow. 1979. "The Triple Agenda of Presidential Debates." *Public Opinion Quarterly* 43 (2): 173–80. https://doi.org/10.1086/268509.

Jamieson, Kathleen Hall, and David S. Birdsell. 1990. *Presidential Debates: The Challenge of Creating an Informed Electorate.* Oxford: Oxford University Press.

Jeffrey, Brooke. 2020. "Second Chance: The Chastened Liberals." In *The Canadian Federal Election of 2019*, edited by Jon H. Pammett and Chris Dornan, 15–41. Montreal: McGill-Queen's University Press.

Jones, Allison. 2015. "Trudeau, Mulcair Reviewing Participation in Leaders' Debate on Foreign Policy." *Globe and Mail.* September 14. https://www.theglobeandmail.com/news/politics/english-only-proposal-may -scuttle-leaders-debate-on-foreign-policy/article26362076/.

Kaid, Lynda Lee, Mitchell S. McKinney, and John C. Tedesco. 2000. *Civic Dialogue in the 1996 Presidential Campaign: Candidate, Media, and Public Voices.* Cresskill: Hampton Press.

Kennedy, Mark. 1988. "TV Debates Get Go-Ahead." *Ottawa Citizen.* October 12.

Kitchener-Waterloo Record. 1993. "Ottawa May Kill Leaders' TV Debate." September 1.

Leaders' Debates Commission. 2020. *Democracy Matters, Debates Count: A Report on the 2019 Leaders' Debates Commission and the Future of Debates in Canada.* https://epe.lac-bac.gc.ca/100/201/301/weekly_acquisitions _list-ef/2021/21-06/publications.gc.ca/collections/collection_2021/bcp-pco/CP22-187-2020-eng.pdf.

Leblanc, Daniel. 2011. "Elizabeth May Excluded from Election Debates." *Globe and Mail*. March 29. https://www.theglobeandmail.com/news/politics/elizabeth-may-excluded-from-election-debates/article574671/.

Leduc, Lawrence. 1990. "Party Strategies and the Use of Televised Campaign Debates." *European Journal of Political Research* 18 (1): 121–41. https://doi.org/10.1111/j.1475-6765.1990.tb00224.x.

———. 1994. "The Leaders' Debates: Critical Event or Non-Event?" In *The Canadian General Election of 1993*, edited by Alan Frizzell, Jon Howard Pammett, and Anthony Westell, 128–41. Ottawa: Carleton University Press.

———. 1997. "The Leaders' Debates: ('...And the Winner Is...')." In *The Canadian General Election of 1997*, edited by Alan Stewart Frizzell and Jon H. Pammett, 207–24. Toronto: Dundurn Press.

Leduc, Lawrence, and Richard Price. 1985. "Great Debates: The Televised Leadership Debates of 1979." *Canadian Journal of Political Science / Revue Canadienne de Science Politique* 18 (1): 135–53. https://doi.org/10.1017/S0008423900029255.

Lipovenko, Dorothy. 1984. "PC, NDP Leaders Accept Invitation to First Debate on Women's Issues." *Globe and Mail*. July 11.

Lipsitz, Keena. 2004. "Democratic Theory and Political Campaigns." *Journal of Political Philosophy* 12 (2): 163–89. https://doi.org/10.1111/j.1467-9760.2004.00196.x.

Lumb, Lionel. 1994. "The Television of Inclusion." In *The Canadian General Election of 1993*, edited by Alan Frizzell, Jon Howard Pammett, and Anthony Westell, 107–23. Ottawa: Carleton University Press.

MacPherson, Don. 2008. "Dion Outsmarts Harper by Supporting May's Bid to Debate; Why Should Duceppe Be Part of the English Debate if the Greens Are Excluded?" *The Gazette*. September 11.

McAndrews, John R., Aengus Bridgman, Peter John Loewen, Daniel Rubenson, Laura B. Stephenson, and Allison Harell. 2020. "Evaluation of the 2019 Federal Leaders' Debates." https://www.debates-debats.ca/en/report/evaluation-2019-federal-leaders-debates/#section_5_5.

McKay, Spencer. 2020. "Canada's Leaders' Debates in Comparative Perspective." Vancouver, BC: Centre for the Study of Democratic Institutions, UBC. http://www.spencermckay.com/wp-content/uploads/2014/02/McKay-Canadas-Leaders-Debates.pdf.

McKinney, Mitchell S. 2005. "Let the People Speak: The Public's Agenda and Presidential Town Hall Debates." *American Behavioral Scientist* 49 (2): 198–212. https://doi.org/10.1177/0002764205279428.

McKinney, Mitchell S., and Diana B. Carlin. 2004. "Political Campaign Debates." In *Handbook of Political Communication Research*, edited by Lynda Lee Kaid. https://doi.org/10.4324/9781410610584-16.

Murphy, Rex. 2004. "Political Debate or Pro Wrestling?" *Globe and Mail*. June 19.

National Party of Canada v. Canadian Broadcasting Corp, 1993 CanLII 7151 (ABKB).

Ottawa Citizen. 1988. "TV Debates Flawed but Not Worthless." October 11.

———. 2005. "Networks Won't Change Format for Debates." December 26.

Owen, Taylor, and Rudyard Griffiths. 2011. "The People's Debates: A Report on Canada's Televised Election Debates." Aurea Foundation.

Priegert, Portia. 1993. "Opposition Charges Tories Want to Kill Election Debates." *The Gazette*. September 1.

Riga, Andy. 2015. "Parlez-Vous Français? The Quality of Party Leaders' French Varies Greatly." *Montreal Gazette*. September 22. https://montrealgazette.com/news/a-look-at-the-quality-of-the-french-spoken-by-party-leaders.

Rogers, Michelle. 2010. "Fair, Informative and Tantalizing: Reforming Federal Election Debates in Canada." Kingston: Centre for the Study of Democracy, Queen's University. https://www.queensu.ca/csdd/sites/csddwww/files/uploaded_files/publications/wps/Reform_Fed_Election_Debates_Canada.pdf.

Sault Star. 2004. "Unfair to Shut Party out of Debates: Leader." June 3.

Thrift, Samantha C. 2013. "Fashion, Flirtation and Fringe Feminists in the News Coverage of the 1984 Leadership Debate." In *Mind the Gaps: Canadian Perspectives on Gender and Politics*, edited by Roberta Lexier and Tamara A. Small, 102–15. Black Point: Fernwood Publishing.

Turcotte, André. 2016. "A Debate About the Debates." In *The Canadian Federal Election of 2015*, edited by Jon H. Pammett and Chris Dornan, 253–74. Toronto: Dundurn.

———. 2020. "A New Experiment for an Old Media Political Event: Leaders' Debates in Canada." In *Routledge International Handbook on Electoral Debates*, edited by Julio Juárez Gámiz, Christina Holtz-Bacha, and Alan Schroeder, 19–28. New York: Routledge/Taylor & Francis Group.

Turkenburg, Emma. 2022. "Televised Election Debates in a Deliberative System: The Role of Framing and Emotions." *Democratic Theory* 9 (1): 1–30. https://doi.org/10.3167/dt.2022.090102.

Waddell, Christopher, and Christopher Dornan. 2006. "The Media and the Campaign." In *The Canadian Federal Election of 2006*, edited by Christopher Dornan and Jon H Pammett, 220–52. Toronto: Dundurn.

Wirth, Christopher, and Sakshi Chadha. 2020. "Federal Court Grants Injunction to Order Leaders' Debate Commission to Accredit Media Organization." Canadian Bar Association. March 16. https://www.cba .org/Sections/Administrative-Law/Articles/2020/Federal-Court-grants-injunction.

CHAPTER THIRTEEN

The Campaign: Elections and Polling in the Twenty-First Century

Christopher Adams

INTRODUCTION

Polling the Canadian electorate goes back to 1941, when American pollster George Gallup established the Toronto office of the Canadian Institute for Public Opinion (CIPO). In many ways it was an extension of Gallup's American Institute for Public Opinion (AIPO). In the CIPO's first year of operations, the Canadian Gallup poll appeared in 27 Canadian newspapers (Robinson 1999, 193n10). Up until that time, Canadians had less-than-reliable ways for assessing the mood of the electorate, such as through media reports about political rallies, letters to the editor, and so forth. The first Canadian Gallup polls to measure Canadian voting intentions appeared during the 1942 national referendum on wartime conscription (i.e., whether the federal government should force Canadians to serve in the military, an explosive issue that divided English-speaking Canadians from French-speaking Quebecers in both world wars).[1] Gallup's final poll on this issue was released two days in advance of the April 27 vote; it correctly predicted a "yes" vote, while overestimating it by just over four percentage points (Creighton 1976, 71; Robinson 1999, 73–4). At least until the 1970s, the CIPO was the only firm to provide polling results on a regular basis for public consumption. This changed during the 1970s and 1980s as pollsters shifted to using advanced telephone survey techniques, modernized fielding centres, and computerized data processing (Adams 2019). The impact of these is discernible when comparing the 1984 federal election, in which only 10 national polls were released to the media, with the 1988 federal election, in which 113 national polls appeared (Pickup 2010, 251; Turcotte 2011, 206).

The most famous fiasco in polling history occurred in 1948, when all the major pollsters confidently predicted that US president Harry Truman, the Democratic candidate, would lose to the Republican governor of New York, Thomas Dewey. A famous photo features the victorious Truman holding aloft a copy of the *Chicago Tribune* with the headline "Dewey Wins."[2] More recently, American pollsters miscalled the 2016 US election, with many reputable forecasters incorrectly saying that Donald Trump would lose. This included Nate Silver's FiveThirtyEight website, which showed

Hilary Clinton's chance of winning over Trump in the range of 70 to 99% (Lohr and Singer 2016). One American polling expert, Sam Wang, said he would eat a bug if Trump won more than 240 electoral votes. Trump won the election with 290 electoral votes, and Wang ate his bug on CNN.[3] Despite concerns about erroneous polling, this chapter shows that polls, when skillfully conducted, are a reliable tool for understanding electorate and party preferences. This chapter also demonstrates how polling is an indispensable tool for candidates and parties to win elections.

DEFINING POLLING

The word "poll" is derived from the early English word "polle," which is the top of a person's head (Safire 1978, 550). Hence the term "poll taxes," which are "head taxes" placed on each person in a specific community. The use of the term for studying voters dates back to the 1800s, when journalists would count heads at political meetings and rallies to gauge the public's mood (Keeter 2021). Examples of how this rough measure served the media include the 1957 federal election, in which the Gallup poll failed to capture Diefenbaker's momentum but in which the media reported on his party's large and boisterous rallies (Wiseman 2022). In the 2015 federal election, the media took note of Justin Trudeau's large rallies, such as a 5,000-plus rally in Brampton, signalling a shift in momentum (Jeffrey 2016, 75). However, polls continue to be the gold standard for assessing voter preferences. They are also used in times other than elections, to assess attitudes and opinions on a wide variety of subject areas, including public policies and current affairs. It is for this reason that Gallup referred to polling as "the pulse of democracy" (Gallup and Rae 1940).

The way Canadians communicate with each other, or communication technology, has always affected how polling was done. In the 1940s and 1950s, many Canadian homes did not have landline telephones, so polling was conducted in person, with interviewers assigned to specific locations for door knocking. By the late 1960s, almost all households had landline phones and long-distance calling no longer required an operator's assistance. Telephone interviewing then became the industry standard from the 1970s onward – at least until the twenty-first century and the widespread use of the internet and cell phones. Then pollsters could no longer rely on landline telephone calling for their work. By 2016, only 67% of Canadian households continued to be equipped with a landline telephone, while 88% of Canadian subscribed to a mobile device (Canadian Radio-television and Telecommunications Commission 2019). By 2020, 84% were using smartphones (Statistics Canada 2021). As of 2020, the total number of mobile subscribers in Canada had grown to 33.1 million (Statista.com n.d.), a large number in a country of just under 37 million (Statistics Canada 2022).

In the early days of telephone interviewing, a polling firm needed only each locale's annually published telephone book for its sample. As more numbers became "unlisted" – that is, removed by the householder from the directory – the use of computers to provide random samples, through random-digit dialing (RDD), became standard during the 1980s and 1990s. Of course, this gave rise to interviewers commonly hearing the refrain, "how did you get this number?" As cellphone usage increased after the turn of the current century, pollsters had no choice but to include cellphones in their samples. One major polling firm, Ipsos, when conducting phone surveys, now ensures that over 70% of the sample includes mobile users (Simpson 2022; Brown 2022).[4]

Another major development is the use of interactive voice response (IVR) systems by such firms as EKOS, Mainstreet Research, and Forum Research. IVR is an updated version of Moviefone, a popular service used by American moviegoers in the 1990s. Using the phone's keypad, the person would punch in a zip code, and the service would provide details about movies showing in neighbourhood theatres (IBM Cloud Education 2021). IVR surveys differ from Moviefone in that they use outbound calling, with respondents reached by automated dialing (DeSilver and Keeter 2015).[5] An IVR survey provides a pre-recorded introduction and a brief series of pre-recorded closed-ended questions, with respondents using their numeric keypads to input their responses (Roos 2008). This automation signifies that many surveys can be completed at great speed while liberating the polling firm from hiring live interviewers located in field centres with their overhead costs. An early adopter of IVR, EKOS used IVR for its 2008 federal election polling, completing 1,000 automated interviews per night (Waddell 2009, 245–6). EKOS also used IVR during the 2013 Liberal Party leadership race, successfully completing 6,455 IVR surveys when contacting 40,000 members and successfully predicting Justin Trudeau's victory over five other candidates on the ballot (Grenier 2014, 26).

The widespread adoption of the internet is the second major recent development in Canadian communications. In 2000, Ipsos reported that 42% of Canadian households did not have internet access (Ipsos-Reid 2001, 7),[6] making online surveys unreliable, particularly for reaching rural and low-income households and senior citizens. However, by 2018, Statistics Canada was reporting that online household access had reached "near-saturation levels," with more than 90% of Canadians having online access (Wavrock 2021, 9, 23). This has significantly influenced how surveys are now done. In 2020, the Canadian Research Insights Council (CRIC) reported that only one in five quantitative research studies was conducted by phone (either by landline or mobile device), while 70% involved the internet (CRIC 2022). Despite this, concerns remain about respondents being honest about their identity, especially when recruited with incentives. Another concern has been the questionable use of "river sampling" by some firms to find respondents, relying on such tools as "banner" and "pop-up" advertising (Steber 2018).

Reputable online pollsters rely on quality panels for their samples. A panel is based on pre-recruited respondents who have agreed to participate in online surveys. They join by receiving online or text-based invitations to complete a membership online survey. According to the market research firm Leger, 70% of their online panelists are recruited through their call centre surveys (Leger Online n.d.). Many other polling firms simply purchase online samples from third parties for their full sampling needs or to augment their own samples. The international firm Lucid uses numerous third-party databases, with access to 1,367,622 pre-recruited Canadians (Lucid 2019). Among the other service providers are Dynata, which has access to 472,880 Canadians (Research Now n.d., 2), Canadian Viewpoint with 300,000 (Canadian Viewpoint n.d.), and Leger with a panel of 400,000 Canadians (Leger Online n.d., 5).

Accessing a large panel allows the pollster to select potential respondents according to specific quotas, such as age, gender, household income, and so forth. Mag Burns, a senior research director with the Angus Reid Institute, a major Canadian online polling firm, describes her firm's approach:

A big national [online] survey would initially be stratified by region and sub-region to ensure good represented geographic coverage. There would also be some specifications, aka. "quotas" set on mainly socio-demographics.

Figure 13.1. Number of Firms Using Specific Modes in Federal Elections, 2000–2021

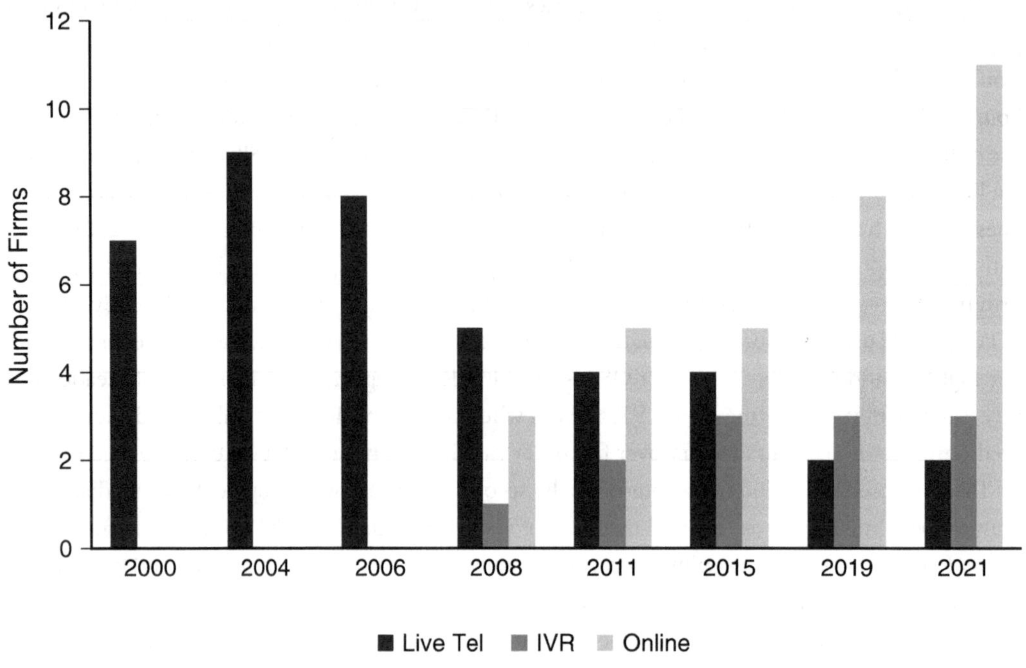

Note: The number of firms for the categories IVR and Online were zero in 2000, 2004, and 2006.

Even then, she reports, there will be unexpected response rates among specific groups. In those cases, "you'd weight after-the-fact" to get "things ideally aligned" with what the sample should be (Burns 2020). That is, the pollster would compare the final sample to the population under study and adjust the weights for each respondent.[7]

An examination of pre-election polling in Figure 13.1 shows the extent to which live phone interviewing has been replaced with IVR and online election surveys. The results are based on the national polls released in the final five days of each campaign. From 2000 to 2006, every firm relied on live telephone interviewing to collect their results (Adams 2022). This changed in 2008, when EKOS used IVR and three other firms used online polling,[8] with all others continuing to use live phone interviewing. In the following federal election of 2011, only a *minority* of firms used live telephone interviewing. Online polling became the most prevalent mode in the 2019 and 2021 federal elections, far outweighing the other two methodologies, with only Nanos Research and Ipsos continuing to use live interviewers. While once thought unreliable, online surveys are now generally considered trustworthy for measuring voter intentions. Charles Breton and colleagues (2017) found this to be the case when studying online polls in the 2015 Canadian federal election.

With all these changes to Canadian polling in recent years, how accurate were the polls in the 2021 federal election? Table 13.1 shows the average results of 10 polling firms that released national polls to the media in the final two days of the campaign. Collectively, the polls were off by a mere 1.1 points from the actual vote for the Liberals (LPC), off by 2.4 points for the Conservatives (CPC),

Table 13.1. Average Results of National Polls and Actual Vote Shares in 2021 Election

	LPC	CPC	NDP	PPC	GPC
Polls	31.5	31.3	18.7	7.0	3.3
Vote	32.6	33.7	17.8	4.9	2.3
Polling difference	−1.1	−2.4	+0.9	+2.1	+1.0

and less than 1 point (.9) for the NDP. They were off by 2.1 and 1.0 points respectively for the People's Party of Canada (PPC) and the Green Party of Canada (GPC). Overall, therefore, the polls proved to be a reliable measure of voter choice in 2021.[9]

THE EVOLVING USES OF POLLING

Not all polls are created for the same purpose. Election polling can be divided into three main categories: media polls, academic polls, and behind-the-scenes party polling. Regarding the first type, in the 2021 federal election, a total of 151 national polls were released by 14 firms.[10] The *Canada Elections Act* requires that these types of polls, at the time of their release, must include information about who is sponsoring the poll, the wording of the questions, the date span in which interviews were conducted, the sampling method and, if applicable, the margin of error (Adams 2019 88–9).

The second category consists of surveys conducted by academics that are chiefly aimed at understanding the dynamics of elections and voting behaviour, including such factors as gender, age, income, ethnicity, and region. The most significant is the Canadian Election Study (CES), which was first launched in 1965 by John Meisel, a political scientist at Queen's University. A direct descendant of the American National Election Survey (ANES), which was first launched in the 1948 US election,[11] the CES continues to be one of the most significant sources for information about Canadian voting behaviour. Indeed, CES data are used in the discussion of voting behaviour in the next chapter.

The third category consists of the more hidden world of party polling. Its importance is described by pollster Michael Marzolini, whose firm Pollara served the Liberals under Jean Chrétien: "Party pollsters try to 'shift the needle' by determining which hot buttons can be pushed and levers pulled that will both solidify the party's core vote and draw support from other parties" (Marzolini 2006, 257). While surveys were used by parties as far back as the 1940s (Robinson 1999),[12] modern party polling really began in the 1960s with a handful of individuals and agencies serving the needs of the Liberals and Progressive Conservatives (PCs), the only two parties with the funds for the regular use of such services (Adams 2010; Geddes 2019). Party polling comes in various forms. One is the national benchmark poll, which is based on a large-scale survey of thousands of voters prior to a campaign's launch. With the large-scale survey, Allan Gregg, who served as the PC's pollster from 1979 to 1993, effectively used segmentation analysis to divide the electorate according to clustering values and attitudes, a technique termed "psychographics," rather than the standard sociodemographic characteristics of age, income, ethnicity, and region.[13] He modelled his work on that done by American pollster Richard Wirthlin, who rose to fame by polling for Ronald Reagan as he climbed the political ladder from actor to governor of California and then president in 1980 and 1984 (Turcotte and Vodrey 2017). Wirthlin counselled Reagan on how to persuade traditionally Democratic voters, such as blue-collar workers and Southern voters, to swing to the Republicans. Gregg, in turn, began using this approach for the 1979 federal election, with such segments labelled "Traditional Conservatives" who could be counted on to support the PCs, "Reluctant Tories" who were disenchanted with the Liberals, and "Little Men and Women" who supported Diefenbaker's PCs in 1958 but had since drifted over to the Liberals and the NDP. Gregg told party strategists that they needed to design their messaging and platform to appeal specifically to these two segments (Courtney 1981, 139, 142). Targeting voters by their values continued to be important. Years later, Tom Flanagan, who worked in many capacities with Stephen Harper for his Conservative Party leadership and in federal campaigns, writes about how the national benchmark poll in the early stages of the 2006 campaign revealed how many Catholic voters, who traditionally voted Liberal, held similar attitudes as Conservative-leaning evangelical Protestants. He correctly concluded that many Catholics would switch to the Conservatives with the appropriate messaging, a strategy that helped Harper gain power (Flanagan 2010).

Another form of party polling is the daily tracking poll. In the 1974 federal election, Martin Goldfarb developed this polling method for Pierre Trudeau's Liberals while conducting his own form of segmentation analysis.[14] At the time, polls were chiefly conducted in person on the doorsteps of Canadian homes. One of Goldfarb's innovations was to employ telephone interviewers located in regional hubs across Canada who collectively conducted 1,000 interviews per night. The completed surveys were placed on airplanes and buses at the end of each evening, with the results tallied in Toronto for the following morning (Adams 2010, 157–8).[15] As the election unfolded, Goldfarb was able to confidently determine the ups and downs of voter support among certain segments and at critical junctures of the campaign, such as immediately following party announcements, new advertising, and media events. This new form of polling was invaluable, because, as one group of political scientists observed, "the 1974 election was not a single event. Rather it was a variety of events produced by a multiplicity of factors which were important to different degrees to groups of voters" (Pammett et al. 1975, 3). Of course, this can be said about every federal election – hence the continuing use of daily tracking in modern elections. However, these are conducted using more moderate daily numbers of 200 or more surveys per day that are continually "rolled up" so that the data can be studied on a week-by-week basis using 1,000 or more interviews over the longer period. As newer data are collected, the older survey results are dropped, thereby making what is now called a "rolling poll."

Yet another form of campaign polling is the riding-specific survey. This is among the oldest forms of polling in Canada, dating back to the 1940s. Such surveys are usually commissioned by parties and candidates to test a potential candidate's viability or to determine where resources should be placed during the campaign. The earliest known example of a riding poll was performed by Canadian Facts and commissioned by Liberal candidate Brooke Claxton in the federal Montreal riding of St. Lawrence–St. George in 1940 (Robinson 1999). Such polls are now routine, especially where swing voters can be found. However, such polls should not be confused with voter identification surveys and for "getting out the vote" (GOTV) (Issenberg 2012, 45–6). These are left to the party staff and volunteers or political consultants. For pollsters, such activity is prohibited by the CRIC, the national organization representing the survey research industry (CRIC 2019). The reason is simple. Using a survey to identify a voter's choice breaches respondent confidentiality. Pollsters therefore will always report their findings in the aggregate, with results broken down by groups, segments, or geography but never by specific household.

To identify voter support, parties traditionally relied on their canvassers to record party preferences when interacting with voters at the doorstep, with the intent of getting them to the polls on election day (Nash 2022). Parties now rely on phone calling either by volunteers or by autodialers for this purpose. The national parties also turn to using "Big Data," which involves connecting the names and addresses on Elections Canada's list of voters with their own list of known supporters and opponents, such as donor lists (both of their own party and those of opponents), lists from past campaigns, and detailed neighbourhood data derived from such sources as the Census. While Big Data procedures might not exactly indicate how a particular individual will vote, the party is able to draw conclusions about the likelihood that those in certain households are supporting a particular party. In 2015 the Liberals effectively used this approach by hiring its first director of analytics, Sean Wiltshire, a former PhD candidate in microbiology and expert in computer modelling and statistics. Brooke Jeffrey (2016), in her study of the 2015 Liberal campaign, argues that by using these data, Liberal candidates were able to deploy their resources effectively.[16]

In addition to using surveys, political parties also use qualitative research which, while not polling, often accompanies survey findings. This is usually in the form of focus groups to gather opinions from targeted populations, test advertising, design the party's platform, and assess the leader's image. Essentially, a focus group consists of six to ten individuals who are recruited to a central location for a series of discussions led by an experienced moderator (Grenville 2018).[17] During elections, focus groups often consist of respondents who are deemed to be potential swing voters, as there is nothing to be learned from those who will not budge from their favourite party. Until recent years, focus groups were held in either focus group facilities or hotel conference rooms. With increased access to the internet among Canadians, online focus groups are now more common, especially with the onset of the pandemic in 2020. Most Canadians are now comfortable using a video camera with Zoom and other online video conferencing platforms. As a result, those in the industry now report that online groups have largely replaced in-person groups. Andrew Enns, an executive vice-president at Leger, reports that now "all government [focus group] work is virtual," in large part because both respondents and client observers find online groups more convenient (Enns 2022). Scott MacKay, a founding partner of Winnipeg-based Probe Research, adds that respondents are more accessible with online groups and can be located anywhere, even faraway northern communities, so long as there is online access (MacKay 2022).[18]

IMPLICATIONS FOR DEMOCRACY

At the heart of good polling is good sampling. Pollsters sample voters from all parts of the voting public, not just the rich or poor, young or old, rural or urban, and so on. For this reason, Gallup referred to a representative sample as having a "miniature electorate" (Gallup and Rae 1940, 73). One problem, however, is that with declining voter turnout, drawing a proper selection of voters from national samples is more difficult. Surveying all those who *can* vote does not automatically translate into a proper sample of those who *do* vote. Voters have become harder to find. In the 1988 federal election, the turnout was 75.3%. In the 2021 federal election, turnout was only 62.6% (Elections Canada 2023), signifying that more than 1/3 of eligible Canadians did not vote. The task is harder for pollsters for provincial elections, where turnout is typically worse. For example, in the British Columbia 2020 provincial election, the turnout was 54.5% (Elections BC 2020), a figure even higher than the 44.1% figure for the 2022 Ontario provincial election (Elections Ontario n.d.). The real problem here is that non-voters are different than voters and tend to belong to different social groupings, including those who are apathetic, alienated, of lower-income households, too busy to vote, or younger in age (Dangerfield 2019). These social segments will naturally have different priorities and attitudes compared to those with higher voting rates. Therefore, sampling too many non-voters for a poll will easily distort the results. When pollsters incorrectly predicted an NDP victory over the Liberals during the 2013 BC provincial election, the post-election analysis was that pollsters captured too many young adults who were supporting the NDP but failed to vote. While the samples properly reflected BC's adult population, they improperly reflected the voting public (Grenier 2014).

With the plethora of election polling from the 1980s onward, concerns have been raised about its negative effects on the democratic process. Complaints include the media's fixation on the "horserace" (i.e., who is winning and losing) rather than on substantial election issues, that voters will abandon parties appearing low in the polls, and that polls dampen turnout when voters believe the outcome is already settled. For minor parties, such as the Green Party or the People's Party of Canada, being low in the polls causes them to be bypassed by the media. In a January 2023 letter from Dugald Lamont, leader of the Manitoba Liberal Party – which held only three seats in the legislature at the time of writing – to a *Winnipeg Free Press* political columnist, Lamont complained:

> Commentators will conclude that, based on a poll, the outcome is fixed.… For us, this means a self-fulfilling prophesy – if we can't get coverage, we can't go up in the polls, and if we can't go up in the polls, we can't get coverage. (Brodbeck 2023, A2)

It was during the 1957 federal election that Progressive Conservative leader John Diefenbaker quipped: "dogs know what to do with polls" (Spencer 1994, 57). Until recent years, many have called for a banning of polls during federal elections, claiming that they distract voters, leading some to abandon their parties of preference if the polls show them losing. In 1986, one government study reported that in prior years "more than twenty Private Members' bills have been introduced in the House of Commons with the purpose of either prohibiting the publication of polls or to control the methodology of polls published in newspapers during campaigns." Another concern is that when the polls report a party is failing, its volunteers become dispirited and fundraising becomes more difficult. On the other hand, polls enhance the democratic process by empowering voters with information to allow them to use their vote strategically. For example, if Party X is their preferred party but is third place in the polls, the voter might choose Party Y if it has a chance in beating Party Z, a party the voter dislikes.

To address concerns about polling, in 1993, Parliament amended the *Canada Elections Act* to prohibit the release of polls from midnight of the Friday prior to the end of voting on election day. As election day in Canadian federal elections occurs on weekdays rather than weekends, this effectively banned the release of polls during the final days of campaigning. This was challenged in court by the Southam and Thomson newspaper chains. After weaving its way through the Ontario provincial courts, the Supreme Court in 1998 ruled that voters have a right to see polls released to the media anytime during an election, except on election day (Jackson and Jackson 2009; Massicotte 2006). The *Canada Elections Act* was subsequently amended to restrict the publication of polls only on election day (Adams 2019). Despite what was thought a long-settled issue, following the historically record-low turnout in the 2022 Ontario provincial election, a 2023 report by Elections Ontario recommended a publication ban on polls two weeks prior to election day (Crawley 2023). Despite the controversies, as this chapter has shown, polling methods continue to change while remaining important tools for media coverage and party strategists.

NOTES

 1 For historical discussions regarding the deeply divisive issue of conscription, see Jones (1981).
 2 The photo can be seen at: https://en.wikipedia.org/wiki/Dewey_Defeats_Truman.
 3 This can be seen online: https://www.cnn.com/2016/11/12/politics/pollster-eats-bug-after-donald-trump-win/index.html.
 4 Another pollster, Curtis Brown with Winnipeg-based Probe Research, reports that while survey studies that are 100% based on telephone interviews are now fairly unusual, for such projects his firm ensures that a minimum of 40% of their sample consists of mobile phone numbers (Brown 2022).
 5 In the US, autodialing is prohibited for contacting mobile users (DeSilver and Keeter 2015).
 6 This study involved 28,000 telephone and in-person interviews in 35 countries. For the three specific countries mentioned here, 900 interviews were conducted in Canada, 1,600 in the US, and 802 in the UK (Ipsos-Reid 2001, 7, 22).
 7 For those unfamiliar with the statistical weighting, a very basic example would be that if only 25% of the sample were women when 50% were expected, hence there being too few women, then each woman would be "weighted up" to count as two respondents when the data are analyzed.
 8 These were AskingCanadians, Angus Reid Strategies, and Ipsos Reid. Ipsos Reid conducted both live phone interviewing and online surveys during this election.
 9 In my own review of all national polls released within the final five days of each federal election from 2000 to 2021, I found little difference between how they performed before 2008 and afterwards. For the elections of 2000, 2004, and 2006, in which *all* polling was done by live telephone interviewers, the average difference between the poll and the actual percentage vote for the winning party was respectively 1.0, 3.6, and 0.8. For those elections after 2008, in which the number of polls done online far outweighed those done via phone for the 2015, 2019, and 2021 elections, the respective differences were 1.8, 1.2, and 0.9. Of the five polls that were done exclusively online in 2021, the difference was only 1.4.
10 This is based on my count of the polls listed by Wikipedia for the 2021 campaign. See https://en.wikipedia.org/wiki/Opinion_polling_for_the_2021_Canadian_federal_election.
11 Unlike other surveys at the time, the ANES did not predict a Truman defeat. Its use of probability sampling for national polls in place of the outdated quota sampling used by Gallup and others helped bring about better polling standards. The ANES was renamed the American Election Study (AES) in 1978 (Adams 2021).
12 The use of constituency polls by the federal Liberals leading up to the 1945 federal election is discussed in Robinson (1999).
13 For a discussion of segment analysis as it relates to marketing research, see Burns and Bush (2010).
14 Goldfarb continued to serve the federal party into the 1980s while pursuing more lucrative marketing research contracts for such Fortune 500 companies as Miller Beer, Xerox, and Ford. I served as a research director serving these clients for the firm in the mid-1990s.

15 In a personal interview, Goldfarb reported that the US Democrats invited both Keith Davey, the national campaign director, and him to present their Canadian polling methodology to Democratic Party strategists.
16 Regarding how these types of efforts have evolved within each party, see Delacourt (2013).
17 Regarding the logistics for setting up a focus group study, see Burns and Bush (2010).
18 For a discussion on online focus group recruiting using social media in Canada, see Wallace et al. (2021).

REFERENCES

Adams, Christopher. 2010. "Polling in Canada: Calling the Elections." In *Mediating Canadian Politics*, edited by Shannon Sampert and Linda Trimble, 151–68. Toronto: Pearson.
———. 2019. "Shifting Targets: Capturing the Electorate's Mood." In *Journal of Parliamentary and Political Law: Special Issue, The Informed Citizens' Guide to Elections*, edited by Gregory Tardi and Richard Balasko, 87–102. Toronto: Thompson Reuters.
———. 2021. "Advances in Sociological 'Truths' and Processing 'Power': Mid-Century Canadian Survey Research and Data Processing." Conference paper presented to the World Association for Public Opinion Research.
———. 2022. "The Canadian Marketing Research Sector: A Quarter Century of Change." Conference paper presented to the World Association for Public Opinion Research.
Breton, Charles, Fred Cutler, Sarah Lachance, and Alex Mierke-Zatwarnicki. 2017. "Telephone versus Online Survey Modes for Election Studies: Comparing Canadian Public Opinion and Vote Choice in the 2015 Federal Election." *Canadian Journal of Political Science* 50 (4): 1005–36. https://doi.org/10.1017/S0008423917000610.
Brodbeck, Tom. 2023. "Struggling Political Leaders Should Look in the Mirror." *Winnipeg Free Press*, January 14.
Brown, Curtis. 2022. Personal Email Communication. June 19.
Burns, Mag. 2020. Personal Email Communication. August 18.
Burns, Alvin C., and Ronald F. Bush. 2010. *Marketing Research*. 6th ed. Boston: Prentice-Hall.
Canadian Radio-television and Telecommunications Commission. 2019. *Communications Monitoring Report 2018*. https://crtc.gc.ca/eng/publications/reports/policymonitoring/2018/cmr1.htm.
Canadian Research Insights Council. 2019. *Public Opinion Research Standards and Disclosure Requirements*. https://www.canadianresearchinsightscouncil.ca/wp-content/uploads/2019/09/CRIC-Public-Opinion-Research-Standards-and-Disclosure-Requirements-1.pdf.
———. 2022. "Canadian Insights Industry Experiences Strong Growth in 2021 – Forecasts Continued Growth in 2022." Media Release. October.
Canadian Viewpoint. n.d. "Online Services." http://canview.com/services-online/#panels.
Courtney, John C. 1981. "Campaign Strategy and Electoral Victory: The Progressive Conservatives and the 1979 Election." In *Canada at the Polls, 1979 and 1980: A Study of the General Elections*, edited by Howard R. Penniman, 121–51. Washington, DC: American Enterprise Institute.
Crawley, Mike. 2023. "Ontario's Election Watchdog Wants Opinion Polls Banned in Run-up to Voting Day." CBC News. April 2. https://www.cbc.ca/news/canada/toronto/ontario-election-opinion-polling-ban-1.6797969.
Creighton, Donald. 1976. *The Forked Road: Canada 1939–1957*. Toronto: McClelland and Stewart.
Dangerfield, Kerry. 2019. "What Current Research Tells Us About Voters and Non-Voters: The Manitoba Experience." In *The Journal of Parliamentary and Political Law: Special Edition 2019, The Informed Citizens' Guide to Elections*, edited by Gregory Tardi and Richard Balasko, 113–27. Toronto: Thompson Reuters.
Delacourt, Susan. 2013. *Shopping for Votes: How Politicians Choose Us and We Choose Them*. Madeira Park: Douglas and McIntyre.
DeSilver, Drew, and Scott Keeter. 2015. "The Challenges of Polling When Fewer People Are Available to Be Polled." Pew Research Center. July 21. https://www.pewresearch.org/fact-tank/2015/07/21/the-challenges-of-polling-when-fewer-people-are-available-to-be-polled/.

Elections BC. 2020. "2020 British Columbia General Election." https://elections.bc.ca/docs/GE42-voting
-stats-infographic.pdf.

Elections Canada. 2023. "Voter Turnout at Federal Elections and Referendums." April 3. https://www
.elections.ca/content.aspx?section=ele&dir=turn&document=index&lang=e.

Elections Ontario. n.d. "General Elections Statistics from the Records." https://results.elections.on.ca/en
/publications.

Enns, Andrew. 2022. Personal Email Communication. December 29.

Flanagan, Thomas. 2010. "Campaign Strategy: Triage and the Concentration of Resources." In *Election*,
edited by Heather McIvor, 155–72. Toronto: Emond Montgomery Publications.

Gallup, George, and Saul Forbes Rae. 1940. *The Pulse of Democracy: The Public-Opinion Poll and How It Works*.
New York: Simon and Schuster.

Geddes, John. 2019. "Who's the Political Genius?" *Maclean's*. September.

Grenier, Éric. 2014. *Tapping into the Pulse: Political Public Opinion Polling in Canada, 2013*. IndieBookLauncher.com.

Grenville, Andrew. 2018. *The Insights Industry: Questioning Everything*. Toronto: Maru/Matchbox.

IBM Cloud Education. 2021. "Interactive Voice Response." March 15. https://www.ibm.com/cloud/learn
/interactive-voice-response.

Ipsos-Reid. 2001. *The Face of the Web, Wave II: 2000–2001*. Vancouver: Ipsos-Reid [Syndicated: used with
permission].

Issenberg, Sasha. 2012. *The Victory Lab: The Secret Science of Winning Elections*. New York: Broadway Books.

Jackson, Robert J., and Doreen Jackson. 2009. *Politics in Canada: Culture, Institutions, Behaviours and Public
Policy*. 7th ed. Toronto: Pearson.

Jeffrey, Brooke. 2016. "Back to the Future: The Resurgent Liberals." In *The Canadian Federal Election of 2015*,
edited by Jon H. Pammett and Christopher Dornan, 57–84. Toronto: Dundurn.

Jones, Richard. 1981. "Politics and Culture: The French Canadians and the Second World War." In *The Second
World War as a National Experience*, edited by Stanley Aster, 82–91. Ottawa: Canadian Committee for the
History of the Second World War.

Keeter, Scott. 2021. "Public Opinion Polling Basics." Pew Research Center. https://www.pewresearch.org
/course/public-opinion-polling-basics/.

Leger Online. n.d. "Born From Research: Panel Book Data Opinion 360" [Brochure].

Lohr, Steve, and Natasha Singer. 2016. "How Data Failed Us in Calling an Election." *New York Times*.
November 10. https://www.nytimes.com/2016/11/10/technology/the-data-said-clinton-would-win-why
-you-shouldnt-have-believed-it.html?smid=nytcore-ipad-share&smprod=nytcore-ipad&_r=0.

Lucid. 2019. *Marketplace: 2019 Book* [Report].

MacKay, Scott. 2022. Personal Interview. December 29.

Marzolini, Michael. 2006. "Public Opinion and the 2006 Election" In *The Canadian Federal Election of 2006*,
edited by Jon Pammett and Christopher Dornan, 253–82. Toronto: Dundurn Press.

Massicotte, Louis. 2006. "Electoral Legislation Since 1997: Parliament Regains the Initiative." In *The
Canadian Federal Election of 2006*, edited by Jon Pammett and Christopher Dornan, 196–219. Toronto:
Dundurn Press.

Nash, Peggy. 2022. *Women Winning Office: An Activist's Guide to Getting Elected*. Toronto: Between the
Lines.

Pammett, Jon, Lawrence LeDuc, Jane Jenson, and Harold Clarke. 1975. *The 1974 Federal Election: A
Preliminary Report*. Occasional Paper No. 4. Ottawa: Department of Political Science, Carleton
University. https://archive.org/details/1974federalelect0000unse/page/64/mode/2up?view=theater.

Pickup, Mark. 2010. "Election Campaign Polls and Democracy in Canada: Examining the Evidence
Behind the Common Claims." In *Voting Behaviour in Canada*, edited by Cameron Anderson and Laura
Stephenson, 242–78. Vancouver: UBC Press.

Research Now. n.d. "Global Panel Sizes." http://sigs.researchnow.com/EU_Emails/UK/14Apr/Panel%20IE
%20Landing%20Page/Global_Panel_Size_IE.pdf.

Robinson, Daniel. 1999. *The Measure of Democracy: Polling, Market Research, and Public Life, 1930–1945*. Toronto: University of Toronto Press.

Roos, Dave. 2008. "How Interactive Voice Response (IVR) Works." HowStuffWorks.com. https://electronics .howstuffworks.com/interactive-voice-response.htm.

Safire, William. 1978. *Safire's Political Dictionary*. New York: Random House.

Simpson, Sean. 2022. Personal Email Communication. 18 June.

Spencer, Dick. 1994. *Trumpets and Drums: John Diefenbaker on the Campaign Trail*. Vancouver: Greystone Books.

Statista.com. n.d. "Number of Mobile Subscribers in Canada from 2010 to 2020." https://www.statista.com /statistics/460060/total-number-of-mobile-subscribers-canada/.

Statistics Canada. 2021. "Smartphone Personal Use and Selected Smartphone Habits by Gender and Age Groups." https://www150.statcan.gc.ca/t1/tbl1/en/tv.action?pid=2210014301.

———. 2022. "2021 Canada Census." https://www150.statcan.gc.ca/n1/daily-quotidien/220209/dq220209a -eng.htm.

Steber, Colson. 2018. "River Sampling vs. Panel Sampling: What's the Difference?" Communications for Research: Market Research Blog, February 15.

Turcotte, André. 2011. "Polls: Seeing Through the Glass Darkly." In *The Canadian Federal Election of 2011*, edited by Jon H. Pammett and Christopher Dornan, 195–218. Toronto: Dundurn Press.

Turcotte, André, and Simon Vodrey. 2017. "Permanent Polling and Governance." In *Votes: Permanent Campaigning in Canada*, edited by Alex Marland, Thierry Giasson, and Anna Lennox Esselment, 127–44. Vancouver: UBC Press.

Waddell, Christopher. 2009. "The Campaign in the Media 2008." In *The Canadian General Election of 2008*, edited by Jon H. Pammett and Christopher Dornan, 217–56. Toronto: Dundurn Press.

Wallace, Rebecca, Elizabeth Goodyear-Grant, and Amanda Bittner. 2021. "Harnessing Technologies in Focus Group Research." *Canadian Journal of Political Science* 54 (2): 335–55. https://doi.org/10.1017 /S0008423921000226.

Wavrock, David, Grant Schellenberg, and Christoph Schimmele. 2021. "Internet-use Typology of Canadians: Online Activities and Digital Skills." Statistics Canada, November 9.

Wiseman, Nelson. 2022. *1950s Canada: Politics and Public Affairs*. Toronto: University of Toronto Press.

PART FOUR

The People

CHAPTER FOURTEEN

Studying Voting Behaviour in Elections: Theory and Explanation

Christian Schimpf, Laura B. Stephenson, and Allison Harell

INTRODUCTION

The focus of this chapter is voting behaviour in elections. The topic is intimately related to the study of elections, in any context, because it focuses on the inputs that produce electoral outcomes – what the voters do when they go to the polls. Those who study voting behaviour seek to understand why voters make the choices they do. That is, what leads someone to prefer candidate A over candidate B? Which considerations matter, and which are ignored? Understanding voting behaviour helps us understand what voters wanted out of an election. If winning candidates and parties take their election as a mandate, then knowing what drives voting behaviour is an important component in assessing the quality of the democratic process.

Understanding individual-level voter behaviour began in earnest with the development of public opinion election surveys in 1940 (Bartels 2010). In subsequent years, various models of vote choice have been developed, compared, and tested in studies of elections around the world. Models have been compared not only across countries, but also at different levels of government and in a single country over time. The findings of these studies shed light on two important aspects of elections: how to understand vote choices and how to understand election outcomes. In other words, *theories* help us understand voters' behaviour and how we can use these models to *explain* what happens in any given election.

DEFINING VOTING BEHAVIOUR

A team of academics at Columbia University ran the first election study in Erie County, Ohio, in the months leading up to the 1940 American election. The findings of this study led to an influential book called *The People's Choice* (Lazarsfeld, Berelson, and Gaudet 1944). That book was designed as an exploration of how individuals react to campaign events and information in shaping their vote.

Their findings pointed to a very basic conclusion – that "[s]ocial characteristics predict political preferences" (Lazarsfeld et al. 1944, 27) – which is far different than what was expected: namely, that campaigns shaped voting. The summary of the Columbia model, as it has become known, is that social group membership largely dictates political preferences.

The focus on social background characteristics has generally fallen out of favour in light of more comprehensive models developed later (see, for example, Campbell et al. 1960; Clarke et al. 2004). However, in 2005, Blais published important research that noted how relevant demographic group membership continues to be for understanding voting behaviour in Canada. His research demonstrated that there was no simple way to account for the importance of support from Catholics and non-European immigrants for the Liberal Party, a finding that had been prominent in previous research. He wrote, "My point is … that we miss something important if we do not examine the group bases of party support" (Blais 2005, 834).

One reason the Columbia model is used less in analyses is that other models incorporate many of the same characteristics while adding others. The Michigan model, for example, first articulated in *The American Voter* (Campbell et al. 1960), introduced a "funnel of causality" as a way of thinking about the factors that contribute to vote choice. Social characteristics may matter, but they are far removed from vote choice. Attitudes about parties, issues, and candidates are the prominent factors in a Michigan vote choice formulation, as these factors are most proximate to the vote.

The American Voter is well-known for introducing the concept of party identification, a long-standing, psychological attachment to a party. Party identification shapes how a citizen understands politics – how they view candidates, how they evaluate parties, and how they understand major political issues (e.g., climate change). Party identification has taken on a life of its own as a factor in voting and politics in general (see Johnston 2006 for a review). There is a general consensus that when a voter forms an attachment to a political party, the attachment matters – a lot. More recent work has examined the social identity aspect of partisanship (Greene 1999; Huddy and Bankert 2017) and how this contributes to attitudes toward out-groups and even polarization (Iyengar and Westwood 2015; Gidron et al. 2020).

The Michigan model made party identification a central component of the study of (American) elections, but the logic of the model, formalized by Miller and Shanks (1996) in the bloc recursive model, has dominated the recent study of Canadian elections as well. Figure 14.1 provides a visual interpretation of how the funnel of causality can be recognized in the stepwise introduction of different "blocs" of variables in a vote choice model (see also Blais et al. 2002; Gidengil et al. 2006; Anderson and Stephenson 2010). The central premise of the bloc recursive model is that factors can be distinguished in terms of their proximity to voting. For example, basic values and partisanship are more distant compared to other factors, such as leader evaluations. Predispositions that are further away from the time of voting can influence behaviour either directly or indirectly by affecting more proximate factors (see Figure 14.1). For example, a social conservative should be less inclined to vote for the Liberal Party. At the same time, they might also be more opposed to climate measures proposed by Liberal Party. Writ large, the model can be seen as a "heuristic device for simplifying a complex and heterogeneous process" (Gidengil et al. 2006, 2). This model is common in analyses of Canadian voting behaviour over the last 20 years (Bélanger and Nadeau 2009; Blais et al. 2002; Fournier et al. 2013; Gidengil et al. 2006; Miller and Shanks 1996).

Figure 14.1. Standard Bloc Recursive Model

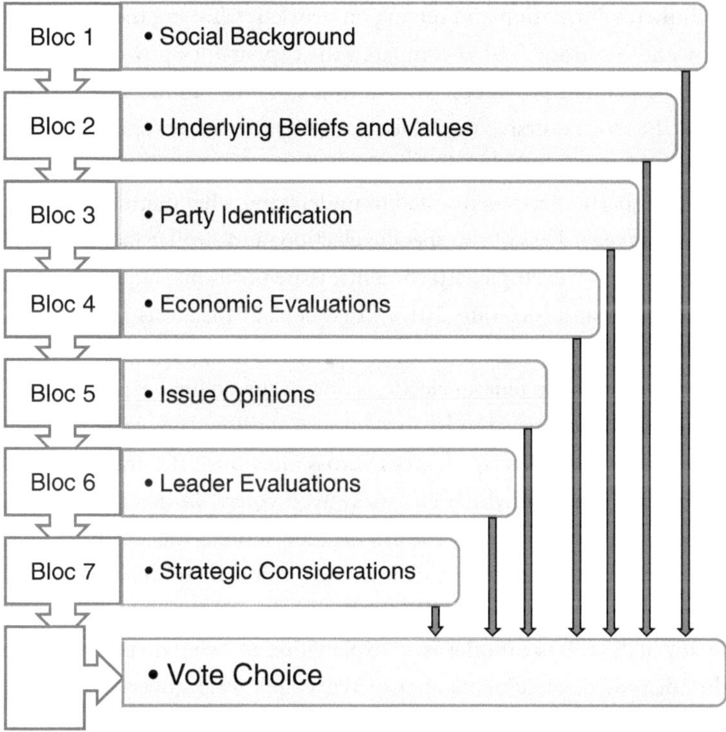

This model is not the only one that has been used to study Canadian elections. The valence model of voting is closely associated with the work of Harold Clarke and various colleagues (Clarke et al. 2004, 2009, 2019). The valence model argues that voters support the candidate or party that is best able to tackle important issues. The concept of "best able" means that party reputation, in terms of affect for the party as well as issue ownership and past performance, matters. The valence model builds on critiques of the spatial model of voting, which, as articulated in Downs (1957), posits that voters prefer the candidate closest to them in issue space. This very basic interpretation of how voters might evaluate candidates and parties has proven useful as a framework for evaluation. Another way of thinking about elections comes from Key (1966) – that voters evaluate the incumbent in terms of whether they have done well or done poorly; if the latter, they seek to, as per the familiar precept, "throw the rascals out." Using the economy as the key metric (as is often assumed) is known as economic voting (Fiorina 1981). Canadian electors are not immune to using economics as a criterion by which to evaluate the governing party (Clarke and Stewart 1996; Daoust and Dassonneville 2018).

Given the variety of vote models, it is worth highlighting work that compares how these models fare in comparison to one another and across different contexts (federal, provincial, and municipal). For example, Clarke, Kornberg, and Scotto (2009) considered which model (focusing in particular on the issue-proximity and valence models, but also analyzing other components) produced the best explanations of vote choice in Canada and the United States. They evaluated in favour of the valence model, arguing that it was so successful because it took into account how individuals made decisions – with limited information and relying on heuristics. Taking the comparisons to the subnational level, Roy and McGrane (2015) compared the explanatory power of the valence and bloc recursive models in Canadian provinces. They found that both models performed similarly, but argued in favour of the bloc recursive model for its ability to uncover specific dynamics and avoid assuming effects that might not hold in all cases. The valence model is more parsimonious while the bloc recursive model is particularly well suited to understand what matters in a specific election.

Yet, voters are voters regardless of the specific election, and similar factors are considered each time they go to the polls. For example, attachments, issue positions, and evaluations matter regularly (c.f. Cutler 2008; Roy and McGrane 2015; Cross et al. 2015; Lucas and Santos 2021). We also see similar factors shaping vote choice over time, though there are interesting changes. For example, evaluating the four Canadian federal elections that occurred between 2000 and 2008, Gidengil et al. (2012) use the bloc recursive model to demonstrate how the electoral fortunes of parties were influenced by factors to different degrees across elections. The model of voting behaviour performed as expected – showing which factors swayed voters, in detail – but by looking across elections the authors were able to identify the importance of social background, for example, to the Liberal Party (which went from winning a majority to a minority to being the Official Opposition during that time). Clarke et al. (2019, xiii) similarly looked across multiple elections (1993–2015) to assess the legitimacy of the valence model as an explanation of "what do elections decide" – namely, that elections do not provide statements about what voters want governments to do so much as take the pulse of what is occurring at a given time. They also found that the model had substantial explanatory power across Canadian elections, leading to a conclusion about continuity.

EVOLUTION OF THE CANADIAN ELECTORATE? THE 2019 AND 2021 ELECTIONS

Since the turn of the century, federal elections in Canada have produced significant change. Examples include the Conservative Party's victory in 2006, the NDP's stunning success under the late Jack Layton, and the landslide election in 2015 that brought the Liberals back to power. Clarke et al. (2019) conclude that the elections have occurred in a context of permanent dealignment, in which voters regularly switch their alliances and votes from one election to the next. Against this background, the 2019 and 2021 Canadian elections stand out, as they produced almost identical results in terms of seats. Although the parties and most leaders stayed the same, the elections took place under very different circumstances. The 2019 election came on the heels of the SNC-Lavalin affair – which resulted from Justin Trudeau pressuring the then-minister of justice and attorney general, Jody Wilson-Raybould, to intervene in a criminal case against construction company SNC-Lavalin – and in the shadow of large-scale climate change protests. The 2019 election marked the first contest for the People's Party of Canada (PPC), a party formed by former Conservative MP Maxime Bernier after he lost the Conservative leadership race in 2017. The incumbent prime minister (Justin Trudeau) was again leading the Liberals, but three other parties entered the 2019 race with a new figure at the helm: the Conservative Party with Andrew Scheer, the NDP led by Jagmeet Singh, and the Bloc

Table 14.1. 2019 and 2021 Canadian Federal Election Results (Popular Vote Share and Seat Count)

Party	2019 Federal Election		2021 Federal Election	
	Popular Vote Share (%)	Seat Count	Popular Vote Share (%)	Seat Count
Liberal	33.1	157	32.6	160
Conservative	34.3	121	33.7	119
New Democratic	16.0	24	17.8	25
Bloc Québécois	7.6	32	7.6	32
Green	6.5	3	2.3	2
People's Party	1.6	0	4.9	0
Turnout	67%		62.6%	

Sources: Elections Canada (Elections Canada 2019, 2021).

Québécois (BQ) under the leadership of Yves-François Blanchet. Throughout the campaign, the Conservative and Liberal parties polled neck and neck in the rest of Canada (ROC) and they also found themselves in a competitive race with the BQ in Quebec. In the end, Trudeau's Liberals won the election but lost the Parliamentary majority they had secured four years earlier. In fact, they secured a lower vote share than the Conservative Party (Table 14.1).

Whereas the 2019 election followed the fixed election schedule established in 2007, the 2021 election was called early on August 15, 2021. At the time, Canada and the world had lived with the realities of the COVID-19 pandemic for over 18 months, including many deaths, closed borders, multiple shutdowns of public life in regions across the country, and severe economic distress for many Canadians. While his party sold Trudeau's early election call as necessary to define the future of the country as it began to recover (partly due to the recently available vaccine), the opposition criticized the prime minister for calling an election during a pandemic. Ahead of the 2021 campaign, polling suggested the Liberals had a sizable lead over the Conservatives, particularly in Quebec, enough to warrant hopes of another majority government. However, the Liberal Party quickly found itself in a tight race with the Conservatives for popular support in the ROC and also fighting off a surging BQ in Quebec. The Liberal Party's favourable poll ratings began to crumble within days of the start of the campaign, particularly in Quebec. The public's initial focus was more on why Canadians were being asked to go to the ballot box during a pandemic than about a vision for Canada's post-pandemic recovery. Despite many ups and downs, Trudeau retained power, as the Liberal Party beat out Erin O'Toole's Conservatives to secure the most parliamentary seats, although, like in 2019, they did not win the most votes. The 2021 election did not bring about the majority the Liberals had hoped for. With the Conservative Party and the NDP barely capitalizing on the Liberal campaign struggles, the election resulted in little change in seat counts – the parliamentary seat outcome was nearly equivalent to the results from the 2019 elections (Table 14.1).

With the two elections taking place in different contexts but yielding nearly identical results, a logical question is: what factors shaped Canadian voters' decisions in 2019 and 2021? Were they the same across these two elections? Answering these questions not only sheds light on the elections, but also on the nature of voting behaviour in Canada generally. We use the multistage bloc recursive model (Miller and Shanks 1996) and draw on the 2019 and 2021 Canadian Election Study (CES)

Table 14.2. Role of Demographics in Voting Decisions in the 2019 and 2021 Canadian Federal Elections (ROC)

	2019					2021				
	LPC	CPC	NDP	Green	PPC	LPC	CPC	NDP	Green	PPC
Catholic	0.06*	−0.05+	0.00	0.00	−0.02**	0.04	−0.03	0.03	−0.01	−0.03*
No religion	0.07**	−0.19**	0.07**	0.05**	−0.00	0.01	−0.16**	0.16**	0.01	−0.01
Religious minority	0.16**	−0.11**	−0.02	−0.01	−0.02	0.08	−0.13**	0.11+	−0.01	−0.03**
Racialized minority	0.09+	−0.03	−0.03	−0.02	−0.01	0.13**	−0.08*	−0.01	−0.00	−0.03
French speaking	0.01	−0.07	−0.05	0.08*	0.02	0.10	−0.16**	−0.06	0.05	0.05
Born outside Canada	0.01	0.02	−0.04+	−0.00	0.02	0.02	0.02	−0.05+	0.02	−0.01
Atlantic resident	0.07+	−0.08*	0.00	0.03	−0.02+	0.10*	−0.02	−0.03	−0.01	−0.03**
Western resident	−0.17**	0.14**	0.03	−0.01	0.01	−0.09**	0.05*	0.04+	0.01	−0.01
Woman	0.03+	−0.09**	0.06**	0.01	0.00	0.05*	−0.08**	0.04+	0.01*	−0.00
Married/partner	−0.05*	0.06**	−0.03	−0.01	0.03**	0.00	0.06*	−0.05*	−0.00	0.01
Union member	0.01	−0.04	0.03	−0.01	0.01	0.01	−0.08**	0.06*	0.01	−0.01
Homeowner	−0.06+	0.11**	−0.04*	0.01	−0.02	−0.00	0.10**	−0.09**	−0.01	−0.00
University degree	0.13**	−0.12**	0.00	0.01	−0.02*	0.11**	−0.03+	−0.04+	0.00	−0.03**
Age group 18–34	−0.05+	0.04	0.00	−0.02	0.03+	−0.04	−0.03	0.07*	−0.00	0.00
Age group 55+	0.05+	−0.02	−0.02	0.01	−0.01+	0.08**	0.04+	−0.08**	0.00	−0.04**
Observations		3,240					2,864			

Notes: Entries show average marginal effects from multinomial regression models. Statistical significance of estimates underlying the average marginal effects is indicated as follows: + p<0.1, * p<0.05, ** p<0.01. Models include additional outcome "Other/spoiled," which is not shown here. All models are weighted.

data (Stephenson et al. 2020 and 2022) to understand and compare voters' rationales.[1] In choosing variables for the models, we mostly follow previous work that used the bloc recursive model (Fournier et al. 2013; Gidengil et al. 2006 and 2012), but we deviate with respect to election-specific issues.[2] We look at the role of demographics, underlying values and beliefs, partisanship, economic perceptions, and the role of leader ratings.[3] For details on the technical procedures, see the Appendix.

To begin, how did demographics structure the vote outside Quebec in 2019 and 2021? Table 14.2 demonstrates that some familiar patterns emerge in both elections. Women were less likely to vote CPC and more likely to vote LPC and NDP than men. Non-religious voters were more likely to vote for a party on the political left, while religious minorities tended to shy away from a Conservative vote. Atlantic Canada voters were more likely to vote Liberal, whereas western Canada was more likely to vote Conservative. While university-educated voters tended to vote Liberal and not Conservative, homeowners and married voters were more likely to vote Conservative.

Yet there are differences across the elections as well. The grey-shaded boxes indicate differences in direction or significance of coefficients between the years. In 2021, religious affiliation did not matter for the Liberal Party vote at all compared to 2019. Historically, the Liberal Party has drawn upon the support of Catholic voters (Blais 2005), but that trend weakened considerably during the 2000s (Gidengil et al. 2012) and disappeared in 2011 (Fournier et al. 2013). It thus seems like

Table 14.3. Role of Underlying Values and Beliefs in Voting Decisions in the 2019 and 2021 Canadian Federal Elections (ROC)

	2019					2021				
	LPC	CPC	NDP	Green	PPC	LPC	CPC	NDP	Green	PPC
Market liberalism	−0.16**	0.29**	−0.14**	−0.02+	0.03**	−0.11**	0.32**	−0.27**	−0.00	0.07**
Moral traditionalism	−0.02	0.15**	−0.11**	−0.03	−0.01	−0.08**	0.18**	−0.13**	−0.02*	0.05**
Political disaffection	−0.24**	0.13**	0.06**	0.03+	0.03**	−0.27**	0.11**	0.10**	−0.00	0.04**
Accommodating Quebec	0.08**	−0.10**	0.01	0.01*	0.00	0.05**	−0.05**	0.01	−0.00	−0.00
Observations			3,240					2,864		

Notes: Entries show average marginal effects from multinomial regression models. Statistical significance of estimates underlying the average marginal effects is indicated as follows: + $p<0.1$, * $p<0.05$, ** $p<0.01$. Models include additional outcome "Other/spoiled," which is not shown here. All models are weighted.

2019 was an outlier in a long-term trend. Interestingly, religious minorities were more likely to vote Liberal in 2019 but NDP in 2021. While non-religious voters consistently shy away from the Conservative Party, they were equally likely to select the Liberals or NDP in 2019, but that support solidified for the NDP in 2021.

The support of racialized minority voters, in favour of the Liberals and opposed to the Conservatives, was starker in 2021 than the previous election. Similarly, union support, insignificant in 2019, re-emerged in 2021 to push voters toward the social democratic NDP and away from the Conservatives. Age differences were more pronounced in 2021 as well, with young voters more likely to vote NDP and older voters more likely to vote Conservative or Liberal. Sociodemographic cleavages, overall, appear more prominent in 2021.

Next, we turn to the role of underlying values and beliefs (Table 14.3), focusing on market liberalism, moral traditionalism, political disaffection, and accommodating Quebec. In previous elections, higher support for market liberalism tended to favour the Conservatives, and this pattern replicated in 2019 and 2021. Market liberalism also increased the probability of voting PPC. Moral traditionalism clearly distinguishes the support of Conservative and NDP voters in both elections, but it decreased the vote for Liberals and increased the likelihood of voting PPC in 2021 as well. Political disaffection disadvantaged the governing party in both elections, with disaffected voters *much* less likely to vote Liberal. And finally, attitudes toward Quebec made one more likely to vote Liberal and less likely to vote Conservative. In general, the values underpinning vote choice in these two elections look largely consistent with previous elections and what we know about ideological differences across the Canadian political parties. If anything, the role of values increased in 2021 with a more polarizing effect for moral traditionalism.

Partisanship features prominently in Canadian politics in terms of its role in attitude formation and political behaviour (Pickup, Stecula, and van der Linden 2020), and our analyses show that the 2019 and 2021 elections were no exception. We focus on respondents who identify with the Liberals, Conservatives, and NDP in the ROC. While some Canadians identify with other parties,

Table 14.4. Role of Partisanship in Voting Decisions in the 2019 and 2021 Canadian Federal Elections (ROC)

	2019			2021		
	LPC	CPC	NDP	LPC	CPC	NDP
LPC	0.39**	−0.23**	−0.06**	0.38**	−0.14**	−0.16**
CPC	−0.19**	0.44**	−0.11**	−0.20**	0.41**	−0.11**
NDP	−0.10**	−0.18**	0.36**	−0.11**	−0.19**	0.36**
Observations		3,240			2,864	

Notes: Entries show average marginal effects from multinomial regression models. Statistical significance of estimates underlying the average marginal effects is indicated as follows: + p<0.1, * p<0.05, ** p<0.01. Models include additional outcome "Other/spoiled," which is not shown here. All models are weighted.

notably the Green Party or even the relatively new PPC, the number of identifiers is small, making empirical analyses difficult. In general, and unsurprisingly, we see that people are more likely to vote for the party they identify with in both 2019 and 2021. For example, the probability of supporting one's own party increases by an average of 36 to 44 percentage points across parties in the ROC in 2019, and 36 to 41 percentage points in 2021. We also see that identifying with one party tends to negatively affect voting for the other parties, particularly on the other side of the political spectrum.

Two elements of economic perspectives are commonly featured in election analyses: egocentric considerations, referring to individuals' own economic situations, and sociotropic considerations, which refer to the perceived development of the national economy. Positive perceptions on both dimensions should lead voters to support the incumbent party, particularly if the leader is the same (c.f. Nadeau and Lewis-Beck 2001). The 2019 and 2021 elections had drastically different economic conditions, as Canada's economy shrank dramatically after the COVID-19-induced lockdowns in the first half of 2020, before recovering somewhat. The national economic perceptions of voters, measured during the election campaigns, reflected these changing circumstances. In 2019, only 41% of Canadians said the economy got worse, whereas 70% said so in 2021. Such negative economic evaluations in 2021 should have been extremely damaging for the governing party. Importantly, no such pattern emerges for personal perceptions (31% in 2019 versus 27% in 2021 said their situation got worse); if anything, personal perceptions were more positive in 2021.

In line with the general expectations, Table 14.5 shows that voters were more likely to vote for the incumbent Liberal Party in their riding the more positive they evaluated Canada's economy in 2019 and 2021. Yet, positive evaluations of the economy were less predictive of voting for other parties in 2021 than in 2019, suggesting that the exceptional circumstances of a global pandemic may have weakened the impact of economic voting. There is also little evidence to suggest that personal economic circumstances played much of a role in vote choice, especially compared to peoples' views of the national economy.

Issues are context- and time-dependent, and they often vary across elections. For our models, we selected issues that featured prominently in the two campaigns. The first two issues concern Canada's approach to refugee and immigrant admission. The 2015 election revealed strong partisan differences concerning immigration and refugee policy (Gravelle 2018). Political geography

Table 14.5. Role of Economic Perspectives in Voting Decisions in the 2019 and 2021 Canadian Federal Elections (ROC)

	2019					2021				
	LPC	CPC	NDP	Green	PPC	LPC	CPC	NDP	Green	PPC
Economic evaluations (national)	0.07**	−0.09**	0.01	0.02**	−0.02*	0.06**	−0.04*	0.00	0.00	−0.02
Economic evaluations (personal)	0.02	−0.03**	0.00	0.01	0.01*	0.00	−0.01	0.01	0.00	−0.01
Observations			3,240					2,864		

Notes: Entries show average marginal effects from multinomial regression models. Statistical significance of estimates underlying the average marginal effects is indicated as follows: + p<0.1, * p<0.05, ** p<0.01. Models include additional outcome "Other/spoiled," which is not shown here. All models are weighted.

generally has prevented major Canadian parties from adopting a strict anti-immigration stance, as there are "densely institutionalized cultural communities" (Taylor 2021, 18) in the Greater Toronto and Hamilton areas that are key to building a winning coalition. Yet the PPC tried to carve out a niche by promising to slash immigration in 2019. There was also the "blackface controversy" in 2019, after photos showing Prime Minister Trudeau wearing brownface makeup at an Arabian Nights theme gala in 2001 emerged, that led to questions about the governing Liberals' commitment to immigration and diversity (Lee et al. 2023). Other issues include the government's handling of the SNC-Lavalin affair, the narrative of Justin Trudeau not keeping his promises (such as electoral reform), and climate change beliefs, the latter pushed onto the agenda by large-scale protests around Canada and globally in the month preceding the 2019 election. By 2021, the SNC-Lavalin affair was in the political rearview while the COVID-19 pandemic lingered; we included measures asking respondents how well the federal government and their own provincial government handled the pandemic instead.

Table 14.6 reveals how several issue positions affected the 2019 and 2021 election outcomes. First, the issue of immigration did not play a substantial role in either election. In 2019 only the People's Party and Green votes were affected – and to a limited degree. Second, issues revolving around the Liberal Party, SNC-Lavalin, and Trudeau's record of keeping election promises consistently affected voters in the ROC. Voters who thought the government handled the SNC-Lavalin affair poorly were less likely to vote for the Liberals, reminiscent of the sponsorship scandal's impact on the Liberal vote in the early 2000s, when negative perceptions of the scandal cost the Liberals approximately 5.5% of the vote in 2004 and 3% of the vote in 2006 (Gidengil et al. 2012, 95–96). In the same way, voters were also less likely to support the Liberals if they thought Trudeau did not keep his election promises. Not surprisingly, the other parties benefited, although not equally.

The election of 2021, in contrast, was dominated by discussions of the ongoing pandemic. Unsurprisingly, those who were more satisfied with how the federal government handled the crisis were more likely to vote for the incumbent party, and they tended to be less likely to vote for either the NDP or the PPC.

Table 14.6. Role of Issue Positions in Voting Decisions in the 2019 and 2021 Canadian Federal Elections (ROC)

	2019					2021				
	LPC	CPC	NDP	Green	PPC	LPC	CPC	NDP	Green	PPC
Immigrant admission	−0.00	0.00	0.00	0.02**	−0.02**	0.01	0.01	−0.00	−0.00	0.00
Trudeau promises	−0.09**	0.04**	0.02*	0.01	0.02**	−0.08**	0.05**	0.03*	0.01*	0.00
SNC-Lavalin handling	−0.03**	0.01	0.01	0.01+	−0.01*					
COVID-19 handling (federal)						0.07**	−0.01	−0.02*	0.00	−0.03**
Climate change beliefs	−0.01	−0.04**	0.03**	0.03**	−0.02**	0.00	−0.02+	0.04**	0.01	−0.02**
Observations			3,240					2,864		

Notes: Entries show average marginal effects from multinomial regression models. Statistical significance of estimates underlying the average marginal effects is indicated as follows: + p<0.1, * p<0.05, ** p<0.01. Models include additional outcome "Other/spoiled," which is not shown here. All models are weighted.

Finally, the issue of climate change had little effect on incumbent support in either election. Climate-skeptic voters were more likely to support parties on the right (CPC and PPC), while belief in climate change led to a higher likelihood of voting NDP, in both elections. Interestingly, Green support was only affected by the climate change issue in 2019, but this is perhaps unsurprising given the collapse of the Green Party in 2021 under new leadership and internal infighting.

The last bloc in our analysis pertains to political leaders. Usually, Canadian party leaders play a crucial role in the spotlight of every election campaign. In some cases, such as the NDP's late Jack Layton, they have played decisive roles in securing the votes necessary for their party to deem an election successful (Fournier et al. 2013), and empirical work suggests that Canadian leaders have always mattered (Bittner 2018). Looking at the results from the 2019 and 2021 elections (Table 14.7), we universally find that the more people like a particular leader, the more likely they were to support the leader's party. The effect of party leader ratings on the vote is most pronounced for Scheer in 2019 and Singh in 2021. We further find that liking one of the major party leaders can also reduce the probability of voting for a party led by someone else. In general, however, these effects tend to be smaller in magnitude than the effect of positive ratings for one's own party.

DEMOCRATIC IMPLICATIONS

Our analysis of the 2019 and 2021 elections outside of Quebec shows that some of the core, long-term factors that are known to underpin vote choice in previous Canadian elections, and around the world, remained key structuring variables of vote choice in 2019 and 2021: sociodemographic cleavages, the importance of values and political identities, and the continued importance of

Table 14.7. Role of Leader Ratings in Voting Decisions in the 2019 and 2021 Canadian Federal Elections (ROC)

Like-Dislike of …	2019					2021				
	LPC	CPC	NDP	Green	PPC	LPC	CPC	NDP	Green	PPC
Scheer (2019) / O'Toole (2021)	−0.12**	0.33**	−0.10**	−0.08**	−0.04**	−0.08**	0.20**	−0.09**	−0.01	−0.01
Trudeau	0.22**	−0.08**	−0.07*	−0.02	−0.03*	0.24**	−0.12**	−0.13**	0.02+	−0.01
Singh	−0.11**	−0.07**	0.23**	−0.01	−0.04**	−0.13**	−0.10**	0.28**	−0.02*	−0.03*
Observations			3,240					2,864		

Notes: Entries show average marginal effects from multinomial regression models. Statistical significance of estimates underlying the average marginal effects is indicated as follows: + $p<0.1$, * $p<0.05$, ** $p<0.01$. Models include additional outcome "Other/spoiled," which is not shown here. All models are weighted.

economic and leader evaluations. This result lends credence to the idea that we can understand elections as being individual events in a sustained series, for which models of voting behaviour are useful guides.

However, despite considerable continuity across the 2019 and 2021 elections, we also found some shifts in the importance of key demographic variables as well as which issues mattered. This suggests that even when little seems to change between elections, context matters and can make a difference for how people make up their minds. In this sense, the two elections reflect a continuation of the challenges voters and parties alike have faced in Canada (Clarke et al. 2019). While there is some level of continuity, the trend of realigning and reimagining winning coalitions from election to election forces parties to adjust their strategy each time while voters may find it hard to predict what to expect from parties. This poses a challenge for democracy in terms of representing the will of the people. If parties fail to understand the wishes of the electorate or develop too broad of a program, voters may find it difficult to understand exactly what they are casting their ballot for. That the Liberal Party squeezed out enough seats to win in two elections despite failing to win the vote share could reflect how creative parties must be to win elections in this context. Ironically, Justin Trudeau's father, Pierre Trudeau, was the last prime minister to lose an election despite winning the most votes in 1979. Since then, voters have become accustomed to seeing the party winning the most votes also end up winning the most seats. If the trend of the 2019 and 2021 elections continues, questions of electoral legitimacy may arise and possibly renew interest in electoral system reform once again.

APPENDIX

We used multinomial regression models to estimate vote choice models for the rest of Canada (ROC). The vote choice variable had six categories and captured whether respondents reported voting for the Liberal Party of Canada (LPC), the Conservative Party of Canada (CPC), the New Democratic Party (NDP), the Green Party of Canada (Green), the People's Party of Canada (PPC), or "other/spoiled voted." We excluded Quebec from the analysis because the party choices differ in that province and the weight of different factors vary in meaningful ways. We use the ROC models here to illustrate how the bloc recursive model works and what it can tell us about voting behaviour outside Quebec.

Following the bloc recursive model's structure, we estimated a series of models and added blocs sequentially. For example, we interpreted the results for economic evaluations based on the model containing the economic perspective variables and all proceeding blocs (social background, underlying beliefs and values, and party identification). This approach does not preclude that adding additional blocs of variables might subsume the effects of specific variables or attenuate them. However, this does not pose a problem here because, as Fournier and colleagues (2013, 878; italics in original) summarize, "the central premise of the block-recursive approach is that the full estimate of a given variable's impact comes *before* causally posterior variables are added." In addition to presenting only selected variables, we also calculated average marginal effects (AMEs) using STATA's dydx margins function. For dummy variables, which we included as factors in the model, the calculated AMEs are the discrete differences in probabilities of voting for a particular party. For continuous variables, the AMEs are derivatives, which represent the increase (decrease) in probabilities of voting for a particular party assuming a constant increase (decrease) in the continuous independent variable. All analyses were weighted, using the weights provided by the CES. Low-quality responses are excluded from the analyses. We excluded duplicated survey IDs, duplicate IP addresses, respondents with failed attention checks, and respondents with an age-birth year mismatch.

NOTES

1 The CES is the longest running national election study in Canada and consists of campaign period and post-election components. We used the 2019 and 2021 CES online surveys. In 2019, the sampling design followed a rolling cross-section format (Johnston and Brady 2002). In 2021, the design was modified so that the sample was stratified in three-day, representative windows throughout the campaign. The CES team collected the online data via the Qualtrics platform, with respondents for 2019 recruited from third-party vendors through Qualtrics and 2021 respondents recruited from Leger Marketing's online panel. Surveys were conducted in both English and French. In both years, the sample is designed to be representative of the Canadian population aged 18 years and older in the 10 provinces. Residents from the territories (Northwest Territories, Yukon Territory, and Nunavut) are excluded from the sampling frame but included in the final sample. The samples were stratified by province, age, gender, and language.

2 Most of the questions used in this study come from the campaign period surveys (CPS). For more details about the questions, see the Appendix. Note that for this study, we relied on a partial sample of the overall dataset. Analyses are limited to those who provided a valid vote choice and answered specific questions, including issue positions of importance. Respondents that did not complete all the questions in the final models were removed from all analyses. This leaves us with 3,218 (ROC) in 2019 and 2,830 (ROC) in 2021.

3 We do not include strategic considerations in our analyses.

REFERENCES

Anderson, Cameron D. 2010. "Economic Voting in Canada: Assessing the Effects of Subjective Perceptions and Electoral Context." In *Voting Behaviour in Canada*, edited by Cameron D. Anderson and Laura B. Stephenson, 139–62. Vancouver: UBC Press.

Anderson, Cameron D., and Laura B. Stephenson. 2010. "The Puzzle of Elections and Voting in Canada." In *Voting Behaviour in Canada*, edited by Cameron D. Anderson and Laura B. Stephenson, 1–39. Vancouver: UBC Press.

Bartels, Larry M. 2010. "The Study of Electoral Behavior." In *The Oxford Handbook of American Elections and Political Behavior*, edited by Jan E. Leighley, 239–61. Oxford: Oxford University Press.

Bélanger, Éric, and Richard Nadeau. 2009. *Le comportement électoral des Québécois*. Montréal: Les Presses de l'Université de Montréal.

Bittner, Amanda. 2018. "Leaders Always Mattered: The Persistence of Personality in Canadian Elections." *Electoral Studies* 54: 297–302. https://doi.org/10.1016/j.electstud.2018.04.013.

Blais, André. 2005. "Accounting for the Electoral Success of the Liberal Party in Canada." *Canadian Journal of Political Science* 38 (4): 821–40. https://doi.org/10.1017/S0008423905050304.

Blais, André, Elisabeth Gidengil, Richard Nadeau, and Neil Nevitte. 2002. *Anatomy of a Liberal Victory: Making Sense of the 2000 Canadian Election*. Peterborough: Broadview Press.

Campbell, Angus, Philip E. Converse, Warren E. Miller and Donald E. Stokes. 1960. *The American Voter*. Chicago: University of Chicago Press.

Clarke, Harold D., Jane Jenson, Larry LeDuc, and Jon Pammett. 2019. *Absent Mandate: Strategies and Choices in Canadian Elections*. Toronto: University of Toronto Press.

Clarke, Harold D., Allan Kornberg, and Thomas J. Scotto. 2009. *Making Political Choices: Canada and the United States*. Toronto: University of Toronto Press.

Clarke, Harold D., David Sanders, Marianne C. Stewart, and Paul Whiteley. 2004. *Political Choice in Britain*. Oxford: Oxford University Press.

Clarke, Harold D. and Marianne C. Stewart. 1996. "Economists and Electorates: The Subjective Economy of Governing Party Support in Canada." *European Journal of Political Research* 29 (2): 191–214. https://doi.org/10.1111/j.1475-6765.1996.tb00648.x

Converse, Philip E., and Georges Dupeux. 1962. "Politicization of the Electorate in France and the United States." *Public Opinion Quarterly* 26 (1): 1–23. https://doi.org/10.1086/267067.

Cross, William P., Jonathan Malloy, Tamara A. Small, and Laura B. Stephenson. 2015. *Fighting for Votes: Parties, the Media, and Voters in an Ontario Election*. Vancouver: UBC Press.

Cutler, Fred. 2008. "Whodunnit? Voters and Responsibility in Canadian Federalism." *Canadian Journal of Political Science* 41 (3): 627–54. https://doi.org/10.1017/S0008423908080761.

Daoust, Jean-François, and Ruth Dassonneville. 2018. "Beyond Nationalism and Regionalism: The Stability of Economic Voting in Canada." *Canadian Journal of Political Science* 51 (3): 553–71. https://doi.org/10.1017/S000842391800001X.

Downs, Anthony. 1957. *An Economic Theory of Democracy*. New York: Harper.

Elections Canada. 2019. "Official Voting Results. Forty-Third General Election." https://www.elections.ca/res/rep/off/ovr2019app/home.html#3.

———. 2021. "General Election. National Results." September 20. https://www.elections.ca/enr/help/national_e.htm.

Fiorina, Morris P. 1981. *Retrospective Voting in American National Elections*. New Haven: Yale University Press.

Fournier, Patrick, Fred Cutler, Stuart Soroka, Dietlind Stolle, and Éric Bélanger. 2013. "Riding the Orange Wave: Leadership, Values, Issues, and the 2011 Canadian Election." *Canadian Journal of Political Science* 46 (4): 863–97. https://doi.org/10.1017/S0008423913000875.

Gidengil, Elisabeth, André Blais, Joanna Everitt, Patrick Fournier, and Neil Nevitte. 2006. "Back to the Future? Making Sense of the 2004 Canadian Election outside Quebec." *Canadian Journal of Political Science* 39 (1): 1–25. https://doi.org/10.1017/S0008423906060069.

Gidengil, Elisabeth, Neil Nevitte, André Blais, Joanna Everitt, and Patrick Fournier. 2012. *Dominance and Decline: Making Sense of Recent Canadian Elections*. Toronto: University of Toronto Press.

Gidron, Noam, James Adams, and Will Horne. 2020. *American Affective Polarization in Comparative Perspective*. Cambridge: Cambridge University Press.

Gravelle, Timothy B. 2018. "Partisanship, Local Context, Group Threat, and Canadian Attitudes towards Immigration and Refugee Policy." *Migration Studies* 6 (3): 448–67. https://doi.org/10.1093/migration/mnx058.

Greene, Steven. 1999. "Understanding Party Identification: A Social Identity Approach." *Political Psychology* 20 (2): 393–403. https://doi.org/10.1111/0162-895X.00150.

Huddy, Leonie, and Alexa Bankert. 2017. "Political Partisanship as a Social Identity." *Oxford Research Encyclopedia of Politics*. https://doi.org/10.1093/acrefore/9780190228637.013.250.

Iyengar, Shanto, and Sean J. Westwood. 2015. "Fear and Loathing across Party Lines: New Evidence on Group Polarization." *American Journal of Political Science* 59 (3): 690–707. https://doi.org/10.1111/ajps.12152.

Johnston, Richard. 2006. "Party Identification: Unmoved Mover or Sum of Preferences?" *Annual Review of Political Science* 9: 329–51. https://www.annualreviews.org/content/journals/10.1146/annurev.polisci.9.062404.170523.

Johnston, Richard, and Henry E. Brady. 2002. "The Rolling Cross-section Design." *Electoral Studies* 21 (2): 283–95. https://doi.org/10.1016/S0261-3794(01)00022-1.

Key, V.O. 1966. *The Responsible Electorate*. Cambridge: Belknap Press.

Lazarsfeld, Paul, Bernard Berelson, and Hazel Gaudet. 1944. *The People's Choice*. New York: Duell, Sloan and Pearce.

Lee, Amber, Allison Harell, Laura Stephenson, Daniel Rubenson, and Peter Loewen. 2023. "Motivated to Forgive? Partisan Scandals and Party Supporters." *Political Psychology* 44 (4): 729–47. https://doi.org/10.1111/pops.12882.

Lucas, Jack, and John Santos. 2021. "Calgary." In *Big City Elections in Canada*, edited by Jack Lucas and R. Michael McGregor, 33–52. Toronto: University of Toronto Press.

Miller, Warren E., and J.M. Shanks. 1996. *The New American Voter*. Cambridge: Harvard University Press.

Nadeau, Richard, and Michael S. Lewis-Beck. 2001. "National Economic Voting in US Presidential Elections." *Journal of Politics* 63 (1): 159–81. https://doi.org/10.1111/0022-3816.00063.

Pickup, Mark, Dominik Stecula, and Clifton van der Linden. 2020. "Novel Coronavirus, Old Partisanship: COVID-19 Attitudes and Behaviours in the United States and Canada." *Canadian Journal of Political Science* 53 (2): 357–64. https://doi.org/10.1017/S0008423920000463.

Roy, Jason, and David McGrane. 2015. "Explaining Canadian Provincial Voting Behaviour: Nuance or Parsimony?" *Canadian Political Science Review* 9 (1): 75–91. https://doi.org/10.1017/S0007123410000505.

Stephenson, Laura B., Allison Harell, Daniel Rubenson, and Peter J. Loewen. 2020. "2019 Canadian Election Study – Online Survey." https://doi.org/10.7910/DVN/DUS88V, Harvard Dataverse, V1.

———. 2022. "2021 Canadian Election Study." https://doi.org/10.7910/DVN/XBZHKC, Harvard Dataverse, V1.

Taylor, Zack. 2021. "The Political Geography of Immigration: Party Competition for Immigrants' Votes in Canada, 1997–2019." *American Review of Canadian Studies* 51 (1): 18–40. https://doi.org/10.1017/psrm.2015.30.

CHAPTER FIFTEEN

Voter Turnout

Stephen E. White

INTRODUCING AND DEFINING VOTER TURNOUT

Most of the things we want democratic elections to accomplish depend on citizens turning out to vote. To be sure, if an election were held and *nobody* showed up at the polls, we would not say the election "worked" in any meaningful sense at all: at the very least, *some* electoral participation is necessary if elections are to fulfill their core functions. For this reason, political scientists are concerned with voter turnout, which is usually defined as either the percentage of eligible voters or the percentage of voting-age people who opt to cast their ballots in democratic elections (the latter is used to measure turnout in political systems where accurate numbers of eligible voters are hard to get) (Solijonov 2016).

In several respects, high voter turnout is desirable. First, voter turnout affects the degree to which elections confer popular control over, and legitimacy to, elected governments. Popular control – "the extent to which citizens can impose their will upon government" (Miller, White, Heywood 1998, 159) – is a crucial function of democratic elections. Citizens need to be able to hold governments accountable, and the threat of being rebuked by the public in periodic elections makes governments more responsive to public opinion (Brooks and Manza 2008). Elections with high voter turnout also enhance the legitimacy of governments, as those governed are more likely to accept a government's right to exercise power when they see that, whether they voted for or against the government, most citizens have enough faith in the "rules of the game" to show up to vote (Anderson et al. 2005). Second, high voter turnout also has implications for representation and equality. Elections have the potential to be a great equalizer in democratic systems when many citizens vote: voting takes less time and effort compared to many other forms of political participation, and citizens are limited to only one vote irrespective of their wealth, knowledge, and other possible advantages (Verba, Schlozman, and Brady 1995). Finally, electoral participation shapes citizens in important ways. Through political participation, citizens learn about issues, government, and their place in the political community – they become "public-spirited" citizens (Pateman 1970, 29).

Low or declining voter turnout can signal an unhealthy democratic system. A longstanding theory, "Tingsten's law of dispersion," posits that whenever turnout is low, voters are less likely to reflect the characteristics and preferences of the broader public (Tingsten 1937; Lijphart 1997). One consequence is that governments elected by a relatively small, unrepresentative subset of the electorate might be less responsive to the desires of most members of the political community. Another concern is the inequalities in "voice" that arise when voters do not reflect the characteristics and preferences of the broader public: some social groups (whether they are defined by class, gender, region, race, or ethnicity) may be underrepresented, while others are overrepresented among voters relative to their size of the population.

Given its significance, it is perhaps surprising that until the late 1990s, scholars paid scant attention to voter turnout in Canada. A precipitous decline in voter turnout in federal and provincial elections in the late twentieth and early twenty-first century, however, led to a new focus on electoral participation as scholars sought to better understand and explain the causes of the decline. This chapter documents that shift in attention and assesses what scholars have learned about voter turnout in Canada. The proliferation of studies of Canadian electoral participation over the last 30 years has broadly shown us the many factors that influence the decision to vote or abstain, but important empirical questions remain about the decline in voter turnout and the implications of electoral participation for other features of democratic government.

EVOLUTION OF THE STUDY OF VOTER TURNOUT IN CANADA

1960–1990: Arrested Development

Although few would argue that voter turnout does not matter, for some time it barely registered as a subject of study in Canada. From the 1960s to the early 1990s, discussions about voter turnout were subsumed in investigations of political participation more generally. Mishler's in-depth study, *Political Participation in Canada* (1979), considers voting as one form of electoral participation, along with such campaign activities as attending rallies, canvassing for candidates, and donating money to parties and campaigns. Moreover, Mishler also devotes considerable attention to such non-electoral activities as contacting public officials, joining voluntary groups, and attending protests. Similarly, Clarke and colleagues' detailed study of Canadian voters, *Political Choice in Canada* (1979), observed very little about voter turnout per se, seeing it as one aspect of political participation. Indeed, their interest was less in political activity than in what might be revealed about orientations to the federal system by examining differences in federal and provincial political participation. They concluded that Canadians were not inclined to participate in one level more than the other, despite their observation that the single largest difference in federal and provincial participation was in rates of voter turnout (Clarke et al. 1979).

Early studies generally painted a rosy portrait of voter turnout in terms of the percentage of eligible Canadians who voted regularly, but they were less upbeat about voting as a form of political participation when compared to other activities. To the extent that scholars assessed Canadian turnout at all, they stressed that it was not the kind of activity that highlighted the best features of democratic citizenship. Van Loon (1970), adapting Milbrath's hierarchy of political participation, saw voting as an undemanding low-commitment activity when compared to joining a party or working on a campaign, and he argued that Canadians' relatively high levels of voting, compared to other activities, did not indicate they were satisfied with politics and government. Rather, Canadians were for the most part political spectators who voted but had little sense that they could influence politics. Subsequent studies largely echoed Van Loon's observations. Mishler notes that most Canadian voters seem to be influenced by "styles and personalities" of candidates rather than by their stances on political issues, and "many of those who do vote display few of the attributes characteristic of the model democrat" (Mishler 1979, 42). Clarke and his colleagues likewise lament what they see as the negative effects of the Canadian party system on citizen participation in federal politics. They argue the brokerage system, wherein Canadian political parties tend to obscure their policy differences, "turns the electoral process into a spectator sport for those who enjoy 'horseraces' rather than an exercise in informed citizen participation" (Clarke et al. 1991, 37).

The lack of attention to turnout, and the emphasis on the (low) quality of electoral participation over turnout rates, might be traced to the same root cause: there was not a lot to say about turnout rates in Canada before the 1990s. Voter turnout in Canada tended to not be high, but certainly not low when compared to other industrial democracies. In one of the very first examinations of voter participation in Canada, Scarrow observed that compared to the United States, turnout was "relatively high" in the first half of the twentieth century, "usually in the 70 percent range" (Scarrow 1961, 352–3). Canadian electoral participation was comparable to turnout in United Kingdom parliamentary elections, where turnout was typically between 70–80% in the twentieth century (Uberoi 2023). Perhaps just as significantly, there was little noteworthy variation across time in Canadian voter turnout levels for most of the twentieth century. As Pammett noted in 1991 (33), "Since the Second World War, it has been normal for three-quarters of the eligible voters to cast ballots in Canadian federal elections. The percentage voting in any given election has varied somewhat from the norm, but has done so within a fairly narrow range." Social scientists are interested in variation across time and place, and voter turnout in Canada did not change much over time and was not markedly different from other places.

1991: The Lortie Commission Studies

Greater attention to voter turnout at the federal level in the late 1980s was prompted by the Royal Commission on Electoral Reform and Party Financing. Eagles (1991) and Pammett (1991) produced analyses on aggregate and individual-level variations in turnout, respectively, as part of the research program for the Commission. That pair of studies is noteworthy for being among the first to empirically test explanations for Canadian electoral participation grounded in broad theories of participation.

In the decades leading up to Eagles, and Pammett's studies, a set of theories had been developing about the determinants of political participation (Blais 2000). The first, and initially most prominent, the calculus of voting model, emphasized the costs and expected benefits of voting and their significance to an individual citizen's decision about whether to vote or abstain: if the latter outweigh the former, a citizen turns out to vote (Downs 1957; Riker and Ordeshook 1968). Other models of participation subsequently emerged, initially to account for particular features of American participation. The socioeconomic status (SES) model, developed to account for enduring differences in political participation among citizens from different socioeconomic backgrounds (Verba, Schlozman, and Brady 1995), argues that time, money, and civic skills are valuable resources that facilitate political participation, and these are related to high education and income. *Mobilization* models stress the role of political parties and other organizations in inducing citizens to participate both by pressuring them to turn out to vote and reducing the costs of voting by providing information and resources that make it easier to cast a ballot (Rosenstone and Hansen 1993). Finally, a less theoretically cohesive school of thought focuses on sociopsychological factors (Blais 2000; Rolfe 2012): this includes motivational factors like political interest, but also social interaction and peer pressure.

Collectively, the studies by Eagles and Pammett would touch on many of these factors. Using data at the federal electoral district level, Eagles examined the roles of socioeconomic resources and political mobilization in voter turnout. His expectation that turnout would be higher in districts with greater concentrations of residents with higher incomes and educations, and those in professional and managerial occupations, was supported by the data (although income exerted a clearer influence than either education or occupation) (Eagles 1991). Eagles also anticipated higher turnout in more competitive districts, where candidates and their parties would make a greater effort to mobilize voters, but the data were less supportive of that hypothesis. Pammett, examining individual-level survey data, also focused on the impact of socioeconomic factors on voting and abstaining. Like Eagles, his results were mixed: there was evidence that higher incomes and professional and managerial occupations were linked with turnout, but education had no noteworthy effect. However, Pammett also considered the high costs associated with voting for some people, which he termed "administrative disenfranchisement" (Pammett 1991, 39). Describing these costs as "the way in which some electoral procedures inhibit voting by presenting difficulties to participation that, although not technically insurmountable, require extra effort," Pammett (1991, 35) found these barriers to be a noteworthy cause of abstention. Pammett also noted two psychological correlates of voter turnout: political interest and a sense of political efficacy – that is, the sense that one can exert an influence on politics.

2001–2010: Voter Turnout Crisis, Renewed Attention, and the Generational Gap

It would be a decade before another significant study of voter turnout in Canada appeared. Indeed, in the years between the Eagles and Pammett studies and Donley Studlar's 2001 investigation of federal and provincial electoral participation, major books on the 1988 and 1997 Canadian elections (Johnston et al. 1992; Nevitte et al. 2000) and the 1992 Canadian referendum on the Charlottetown Accord (Johnston et al. 1996) were silent on the matter of voter turnout. Studlar's study of federal and provincial turnout over the 1945–1998 period demonstrated that many of the aggregate determinants of turnout were largely similar at both the federal and provincial levels in Canada, and, consistent with Eagles' earlier work (Eagles 1991), "political variables" (for example, those related to how parties mobilize voters by urging them to vote) were less important than sociodemographic factors in determining turnout (Studlar 2001, 316).

However, greater attention to this phenomenon did not occur until a clear pattern of declining voter turnout emerged at the federal level around the turn of the last century. Figure 15.1 illustrates this dynamic. From 1988 and 2008, federal turnout fell in six consecutive elections from 75.3% to 58.8% – a staggering annualized rate of 0.825%. It is worth noting as well that provincial election

Figure 15.1. Turnout in Canadian Federal Elections, 1945–2021

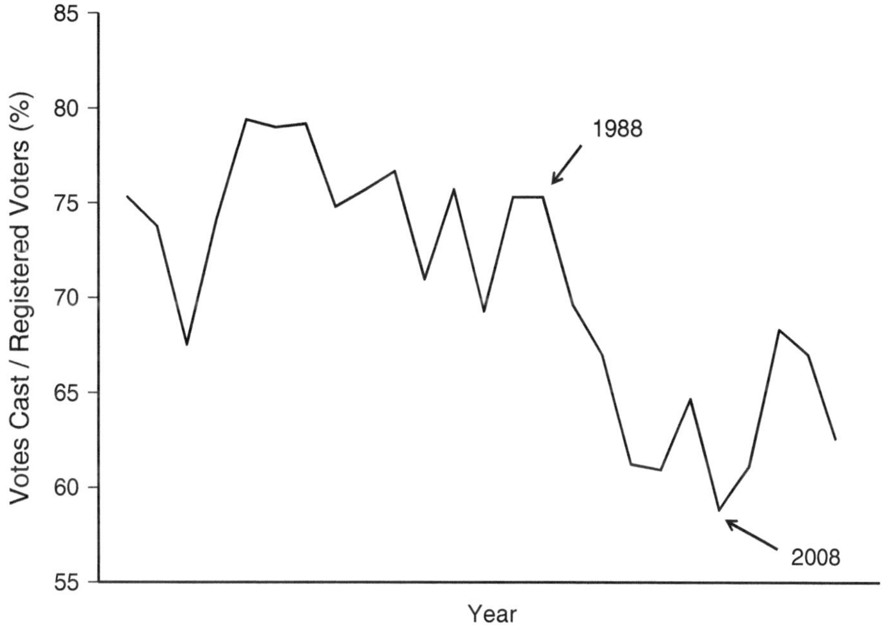

Source: Elections Canada.

turnout also generally declined during this period, and indeed the drop in some provinces appears to have preceded the federal decline. For example, in Canada's two most populous provinces, Ontario and Quebec, provincial voter turnout fell at an annual rate of 0.51% and 0.22%, respectively, in the period from 1970 to 1994. The decline continued in the period from 1995 to 2019, with annualized turnout declines of 0.39% and 0.35% in Ontario and Quebec.[1]

A flurry of research followed in the early 2000s as researchers sought to account for plummeting electoral participation in Canada. The most prominent and enduring of these explanations hinged on a unique combination of factors: generational change and citizens' sense of civic duty (Blais et al. 2004). Scholars in Canada (Pammett 1991; Rubenson et al. 2004) and elsewhere (Franklin, Lyons, and Marsh 2004) had long noted that older citizens demonstrated a greater propensity to vote. This was often attributed to movement through the life course: older voters are more deeply embedded in their communities and because they are more likely to have careers and families, they are more likely to view the electoral stakes as being significant. However, a person's age can stand for any number of things, including the period in which they were born and raised; one broad set of social scientific theories argues that the social, economic, and political environment to which people are exposed in the early, "impressionable" years of life – sometime between adolescence and early adulthood – leaves a lasting imprint on their attitudes and beliefs. Since social, economic, and political environments change over time, generations can emerge with unique attitudes and beliefs that distinguish them from earlier and subsequent generations (Sears and Brown 2013).

Blais and colleagues (2002 and 2004) argued that much of the difference in voter turnout between young and old Canadians could be credited to generational change: the "impressionable years" of younger voters had fostered attitudes and beliefs that did not promote political participation. Using data from multiple Canada election studies, Blais and colleagues (2002) empirically demonstrated that some of the age difference in turnout was in fact a generational difference. Age mattered, to be sure, but even greater were differences in the propensity to vote between more and less recent generations, or *birth cohorts* – groups of people born and raised in the same period and subject to shared environmental influences. Successive new generations have been less and less likely to vote than earlier generations. Moreover, Blais and colleagues (2002) were able to show that most of the aggregate decline in turnout from 1988 to 2000 could be explained by *generational replacement*, or the entry into the electorate of new generations of citizens with a low propensity to vote, and the gradual exit of older generations who were more inclined to vote.

What was the reason for this generational difference? In another study, Blais and colleagues (2004) focused on a factor that had to that point received only a modest amount of attention: the idea that citizens in democratic countries feel they have a moral obligation to vote, that to not vote is simply *wrong*. Mishler (1979, 42) had long ago noted that "[f]or many citizens the act of voting appears to be regarded as *little more* than a civic obligation" [emphasis added], but Blais had subsequently investigated a sense of civic duty as a motivation to vote in a book-length treatment of voter turnout and determined that "[d]uty is the overriding motivation for a clear majority of voters" (Blais 2000, 112). Blais and colleagues' 2004 study, "Where Does Turnout Decline Come From?," considered whether generational differences in orientations to voting as a moral duty might account for declining voter turnout in Canada. It showed that most of the generational differences in turnout could be explained by more recent birth cohorts' lower sense of duty and relative inattentiveness to politics.

The generational account of turnout decline appears to have been widely accepted – that is, few have offered alternative explanations for the decline that do not implicate birth cohort differences. One notable exception was Black's (2003) argument that changes in voter registration in the late 1990s negatively affected turnout. Black did not oppose the generational argument, but instead contended that another factor contributing to the decline was the shift from enumeration – the practice of canvassing from door to door at the time of an election to verify and record who was eligible to vote – to using a permanent register of electors in the Canadian federal election of 2000. The use of a permanent register, Black argued, imposes non-trivial voter registration costs on those who are not already on the register.

Aside from Black's argument, research in the first decade of the 2000s focused on alternative explanations for the generational gap in Canadian voter turnout. The three most prominent alternative explanations focus on the competitiveness of elections (Johnston, Matthews, and Bittner 2007), media consumption and civic literacy (Milner 2003), and broader sociocultural change (Howe 2010). Adapting the theoretical arguments of Franklin (2004) and Plutzer (2002), Johnston, Matthews, and Bittner (2007) demonstrated that from 1988 to 2004, newly eligible voters were particularly sensitive to the level of competition in their federal electoral district: the less competitive, the less likely they were to vote. For Milner (2004), a lack of civic literacy among recent generations is the problem. Indeed, his research, like that of others (Wattenberg 2015), showed that at the national level, newspaper consumption is linked to a more politically informed citizenry and to higher turnout, whereas television consumption appeared to have the opposite effects. "When it comes to explaining declining turnout," he argues, "the analysis suggests that a major factor explaining such diminishing in political participation in the United States, Canada, the United Kingdom and other countries where this has

Figure 15.2. "Voting Is a Duty" by Birth Cohort

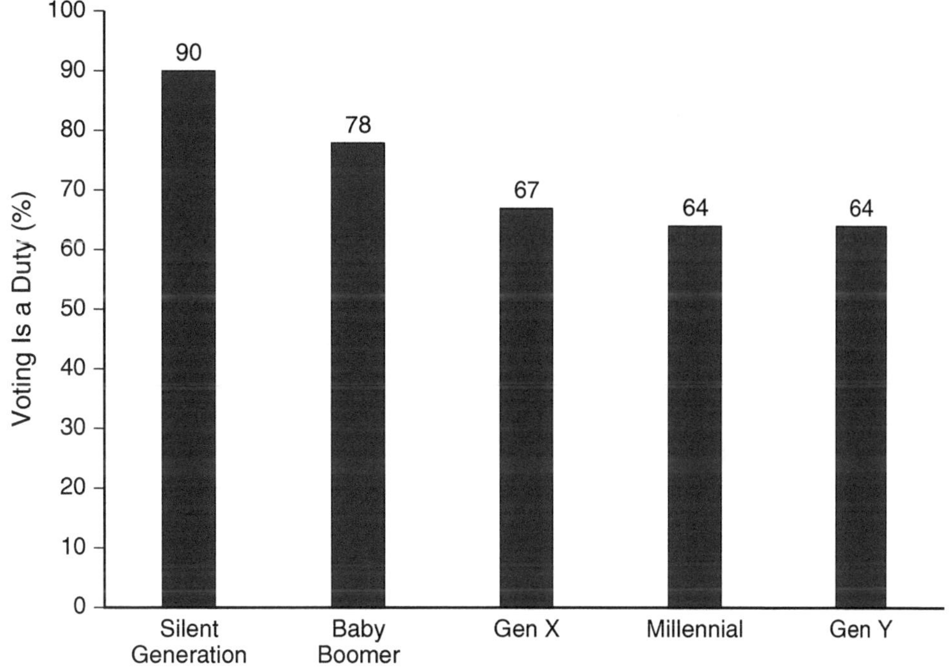

Source: 2021 Canadian Election Study.

been taking place has been the arrival at maturity of generations for whom reading the newspaper is not part of their normal daily lives" (Milner 2004, 185). Howe (2010) contends that younger generations' withdrawal from politics is caused by factors outside of politics. For Howe, the development and subsequent entrenchment of adolescence as a distinct life stage over the course of the twentieth century can account for these generational differences in political engagement. Younger people are increasingly individualistic in ways that are not conducive to electoral participation.

While none of these generational explanations are necessarily mutually exclusive, none seems as persuasive as the civic duty account. More recently, Blais and Rubenson, analyzing a vast amount of information – individual-level data from 83 elections in eight countries, district-level data from more than 30 years of British elections, and panel data from US presidential elections – concluded that generational effects on voter turnout are pervasive, and changes in political norms and values (including civic duty) is the primary cause (Blais and Rubenson 2013).

The evidence from the most recent Canadian Election Study in 2021 suggests that sense of civic duty remains a powerful explanation for turnout in Canada. When asked whether they personally viewed voting first and foremost as a duty or a choice, 71% of respondents said it was a duty and only 29% said it was a choice.[2] Those views were strongly related to reported turnout: 94% of respondents who stated that voting was a duty reported voting in the September 2021 federal election, whereas only 69% of those who stated that voting was a choice reported voting. Moreover, as Figure 15.2 illustrates, there are stark generational differences in views about voting as a duty. Nine in ten members of the so-called "Silent

Generation" (those born before the end of World War II) believe voting is a duty rather than a choice, whereas only 78% of "Baby Boomers" (born 1945–1964), 67% of "Generation X" (born 1965–1979), and 64% of "Millennials" (born 1980–1996) and "Generation Y" (born after 1996) believe voting is a duty.

2010–2023: New Directions

Significantly, the flurry of research activity focused on voter turnout in Canada in the early 2000s also seems to have had a lasting impact. Efforts to better understand the nature of the sense of duty to vote and related factors has been one significant area of research, and that work has extended well beyond Canada. However, research has also grown in other areas, including the costs and benefits of voting, provincial voter turnout, and heterogeneity in turnout among different social groups.

Recent research on the origins and consequences of the sense of duty to vote has furthered our understanding of its pivotal role in voting, but it has also drawn attention to the role of social norms and social pressure more generally. Galais (2018) uses a unique set of panel data that tracked participants from childhood to young adulthood to show the importance of early socialization, especially the role of family socialization, in the development of a strong sense of civic duty among young Canadians. Other work has sought to understand the effects of social pressure and conformity on electoral participation. Blais, Galais, and Coulombe (2019), for example, use studies in British Columbia and Quebec to demonstrate that social pressure can influence turnout: knowing that friends and family are voting, especially one's spouse or partner, is a strong incentive to vote. A person's degree of conformity – that is, their willingness to change behaviour to match the behaviour of those around them – also appears to be important: "conformist voters have an added incentive to 'follow the pack' and vote when turnout is high while abstain when turnout is low" (Blais and Hortala-Vallve 2021, 1395).

Other research has turned back to the effects of the perceived costs and expected benefits of voting. Sevi and Blais (2022), for example, find that Canadian voters who learn the cost of voting is low in one election will then apply that lesson to subsequent elections. Santana and Aguilar (2021) show a gender gap in the perceived costs of voting in Canada and other countries: women, and especially women with children, see the costs of voting as higher. Even seemingly trivial costs matter, as Stockemer and Wigginton (2018) demonstrate: examining federal elections from 2004 to 2015, they show that more precipitation and lower temperatures reduce turnout in federal elections. Other have considered how voting procedures and regulations might raise or lower the costs of voting. Goodman and Stokes (2020), for instance, show that Ontario municipalities that use internet voting have higher voter turnout because of the relatively lower costs in terms of time and effort to vote online. The expected benefits of voting also have clear effects: Using 2019 Canadian Election Study data, Cutler et al. (2022) find that citizens' stated likelihood of voting increases with their preferred party's perceived chances of winning in their federal electoral district. Caruana and colleagues (2015) find citizens are motivated to turn out to defeat parties they particularly dislike.

Recent work has also sought to examine whether the many factors that influence voter participation operate differently for members of particular social groups, particularly members of historically marginalized communities. As mentioned, Santana and Aguilar (2021) show that Canadian men and women perceive the costs of voting differently. Dabin, Daoust, and Papillon (2019) find that turnout in Indigenous communities in federal elections from 2006 to 2015 was higher in districts with Indigenous candidates. However, in some instances, members of historically marginalized groups behave in much the same way as the rest of the population, despite their varied experiences. Armstrong, Alcantara, and Kennedy (2021), for example, unexpectedly found that the size of electorates in five Inuit communities affected federal turnout in much the same way as in the rest of Canada: districts with smaller populations generally had higher turnout. White (2023) found that Canadian immigrants exhibited the same "generational" turnout pattern in federal elections as their Canadian-born co-citizens.

CONCLUSION

While voter turnout in Canadian federal elections appeared to rebound in 2015 and 2019, it is far from certain that the long-term decline in electoral participation has slowed or reversed. After reaching lows of 58.8% and 61.1% in 2008 and 2011, respectively, turnout rose to 68.3% and 67% in the 2015 and 2019 federal contests. However, turnout fell once again to 62.6% in the 2021 federal election (although it is unclear the extent to which the COVID-19 pandemic was responsible for lower turnout in that election). Moreover, turnout trends in some provinces remain particularly worrisome. As detailed earlier, Ontario and Quebec have witnessed a long-term decline in provincial voter turnout since the 1970s. In the 2022 Ontario provincial election, turnout reached an unprecedented low of only 44%. Quebec voter turnout in the last two provincial elections (2018 and 2022) was only 66% – the second-lowest turnout in the last 50 years. In British Columbia, turnouts in the last three provincial elections rank as the lowest (54% in 2020) and third and fourth lowest (61% and 57% in 2017 and 2013, respectively) in the last 50 years.

Despite the growth in research, several "big picture" questions about voter turnout in Canada remain. First, are the ultimate sources of turnout decline in Canada rooted in politics or something else? It seems clear that falling turnout in Canada is a consequence of generational replacement and that more recent generations have a weaker sense of civic duty. Moreover, Canada does not appear to be unique in this regard. But *why* do more recent generations have a weaker sense of civic duty? No one has yet offered a satisfying answer to that question. To what extent is that weakened sense of civic duty the result of distinctly political factors (for example, the changing relationship between citizens and the state) and to what extent is it a feature, or perhaps even a by-product, of broader social changes? Low turnout and a waning sense of civic duty might be symptoms of deeper problems in established democratic systems like Canada. Galais (2018) and others have started the work of better understanding the origins of the sense of duty, and perhaps this, rather than turnout per se, ought to be the focus of more research. Why is this important? When it comes to identifying solutions to declining turnout, understanding the extent to which the root causes are located within the political system or within society more broadly is crucial.

Second, the continuing inattention to voter turnout at the provincial level is striking. There has been some progress. The Armstrong, Alcantara, and Kennedy (2021) study of Inuit communities mentioned earlier, for example, examines turnout at provincial, regional, and federal levels. Siaroff and Wesley (2015) and Thorlakson (2015) have investigated provincial turnout. Examining every provincial election from 1965 to 2014, Siaroff and Wesley (2015) find turnout is higher in competitive elections and systems with multipartism, in provinces where the working class is more mobilized, and in provinces where identification with the provincial community is strong. Likewise, Thorlakson (2015, 164) uses individual-level and contextual data to show that "interest in provincial politics is one of the strongest predictors of high provincial turnout relative to federal turnout." Nevertheless, we know much less about provincial turnout than federal turnout.

Third, what have been the *consequences* of voter turnout in Canada? Far less is known about this. Does electoral participation foster good citizenship, as Pateman (1970) suggests? What is its impact on political efficacy, interest, and knowledge in Canada? There is some evidence of a positive effect of turnout on political efficacy in the United States (Clark and Acock 1989; Finkel 1985 and 1987). However, determining causality is a significant challenge: does behaviour cause attitudes, or do attitudes cause behaviour? Kostelka and Blais (2018) demonstrate that turning out to vote in national and subnational elections is associated with greater satisfaction with democracy. Quintelier and van Deth (2014) show that political engagement has positive effects on political efficacy and other political attitudes in Belgium. Could the same be true in Canada? Blais and colleagues (2004) and Stockemer and Rocher (2017), for example, show a link between political knowledge and turnout, but to what extent does knowledge foster participation, and to what extent does electoral participation actually motivate Canadians to learn more about politics? There are also questions about the effects of turnout on representation and equality. Examining the 2000 Canadian Election Study, Rubenson and colleagues (2007) found that across a broad range of policy areas, voter opinions were not appreciably different from those of non-voters. They concluded that "[v]oters' opinions are, by and large, representative of the larger population and universal turnout would not have changed the election result" (Rubenson et al. 2007, 589), but recent work by Godbout and Turgeon (2019) challenges the claim that the preferences of Canadian voters mirror those of the broader population. Moreover, as turnout has declined, there is good reason to be concerned that this problem with representation has grown. Finally, does high turnout enhance the legitimacy of elected governments in Canada? Early studies suggested participation did in fact promote support for elections (Nadeau and Blais 1993), but at the same time supporting a winning candidate or party, either locally or nationally, boosts satisfaction with democracy in Canada (Blais and Gelineau 2007).

NOTES

1 Calculated by the author from provincial data.
2 The question wording is: "People have different views about voting. For some, voting is a *duty*. They feel that they should vote in every election. For others, voting is a *choice*. They only vote when they feel strongly about that election. For you personally, is voting *first and foremost* a Duty or a Choice?" Data were weighted according to province, as well as gender, age group, and education level using the weight variable pes21_weight_general_all. The number of observations is 14,734.

REFERENCES

Anderson, C.J., A. Blais, S. Bowler, T. Donovan, and O. Listhaug. 2005. *Losers' Consent: Elections and Democratic Legitimacy*. Oxford: Oxford University Press.
Armstrong, D.A., C. Alcantara, and J. Kennedy. 2023. "Exploring the Effects of Electorate Size on Indigenous Voter Turnout." *Politics, Groups, and Identities* 11 (1): 98–107. https://doi.org/10.1080/21565503.2021.1926297.

Black, J.H. 2003. "From Enumeration to the National Register of Electors: An Account and an Evaluation." *Choices* 9 (7). https://irpp.org/research-studies/choices-vol9-no7/.

Blais, A. 2000. *To Vote or Not to Vote?: The Merits and Limits of Rational Choice Theory*. Pittsburgh: University of Pittsburgh Press.

Blais, A., C. Galais, and M. Coulombe. 2019. "The Effect of Social Pressure from Family and Friends on Turnout." *Journal of Social and Personal Relationships* 36 (9): 2824–41. https://doi.org/10.1177/0265407518802463.

Blais, A., and F. Gélineau. 2007. "Winning, Losing, and Satisfaction with Democracy." *Political Studies* 55 (2): 425–41. https://doi.org/10.1111/j.1467-9248.2007.00659.x.

Blais, A., E. Gidengil, R. Nadeau, and N. Nevitte. 2002. *Anatomy of a Liberal Victory: Making Sense of the Vote in the 2000 Canadian Election*. Toronto: University of Toronto Press.

Blais, A., E. Gidengil, and N. Nevitte. 2004. "Where Does Turnout Decline Come From?" *European Journal of Political Research* 43 (2): 221–36. https://doi.org/10.1111/j.1475-6765.2004.00152.x.

Blais, A., and R. Hortala-Vallve. 2016. "Are People More of Less Inclined to Vote When Aggregate Turnout is High?" In *Voting Experiments*, edited by A. Blais, J.F. Laslier, and K. Van der Straeten, 117–25. Cham: Springer.

Blais, A., and D. Rubenson. 2013. "The Source of Turnout Decline: New Values or New Contexts?" *Comparative Political Studies* 46 (1): 95–117. https://doi.org/10.1177/0010414012453032.

Brooks, C., and J. Manza. 2008. *Why Welfare States Persist: The Importance of Public Opinion in Democracies*. Chicago: University of Chicago Press.

Caruana, N.J., R.M. McGregor, and L.B. Stephenson. 2015. "The Power of the Dark Side: Negative Partisanship and Political Behaviour in Canada." *Canadian Journal of Political Science/Revue canadienne de science politique* 48 (4): 771–89. https://doi.org/10.1017/S0008423914000882.

Clarke, H.D. and A.C. Acock. 1989. "National Elections and Political Attitudes: The Case of Political Efficacy." *British Journal of Political Science* 19 (4): 551–62. https://doi.org/10.1017/S0007123400005639.

Clarke, H.D., J. Jenson, L. LeDuc, and J.H. Pammett. 1979. *Political Choice in Canada*. Toronto: McGraw-Hill Ryerson.

Clarke, H.D., J. Jenson, L. LeDuc, and J.H. Pammett. 1991. *Absent Mandate: Interpreting Change in Canadian Elections*. 2nd ed. Toronto: McGraw-Hill Ryerson.

Cutler, F., A. Rivard, and A. Hodgson. 2022. "Why Bother? Supporters of Locally Weaker Parties Are Less Likely to Vote or to Vote Sincerely." *Canadian Journal of Political Science/Revue canadienne de science politique* 55 (1): 208–25. https://doi.org/10.1017/S0008423921000755.

Dabin, S., J.F. Daoust, and M. Papillon. 2019. "Indigenous Peoples and Affinity Voting in Canada." *Canadian Journal of Political Science/Revue canadienne de science politique* 52 (1): 39–53. https://doi.org/10.1017/S0008423918000574.

Downs, A. 1957. *An Economic Theory of Democracy*. New York: Harper and Row.

Eagles, M. 1991. "Voting and Non-Voting in Canadian Federal Elections: An Ecological Analysis." In *Voter Turnout in Canada*, edited by H. Bakvis, 3–32. Toronto: Dundurn Press.

Finkel, Steven E. 1985. "Reciprocal Effects of Participation and Political Efficacy: A Panel Analysis." *American Journal of Political Science* 29 (4): 891–913. https://doi.org/10.2307/2111186.

Finkel, Steven E. 1987. "The Effects of Participation on Political Efficacy and Political Support." *Journal of Politics* 49 (3): 441–64. https://doi.org/10.2307/2131308.

Franklin, Mark N. 2004. *Voter Turnout and the Dynamics of Electoral Competition in Established Democracies since 1945*. Cambridge: Cambridge University Press.

Franklin, M.N., P. Lyons, and M. Marsh. 2004. "Generational Basis of Turnout Decline in Established Democracies." *Acta politica* 39: 115–51. https://doi.org/10.1057/palgrave.ap.5500060.

Galais, C. 2018. "How to Make Dutiful Citizens and Influence Turnout: The Effects of Family and School Dynamics on the Duty to Vote." *Canadian Journal of Political Science/Revue canadienne de science politique* 51 (3): 599–617. https://doi.org/10.1017/S0008423918000021.

Godbout, J.F., and M. Turgeon. 2012. "The Preferences of Voters and Non-voters in Canada (1988–2008)." In *Duty and Choice: The Evolution of the Study of Voting and Voters*, edited by P.J. Loewen and D. Rubenson, 81–104. Toronto: University of Toronto Press.

Goodman, N., and L.C. Stokes. 2020. "Reducing the Cost of Voting: An Evaluation of Internet Voting's Effect on Turnout." *British Journal of Political Science* 50 (3): 1155–67. https://doi.org/10.1017/S0007123417000849.

Howe, P. 2010. *Citizens Adrift: The Demographic Disengagement of Young Canadians*. Vancouver: UBC Press.

Johnston, R., A. Blais, H.E. Brady, and J. Crete. 1992. *Letting the People Decide: The Dynamics of Canadian Elections*. Stanford: Stanford University Press.

Johnston, R., A. Blais, E. Gidengil, and N. Nevitte. 1996. *The Challenge of Direct Democracy: The 1992 Canadian Referendum*. Montreal: McGill-Queen's University Press.

Johnston, R., J.S. Matthews, and A. Bittner. 2007. "Turnout and the Party System in Canada, 1988–2004." *Electoral Studies* 26 (4): 735–45. https://doi.org/10.1016/j.electstud.2007.08.002.

Kostelka, F., and A. Blais. 2018. "The Chicken and Egg Question: Satisfaction with Democracy and Voter Turnout." *PS: Political Science & Politics* 51 (2): 370–76. https://doi.org/10.1017/S1049096517002050.

Lijphart A. 1997. "Unequal Participation: Democracy's Unsolved Dilemma." *American Political Science Review* 91 (1): 1–14. https://doi.org/10.2307/2952255.

Miller, W.L., S. White, and P. Heywood. 1998. *Values and Political Change in Postcommunist Europe*. London: Palgrave Macmillan.

Milner, H. 2003. "Civic Literacy in Global Civil Society: Excluding the Majority from Democratic Participation." In *Global Civil Society and its Limits*, edited by G. Laxer and S. Halperin, 189–209. London: Palgrave Macmillan.

———. 2004. "'Reading More Newspapers and Voting Less?' A Rejoinder to Pattie and Johnston." *Canadian Journal of Political Science/Revue canadienne de science politique* 37 (1): 185–88. https://doi.org/10.1017/S0008423904040090.

Mishler, W. 1979. *Political Participation in Canada: Prospects for Democratic Citizenship*. Toronto: Macmillan of Canada.

Nadeau, R., and A. Blais. 1993. "Accepting the Election Outcome: The Effect of Participation on Losers' Consent." *British Journal of Political Science* 23 (4): 553–63. https://doi.org/10.1017/S0007123400006736.

Nevitte, N., A. Blais, E. Gidengil, and R. Nadeau. 2000. *Unsteady State: The 1997 Canadian Federal Election*. Don Mills: Oxford University Press.

Pammett, J.H. 1991. "Voter Turnout in Canada." In *Voter Turnout in Canada*, edited by H. Bakvis, 33–60. Toronto: Dundurn Press.

Pateman, C. 1970. *Participation and Democratic Theory*. Cambridge: Cambridge University Press.

Plutzer, E. 2002. "Becoming a Habitual Voter: Inertia, Resources, and Growth in Young Adulthood." *American Political Science Review* 96 (1): 41–56. https://doi.org/10.1017/S0003055402004227.

Quintelier, E. and J.W. Van Deth. 2014. "Supporting Democracy: Political Participation and Political Attitudes. Exploring Causality Using Panel Data." *Political Studies* 62 (1): 153–71. https://doi.org/10.1111/1467-9248.12097.

Riker, W.H., and P.C. Ordeshook. 1968. "A Theory of the Calculus of Voting." *American Political Science Review* 62 (1): 25–42. https://doi.org/10.2307/1953324.

Rolfe, M. 2012. *Voter Turnout: A Social Theory of Political Participation*. New York: Cambridge University Press.

Rosenstone, S.J., and John Mark Hansen. 1993. *Mobilization, Participation, and Democracy in America*. New York: Macmillan.

Rubenson, D., A. Blais, P. Fournier, E. Gidengil, and N. Nevitte. 2004. "Accounting for the Age Gap in Turnout." *Acta Politica* 39: 407–21. https://doi.org/10.1057/palgrave.ap.5500079.

———. 2007. "Does Low Turnout Matter? Evidence from the 2000 Canadian Federal Election." *Electoral Studies* 26 (3): 589–97.

Santana, A., and S. Aguilar. 2021. "How Costly Is Voting? Explaining Individual Differences in the Cost of Voting." *Journal of Elections, Public Opinion and Parties* 31 (1): 119–39. https://doi.org/10.1080/17457289.2019.1658196.

Scarrow, H.A. 1961. "Patterns of Voter Turnout in Canada." *Midwest Journal of Political Science* 5 (4): 351–64.

Sears, D.O., and C. Brown. 2013. "Childhood and Adult Political Development." In *The Oxford Handbook of Political Psychology*, 2nd ed., edited by L. Huddy, D.O. Sears, and J.S. Levy, 59–95. Oxford: Oxford University Press.

Sevi, S., and A. Blais. 2022. "Does Voting in One Election Reduce the Expected Cost of Voting in Subsequent Elections?" *Canadian Journal of Political Science/Revue canadienne de science politique* 55 (2): 486–95. https://doi.org/10.1017/S0008423922000063.

Siaroff, A., and J.J. Wesley. 2015. "Comparative Voter Turnout in the Canadian Provinces since 1965: The Importance of Context." *Canadian Political Science Review* 9 (1): 147–63. https://doi.org/10.24124/c677/20151206.

Solijonov, A. 2016. *Voter Turnout Trends Around the World*. Stockholm: International Idea.

Stockemer, D., and F. Rocher. 2017. "Age, Political Knowledge and Electoral Turnout: A Case Study of Canada." *Commonwealth & Comparative Politics* 55 (1): 41–62. https://doi.org/10.1080/14662043.2017.1252896.

Stockemer, Daniel, and Michael Wigginton. 2018. "Fair Weather Voters: Do Canadians Stay at Home When the Weather Is Bad?" *International Journal of Biometeorology* 62: 1027–37. https://doi.org/10.1007/s00484-018-1506-6.

Studlar, D.T. 2001. "Canadian Exceptionalism: Explaining Differences Over Time in Provincial and Federal Voter Turnout." *Canadian Journal of Political Science/Revue canadienne de science politique* 34 (2): 299–319. https://doi.org/10.1017/S0008423901777918.

Thorlakson, L. 2015. "Explaining the Federal-Provincial Turnout Gap in the Canadian Provinces." *Canadian Political Science Review* 9 (1): 164–76. https://doi.org/10.24124/c677/20151207.

Tingsten H. 1937. *Political Behavior: Studies in Election Statistics*. London: PS King & Son, Ltd.

Uberoi, Elise. 2023. *Turnout at Elections. House of Commons Library Research Briefing.* Number 8060, January 10. https://researchbriefings.files.parliament.uk/documents/CBP-8060/CBP-8060.pdf.

Van Loon, Rick. 1970. "Political Participation in Canada: The 1965 Election." *Canadian Journal of Political Science/Revue canadienne de science politique* 3 (3): 376–99. https://doi.org/10.1017/S0008423900029784.

Verba, S., K.L. Schlozman, and H.E. Brady. 1995. *Voice and Equality: Civic Voluntarism in American Politics*. Cambridge: Harvard University Press.

Wattenberg, M.P. 2015. *Is Voting for Young People?* 4th ed. London: Routledge.

White, S.E. 2023. "Immigrant Voter Turnout and Time: Does Period of Arrival Matter More than Length of Stay?" *International Migration* 61 (6): 118–22. https://doi.org/10.1111/imig.13150.

CHAPTER SIXTEEN

Gender and Elections

Melanee Thomas

DEFINITION: WHAT IS GENDER?

Political science research, including research about elections, often (though erroneously) presents gender as synonymous with women. While perhaps understandable from a historical perspective, this conflation obfuscates gender's complex effects on elections in Canada and elsewhere.

Gender is a social construct created by people's interactions with one another; through these interactions, the boundaries about genders become accepted and defined. For elections scholars, at least two aspects of gender are salient. First, how people view and understand their own gender helps structure their behaviour, including if and how they vote (Gidengil 2007; Blais 2000), and their ambition for and interest in a political career (Pruysers and Blais 2019; Thomas 2012). Second, people use a candidate or leader's perceived gender to evaluate them (Cutler 2002; Trimble 2017).

These gendered evaluations are not neutral. Instead, they are based on stereotypic expectations about "appropriate" and "expected" behaviour for women and men (Schneider and Bos 2019). For example, because caring roles are disproportionately filled by women – think stay-at-home parents and nurses – the traits associated with being good at these caring roles are associated with women in general. Similarly, roles that are disproportionately filled by men tend to be associated less with care and compassion, more with strength and aggression. These social roles generate stereotypes – broad, blunt, overgeneralizations about a group – that subsequently proscribe traits and behaviours that are expected of someone because of their gender, regardless of the roles they actually fill. Individuals can then be sanctioned by others if their roles or behaviour are perceived to violate these stereotypical gender roles (Schneider and Bos 2019).

This is a key explanation for why women are evaluated differently in politics than men. Politicians are expected to be charismatic, ambitious, and strong; these traits align more closely with stereotypic expectations of men than women. Indeed, women in politics are stereotyped as having very few positive traits associated with politicians, women in general, or women professionals. As a result, unlike men, women in politics "are [stereotypically] defined more by their deficits than their strengths" (Schneider and Bos 2014, 260).

This pattern extends to women's perceived capacity for politics in general. About one in five Canadians, regardless of their ideology, partisanship, age, or education, agree that men are "naturally better" leaders than women and that women are both "too emotional" and "too nice" for politics (Chen et al. 2023). Knowing this makes it perhaps less surprising that Canadian electoral politics is still stereotyped as masculine and dominated by white men (Ouellet, Shiab, and Gilchrist 2021; Johnson et al. 2021b).

This context helps explain why analyses of gender and politics predominantly focus on women, rather than on men or gender identities beyond the binary. Men are viewed as the political norm, in part because their considerable overrepresentation in politics is not often problematized in politics or in research about it. As a result, women are viewed as "deviant" when they take, on average, different views, values, and beliefs or are differently engaged in politics than are men. While focusing on these gaps has produced significant insights, it also presents women and men as more homogenous groups than they are (Gidengil 2007) while ignoring gender identities beyond the binary.[1] With these caveats in mind, it is to that early research we now turn.

EVOLUTION – STUDYING GENDER, VOTERS, AND CANDIDATES OVER TIME

> Insofar as anyone constructs a world of politics or work the builders are men. This is the ultimate insult accorded the woman voter. But it is not, as we have endeavored to show, the only one. (Goot and Reid 1975, 35)

> We have also been witnessing the growing salience of – and sensitivity to – groups that have stood at the margins of the political mainstream. These include racial minorities and women. (Blais et al. 2002, 102)

Sexist Scientism: Studying Gender and Voters

Early studies of voting behaviour marked women as Schrödinger's Voter. Denied franchise rights as late as 1960 in Canada (Janovicek and Thomas 2018),[2] foundational texts on voting behaviour (Almond and Verba 1963; Campbell et al. 1960) argue that women voters "had little or no impact on politics" (Goot and Reid 1975, 5). Yet others argue that elections turned on women's support, such that leaders including Charles de Gaulle and Dwight Eisenhower owed their election to women. Women's voting behaviour either was so trivial that it was seen to have "no intrinsic importance" (Duverger 1955, quoted in Goot and Reid 1975, 5) or, it seems, was the reason why a country got "stuck," so to speak, with a particular election outcome. More detailed studies of early voting behaviour either ignored women entirely, castigated their motives and actions as "fickle," and/or explicitly argued that women's behaviour was dictated by the preferences of their fathers, husbands, or, if single, the man acting as the head of their household (Goot and Reid 1975). This early work is sexist in that it clearly views women as less worthy of study than men. It also argues that this sexist approach was ostensibly objective and unbiased because of its use of the scientific method, survey research, and quantitative analysis. Characterizing this early work as sexist scientism, as Goot and Reid did, is apt indeed.

Table 16.1. Monographs in Canada, 1962–2019: Gender and Election

Author(s)	Title	Publication Year	Index Mentions: Women	Index Mentions: Gender	Substantive Content
John Meisel	*The Canadian General Election of 1957*	1962	No	No	None
Harold Clarke, Jane Jenson, Lawrence LeDuc, and Jon Pammett	*Absent Mandate: The Politics of Discontent in Canada*	1984	No	No	None
Harold Clarke, Lawrence LeDuc, Jane Jenson, and Jon Pammett	*Absent Mandate: Interpreting Change in Canadian Elections*	1991	No	No	None
Richard Johnston and André Blais	*Letting the People Decide: Dynamics of a Canadian Election*	1992	No	No	None
Harold Clarke, Jane Jenson, Lawrence LeDuc, and Jon Pammett	*Absent Mandate: Canadian Electoral Politics in an Era of Restructuring*	1996	No	N=5	Gender gaps in prioritizing unemployment are observed; otherwise, gender is used as a sociodemographic control and is not analyzed.
André Blais, Elisabeth Gidengil, Richard Nadeau, and Neil Nevitte	*Anatomy of a Liberal Victory*	2000	N=37	N=17	Gender is presented as a key social cleavage, similar to religion and region; as a result, has meaningful analyses of women's voting behaviour throughout the book.
Elisabeth Gidengil, Neil Nevitte, André Blais, Joanna Everitt, and Patrick Fournier	*Dominance & Decline: Making Sense of Recent Canadian Elections*	2012	N=4	N=4	Gender presented as a "consequential factor" that explains election outcomes through gender gaps in value differences, political behaviour, and vote choice.
Harold Clarke, Jane Jenson, Lawrence LeDuc, and Jon Pammett	*Absent Mandate: Strategies and Choices in Canadian Elections*	2019	No	No	None

There are a few ways to trace how gender has been applied to electoral behaviour in Canada. Many foundational studies are published as monographs that use the Canadian Election Study, or CES (recall Chapter 14), to explain a given election outcome while applying and extending theories of voting behaviour to the Canadian context. These are listed in Table 16.1.[3] Most completely ignore women and gender as substantive analytical categories; another merely uses gender as a sociodemographic control. Only two of these – Blais and colleagues' *Anatomy of a Liberal Victory*, published in 2000 and Gidengil and colleagues' *Dominance and Decline*, published in 2012 – treat gender as a meaningful basis for analysis. Here, gender is measured as a binary (e.g., women and men) and presented as a social cleavage akin to region, religion, and ethnicity. Significant and meaningful gender gaps in how Canadians feel about issues, values and beliefs, economic voting, and vote choice show that gender is a "consequential" factor in Canadian elections (Gidengil et al. 2012). Yet, as is apparent from Clarke and colleagues (2019), it is (incredibly) still possible to publish a full monograph on electoral behaviour in Canada without mentioning women or gender once.

Gender is consequential for Canadian voters because women and men tend to differ, on average, in their values, beliefs, and issue positions, in political engagement, and in vote choice. Women tend to be more left-leaning in their values and beliefs than men, with women being more skeptical of market conservatism than men, and men being more socially conservative than women (Gidengil et al. 2012 and 2004; Gidengil 1995). These gender gaps help inform gender differences in partisanship, leader evaluations, and ultimately vote choice (Gidengil et al. 2012; Blais et al. 2002).

When women and men hold the same values or take the same issue positions, their reasons for doing so can differ, too. For example, some argue that a commitment to feminism and gender equality pushes women to the left. This was hypothesized to create an episodic tension on some issues, particularly connected to morality or tradition, when feminism or commitment to gender equality came into conflict with other identities, such as religion (O'Neill 2001). More recent research shows that many gender gaps in attitudes and issue positions disappear for women who report that their gender is not very important to how they see themselves. In contrast, women who "prioritize their gender identity more" tend to identify more with the left and take more left-leaning positions on issues (Bittner and Goodyear-Grant 2017, 574).

Much of this research on gender gaps focuses on what might be different about women's particular situation that may lead them to engage differently with politics than men, as well as on how larger gendered structures act to help produce these gender gaps. For example, situational factors highlight how a particular woman's occupation, family circumstances, educational attainment, and the like affect her interactions with politics. Structural factors address larger cultural ideas about the appropriateness of women's participation in the labour force and politics, as well as how open to gender equity a society might be. Situational and structural factors are presented as explanations for both the presence and variability of gender gaps over time (Inglehart and Norris 2000; Erickson and O'Neill 2002). This approach accepts, albeit in varying degrees, that men's position is the "norm." In so doing, it looks for explanations for gender gaps that focus on what's "different" about women compared to men.

This focus is much clearer in research that examines gender gaps in political engagement, such as political interest, knowledge, efficacy, and ambition. All these forms of political engagement are generally associated with higher levels of participation, suggesting that if gender gaps in political engagement close, then so too would other gender gaps in activities such as running for office. Notably, in Canada, women are more likely than men to vote and have been for some time (Elections Canada 2022; see also Stockemer and Sundstrom 2023). It is striking, then, though perhaps less surprising, that other gender gaps in political engagement are stable in the face of significant changes to gendered situational and structural factors over time. Instead, sexism appears to help explain why women appear less interested in politics than men, both with respect to biased scholarship (Glenn and Grimes 1968), as well as with respect to how women in the past have perceived their own political interest (Bennett and Bennett 1989). Women appear to know less about politics than men, but these political knowledge measures are biased in at least two ways. First, men are more reluctant than women to say "I don't know," even when that's the honest answer. Second, most measures of political knowledge included in election studies focus on naming politicians – something men tend to do better than women. When questions focus on policy knowledge, women tend to outperform men (Stolle and Gidengil 2010). In general, while some research suggests that gender gaps in socioeconomic resources may explain why women are less politically engaged than men (Burns, Schlozman, and Verba 2001), evidence from Canada shows that changing women's situational or larger structural factors cannot explain much about these gender gaps in political engagement over time (Thomas 2012).

Research into one particular gender gap in political engagement – political ambition – tends to take a different approach. Unlike political interest, knowledge, and efficacy, ambition for a career in electoral politics is relatively uncommon for women and men alike. Here, research shows that negative gender stereotypes about women and politics explain much of this gender gap. For example, in experimental settings, women exposed to negative stereotypes report much lower levels of political ambition than women presented with more neutral content about politics (Pruysers and Blais 2017). Similarly, when men are presented with experimentally manipulated news content that sexually trivializes a man in politics, men's levels of ambition drop to women's. Women's political ambition, by contrast, does not appear to change when they read a news story that objectifies women politicians (Pruysers, Thomas, and Blais 2020). This may be because sexist stereotypes about women are still relatively common in Canadian politics (Chen et al. 2023).

In focusing on gender gaps, research investigating gender and voters in Canada has two serious pitfalls. First, by focusing on the differences between women and men, it ignores the significant diversity among women, as well as areas where women and men may be in broad agreement (Gidengil 2007). Unsurprisingly, given the content in Chapter 17, few studies examine how gender and other forms of diversity interact in Canadian politics, particularly with respect to race. Those that do focus on Indigeneity, immigration, or sexual orientation. For example, settler colonialism generates significantly different gender gaps among Indigenous persons than it does amongst settlers, even though some of these gender gaps (e.g., in vote choice) appear similar on the surface (Harell and Panagos 2013). Immigrant women are significantly less likely to participate in politics than women who were born in Canada; this gap is smallest for immigrant women with strong social networks that help them generate access to socioeconomic resources (Gidengil and Stolle 2009). And while gender affinity effects – voting for someone because of a shared gender – are weak for women in Canada (Goodyear-Grant and Croskill 2011), there is some evidence to suggest that non-LGBT women were more likely to support a political party when it chose an out lesbian as its leader (Albaugh and Baisley 2023; also see Chapter 19). These nuances and complexities of women's voting behaviour are missed when research focuses only on gender gaps between women and men.

Research lags, too, with respect to how gender affects men's voting behaviour. This may be an artifact of taking men's behaviour as the "default" or "norm," as outlined above. Certainly, research documenting gender gaps shows how men's values, beliefs, and issue positions are different than women's. Yet, research examining men and masculinity generates important insights in its own right. Men are more likely to adopt positions on the political right, dismiss men's overrepresentation (and women's underrepresentation) as a problem, and prefer men in positions of political leadership (Bittner and Goodyear-Grant 2017), particularly after men are told a woman has beaten them in an experimental competition (Mansell et al. 2022). This perceived threat to men's masculinity, relative performance, and status increases men's reported sexism (Mansell et al. 2022) and is also associated with vote choice (Mutz 2018; Gidengil and Stolle 2021). But, like women, men are not a monolith and the men whose behaviour best fits these patterns are strongly committed to a narrow, heterosexist version of masculinity. LGBT men do not appear to fit this pattern (Albaugh and Baisley 2023).

Stalled: Studying Gender, Parties, and Candidates

It would be tempting to assume that after women were granted franchise rights, it was as if a switch flipped and women's presence as candidates for public office and as elected representatives steadily increased. A cursory glance at Figure 16.1, which tracks the proportion of women candidates and MPs in federal elections in Canada over time, suggests this may not be an unreasonable conclusion. Yet while women's presence as candidates and MPs has increased over time, it has also stalled and backslid. Understanding why is key to understanding how gender shapes campaigns and elections in Canada.

In the first elections after Confederation, women's right to vote and run for office in Canada varied, with property and race-based exclusions. Depending on which part of Canada they lived in, white women were able to vote and run for office decades before women of South and East Asian descent, as well as women who practised some non-Christian religions. Until 1960, Indigenous women who wanted to run for office had to relinquish their treaty rights (Janovicek and Thomas 2018; see Chapter 18). Other legal restrictions on women's ability to participate in public life, such as their ability to work, study, and access credit, were all restricted until at least the mid-twentieth century (Royal Commission on the Status of Women in Canada 1970). It is not surprising, then, that until those restrictions were eliminated, few women were nominated as candidates for public office.[4]

There are several reasons why it matters that fewer women run for office and, by extension, are elected to public office in Canada than men, all of which connect to ideas about what it means to be represented in a democracy. One of the most widely used measures of representation is descriptive representation, which simply asks how well candidates and/or MPs mirror the population they are supposed to represent (Pitkin 1967). Descriptive representation is useful because it is relatively objective and easy to measure. Large differences between a group's proportion of the population and their presence as candidates or elected representatives may be a cue that systemic bias and prejudice are barriers that make it harder for members of that group to participate in politics.

Skeptical readers may observe that representation cannot be confined to someone's identities. It is active and must also include what representatives do. This is true, but it would be an error to use this critique to create a false dichotomy between who candidates and MPs are and what they do. Research

Figure 16.1. Percentage of Women Candidates and Elected in Federal Elections by Party, 1917–2021

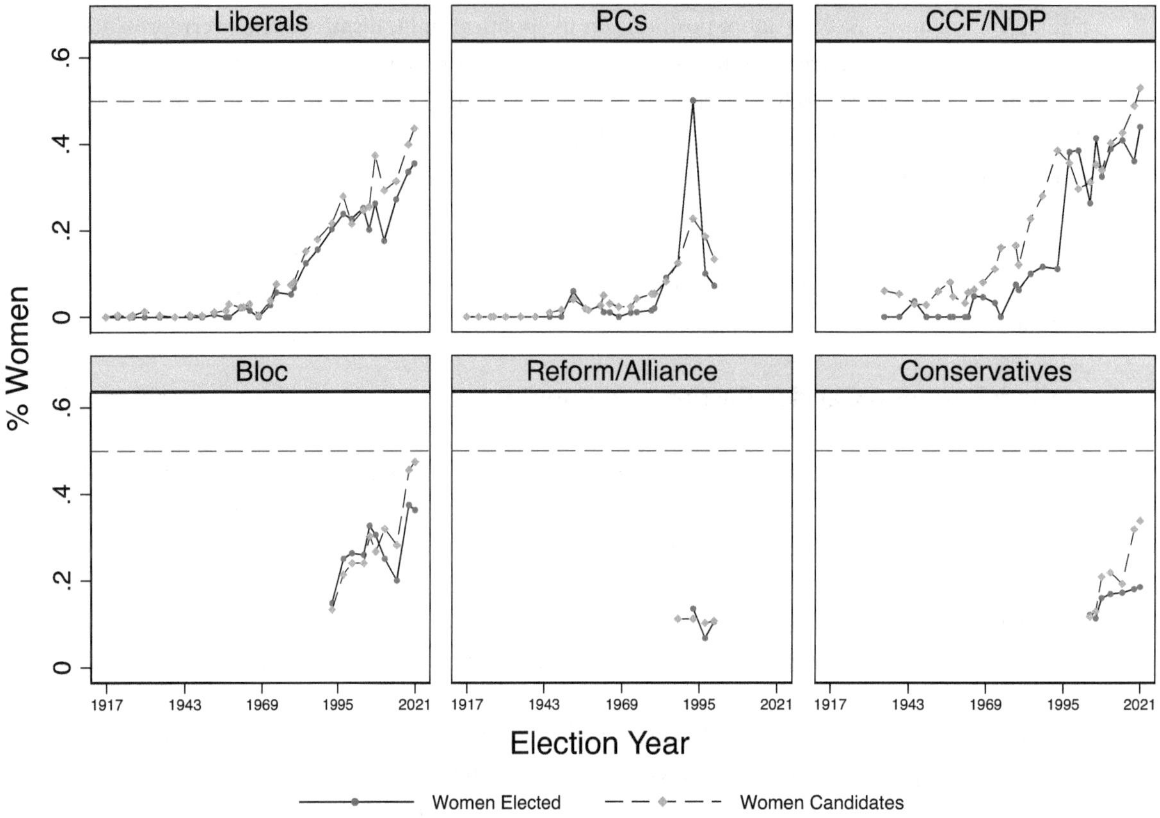

Source: Calculated from Sevi (2019).

clearly and consistently shows that in Canada – a system where political institutions can place severe constraints on candidates and MPs to act for a group (versus, say, their political party) – women representatives still substantively speak to and act on issues that disproportionately affect women or are gendered than do men (Tremblay 1998; Rayment 2024, Rayment and McCallion 2023). This is largely due to policy-relevant differences in lived experiences (Mansbridge 1999). As a result, while some representatives are better placed than others (Childs and Krook 2009), the relationship between who candidates and MPs are and what they do is best seen as a "both-and" rather than an "either-or."

While the proportion of women candidates in Canadian federal elections has been steadily growing over time, albeit with some bumps and backsliding, Figure 16.1 shows that the successful election of women is much more volatile. Despite persistent sexism in Canadian politics, as noted above, the reason more women run than are elected is *not* because Canadian voters seem to be unwilling to vote for women candidates (Sevi, Arel-Bundock, and Blais 2019). Instead, the answer lies within the organizations responsible for nominating candidates and contesting elections: political parties.

Women are less likely than men to be party members and in general, parties have been slow to integrate women as fully into positions of power and influence internally as they do men (Young 2000; Cross, Pruysers, and Currie-Wood 2022; Young and Cross 2003). It is perhaps unsurprising, then, that most federal parties in Canada do a poor job of nominating women as candidates. Even though the majority of candidates are acclaimed (Cross 2004), parties are more likely to create contexts where women seek nomination when women serve in leadership roles, such as local district association president, and when nomination contests are opened early and stay open for a longer period of time (Cheng and Tavits 2011; Cross and Pruysers 2019). Some party organizers are candid that, in working to create this context, they have to say no to acclaiming the volunteers who first come forward to run: typically older white, able-bodied men (Thomas 2019). Indeed, even though white men are only about a third of Canada's population, they are still a majority of federal candidates (Johnson et al. 2021a; Ouellet, Shiab, and Gilchrist 2021).

Women who are nominated as candidates face an additional hurdle: nearly every political party is likely to nominate them in a district they are set to lose. Between 2004 and 2011, an absolute majority of women were candidates in a district their party was almost guaranteed to lose. While this was also true for a plurality of men, men were also significantly more likely to run in strongholds their party was almost guaranteed to win. This pattern of nominating men in known winnable seats and women in lost-cause districts extended to open seats and to incumbents (Thomas and Bodet 2013). This is one reason why incremental increases in women's candidacies have not translated comparably into women's increased presence in the House of Commons. This pattern does not only exist for women candidates at the federal level but also across all provinces and levels of government (Trimble, Arscott, and Tremblay 2013; Tolley 2011), women party leaders and premiers (O'Neill, Pruysers, and Stewart 2021; Thomas 2018), visible and racialized minorities (Tolley 2023), and LGBT candidates (Baisley and Albaugh 2022), suggesting a distinct difference between the rhetoric and action within some parties (see also Chen et al. 2023).

Several things, then, are true at once: women are less ambitious for public office than are men, but enough women are interested in running as candidates that parties could nominate proportions of women, men, nonbinary, and genderqueer folks that match their presence in the population (Ashe and Stewart 2012). Political parties nominate women systematically in districts they are less likely to win, and yet evidence also suggests that when women run, they win. Taken together, these factors motivate civil society organizations such as *Equal Voice* (2023) and *Ask Her* (2023) to focus some of their activities on women-only campaign schools.

IMPLICATIONS FOR DEMOCRACY

Over a century after the first woman was elected to serve as an MP, women remain underrepresented and disadvantaged in Canadian electoral politics: men are far more likely to be nominated as candidates and elected as MPs, especially if they are white. Women are more likely than men to vote, but when women's values, beliefs, issue preferences, and vote choice differ from men's, women are still presented (tacitly and, at times, explicitly) as deviant. As many as one in five Canadians are willing to report they think men are "naturally" better leaders than women and that women are "too emotional" and "too nice" for politics. Research shows, though, that many more think these things but know better than to say them out loud (Chen et al. 2023). In sum, gender systemically structures Canadian electoral politics, and sexism systemically biases it.

Democracies that are systemically biased are incomplete at best and failing at worst. Canadian democracy is arguably somewhere in between, though there are signs suggesting that, at least with respect to gender, Canadian democracy is not healthy. The content presented throughout this chapter documents only some of the ways in which Canadian democracy is gendered in general and biased against women. One measure of a healthy democracy could be the extent to which people want to change this. Among Canadians, it is well established (and noted above) that men are much less concerned about this problem than women.

This is mirrored across political parties. While most federal parties indicate that gender equality is a reasonable goal, they differ on the extent to which they will advocate for it, especially regarding specific policies and interventions. When asked about the extent to which federal parties support or oppose gender equality, particularly with respect to "implementing special measures for women," most federal parties – that is, the NDP, Greens, Liberals, and the Bloc Québécois – are seen to be largely very supportive. By contrast, the Conservative Party of Canada is not only perceived to be most likely to "dismiss the idea of gender equality and special laws aimed at achieving it as efforts of enforcing so-called gender ideology" (Wiesehomier et al. 2022, 10), but also the only party to be oriented more toward opposing gender equality than supporting it (see also Thomas 2017).

Another trend being seen in democracies, including Canada, is a rise in gender-based political violence. Gender-based political violence takes several forms; the most common in Canada is psychological violence, where communications (e.g., phone calls, emails, social media posts and comments, in-person conversations) threaten women politicians with physical or sexual violence, castigate them with hostility (e.g., epithets), or otherwise indicate that women do not belong in politics because they are women. In Canada, women MPs have been followed home by hostile members of the public (Mosleh and Ballingal 2022), been told to "fuck off" in front of their children coming out of a movie theatre (Rabson 2019), and had funerals arranged for them by members of the public, among other death threats (Trynacity 2018). While writing this chapter, I met with a parliamentary secretary responsible, in part, for the status of women; she reported that most women MPs now wear panic buttons routinely, at least while in Ottawa. This is distinct from the expected rough and tumble of politics in both its vitriol and to whom it is directed (Krook 2020). The point of this violence is to prevent women from doing political work.

Again, it is worth asking what it means for Canadian democracy if (1) these threats are credible and candidates and politicians are at elevated risk of violence *because they are women*, or (2) even if the threats are not credible, the context is such that some, including those responsible for the security of elected representatives, genuinely believe them to be true.

Ultimately, Canadian electoral politics cannot be healthy until women are fully integrated in a genuine, unbiased manner. Similarly, the study of Canadian electoral politics will be biased until gender is comparably integrated. It is possible to see that there is a long way for both to go without diminishing current and past gender equity gains.

NOTES

1 Research investigating gender identities beyond women and men is still in its nascence in political science in general, and the study of electoral politics in Canada is no exception to this. The field's main research tool – the Canadian Election Study – included a nonbinary gender identity first in 2019 (Stephenson et al. 2020); similarly, trans and nonbinary candidates were first presented to Canadians as nominated individuals in the 2019 federal election (Johnson et al. 2021a), though nonbinary candidates were elected to provincial legislatures prior to this (see Thomas 2019). Statistics Canada did not include explicit categories for nonbinary and transgender people in their data collections until 2021 (Government of Canada 2021). Studying gender and elections beyond the binary will certainly be a fruitful avenue for future research.

2 Gendered exclusions on suffrage rights in Canada are complex. In general, though with some variations due to property ownership, women were excluded from voting in the nineteenth century in Canada. Campaigns to extend suffrage rights to women in the twentieth century were connected to the expansion of the settler state and explicitly to white supremacy. The vote was extended to women in Canada first in the Prairie provinces, in part for political expediency (Carter 2021). White women in Quebec were the last to be enfranchised in 1940, while race-based exclusions prevented Asian women from voting until the late 1940s and Indigenous women from voting until the Bill of Rights was passed in 1960 (Janovicek and Thomas 2018). A comprehensive overview of this history is available through the Women's Suffrage and the Struggle for Democracy Series, edited by Veronica Strong-Boag and published by UBC Press. For more information, see https://www.ubcpress.ca/womens -suffrage-and-the-struggle-for-democracy?per-page=20.

3 A series of edited collections aptly titled *The Canadian General Election of [YEAR]* or *The Canadian Federal Election of [YEAR]* is also routinely published. These typically address each party's campaign, with additional chapters featuring analyses of the media, polls, and other thematic topics. A chapter on gender has been included once, in 2015 (O'Neill and Thomas 2016).

4 These restrictions are the rationale for focusing early studies of gender and voting behaviour around situational and structural factors, as outlined in the previous section.

REFERENCES

Albaugh, Quinn M., and Elizabeth Baisley. 2023. "Gender and LGBT Affinity Effects: The Case of Ontario Premier Kathleen Wynne." *Politics & Gender* 19 (4): 1156–79. https://doi.org/10.1017 /S1743923X23000302.

Almond, Gabriel A., and Sidney Verba. 1963. *The Civic Culture: Political Attitudes and Democracy in Five Nations.* Princeton: Princeton University Press.

Ashe, Jeanette, and Kennedy Stewart. 2012. "Legislative Recruitment: Using Diagnostic Testing to Explain Underrepresentation." *Party Politics* 18 (5): 687–707. https://doi.org/10.1177/1354068810389635.

Ask Her YYC. 2023. "What We Do." https://askheryyc.org.

Baisley, Elizabeth, and Quinn M. Albaugh. 2022. "What Explains Gaps in District Competitiveness? The Case of LGBTQ Candidates." *Working Paper.*

Bennett, Linda L.M., and Stephen Earl Bennett. 1989. "Enduring Gender Differences in Political Interest: The Impact of Socialization and Political Dispositions." *American Politics Quarterly* 17 (1): 105–22. https://doi.org/10.1177/1532673X8901700106.

Bittner, Amanda, and Elizabeth Goodyear-Grant. 2017. "Digging Deeper into the Gender Gap: Gender Salience as a Moderating Factor in Political Attitudes." *Canadian Journal of Political Science/Revue Canadienne de Science Politique* 50 (2): 559–78. https://doi.org/10.1017/S0008423917000270.

Blais, André. 2000. *To Vote or Not to Vote: The Merits and Limits of Rational Choice Theory.* Pittsburgh: University of Pittsburgh Press.

Blais, André, Elisabeth Gidengil, Richard Nadeau, and Neil Nevitte. 2002. *Anatomy of a Liberal Victory: Making Sense of the Vote in the 2000 Canadian Election.* Toronto: University of Toronto Press.

Burns, Nancy, Kay Lehman Schlozman, and Sidney Verba. 2001. *The Private Roots of Public Action: Gender, Equality, and Political Participation.* Cambridge: Harvard University Press.

Campbell, Angus, Philip E. Converse, Warren E. Miller, and Donald E. Stokes. 1960. *The American Voter.* Oxford: John Wiley.

Carter, Sarah. 2021. *Ours by Every Law of Right and Justice: Women and the Vote in the Prairie Provinces.* Vancouver: UBC Press.

Chen, Philip, Melanee Thomas, Allison Harell, and Tania Gosselin. 2023. "Explicit Gender Stereotyping in Canadian Politics." *Canadian Journal of Political Science* 56 (1): 209–21. https://doi.org/10.1017/S0008423922000890.

Cheng, Christine, and Margit Tavits. 2011. "Informal Influences in Selecting Female Political Candidates." *Political Research Quarterly* 64 (2): 460–71. https://doi.org/10.1177/1065912909349631.

Childs, Sarah, and Mona Lena Krook. 2009. "Analysing Women's Substantive Representation: From Critical Mass to Critical Actors." *Government and Opposition* 44 (2): 125–45. https://doi.org/10.1111/j.1477-7053.2009.01279.x.

Clarke, Harold D., Jane Jenson, Lawrence LeDuc, and Jon H. Pammett. 2019. *Absent Mandate: Strategies and Choices in Canadian Elections.* Toronto: University of Toronto Press.

Cross, William P. 2004. *Political Parties. Canadian Democratic Audit 2.* Vancouver: UBC Press.

Cross, William P., and Scott Pruysers. 2019. "The Local Determinants of Representation: Party Constituency Associations, Candidate Nomination and Gender." *Canadian Journal of Political Science/Revue Canadienne de Science Politique* 52 (3): 557–74. https://doi.org/10.1017/S0008423919000064.

Cross, William P., Scott Pruysers, and Rob Currie-Wood. 2022. *The Political Party in Canada.* Vancouver: UBC Press.

Cutler, Fred. 2002. "The Simplest Shortcut of All: Sociodemographic Characteristics and Electoral Choice." *Journal of Politics* 64 (2): 466–90. https://doi.org/10.1111/1468-2508.00135.

Elections Canada. 2022. "Turnout by Gender – Estimation of Voter Turnout by Age Group and Gender at the 2021 General Election." July 13. https://www.elections.ca/content.aspx?section=res&dir=rec/eval/pes2021/evt&document=p6&lang=e#ftn10.

Equal Voice. 2023. "Equal Voice." https://equalvoice.ca/.

Erickson, Lynda, and Brenda O'Neill. 2002. "The Gender Gap and the Changing Woman Voter in Canada." *International Political Science Review* 23 (4): 373–92. https://doi.org/10.1177/0192512102023004003.

Gidengil, Elisabeth. 1995. "Economic Man – Social Woman? The Case of the Gender Gap in Support for the Canada-United States Free Trade Agreement." *Comparative Political Studies* 28 (3): 384–408. https://doi.org/10.1177/0010414095028003003.

———. 2007. "Beyond the Gender Gap: Presidential Address to the Canadian Political Science Association, Saskatoon, 2007." *Canadian Journal of Political Science / Revue Canadienne de Science Politique* 40 (4): 815–31. https://doi.org/10.1017/S0008423907071181.

Gidengil, Elisabeth, Andre Blais, Neil Nevitte, and Richard Nadeau. 2004. *Citizens.* Canadian Democratic Audit Series. Vancouver: UBC Press.

Gidengil, Elisabeth, Neil Nevitte, Andre Blais, Joanna Everitt, and Patrick Fournier. 2012. *Dominance and Decline: Making Sense of Recent Canadian Elections.* Toronto: University of Toronto Press.

Gidengil, Elisabeth, and Dietlind Stolle. 2009. "The Role of Social Networks in Immigrant Women's Political Incorporation." *International Migration Review* 43 (4): 727–63. https://doi.org/10.1111/j.1747-7379.2009.00783.x.

———. 2021. "Beyond the Gender Gap: The Role of Gender Identity." *Journal of Politics* 83 (4): 1818–22. https://doi.org/10.1086/711406.

Glenn, Norval D., and Michael Grimes. 1968. "Aging, Voting, and Political Interest." *American Sociological Review* 33 (4): 563–75. https://doi.org/10.2307/2092441.

Goodyear-Grant, Elizabeth, and Julie Croskill. 2011. "Gender Affinity Effects in Vote Choice in Westminster Systems: Assessing 'Flexible' Voters in Canada." *Politics & Gender* 7 (2): 223–50. https://doi.org/10.1017/S1743923X11000079.

Goot, Murray, and Elizabeth Anne Reid. 1975. *Women and Voting Studies: Mindless Matrons or Sexist Scientism?* Sage Professional Papers in Contemporary Political Sociology. No. 06-008. London: Sage Publications.

Government of Canada. 2021. "Gender of Person." Statistics Canada. October 18. https://www23.statcan.gc.ca/imdb/p3Var.pl?Function=DEC&Id=410445.

Harell, Allison, and Dimitrios Panagos. 2013. "Locating the Aboriginal Gender Gap: The Political Attitudes and Participation of Aboriginal Women in Canada." *Politics & Gender* 9 (4): 414–38. https://doi.org/10.1017/S1743923X1300038X.

Inglehart, Ronald, and Pippa Norris. 2000. "The Developmental Theory of the Gender Gap: Women's and Men's Voting Behavior in Global Perspective." *International Political Science Review / Revue Internationale de Science Politique* 21 (4): 441–63. https://doi.org/10.1177/0192512100214007.

Janovicek, Nancy, and Melanee Thomas. 2018. "Canada: Uneven Paths to Suffrage and Women's Electoral Participation." In *The Palgrave Handbook of Women's Political Rights*, edited by Susan Franceschet, Mona Lena Krook, and Netina Tan, 169–84. Basingstoke: Palgrave MacMillan.

Johnson, Anna, Erin Tolley, Melanee Thomas, and Marc André Bodet. 2021a. *Dataset on the Demographics of Canadian Federal Election Candidates (2008–2019)*. https://doi.org/10.7910/DVN/MI5XQ6: Harvard Dataverse, V1.

———. 2021b. "A New Dataset on the Demographics of Canadian Federal Election Candidates." *Canadian Journal of Political Science* 54 (3): 717–25. https://doi.org/10.1017/S0008423921000391.

Krook, Mona Lena. 2020. *Violence against Women in Politics*. Oxford: Oxford University Press.

Mansbridge, Jane. 1999. "Should Blacks Represent Blacks and Women Represent Women? A Contingent 'Yes.'" *Journal of Politics* 61 (3): 628–57. https://doi.org/10.2307/2647821.

Mansell, Jordan, Allison Harell, Melanee Thomas, and Tania Gosselin. 2022. "Competitive Loss, Gendered Backlash and Sexism in Politics." *Political Behavior* 44 (1): 455–76. https://doi.org/10.1007/s11109-021-09724-8.

Mosleh, Omar, and Alex Ballingal. 2022. "Fear, Loathing and 'Anti-Politics': Inside the New Reality for Canadian Politicians." *Toronto Star*, July 16. https://www.thestar.com/politics/federal/2022/07/16/fear-loathing-and-anti-politics-inside-the-new-reality-for-canadian-politicians.html.

Mutz, Diana C. 2018. "Status Threat, Not Economic Hardship, Explains the 2016 Presidential Vote." *Proceedings of the National Academy of Sciences* 115 (19): E4330–39. https://doi.org/10.1073/pnas.1718155115.

O'Neill, Brenda. 2001. "A Simple Difference of Opinion? Religious Beliefs and Gender Gaps in Public Opinion in Canada." *Canadian Journal of Political Science / Revue Canadienne de Science Politique* 34 (2): 275–98. https://doi.org/10.1017/S0008423901777906.

O'Neill, Brenda, Scott Pruysers, and David K. Stewart. 2021. "Glass Cliffs or Partisan Pressure? Examining Gender and Party Leader Tenures and Exits." *Political Studies* 69 (2): 257–77. https://doi.org/10.1177/0032321719880316.

O'Neill, Brenda, and Melanee Thomas. 2016. "Because It's 2015: Gender and the 2015 Federal Election." In *The Canadian Federal Election of 2015*, edited by Christopher Dornan and Jon H. Pammett, 275–304. Toronto: Dundurn Press.

Ouellet, Valérie, Naël Shiab, and Sylvène Gilchrist. 2021. "White Men Make up a Third of Canada's Population but a Majority of MPs – Here's Why." Radio-Canada. https://ici.radio-canada.ca/info/2021/elections-federales/minorites-visibles-diversite-autochtones-racises-candidats-politique/en.

Pitkin, Hanna Fenichel. 1967. *The Concept of Representation*. Berkeley: University of California Press.

Pruysers, Scott, and Julie Blais. 2017. "Why Won't Lola Run? An Experiment Examining Stereotype Threat and Political Ambition." *Politics & Gender* 13 (2): 232–52. https://doi.org/10.1017/S1743923X16000544.

———. 2019. "Narcissistic Women and Cash-Strapped Men: Who Can Be Encouraged to Consider Running for Political Office, and Who Should Do the Encouraging?" *Political Research Quarterly* 72 (1): 229–42. https://doi.org/10.1177/1065912918786040.

Pruysers, Scott, Melanee Thomas, and Julie Blais. 2020. "Mediated Ambition? Gender, News and the Desire to Seek Elected Office." *European Journal of Politics and Gender* 3 (1): 37–59. https://doi.org/10.1332/251510819X15701058119488.

Rabson, Mia. 2019. "Threats, Abuse Move from Online to Real World, McKenna Now Requires Security." CBC News. September 7. https://www.cbc.ca/news/politics/threats-abuse-move-from-online-to-real-world-mckenna-now-requires-security-1.5274766.

Rayment, Erica. 2024. *What Women Represent: The Impact of Women in Parliament.* Toronto: University of Toronto Press.

Rayment, Erica, and Elizabeth McCallion. 2023. "Contexts and Constraints: The Substantive Representation of Women in the Canadian House of Commons and Senate." *Representation* 60 (1): 117–33. https://doi.org/10.1080/00344893.2023.2173283.

Royal Commission on the Status of Women in Canada. 1970. *Report of the Royal Commission on the Status of Women in Canada.* Ottawa: Information Canada.

Schneider, Monica C., and Angela L. Bos. 2014. "Measuring Stereotypes of Female Politicians." *Political Psychology* 35 (2): 245–66. https://doi.org/10.1111/pops.12040.

———. 2019. "The Application of Social Role Theory to the Study of Gender in Politics." *Political Psychology* 40 (S1): 173–213. https://doi.org/10.1111/pops.12573.

Sevi, Semra. 2019. "Who Runs? Canadian Federal and Ontario Provincial Candidates since 1867." *Canadian Journal of Political Science* 54 (2): 471–76. https://doi.org/10.7910/DVN/ABFNSQ.

Sevi, Semra, Vincent Arel-Bundock, and André Blais. 2019. "Do Women Get Fewer Votes? No." *Canadian Journal of Political Science / Revue Canadienne de Science Politique* 52 (1): 201–10. https://doi.org/10.1017/S0008423918000495.

Stephenson, Laura B., Allison Harell, Daniel Rubenson, and Peter John Loewen. 2020. *2019 Canadian Election Study – Online Survey.* https://doi.org/10.7910/DVN/DUS88V: Harvard Dataverse, V1.

Stockemer, Daniel, and Aksel Sundstrom. 2023. "The Gender Gap in Voter Turnout: An Artefact of Men's Over-reporting in Survey Research?" *British Journal of Politics and International Relations* 25 (1): 21–41. https://doi.org/10.1177/13691481211056850.

Stolle, Dietlind, and Elisabeth Gidengil. 2010. "What Do Women Really Know? A Gendered Analysis of Varieties of Political Knowledge." *Perspectives on Politics* 8 (1): 93–109. https://doi.org/10.1017/S1537592709992684.

Thomas, Melanee. 2012. "The Complexity Conundrum: Why Hasn't the Gender Gap in Subjective Political Competence Closed?" *Canadian Journal of Political Science / Revue Canadienne de Science Politique* 45 (2): 337–58. https://doi.org/10.1017/S0008423912000352.

———. 2017. "Women and Federal Conservative Parties in Canada, 1993-2013." In *The Blueprint: Conservatives and Canadian Politics, 1993-2013*, edited by Joanna Everitt and J.P. Lewis. Toronto: University of Toronto Press.

———. 2018. "In Crisis or Decline? Selecting Women to Lead Provincial Parties in Government." *Canadian Journal of Political Science / Revue Canadienne de Science Politique* 51 (2): 379–403. https://doi.org/10.1017/S0008423917001421.

———. 2019. "Governing as If Women Mattered: Rachel Notley as Alberta Premier." In *Doing Politics Differently? Women Premiers in Canada's Provinces and Territories*, edited by Sylvia Bashevkin, 250–71. Vancouver: UBC Press.

Thomas, Melanee, and Marc André Bodet. 2013. "Sacrificial Lambs, Women Candidates, and District Competitiveness in Canada." *Electoral Studies* 32 (1): 153–66. https://doi.org/10.1016/j.electstud.2012.12.001.

Tolley, Erin. 2011. "Do Women 'Do Better' in Municipal Politics? Electoral Representation across Three Levels of Government." *Canadian Journal of Political Science / Revue Canadienne de Science Politique* 44 (3): 573–94. https://doi.org/10.1017/S0008423911000503.

———. 2023. "Gender Is Not a Proxy: Race and Intersectionality in Legislative Recruitment." *Politics & Gender* 19 (2): 373–400. https://doi.org/10.1017/S1743923X22000149.

Tremblay, Manon. 1998. "Do Female MPs Substantively Represent Women? A Study of Legislative Behaviour in Canada's 35th Parliament." *Canadian Journal of Political Science / Revue Canadienne de Science Politique* 31 (3): 435–65. https://doi.org/10.1017/S0008423900009082.

Trimble, Linda. 2017. *Ms. Prime Minister: Gender, Media, and Leadership.* Toronto: University of Toronto Press.

Trimble, Linda, Jane Arscott, and Manon Tremblay, eds. 2013. *Stalled: The Representation of Women in Canadian Governments.* Vancouver: UBC Press.

Trynacity, Kim. 2018. "11 Death Threats Made against Alberta Premier Rachel Notley, Government Security Records Show." CBC News. May 4. https://www.cbc.ca/news/canada/edmonton/notley -premier-threats-security-1.4644989.

Wiesehomier, Nina, Kenneth Benoit, Matthew Singer, and Saskia Ruth-Lovell. 2022. *Political Representation, Executives, and Political Parties Survey Summary (PREPPS) Data Guide.* Data from Expert Surveys in 31 EUR + Countries, 2020–2021.

Young, Lisa. 2000. *Feminists and Party Politics.* Vancouver: UBC Press.

Young, Lisa, and William P. Cross. 2003. "Women's Involvement in Canadian Political Parties." In *Women and Electoral Politics in Canada*, edited by Manon Tremblay and Linda Trimble, 92–109. Don Mills: Oxford University Press.

CHAPTER SEVENTEEN

Racialized Canadians in Politics

Asif Hameed and Erin Tolley

DEFINING RACIALIZATION

Multiculturalism is a thread that runs deep through Canadians' collective identity. "A nation of immigrants," "diversity, our strength," and "a mosaic, not a melting pot" are just a few of the familiar taglines. Beyond the sloganeering is a more complicated story about the economic, social, and political realities of race in Canada.

In Canada, those who identify as racialized are more likely than others to live in poverty, experience discrimination, be stopped by police, and die by homicide (Block and Galabuzi 2018; Moreau 2022; Wang and Moreau 2022; Wortley and Owusu-Bempah 2011). In 2020, after George Floyd, a Black man, was murdered by Minneapolis police officers, Black Lives Matter highlighted longstanding racial disparities in sustained protests calling for increased racial equality. Between 2019 and 2020, police-reported racially motivated hate crimes spiked in Canada by 80%; Black Canadians are more likely to experience racially motivated hate crimes than any other group (Wang and Moreau 2022). In the wake of the COVID-19 pandemic, hate crimes targeting Canadians of East and Southeast Asian descent rose by 301% (Wang and Moreau 2022). This rise in hate crimes could be indicative of the backlash that frequently follows demands for racial equality. Confronted with a changing social order, (white) Canadians may retaliate violently to reset what they erroneously view as a natural racial hierarchy; commentators have called this phenomenon "whitelash" (Smith 2020).

In this chapter, we use the term "racialized" to refer to individuals who are not Indigenous peoples and who identify as non-Caucasian or non-white in race or colour. We prefer this term to other alternatives for two reasons. First, although many institutions continue to use the term "visible minority," this descriptor problematically centres whiteness as the invisible norm, a limitation even Statistics Canada has acknowledged. Second, by using the language of racialization, we highlight the dynamic, socially constructed processes that create racial categories and imbue them with significance. Race is not biological or inherent; as a longtime researcher of racial dynamics in Canada puts it, race is a verb, not a noun (Fleras 2014). That said, one limitation of an aggregate term like "racialized" is that it combines many groups – all with distinctive characteristics based on race, national origin, language, and religion – into a single category, thus rendering this heterogeneity invisible.

Some observers (including many Canadian political scientists) use "ethnicity" as a synonym for race. The two concepts overlap, but they are distinct. Ethnicity is our cultural identity: our language, customs, and practices. Each of us chooses our ethnicity, and it can change over time. Race, by contrast, is most often externally ascribed. Although there is no genetic basis for it, race is understood as something individuals are born with: it is inherited, immutable, and based on characteristics we do not choose and cannot change. A focus on ethnic and territorial cleavages, such as those between the Québécois and *les canadiens*, once dominated Canadian political science, but the country's increased racial diversity is bringing racial identity to the fore (Nath 2011; Nath et al. 2018; Thompson 2008).

Nonetheless, the discipline's intellectual history means there is still very little research tracing political differences between white and racialized Canadians, or among racialized Canadians themselves. Until 2021, the Canadian Election Study (CES), which has been conducted since 1965 and is the largest source of data on elections and politics in Canada, had not ever included a question on respondents' racial identification. As a result, we knew very little about how race influences vote choice, voter turnout, partisan identification, or policy preferences. Political science is not alone in its relative silence on race. For example, the Library of Parliament publishes data on the gender and Indigenous background of parliamentarians, but they include no information on their race.

Canadian political science has alternated between ignoring race as a salient marker of political difference or suboptimally inferring it using other characteristics, such as ethnicity, immigration status, or language. The lack of systematic data on race in Canadian politics is one roadblock to understanding how race influences electoral campaigns and outcomes. It also means researchers mostly rely on American theories that are frequently not transferable given different political systems, varying political geography, and idiosyncratic approaches to categorizing and classifying racial groups. When we fail to count race, we fail to account for race.

Race has political consequences. We cannot understand core democratic tenets, like equality, representation, and legitimacy, if we do not understand race. This lack of understanding has very real consequences. For example, a 2022 Abacus survey found that the rising cost of living surpassed health care and the economy as the most important issues facing Canadians, with housing affordability not far behind (Anderson and Coletto 2022). Federal and provincial governments have enacted a slate of policies to encourage housing construction and offer down payment assistance, which Prime Minister Trudeau said would "unlock homeownership for the middle class," but these policies do little to address the roadblocks to home ownership disproportionately faced by racialized Canadians (Statistics Canada 2023). This disparity is an outgrowth of a historical racial cleft in property ownership in Canada, which has been exacerbated by discriminatory lending practices and a persistent wage gap between white and racialized Canadians. Racially undifferentiated policymaking has contributed to racially differentiated outcomes.

A central insight of research on descriptive representation is that the characteristics of elected officials should mirror those of the electorate (Mansbridge 1999; Phillips 1998; Pitkin 1972). The match need not be perfect, but there is some expectation of a "rough correspondence" (Phillips 2017). Such representation is particularly important for groups whose shared interests have historically been excluded from a country's economic, political, and social life (Mansbridge 1999). When these groups do not have an institutional voice, there is a risk that government decisions will be partial and not meet the needs of a diverse population. Even more worryingly, excluded citizens may view institutions with suspicion, which can impede perceptions of institutional legitimacy and decrease support for policy initiatives. Finally, the lack of demographic role models shapes the political attitudes and aspirations of young people, laying a foundation for their futures (Bos et al. 2021; Campbell and Wolbrecht 2006). As the saying goes: if you don't see it, you can't be it. For these reasons, political inclusion is an important indicator of democratic health (Cross 2011).

EVOLUTION OF PARTICIPATION OF RACIALIZED CANADIANS IN ELECTORAL POLITICS

Many of us think of politics as a neutral arena, one where the rules apply equally to all. But Canada's political history is rooted in processes, institutions, and legislation that are foundationally discriminatory. Rex Wood's portrait of the Fathers of Confederation depicts 36 propertied white men who crafted a political union to represent their own interests. Rules around who could vote and run for office were also exclusionary: Chinese Canadians and Indigenous peoples were denied these rights at various points, and it was not until 1960 that Canada's racial restrictions on the franchise were removed (Elections Canada 2021). Accordingly, it is difficult to separate Canada's past from its present: the threads of the country's racist past are woven into today's fabric, which has been remarkably durable.

Elected Representatives

Most early studies of diversity in Canadian politics focused on the representation of those who were neither British nor French (Ogmundson and McLaughlin 1992). Between 1867 and 1964, just 97 MPs of non-British or non-French origin were elected to the House of Commons; most of these were German, Ukrainian, or Jewish (Stasiulis and Abu-Laban 1991). In 1957, Douglas Jung, a Progressive Conservative from Vancouver Centre, became the first racialized Canadian elected to the House of Commons, but members of Parliament (MPs) remained mostly white and of European origin until the late 1980s (Pelletier 1991; Stasiulis and Abu-Laban 1991). As Canada's population became more racially diverse, the proportion of racialized MPs also began to increase (see Figure 17.1). By 2021, a total of 53 (15.7%) MPs were racialized. The first racialized women entered the House of Commons in 1993 when Jean Augustine and Hedy Fry were elected. Following the 2021 election, 18 (5.3%) MPs were racialized women, and 35 (10.4%) were racialized men.

Figure 17.1. Racialized Members of Parliament, 1988–2021

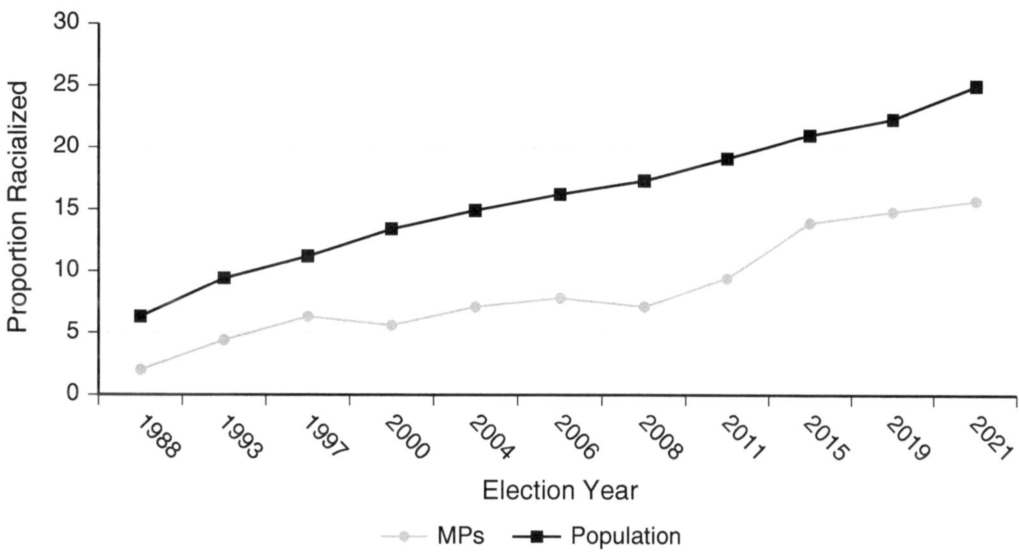

Sources: Pelletier (1991); Black and Hicks (2006); Black (2008, 2020); Tolley et al. (2022); population data drawn from the Canadian Census.

Although the proportion of racialized MPs is the highest it has ever been in Canada's history, it still does not reflect the diversity of the Canadian population. What explains this representational shortfall? In what follows, we focus on two aspects that are central to electoral outcomes: voters and campaigns.

Voters

The proportion of the Canadian population that identifies as racialized has grown from around 6% in the early 1980s to 25% as of the 2021 Census (Statistics Canada 2022). Canada's immigration intake has shifted from predominantly European source countries to, increasingly, those in Asia and Africa. This shift, along with higher birth rates among racialized Canadians, has altered the racial composition of the electorate. Racialized Canadians are now a significant and growing segment of the electorate, with South Asian, Chinese, and Black Canadians accounting for 16% of the country's total population.

Racialized Canadians are also a predominately urban cohort, with over 95% living in cities compared to just under 74% of the general population; nearly 70% of racialized Canadians reside in Toronto, Vancouver, or Montreal and their surrounding areas. This trend toward urbanization has had important impacts on the voting power of racialized Canadians. As Kelly Saunders points out in Chapter 5, independent provincial electoral commissions oversee the drawing of federal electoral boundaries every 10 years. Although the preservation of voting equality rights is one component of the commissioners' work, the country's varying geography – including sparsely populated rural and northern communities – means there is often significant population variance across districts (Courtney 2001). The Supreme Court of Canada has upheld this population variance, arguing the right to vote does not require a strict adherence to the principle of one-person, one-vote, but instead only a guarantee of "effective representation" (Pal and Choudhry 2007). As a result, electoral maps systematically underrepresent some voters, with the votes of those living in urban areas worth less than those living in rural areas (Courtney 2001; Pal and Choudhry 2007).

Inequality in voting power is not race-neutral, because the districts in which urban voters are proportionately underrepresented are also where an overwhelming majority of racialized Canadians reside. As Pal and Choudhry (2007, 3) succinctly put it, "Promoting the interests of Canada's rural minority and the minority of Canadians who live in smaller provinces necessarily comes at the cost of the interests of a visible minority." The voting power of racialized Canadians has been reduced because of urban vote dilution and the overrepresentation of rural voters in Parliament.

Even so, political parties have long taken notice of social cleavages and worked to translate these into discernable voting blocks. Historian Christian Champion (2006) has documented efforts to court "our ethnic friends" in both the Liberal and Conservative parties. John Diefenbaker's "unhyphenated Canadianism" and *Bill of Rights* were policies meant to appeal to non-British and non-French voters, while Liberal organizers in the 1960s identified friendly ethnic associations and "annual ethnic ceremonies" that they could attend to broaden their base of appeal. Campaign appearances at gurdwaras and mosques, advertisements in minority language media, and outreach to community associations are now run-of-the-mill campaign tactics most evident in suburban areas surrounding the country's most diverse cities, including Toronto, Montreal, and Vancouver but also Edmonton and Calgary.

These tactics make sense in many ways: racialized voters are an identifiable and often highly engaged segment of the electorate. For example, on average, South Asian Canadians make higher-than-average financial contributions to political parties and candidates; these donations fund the signage, advertisements, and polling that are the hallmarks of modern campaigns (Besco and Tolley 2022). Racialized voters have varied partisan attachments, and there are only a small number of districts where any racialized group makes up even 1/3 of the population, so ethnic outreach strategies are usually a series of microtargeting efforts. This approach has been especially apparent in the Conservative Party, which segmented so-called ethnic voters sympathetic to Conservative priorities and tailored the party's agenda to appeal specifically to them (Tolley 2017).

Research finds that although racialized voters are not homogeneous in their preferences and political priorities, they tend to feel a closer affinity with candidates from their own and other minority racialized groups than with white candidates. This generalized racial affinity is highest among racialized voters who identify strongly with their own ethnocultural group (Besco 2019). As an example, voters who self-identify strongly as Chinese Canadian are more likely to support a South Asian candidate than voters who only weakly identify as Chinese Canadian. Parties have been able to leverage these so-called "rainbow coalitions" in districts with large racialized populations but where no one group makes up a majority.

Under Stephen Harper's leadership, much was made of the Conservatives' inroads into electoral districts with large immigrant populations, with one popular account referring to the trend as the "big shift" (Bricker and Ibbitson 2013). This shift was primarily driven by an evolution in the voting preferences of (mostly white) European-origin immigrants who turned toward the Conservatives (Harell 2013), rather than an exodus of racialized supporters from the Liberal Party (Blais 2005).

Although many racialized Canadians are actively engaged in electoral politics, aggregate voter turnout tends to be lower for racialized Canadians than for others (Reitz and Banerjee 2007; Tolley and Rayment 2021). Immigration patterns explain some of this difference (Bilodeau and Kanji 2006; Jedwab 2006), but even among those born in this country, racialized Canadians vote at lower rates than white Canadians. The reasons for disparities in voter turnout are multifaceted: accessibility, interest in politics, engagement by parties, and information about voting and politics can all shift voting rates. Prejudice also matters. Research in other countries shows that while racial discrimination in policy settings or institutions seems to motivate political engagement, those who experience interpersonal discrimination – that is, racism at the hands of their peers – are less likely to vote than those who have not experienced racial prejudice (Besco et al. 2022; Oskooii 2016, 2020).

Most Canadian research finds little evidence that voters discriminate directly against candidates on account of their racial background (Black and Erickson 2006; Tossutti and Najem 2002), but this conclusion is not an absolution: indeed, there is ample evidence of racism and racist attitudes in Canada (Besco and Tolley 2018). Why does that discrimination not appear in electoral results? One reason is that vote choice is mostly driven by one's preference for a party or its leader, and this preference is likely to wash away all but the most discriminatory impulses against one's local candidate (Allen Stevens et al. 2019; Blais et al. 2003).

Although racial discrimination might not influence election results in a direct way, race structures the vote in other ways. At the most basic level, a candidate's race provides voters with a demographic cue or, as Cutler (2002) puts it, "the simplest shortcut of all." In the absence of other information, voters tend to see racialized candidates as more ideologically liberal, more interested in policy issues like immigration and multiculturalism, and less qualified to hold public office than their white counterparts (Haynie 2002; McDermott 1998; Zilber and Niven 2000). Moreover, because the prototypical politician continues to be a white male, many voters still associate whiteness and masculinity with electoral capability and success (Tolley 2016).

Finally, although there is little evidence of aggregate electoral discrimination, racialized candidates are disadvantaged when they run for right-leaning parties. Besco (2020) shows that Conservative voters defect from the party when their district candidate is racialized, an effect that he refers to as "friendly fire" and which is not apparent in any other party. Racialized candidates who run for right-leaning parties thus experience an electoral penalty, an outcome that may dampen either their enthusiasm for running for those parties or the parties' enthusiasm for nominating them.

Perceptions of candidates are driven by many factors. One important factor is the media, who serve as the link between voters and the campaign. The media are not simply a conduit; rather, they help to highlight the issues they view as most pressing and the decision criteria that are most salient. These choices are often implicit, sometimes unintentional, but definitely not neutral. For example, research finds the media cover racialized candidates differently than their white counterparts. In comparison to white candidates, the media focus more on racialized candidates' sociodemographic characteristics than their policy interests and present these candidates as less electorally viable even when their qualifications are equivalent to those of white candidates. This process is known as racial mediation (Tolley 2016). Meanwhile, stereotypes about race and gender intersect to shape the media's coverage of racialized women in politics, including a focus on their novelty and exoticism, their perceived loyalty, and adherence to model minority stereotypes (Tolley 2019a). Racialized framing is consistent with news values that prioritize coverage that is unconventional, sensational, or conflictual. This coverage shapes how voters understand politics and assess the candidates before them.

Campaigns

Despite Canada's diversity, race and immigration issues have largely not been central features of most electoral campaigns (Black and Hicks 2008; Marwah et al. 2013). Researchers attribute this absence to Canada's political geography and generally high levels of support for immigration and multiculturalism (Besco and Tolley 2018; Reitz 2011; Taylor 2021). These factors have made it politically dangerous for parties to campaign on an anti-diversity platform. To form government, parties need to win the ridings in which large numbers of racialized Canadians live. Most parties have therefore been reluctant to turn immigration and multiculturalism into electoral wedge issues (Black and Hicks 2008). Those that have – notably the Reform Party – have watched their electoral ambitions evaporate.

In recent campaigns, parties have deviated somewhat from this consensus, and diversity issues have been more central. In the 2015 campaign, the Conservative Party dug in on plans to ban the wearing of the niqab at citizenship ceremonies and promised to set up a tipline for reporting "barbaric cultural practices." The New Democrats, meanwhile, pledged support for the niqab, a stance that likely contributed to the party's implosion in Quebec, where secularism and religious symbols have long been a political cudgel. Observers suggest the Conservatives may have moved too far to the right in 2015; with the New Democrats leaking support, the Liberals ultimately prevailed (Kymlicka 2021; Tasker 2016; Tolley 2017).

Four years later, in 2019, a key plank of the Conservative campaign was a promise to end "illegal immigration." Footage of asylum seekers arriving at a border crossing near Roxham Road in rural Quebec provided a vivid backdrop for parties to discuss tougher immigration laws. One thematic section of the English-language leaders' debate in October 2019 was titled "Polarization, human rights, immigration," underscoring the political malaise increasingly associated with migration policy. The leaders focused much of their attention in this segment of the debate on Quebec's secularism law – commonly referred to as Bill 21 – which prohibits public-sector workers, including teachers, police officers, judges, and provincial lawyers from wearing religious symbols such as turbans, hijabs, and crucifixes.

Meanwhile, in mid-September, *TIME* magazine released a 2001 photo of Trudeau at a costume party; he was dressed as a character from the movie Aladdin and wearing a turban, robe, and dark makeup on his face and hands. A second photo depicted Trudeau in a talent show; he was performing Harry Belafonte's version of the Jamaican folk song "Day-O," wearing blackface and an afro wig. After *TIME* published its story, a video was released showing Trudeau in the 1990s, again in blackface. Trudeau's image as a guardian of diversity was eroded by these incidents and by the high-profile departures of Jody Wilson-Raybould, an Indigenous woman, and Celina Caesar-Chavannes, a Black woman, from the Liberal caucus shortly before the 2019 election; both women were vocally critical of Trudeau's leadership.

By the 2021 campaign, race and diversity seemed to have fallen off the political agenda, with one reporter noting, "some voters are left wondering why the social and racial reckoning once dominating headlines has turned into a fringe issue among federal leaders" (Khan 2021). Although the parties' platforms made various appeals to historically marginalized groups, most of these promises were generic, not costed, or part of a broader economic, environmental, or social policy agenda rather than goals in their own right (Tolley et al. 2022). Quebec's secularism law was raised once again in the English-language leaders' debate, but rather than focusing on the substance of the issue, the party leaders zeroed in on whether the moderator's characterization of the legislation as "discriminatory" was unfair (Tolley et al. 2022). The prominence of diversity issues in campaigns has thus waxed and waned over time.

Alongside this issue evolution, the diversity of candidate slates has increased (see Figure 17.2), and political parties seem to have become more cognizant of the necessity – and benefits – of recruiting racialized candidates (Johnson et al. 2021; Tolley 2023; Tolley et al. 2022). The 2021 election saw more racialized candidates running than ever before; across the major parties, 21.9% of all office seekers were racialized, and 10% of candidates were racialized women or nonbinary, compared to 31% who were white women or nonbinary (Tolley et al. 2022). Despite this, as Figure 17.1 shows, diversity in the House of Commons edged up only slightly, in part because racialized candidates are disproportionately nominated in districts where their parties are less electorally competitive (Lapointe et al. 2024; Tolley et al. 2022). Although parties are rhetorically committed to candidate diversity, even when they have the opportunity to select racialized candidates, they frequently choose not to do so, or do so in only the most diverse ridings, and there is some evidence that they funnel party resources – including more money – to districts where white male candidates have been nominated (Ouellet et al. 2021; Tolley 2023).

Strategies to recruit more diverse candidates vary across the major parties. The New Democrats are the most explicit and have committed to an aggregate target for candidates from a variety of equity-seeking groups. The Liberals and Greens both require electoral districts to consider candidate diversity in their recruitment and nomination processes, while the Conservatives have adopted more of a free-market approach (Thomas and Morden 2019). Given these variations, it is somewhat counterintuitive that the proportion of racialized candidates across each of the major parties differed very little, at least not until 2019. This result contrasts sharply from the experience of women candidates, where the New Democrats have long embraced gender diversity (Johnson et al. 2021; Tolley 2019b; see also Chapter 16 in this volume).

In any given institution, where there is more power and prestige, there is typically less diversity, a phenomenon that has been called the vertical mosaic, the law of increasing disproportion, or the law of minority attrition (Porter 1965; Putnam 1976; Taagepera 1994). In Canada, the theory holds, and only a handful of racialized Canadians have ascended to leadership roles. One analysis of provincial and federal leadership contests found that no major party selected a racialized leader during the 1990s, and in the past 20 years, just 13% of federal and provincial leaders have been racialized or Indigenous (Grenier 2020). There have been just three racialized leaders of major federal parties in the country's history: Vivian Barbot for the Bloc Québécois, Jagmeet Singh for the New Democrats, and Annamie Paul for the Green Party. Federally, no racialized person has led a party with status as the government or Official Opposition, and just one, Singh, has served for more than a year.

Singh's selection as New Democratic leader in 2017 is one explanation for the increasing number of racialized candidates running under the party's banner. Candidate selection is devolved to local

Figure 17.2. Distribution of Racialized Candidates across Federal Political Parties, 2008–2021

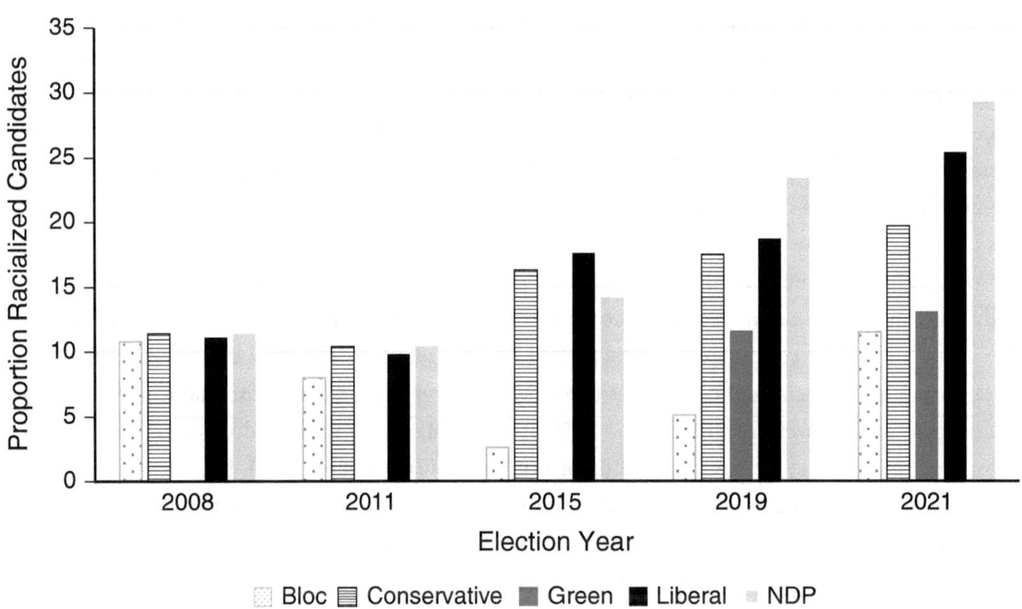

Source: Johnson et al. (2021); Tolley et al. (2022). Note that data on racial diversity in the Green Party was not collected prior to 2019.

electoral district associations in Canada; 75% of local party presidents are white and male (Tolley 2019b). Given these dynamics, the presence of a racialized leader may help to broaden the pool of prospective candidates and signal that the party is open to diversity. Still, a racialized leader on the national stage remains rare, and entrenched perceptions of suitability of office do not shift overnight.

Early in his tenure, Singh was heckled as a supposed sympathizer of the Muslim Brotherhood, and in 2019, a man approached him during a campaign stop in Montreal's Atwater Market to advise, "You should really cut your turban off and you [would] look like a Canadian." In response, Singh replied, "I think Canadians look like all sorts of people. That's the beauty of Canada," to which the voter retorted, "In Rome, you do as the Romans do" (Connolly 2019). Meanwhile, Annamie Paul, the first Black Jewish woman to lead a federal party, called the experience the "worst period" of her life (Tasker 2021). Negative public responses to racialized difference in politics are a powerful reminder of the durability of Canada's racial hierarchy.

IMPLICATIONS FOR DEMOCRACY

Although Canadians often distinguish their country's own racial history from the more explicit examples of slavery and segregation in the United States, our political record shows that we are not immune from racism. Canadian democracy has been shaped by the intersection between race and electoral politics, with notable implications for representation, policymaking, and discourse.

After a long period of electoral underrepresentation, the House of Commons is experiencing a historic high in the number of racialized MPs. This trend has the potential to facilitate the participation and articulation of minority interests in governance, to build trust, and to increase the legitimacy of the state in the eyes of those who have been traditionally marginalized from it. These are all positives.

Nonetheless, the presence of a few more diverse faces in Parliament is not a substitute for widespread structural change. Efforts to increase racialized representation are often utilitarian, even tokenizing, with descriptive representation becoming a box to check so that parties can win seats in diverse urban ridings. One outcome of this focus is that racialized communities living *outside* these so-called battleground districts rarely see themselves mirrored in their representatives. There is evidence of diversity in politics – some descriptive representation – but that has not yet translated fully into substantive representation in the form of more equitable and inclusive policies (Pitkin 1972).

Moreover, while there are more racialized Canadians in the legislative branch, the arenas with the most authority and power exist largely as white spaces. Party leaders are mostly white; so too are most cabinet ministers and senior officials in the bureaucracy (Griffith 2017). Representative government remains unrepresentative, and the relative absence of racial diversity in positions of political power squares awkwardly with Canadians' perception of themselves as multicultural, open, and tolerant. This pattern also raises questions about the perspectives that have influence and agency. When policymakers lack lived experience with racism and discrimination, policy regimes may ignore these realities or, even worse, contribute to them.

Entrenched across all policy areas is what W.E.B. DuBois famously called "the colour line," or the division between racial privilege and oppression. In Canada, the colour line appears in policies that are, on their face, neutral, but racially differentiated in practice. For example, the Mulroney and Harper governments passed sweeping tough-on-crime bills that implicitly and disproportionately targeted and incarcerated Black Canadians for drug-related charges, even though evidence shows white Canadians engaged in more drug-related activities, including trafficking and illicit consumption (Khenti 2014). During this time, there were almost no Black MPs in office. Similarly, the years following the September 11 attacks saw an increased level of scrutiny, surveillance, and threat-perception of Muslim Canadians from the state under successive governments, justifying incursion into citizens' lives and contributing to a mistrust that persists to this day (Dhamoon and Abu-Laban 2009; Wilkins-Laflamme 2018). These programs were developed in a time when the governing party had only *two* Muslim voices. Despite the pervasiveness of institutional discrimination, racialized Canadians express high levels of institutional trust and confidence in democracy in Canada, even higher than their white counterparts (Hwang 2017; Thurton 2022), but research shows that trust can be lost in the face of perceived or experienced discrimination (Bilodeau 2017).

A recent survey by the Angus Reid Institute found that while the proportion of Canadians taking pride in greater diversity has increased since the 1990s, there is a significant bloc of skepticism. According to these data, just over half of Canadians (51%) embrace diversity and view racism as a major problem, while a near equal number (49%) see racism as a minor or even nonexistent issue. This latter group mostly consists of white men over the age of 55 from the prairies, who support parties on the political right (Angus Reid Institute 2021). Other research characterizes Canadians as "conditional multiculturalists" who are not overtly opposed to immigration and diversity but whose acceptance comes with strings attached (Besco and Tolley 2018).

Populism and xenophobic nationalism have become a central part of the political zeitgeist, with Brexit and the Trump presidency mainstreaming the once political fringe. Inherent within the politics of the alt-right is a clear animus toward racial difference, one that is fuelled by a resentment toward diversity and multiculturalism (Perry et al. 2019). The 2022 occupation of Parliament Hill and key arteries along the US-Canada border by the so-called Freedom Convoy illustrated the brazenness of this hostility and showed that Canada is not immune to polarization (Graves and Smith 2020). Protestors in Ottawa waved Nazi and Confederate flags on the steps of Parliament, while armed militias at Coutts Crossing along the Alberta-Montana border wore the insignia of the Diagolon movement, which is dedicated to instigating a race war in Canada. Some elected officials hesitated to denounce the protestors or sympathized with their claims, while others framed the use of racist symbols as an aberration rather than indicative of a new level of hostility and exclusion.

In their dynamics, discourse, and outcomes, elections have helped to cement Canada's vertical mosaic. Successive campaigns have returned parliaments that do not adequately capture the country's racial diversity. These parliaments continue to enact policies whose outcomes differentially affect racialized and white Canadians. Electoral procedures, while ostensibly neutral, also have racially differentiated effects. As this chapter has shown, these effects are evident in candidate recruitment, party leadership, the drawing of electoral boundaries, and media coverage. Although multiculturalism in Canada is frequently referred to as a tapestry or mosaic, political campaigns are usually characterized by battle metaphors. For racialized Canadians, the metaphor that is perhaps most apt is the one that highlights just how uneven the playing field really is.

ACKNOWLEDGEMENT

This research was undertaken, in part, thanks to funding from the Canada Research Chairs Program.

REFERENCES

Allen Stevens, Benjamin, Md Mujahedul Islam, Roosmarijn de Geus, Jonah Goldberg, John R. McAndrews, Alex Mierke-Zatwarnicki, Peter John Loewen, and Daniel Rubenson. 2019. "Local Candidate Effects in Canadian Elections." *Canadian Journal of Political Science* 52 (1): 83–96. https://doi.org/10.1017/S0008423918000367.

Anderson, Bruce, and David Coletto. 2022. "Conservatives Lead Liberals by 3; Liberals Trail on Cost of Living and the Economy." Abacus Data. November. https://abacusdata.ca/canadian-politics-november-2022/.

Angus Reid Institute. 2021. "Diversity and Racism in Canada: Competing Views Deeply Divide Country Along Gender, Generational Lines." https://angusreid.org/wp-content/uploads/2021/06/2021.06.21_Diversity_Racism.pdf.

Besco, Randy. 2019. *Identities and Interests: Race, Ethnicity, and Affinity Voting*. Vancouver: UBC Press.

———. 2020. "Friendly Fire: Electoral Discrimination and Ethnic Minority Candidates." *Party Politics* 26 (2): 215–26. https://doi.org/10.1177/1354068818761178.

Besco, Randy, Sergio Garcia-Rios, Julius Lagodny, Nazita Lajevardi, Kassra Oskooii, and Erin Tolley. 2022. "Fight Not Flight: The Effects of Explicit Racism on Minority Political Engagement." *Electoral Studies* 80: 102515. https://doi.org/10.1016/j.electstud.2022.102515.

Besco, Randy, and Erin Tolley. 2018. "Does Everyone Cheer? The Politics of Multiculturalism in Canada." In *Federalism and the Welfare State in a Multicultural World*, edited by Elizabeth Goodyear-Grant, Richard Johnston, Will Kymlicka, and John Myles, 291–318. Kingston: McGill-Queen's University Press.

———. 2022. "Ethnic Group Differences in Donations to Electoral Candidates." *Journal of Ethnic and Migration Studies* 48 (5): 1072–94. https://doi.org/10.1080/1369183X.2020.1804339.

Bilodeau, Antoine. 2017. "Mobilisation or Demobilisation? Perceived Discrimination and Political Engagement among Visible Minorities in Quebec." *Political Science* 69 (2): 122–38. https://doi.org/10.1080/00323187.2017.1332955.

Bilodeau, Antoine, and Mebs Kanji. 2006. "Political Engagement among Immigrants in Four Anglo-democracies." *Electoral Insight* 8 (2): 43–49. https://www.elections.ca/content.aspx?section=res&dir=eim/issue19&document=p8&lang=e.

Black, Jerome H. 2008. "The 2006 Federal Election and Visible Minority Candidates: More of the Same?" *Canadian Parliamentary Review* 30 (3): 30–36. http://revparl.ca/31/3/31n3_08e_Black.pdf.

———. 2020. "Visible Minority Candidates and MPs in the 2019 Federal Election." *Canadian Parliamentary Review* 43 (2): 17–23. https://www.revparlcan.ca/en/visible-minority-candidates-and-mps-in-the-2019-federal-election/.

Black, Jerome H., and Lynda Erickson. 2006. "Ethno-racial Origins of Candidates and Electoral Performance: Evidence from Canada." *Party Politics* 12 (4): 541–61. https://doi.org/10.1177/1354068806064733.

Black, Jerome H., and Bruce M. Hicks. 2006. "Visible Minority Candidates in the 2004 Election." *Canadian Parliamentary Review* 29 (2): 26–31. http://revparl.ca/29/2/29n2_06e_Black.pdf.

———. 2008. "Electoral Politics and Immigration in Canada: How Does Immigration Matter?" *Journal of International Migration and Integration* 9 (3): 241–67. https://doi.org/10.1007/s12134-008-0069-5.

Blais, André. 2005. "Accounting for the Electoral Success of the Liberal Party in Canada." *Canadian Journal of Political Science* 38 (4): 821–40. https://doi.org/10.1017/S0008423905050304.

Blais, André, Elisabeth Gidengil, Agnieszka Dobrzynska, Neil Nevitte, and Richard Nadeau. 2003. "Does the Local Candidate Matter? Candidate Effects in the Canadian Election of 2000." *Canadian Journal of Political Science* 36 (3): 657–64. https://doi.org/10.1017/S0008423903778810.

Block, Sheila, and Grace-Edward Galabuzi. 2018. *Persistent Inequality: Ontario's Colour-coded Labour Market*. Toronto: Canadian Centre for Policy Alternatives.

Bos, Angela L., Jill S. Greenlee, Mirya R. Holman, Zoe M. Oxley, and J. Celeste Lay. 2021. "This One's for the Boys: How Gendered Political Socialization Limits Girls' Political Ambition and Interest." *American Political Science Review* 116 (2): 484–501. https://doi.org/10.1017/S0003055421001027.

Bricker, Darrell, and John Ibbitson. 2013. *The Big Shift: The Seismic Change in Canadian Politics, Business, and Culture and What It Means for Our Future*. Toronto: HarperCollins.

Campbell, David E., and Christina Wolbrecht. 2006. "See Jane Run: Women Politicians as Role Models for Adolescents." *Journal of Politics* 68 (2): 233–47. https://doi.org/10.1111/j.1468-2508.2006.00402.x.

Champion, Christian P. 2006. "Courting 'Our Ethnic Friends': Canadianism, Britishness, and New Canadians, 1950–1970." *Canadian Ethnic Studies Journal* 38 (1): 23–46.

Connolly, Amanda. 2019. "Jagmeet Singh Confronted by Man Who Tells Him: 'Cut Your Turban Off.'" *Global News*. October 4. https://globalnews.ca/news/5980241/jagmeet-singh-confronted-over-turban-montreal/.

Courtney, John C. 2001. *Commissioned Ridings: Designing Canada's Electoral Districts*. Montreal: McGill-Queen's University Press.

Cross, William, ed. 2011. *Auditing Canadian Democracy*. Vancouver: UBC Press.

Cutler, Fred. 2002. "The Simplest Shortcut of All: Sociodemographic Characteristics and Electoral Choice." *Journal of Politics* 64 (2): 466–90. https://doi.org/10.1111/1468-2508.00135.

Dhamoon, Rita, and Yasmeen Abu-Laban. 2009. "Dangerous (Internal) Foreigners and Nation-Building: The Case of Canada." *International Political Science Review* 30 (2): 163–83. https://doi.org/10.1177/0192512109102435.

Elections Canada. 2021. *A History of the Vote in Canada.* 3rd ed. Ottawa: Chief Electoral Office of Canada.

Fleras, Augie. 2014. *Racisms in a Multicultural Canada: Paradoxes, Politics, and Resistance.* Waterloo: Wilfrid Laurier University Press.

Graves, Frank, and Jeff Smith. 2020. *Northern Populism: Causes and Consequences of the New Ordered Outlook.* Calgary: Canadian Global Affairs Institute.

Grenier, Éric. 2020. "When It Comes to Leadership, Canada's Political Parties Aren't Getting More Diverse." CBC News. June 9. https://www.cbc.ca/news/politics/grenier-leadership-diversity-1.5603626.

Griffith, Andrew. 2017. "Diversity in the Public Service's Executive Ranks." *Policy Options.* October 16. https://policyoptions.irpp.org/magazines/october-2017/diversity-in-the-public-services-executive-ranks/.

Harell, Allison. 2013. "Revisiting the 'Ethnic' Vote: Liberal Allegiance and Vote Choice among Racialized Minorities." In *Parties, Elections and the Future of Canadian Politics*, edited by Amanda Bittner and Royce Koop, 140–60. Vancouver: UBC Press.

Haynie, Kerry. 2002. "The Color of Their Skin or the Content of Their Behavior? Race and Perceptions of African American Legislators." *Legislative Studies Quarterly* 27 (2): 295–314. https://doi.org/10.2307/3598532.

Hwang, M.M.H. 2017. "Ethnicity and Political Trust in Canada: Is There a Deepening Divide?" *Canadian Journal of Sociology* 42 (1): 23–54. https://doi.org/10.29173/cjs25734.

Jedwab, Jack. 2006. "The 'Roots' of Immigrant and Ethnic Voter Participation in Canada." *Electoral Insight* 8 (2): 3–9. https://www.elections.ca/content.aspx?section=res&dir=eim/issue19&document=p2&lang=e.

Johnson, Anna, Erin Tolley, Melanee Thomas, and Marc André Bodet. 2021. "A New Dataset on the Demographics of Canadian Federal Election Candidates." *Canadian Journal of Political Science* 54 (3): 717–25. https://doi.org/10.1017/S0008423921000391.

Khan, Ahmar. 2021. "Canada Election: Black, Indigenous Voters Lament Leaders Shying Away from Race-Based Issues." *Global News.* September 17. https://globalnews.ca/news/8194241/black-Indigenous-voters-federal-election.

Khenti, Akwatu. 2014. "The Canadian War on Drugs: Structural Violence and Unequal Treatment of Black Canadians." *International Journal of Drug Policy* 25 (2): 190–95. https://doi.org/10.1016/j.drugpo.2013.12.001.

Kymlicka, Will. 2021. "The Precarious Resilience of Multiculturalism in Canada." *American Review of Canadian Studies* 51 (1): 122–42. https://doi.org/10.1080/02722011.2021.1878544.

Lapointe, Valérie, Benjamin Ferland, and Luc Turgeon. 2024. "Still Sacrificial Lambs? Yes! Minority Groups in Canadian Federal Elections, 2015–2021." *Electoral Studies* 87: 102717. https://doi-org.proxy.library.carleton.ca/10.1016/j.electstud.2023.102717

Mansbridge, Jane. 1999. "Should Blacks Represent Blacks and Women Represent Women? A Contingent 'Yes.'" *Journal of Politics* 61 (3): 628–57. https://doi.org/10.2307/2647821.

Marwah, Inder, Triadafilos Triadafilopoulos, and Stephen White. 2013. "Immigration, Citizenship and Canada's New Conservative Party." In *Conservatism in Canada*, edited by James Farney and David Rayside, 95–119. Toronto: University of Toronto Press.

McDermott, Monika L. 1998. "Race and Gender Cues in Low-information Elections." *Political Research Quarterly* 51 (4): 895–918. https://doi.org/10.1177/106591299805100403.

Moreau, Greg. 2022. "Police-reported Crime Statistics in Canada." *Juristat* (Catalogue no. 85-002-X). https://www150.statcan.gc.ca/n1/en/catalogue/85-002-X202200100013.

Nath, Nisha. 2011. "Defining Narratives of Identity in Canadian Political Science: Accounting for the Absence of Race." *Canadian Journal of Political Science* 44 (1): 161–93. https://doi.org/10.1017/S0008423910001071.

Nath, Nisha, Ethel Tungohan, and Megan Gaucher. 2018. "The Future of Canadian Political Science: Boundary Transgressions, Gender and Anti-Oppression Frameworks." *Canadian Journal of Political Science* 51 (3): 619–42. https://doi.org/10.1017/S0008423918000197.

Ogmundson, R., and J. McLaughlin. 1992. "Trends in the Ethnic Origins of Canadian Elites: The Decline of the BRITS?" *Canadian Review of Sociology* 29 (2): 227–42. https://doi.org/10.1111/j.1755-618X.1992.tb02437.x.

Oskooii, Kassra A.R. 2016. "How Discrimination Impacts Sociopolitical Behavior: A Multidimensional Perspective." *Political Psychology* 37 (5): 613–40. https://doi.org/10.1111/pops.12279.

———. 2020. "Perceived Discrimination and Political Behavior." *British Journal of Political Science* 50 (3): 897–92.

Ouellet, Valérie, Naël Shiab, and Sylvène Gilchrist. 2021. "White Men Make Up a Third of Canada's Population but a Majority of MPs — Here's Why." CBC News. August 26. https://ici.radio-canada.ca/info/2021/elections-federales/minorites-visibles-diversite-autochtones-racises-candidats-politique/en.

Pal, Michael, and Sujit Choudhry. 2007. "Is Every Ballot Equal? Visible-minority Vote Dilution in Canada." *IRPP Choices* 13 (1): 1–30. https://irpp.org/research-studies/choices-vol13-no1/.

Pelletier, Alain. 1991. "Politics and Ethnicity: Representation of Ethnic and Visible-Minority Groups in the House of Commons." In *Ethno-cultural Groups and Visible Minorities in Canadian Politics: The Question of Access*, edited by Kathy Megyery. Toronto: Dundurn.

Perry, Barbara, Tanner Mirrlees, and Ryan Scrivens. 2019. "The Dangers of Porous Borders." *Journal of Hate Studies* 14 (1): 53–75. https://doi.org/10.33972/jhs.124.

Phillips, Anne. 1998. *The Politics of Presence*. Oxford: Oxford University Press.

———. 2017. "The Politics of Presence: Do Politicians Represent Us?" *LSE Politics*. September 6. https://blogs.lse.ac.uk/government/2017/09/06/the-politics-of-presence-do-politicians-represent-us/.

Pitkin, Hanna F. 1972. *The Concept of Representation*. Berkeley: University of California Press.

Porter, John. 1965. *The Vertical Mosaic: An Analysis of Social Class and Power in Canada*. Toronto: University of Toronto Press.

Putnam, Robert D. 1976. *The Comparative Study of Political Elites*. Englewood Cliffs: Prentice-Hall.

Reitz, Jeffrey G. 2011. *Pro-immigration Canada: Social and Economic Roots of Popular Views*. Montreal: Institute for Research on Public Policy.

Reitz, Jeffrey, and Rupa Banerjee. 2007. "Racial Inequality, Social Cohesion and Policy Issues in Canada." In *Belonging? Diversity, Recognition and Shared Citizenship in Canada*, edited by Keith Banting, Thomas J. Courchene, and F. Leslie Seidle, 489–527. Montreal: Institute for Research on Public Policy.

Smith, Terry. 2020. *Whitelash: Unmasking White Grievance at the Ballot Box*. New York: Cambridge University Press.

Stasiulis, Daiva K., and Yasmeen Abu-Laban. 1991. "The House the Parties Built: (Re)constructing Ethnic Representation in Canadian Politics." In *Ethno-cultural Groups and Visible Minorities in Canada Politics: The Question of Access*, edited by Kathy Megyery, 3–99. Toronto: Dundurn.

Statistics Canada. 2022. *2021 Census of Population*. Catalogue no. 98-316-X2021001. Ottawa: Statistics Canada. https://www12.statcan.gc.ca/census-recensement/2021/dp-pd/prof/index.cfm?Lang=E.

———. 2023. "Housing Conditions among Racialized Groups: A Brief Overview." *The Daily*. Ottawa: Statistics Canada. https://www150.statcan.gc.ca/n1/daily-quotidien/230123/dq230123b-eng.htm.

Taagepera, Rein. 1994. "Beating the Law of Minority Attrition." In *Electoral Systems in Comparative Perspective: Their Impact on Women and Minorities*, edited by Wilma J. Rule and Joseph Zimmerman, 236–45. Westport: Greenwood Press.

Tasker, John Paul. 2016. "NDP Dropped 20 Points in 48 Hours After Supporting the Niqab, Tom Mulcair Says." CBC News. February 13. http://www.cbc.ca/news/politics/thomas-mulcair-accepts-responsibility-1.3446241.

———. 2021. "Annamie Paul Is Stepping Down as Green Party Leader." CBC News. September 27. https://www.cbc.ca/news/politics/annamie-paul-stepping-down-green-leader-1.6190793.

Taylor, Zack. 2021. "The Political Geography of Immigration: Party Competition for Immigrants' Votes in Canada, 1997–2019." *American Review of Canadian Studies* 51 (1): 18–40. https://doi.org/10.1080/02722011.2021.1874732.

Thomas, Paul E.J., and Michael Morden. 2019. *Party Favours: How Federal Election Candidates are Chosen.* Toronto: Samara Centre for Democracy.

Thompson, Debra. 2008. "Is Race Political?" *Canadian Journal of Political Science* 41 (3): 525–47. https://doi.org/10.1017/S0008423908080827.

Thurton, David. 2022. "Black Canadians Twice as Likely to Trust the Government — but Less Likely to Trust Police: Survey." CBC News. April 19. https://www.cbc.ca/news/politics/back-canadians-trust-government-survey-1.6422675.

Tolley, Erin. 2016. *Framed: Media and the Coverage of Race in Canadian Politics.* Vancouver: UBC Press.

———. 2017. "Partisan Players or Political Pawns: Immigrants, Minorities and Conservatives in Canada." In *The Blueprint: Conservative Parties and Their Impact on Canadian Politics*, edited by J.P. Lewis and Joanna Everitt, 101–28. Toronto: University of Toronto Press.

———. 2019a. "Breaking the Concrete Ceiling: Media Portrayals of Racialized Women in Politics." In *Gendered Mediation: Identity and Image Making in Canadian Politics*, edited by Angelia Wagner and Joanna Everitt, 106–26. Vancouver: UBC Press.

———. 2019b. "Who You Know: Local Party Presidents and Minority Candidate Emergence." *Electoral Studies* 58: 70–79. https://doi.org/10.1016/j.electstud.2019.02.007.

———. 2023. "Gender Is Not a Proxy: Race and Intersectionality in Legislative Recruitment." *Politics & Gender* 19 (2): 373–400. https://doi.org/10.1017/S1743923X22000149.

Tolley, Erin, Aneurin Bosley, and Nana aba Duncan. 2022. "Still Not There: Diversity and Inclusion in the 2021 Canadian Election Campaign." In *The Canadian Federal Election of 2021*, edited by Jon H. Pammett and Christopher Dornan, 192–219. Montreal: McGill-Queen's University Press.

Tolley, Erin, and Erica Rayment. 2021. "Mississauga." In *Big City Elections in Canada*, edited by Jack Lucas and R. Michael McGregor, 147–68. Toronto: University of Toronto Press.

Tossutti, Livianna S., and Tom Pierre Najem. 2002. "Minorities and Elections in Canada's Fourth Party System: Macro and Micro Constraints and Opportunities." *Canadian Ethnic Studies* 34 (1): 85–111.

Wang, Jing Hui, and Greg Moreau. 2022. "Police-reported Hate Crime in Canada, 2020." *Juristat* (Catalogue no. 85-002-X). https://www150.statcan.gc.ca/n1/pub/85-002-x/2022001/article/00005-eng.htm.

Wilkins-Laflamme, Sarah. 2018. "Islamophobia in Canada: Measuring the Realities of Negative Attitudes Toward Muslims and Religious Discrimination." *Canadian Review of Sociology / Revue canadienne de sociologie* 55 (1): 86–110. https://doi.org/10.1111/cars.12180.

Wortley, Scot, and Akwasi Owusu-Bempah. 2011. "The Usual Suspects: Police Stop and Search Practices in Canada." *Policing and Society* 21 (4): 395–407. https://doi.org/10.1080/10439463.2011.610198.

Zilber, Jeremy, and David Niven. 2000. *Racialized Coverage of Congress: The News in Black and White.* Westport: Praeger.

CHAPTER EIGHTEEN

Validating the Canadian Electoral Process or Indigenous Nationhoods? The Complexities of First Nations, Métis, and Inuit Participation in Canadian Federal Elections

Chadwick Cowie

INTRODUCTION

In October of 2015, Indigenous participation and representation in a Canadian federal election attained levels that had not been reached previously. Although one can argue that Indigenous voting has gone down since 2015, Indigenous representation in candidates, provincial legislatures, as well as in the House of Commons has been steadily climbing. The question of Indigenous participation has consistently been viewed through a Canadian lens – one that reflects upon them as Canadian citizens while ignoring how citizenship has been used in a negative way to not only prevent them from having a say but also to exploit them for state interests rather than as equal citizens or dual citizens of the Canadian state and their own nations (see Cowie 2023 and 2024).

Therefore, this chapter assesses Indigenous participation in Canadian federal elections from 1867 to 2015 – the latter marking the highest turnout for Indigenous voters. To fully consider Indigenous forms of participation in relation to the Canadian state, I look to evaluate Indigenous impacts, or lack thereof, on Canadian elections, the evolution of Indigenous participation, as well as its implications by specifically considering First Nations, Métis, and Inuit separately between 1867 and 1991. Additionally, I consider Indigenous engagement in Canadian elections between 1991 to 2015 to better understand the literature that has emerged on Indigenous involvement in Canadian elections from 2019 to the present. This chapter asserts that although participation has had some positive impacts for First Nations, Métis, and Inuit peoples, there is a general lack of public understanding as to why Indigenous electoral involvement is a complicated topic that requires awareness of the Canadian state's encroachment upon them.

DEFINING INDIGENOUS PEOPLES IN RELATION TO THE CANADIAN STATE

In defining Indigenous peoples and nations who share territory with the Canadian state, it is important to understand that there are over 50 nations and confederacies. Use of the term *Indigenous* when referencing the first inhabitants of North America has grown over the last two decades due to the work of the United Nations – specifically the working group on Indigenous peoples and rights. This group looked to the term *Indigenous* as not only a way for Indigenous peoples to define themselves but also to counter the long history of being defined by those who did not belong to their nation, culture, or their territory. The Canadian state has also, over the last decade, moved toward the term *Indigenous* and connecting it to *Aboriginal*, which encompasses First Nations, Métis, and Inuit peoples and is the term used within Canadian state legal documents and the *Constitution Act, 1982*.

The term *First Nations* tends to reflect those nations who entered agreements and treaties with European nations and, eventually, the Canadian state on behalf of the Crown. Over time, European representatives, settlers, and Canadian officials and citizens used the term *Indian* when referring to First Nations, which represented various nations and confederacies of peoples. Examples include the Innu, the Wabanaki Confederacy, the Nehiyaw, Anishinaabeg, Dene, Siiksikaawa, Squamish, Haida, and the Tlingit. Treaties and agreements formulated with First Nations tend to fall into four categories, namely the "Peace and Friendship," pre-Confederation, Numbered, and modern treaties.

The first three types of treaties span a period from the 1600s to 1923, with modern treaties beginning in 1974. Despite First Nations having their own forms of citizenship, governance, legal systems, and societal, cultural, and spiritual structures under section 91(24) of the *Constitution Act, 1867*, the Canadian state further, and unilaterally, defined who qualified as First Nations, specifically under the definition of *Indian*. This definition, paired with colonial laws, allowed for the Canadian state to cement its control and authority over First Nations and whom it deemed to fulfill its criteria. Such controls and criteria will be discussed further in this chapter.

The history of the Métis has been expressed by some to date back as far as the late 1700s, but in relation to the Canadian state it tends to focus on the transfer of Rupert's Land to the Canadian state, which was met with resentment and opposition from the Métis. Métis community opposition specifically related to not being included in the negotiations and further anger only grew when Canadian land surveyors were sent to divide up the land for settlement. In turn, the Métis pushed back on Canadian encroachment, leading to the Métis-led Red River Resistance.[1] A provisional government, led by Louis Riel, was formed. The Riel provisional government had drafted a "List of Rights," which included recognition and protection of the French language, religious rights for both Catholics and Protestants, and recognition of Métis homesteads (Chartrand 2021, 46). The List of Rights was central to negotiations between the Riel provisional government and the Canadian state. Riel government representatives were able to secure much of their List of Rights, which led the Macdonald government and the House of Commons to pass the *Manitoba Act* of 1870 and to create the province of Manitoba on July 15, 1870 (Wardaugh 2021; Chartrand 2021; Kermoal 2021; Teillet 2021). Manitoba's creation granted voting rights to Métis men, who thus were able to participate in future federal Canadian elections right away, unlike First Nations people.

If looking at a present-day map of the Canadian state, Inuit territories are reflected as four regions: Nunatsiavut, Nunavik, Nunavut, and Inuvialuit. The Inuit have spanned these regions for centuries and participated in their own forms of legal, political, and socioeconomic structures. Settler societies and the Canadian state have given little attention or understanding to Inuit governance structures. During the 1930s, a jurisdictional feud over who was responsible for the Inuit came to a head between the province of Quebec and the Canadian state. The jurisdictional feud between Quebec and Canada would lead to the 1939 Supreme Court of Canada ruling that all Inuit within the boundaries of the Canadian state were the responsibility of the federal government. Like First Nations, the Inuit did not participate in the decision making or discussion over whose jurisdiction they were under – nor was their own agency even considered.

According to 2021 Canadian statistics, there are 1,048,400 First Nations, 624,200 Métis, and around 64,200 Inuit. Thus, when considering a collective number, Canada recognizes around 1,736,800 Indigenous peoples whom the Canadian state deems within its borders. These numbers do not include those whom First Nations may also deem as belonging to their communities, nations, and confederacies and further highlights the colonial relationship with the Canadian state that unilaterally defines who is First Nations and who is not. It is important to understand such unilateral decision making in defining not only Inuit, Métis, and First Nations, but also those considered Indigenous and guaranteed rights under the *Constitution Act, 1982,* as it does impact understandings of Indigenous participation not only in the Canadian state but also in elections.

EVOLUTION OF INDIGENOUS PARTICIPATION IN CANADA

Wards of the State to Conflict over Involvement: First Nations' Participation

Most of the literature and research that exists regarding First Nations[2] political engagement from the formation of the Dominion of Canada to the present reflects the idea that First Nations could only participate when the settler majority considered them "civilized" or through the view of belonging to the Canadian state as citizens of said state. As Kirkby (2019, 498, 503) highlights, "the full story of the [First Nations] franchise remains untold because most historians assume there is no story to tell." Following the formation of the Dominion, "Indian men at first remained disenfranchised due to their inability to meet the various provincial property tests while living on reserves." This, alongside the *Gradual Civilization Act* of 1857 deterred other First Nations men from participating in elections, as a First Nations man would have to renounce his identity and "become severed from his nation" (Kirkby 2019, 503). The John A. Macdonald government sought to hasten the process of assimilation by introducing the *Gradual Enfranchisement Act* (GEA) in 1869.

The introduction of the *Indian Act* in 1876 by the Mackenzie Liberal government also furthered the aims of the GEA and extended the hand of the Canadian government over the lives of First Nations peoples. The *British North America* (*BNA*) *Act*, under section 91(24), gave unilateral control of First Nations (Indians) to the newly formulated federal government. Although the *Indian Act* was used to dictate and control First Nations people, it also offered the ability for First Nations men who had property to vote.

With regard to the 1887, 1891, and 1896 elections, Kirkby (2019) highlights that the ability of First Nations men to participate in the three elections was purely by coincidence and a loophole that would disappear by 1900. Representatives from rural areas of Ontario were the key supporters of First Nations voting, and this support very much relates to the fact that First Nations' support benefited them. In 1884, the Macdonald government tightened the rules, requiring First Nations men who were planning to vote to prove the territory under their name was indeed theirs – this required a three-year probation. Thus, First Nations men had direct impact in the 1887 Canadian election and assisted with a slim win for the Conservative Party due to Anishinaabeg men voting in several Ontario ridings.

In 1898, the Laurier government fulfilled one of its promises that related to amending the *Elections Act* (Kirkby 2019). Included in these amendments was the removal of any and all Status First Nations men with property from having the franchise and participating politically unless they were also deemed civilized and gave up their identity (or status).[3] This rule would remain in force for the next 62 years.[4]

In 1960, the Diefenbaker government enacted full enfranchisement, granting First Nations men and women the right to vote federally without having to give up their identity (Cowie 2013 and 2021). Although Diefenbaker enacted such changes, they were not taken in recognition of Indigenous people as dual citizens of both their nations and the Canadian state, but rather solely as Canadians to whom granting citizenship would lead to equality. Almost a full four months after enfranchisement, the Michi Saagiig Nishnaabeg[5] communities of Curve Lake and Hiawatha, located in the district of Peterborough, were the first to be able to cast ballots on-reserve in a by-election, after losing their ability to do so in 1898. Little to no data exist as to how high the voter turnout was.

Another key moment for Indigenous participation occurred in 1968 with Leonard Marchand's victory in the district of Kamloops-Cariboo. He was not only the first Status–First Nations person to be elected to the House of Commons, but also the first Indigenous person to become a parliamentary secretary (Marchand and Hughes 2000).

Tyranny of the English Majority to Ongoing Recognition: The Métis

Métis voices came to the House of Commons in 1871, when Pierre Delorme and Angus McKay were elected in Manitoba. Although the elections of Delorme and McKay are significant for Indigenous participation and representation in Canada's federal electoral process, their time in the House was short as neither sought re-election in 1872 – reasoning for not running again is not provided.

A 1948 by-election in the former federal district of Rosthern led to the official return of Métis representation in the House of Commons, when Liberal William Boucher won, and he was re-elected in the 1949 election. Métis representative Roger Teillet was elected in 1962 in the district of St. Boniface for the Liberals, and in 1963, Eugène Rhéaume was elected in the Northwest Territories for the PCs. Teillet also became the first Métis/Indigenous person to serve as minister of veterans affairs in 1963 (Barkwell n.d.b). After Teillet's 1968 nomination loss and decision not to run in said election, Métis representation in the House of Commons would be nonexistent until 1972, when Wally Firth was elected for the NDP in the Northwest Territories (DBPedia n.d.). Like Boucher and Rhéaume, little is recorded regarding Firth's time in the House of Commons between 1972 and 1979.

Métis MPs returned to the House in the 1980 election with Cyril Keeper's win as the NDP candidate in the electoral district of Winnipeg–St. James (Barkwell, n.d.a). Keeper's win in 1980 is important as he was the only Métis individual in the House of Commons during the planning of the Charter and the *Constitution Act, 1982.* Keeper lost his re-election bid in the 1988 election.

Human Flagpoles to Self-Representation in the House of Commons: The Inuit

Inuit participation has taken many forms when we assess their relation to their territory, contact with settler societies, and the Canadian state. Unlike First Nations and Métis, Inuit engagement did not come to the fore when relating to Canada until the 1920s.

Between 1867 and 1934, little focus was given to the Inuit – nor was electoral participation pursued or sought. In fact, the Canadian state, under R.B. Bennett's Progressive Conservative government, sought to prevent any Inuit participation with the *Dominion Franchise Act* of 1934. The *Dominion Franchise Act* effectively made it illegal for Inuit to vote in Canadian federal elections, leaving the power of who became the elected representative for the Inuit territories to that of non-Inuit citizens of Canada (Milen 1991; Tester 2017).

It was only under Louis St. Laurent that the Canadian state extended citizenship and enfranchisement to the Inuit in 1950. Granting citizenship to Inuit lent greater credibility to Canadian sovereignty, whether the Inuit agreed to become Canadian citizens or not. Furthermore, the Canadian state continued to dictate and control much of everyday Inuit life, and the ability for Inuit to vote until the late 1970s (including in the 1953 federal election) was limited due to the unwillingness of the Canadian state to send ballots and ballot boxes to Inuit territories (Milen 1991; Cowie 2013 and 2021). Federal reluctance to ensure voting infrastructure was available in Inuit communities post-1950 highlights how the Inuit were not viewed as equal citizens but instead chiefly used to continue Canadian territorial claims in the north – they were essentially seen as human flagpoles.

The 1979 election was also a historic election for Inuit participation as it marked the election of not only the first Inuk MP, but also the first Inuk MP for the district with a majority of Inuit people living within it: Nunatsiaq – which has continued to be represented by an Inuk MP since (Milen 1991; Cowie 2013 and 2021). Peter Ittinuar was re-elected as an NDP MP in the 1980 election and was a key voice for the Inuit during the discussions and patriation in 1982. Ittinuar used his position to push the Pierre Trudeau government not only on the rights of Inuit but also for a land claim agreement to be formulated for the area he represented. After getting the Trudeau government to agree, Ittinuar in turn crossed the floor and joined the Liberal caucus in 1982 (Nunavut Tunngavik 2018). It is worth wondering whether the creation of Nunavut would have occurred had Ittinuar not been an MP at the time of patriation. Although Ittinuar's work was a key component to the Nunavut Land Claims process, he was not re-elected in the 1984 election.

Inuit participation in the Canadian electoral process continued with the election of Thomas Suluk (PC) in Nunatsiaq. As a backbencher, Suluk's focus was primarily on the continued movement of the Nunavut Land Claims process. He opted to not seek re-election in 1988 (Parliament of Canada n.d.). Jack Anawak was elected as a Liberal MP in the 1988 election (Bell 1997; Geddes 2019). Anawak's win, alongside that of First Nations MPs Blondin-Andrew and Littlechild, marked the first time three Indigenous MPs were elected to the House of Commons in the same federal election – and they were also sitting MPs when the Mulroney government promised a Royal Commission on Aboriginal Peoples (RCAP) following the 1990 Kanien'kéha:ka resistance at Kanehsatà:ke.

RCAP to Historic Turnout: First Nations, Métis, and Inuit Participation, 1991–2015

The 1990s brought a notable period of assessment and debate on the Indigenous/Canadian relationship, as well as how to increase Indigenous presence and participation in Canada's electoral process. There were numerous initiatives by parties and the government to increase Indigenous engagement.

What is noticeable for Indigenous participation and representation relative to the 1993 election is how many Indigenous MPs were elected and re-elected. Both Anawak and Blondin-Andrew were re-elected, and a third Indigenous Liberal MP was elected for Churchill: Elijah Harper (Hicks 1996). Harper's election victory marked the first time a Cree person was elected as well as the first time three Indigenous MPs had been elected under a single party. Willie Littlechild, the other Indigenous incumbent, opted to not run for re-election.

Although three Indigenous MPs were originally elected in 1993, a by-election in March 1996 would mark the first time in Canadian politics that four Indigenous people would not only sit in the House of Commons but do so on the governing benches. The election victory of Lawrence O'Brien, who was Métis, in the electoral district of Labrador also marked the first time that First Nations, Métis, and Inuit were each represented in the House of Commons at the same time. Moreover, they were MPs when the RCAP's findings and recommendations were released that November.

Amid the tabling of the RCAP's findings and recommendations, the Canadian state was also facing large financial deficits, a lowered credit rating, exhaustion from the mega-constitutional period of the 1980s and early 1990s, as well as secessionist woes with Quebec. In turn, the Chrétien Liberal government was not keen on pushing forth RCAP's recommendations, citing concerns over the costs of implementation. Rather than implementing the Commission's recommendations, such as those focused on bridging the socioeconomic gap related to funding for First Nations, Métis, and Inuit, funding caps implemented in the March 1996 federal Canadian budget were retained. Although there seems to have been little pushback by the Indigenous MPs at the time, fiscal austerity dominated the 1996 and 1997 budgets, and the 1997 federal election brought forth only minor changes in Indigenous participation and representation.

The 1997 federal election resulted in another majority for Chrétien and continued representation by four Indigenous MPs in the House of Commons. Both Blondin-Andrew and O'Brien were re-elected, though Harper, seeking a second term, was defeated (Government of Canada 1997). Additionally, Anawak chose to retire from federal politics, but the Liberals kept their hold on the northern electoral district with the election of Nancy Karetak-Lindell (ICT Staff 2011). Karetak-Lindell's win in Nunavut was a historic moment not only for Inuit representation but specifically for representation of Indigenous women. Karetak-Lindell's win marked the first time an Inuk woman was elected to the House of Commons and also the first time that two Indigenous women were MPs at the same time. Little change occurred in relation to Indigenous participation or representation between the 1997 and 2000 elections. In fact, Indigenous engagement in voting or volunteering during the 1993, 1997, and 2000 federal Canadian elections was not assessed or tracked; thus, the impact of Indigenous people's turnout and influence in specific districts, including their satisfaction or dissatisfaction with the Canadian state, is unknown.

Liberal leader Paul Martin actively pushed for the recruitment of Indigenous candidates to run for the Liberals (ICT Staff 2011). Martin often expressed that First Nations, Métis, and Inuit understood their needs and the issues facing them better than non-Indigenous people and thus their voices, presence, and input was crucial (Smith 2006). In other words, Martin's approach shifted toward partnership, where Indigenous peoples were to be included and at the table as equals within the Canadian state. Martin's commitment to nation-to-nation relations, as well as increased representation of Indigenous peoples, did produce results in the 2004 election. Although Elections Canada had already established an Aboriginal Community Relations Officer Program (ACROP) and an Aboriginal Elder and Youth Program (AEYP) in the 1990s, there was a focus in the 2004 election on party outreach and relationship building. For instance, the 2004 federal election had a total of 27 Indigenous candidates (Vongdouangchanh 2004), and five of them were elected to the House of Commons. In turn, that election brought forth some important "firsts." Both Bernard Cleary and Peter Smith's wins marked the first Indigenous candidates to be elected from electoral districts in Quebec. Cleary also became the first Innu elected in Canadian electoral history (Vongdouangchanh 2004) and the first Indigenous person was elected under the Bloc Québécois (Ladner and McCrossan 2007).

Additional supports were put in place through Elections Canada to increase the number of ballot boxes available not only within Indigenous communities but also in urban centres with high numbers of Indigenous peoples. For instance, the 2006 election witnessed an increase in advanced voting options for Indigenous communities as well as ballot boxes at Indigenous Friendship Centres (Smith 2006). Furthermore, education sessions were offered to increase Indigenous voter turnout, and party outreach aimed to increase Indigenous candidacies. In relation to the number of Indigenous candidates, there was a small decrease from the previous 27 in 2004 to a total of 20 in 2006. When looking at Indigenous candidates within the political parties, the Liberals led again with 16, an increase of five from 2004. The Conservatives and NDP both had five candidates each – a decrease of three for the NDP and an increase of two for the Conservative Party. The Greens had three Indigenous candidates while the BQ had one (Smith 2006). The House of Commons continued to have only five Indigenous MPs following the 2006 election. Karetak-Lindell and Todd Russell were re-elected in their districts, while Cleary, Smith, and Blondin-Andrew each lost their seats. Cree MPs Gary Merasty of Desnethé-Missinippi-Churchill River and Tina Keeper of Churchill won seats for the Liberals. Conservative candidate Rod Bruinooge, a member of the Métis Nation, was also elected for Winnipeg South. He became the sole Indigenous MP in a minority government led by Stephen Harper.

The start of the Harper Conservative government in January 2006 brought forth change in policy and relations between Indigenous peoples and the Canadian state. The Harper government opted to cut funding for Indigenous languages and continued to impose the 2% funding cap that had been in place since the Chrétien years. Further cuts were made to Indigenous engagement initiatives relating to voting and federal elections – almost all such activities implemented by the Martin government were removed prior to the 2008 election, including early voting at Friendship Centres and programs in place to engage Elders and youth (Ladner and McCrossan 2007; Cowie 2013). Lastly, changes to the *Elections Act* in 2007 further complicated Indigenous participation in the 2008 election as new rules made it difficult for Indigenous voters to validate their location and led to lower turnout in key ridings such as Nunavut, Labrador, and Desnethé-Missinippi-Churchill River.[6]

Although Indigenous turnout declined in the 2008 federal election, there were historic firsts as well. Shelly Glover's win marked the election of a Métis woman for the first time. Additionally, Glover, Bruinooge, Rob Clarke, and Leona Aglukkaq's wins also marked the first time four Indigenous MPs were elected to the Conservative caucus. Liberal Russell was re-elected in the district of Labrador. Following the 2008 federal election, the Harper government continued to push forth with a top-down approach to Indigenous communities, policies, and relations.

The 2011 election witnessed a dramatic shift in Canadian politics and a couple of firsts for Indigenous participation as well. Regarding overall Indigenous engagement, there was again an increase in the number of Indigenous people seeking election – in total, 35 Indigenous candidates. In addition to the four Indigenous Conservative incumbents, Peter Penashue, a member of the Innu Nation, sought to represent the district of Labrador. All five Indigenous Conservative candidates won their seats, marking the highest number of Indigenous MPs elected to the Conservative caucus to date (Ladner and McCrossan 2007; Cowie 2013). However, Penashue's win meant Russell's loss and with it any Indigenous representation in the Liberals (Jeffrey 2011). However, Romeo Saganash and Jonathan Genest-Jourdain were both elected as NDP MPs in the "orange wave" that saw the NDP form the Official Opposition (Pammett and Dornan 2011). Therefore, the 2011 federal election was significant not only for being another political earthquake in Canadian politics, with the NDP forming opposition and the Liberal Party being reduced to third-party status, but also because the number of Indigenous MPs jumped from five to seven. Lastly, the Conservatives won their majority – allowing the Harper government to continue its top-down approach to policy and relations with Indigenous nations.

In turn, there was an increase in actions among Indigenous peoples – including new instances of protesting, educating, and consideration for casting a ballot in the next federal election (Cowie 2012). The first step was the response by Indigenous peoples to Bill C-45 as well as other legislation that had been pushed, or planned, by the Harper government (McAdam 2014; Kino-nda-niimi Collective 2014; Kinew 2014; Coates 2015; Gottardi 2020). The response to such legislation was the creation of the Idle No More movement, led by Sylvia McAdam, Jess Gordan, Nina Wilson, and Sheelah McLean.

Idle No More began with a focus on concerns regarding the removal of environmental protections as well as the changes to Indigenous consultation and land leasing in relation to Bill C-45 (Wootherspoon and Hansen 2013; Kinew 2014; Kino-nda-niimi Collective 2014; Coates 2015; Gottardi 2020). Like the Arab Spring, the use of social media was an important component of the mobilizing and organizing strategy of Idle No More. Social media was also key for expressing Idle No More's purpose and reaching people not only in every corner of Turtle Island, but also around the world. Between December 21 and 23, 2012, round dances and rallies occurred in multiple cities throughout Canada and, in solidarity, around the world. Events took place in major cities such as Toronto and Montreal, as well as smaller or northern cities and towns such as Iqaluit, Prince Albert, and Peterborough.

Such mobilization from Idle No More also crossed over into Canadian federal politics – especially with the release of the Truth and Reconciliation Commission (TRC)'s findings, the introduction of Bill C-51, and the engagement of some political parties. Such conversation was further bolstered by the Liberals and NDP as they prepared for the 2015 federal election. Thus, by the spring and summer of 2015, the NDP, Liberals, and Greens sought to strengthen inroads among Indigenous peoples not only to build a relationship with peoples who have traditionally felt unheard but to secure votes from Canadians and Indigenous voters alike.

Ultimately, a record number of Indigenous candidates would seek seats in the 2015 election: 4 Conservative, 10 Green, 18 Liberal,[7] and 22 NDP (Fontaine 2015). Fontaine, in highlighting the record number of candidates, explains that this was "up 23% from the 2011 election, when there were 31 [I]ndigenous candidates." Additionally, after the formation of Idle No More, the Liberals, NDP, and Greens began meeting with Indigenous peoples and organizations to recruit Indigenous candidates and volunteers and to formulate policies for their platforms that related to First Nations, Métis, and Inuit.

Such relationship building from the opposition parties, alongside the five Indigenous incumbents, meant that there was, at minimum, 13 different nations who had members running for a seat in the House of Commons in 2015, alongside four candidates who simply self-identified as "mixed." Of the Indigenous candidates listed, 12 identified as Métis and another 10 as Nehiyaw. Another 6 of the candidates self-identified as Nishnaabeg, 5 as Inuit, 3 as Innu, and 2 each self-identified as L'nu and Dene. One candidate each self-identified as being connected to the following nations: Carrier, Nuu-Chah-nut, Kwakwaka'wakw, Nakota, Tr'ondëk Hwëch'in, Gitxsan, Tsleil-Waututh, and Abanaki (Fontaine 2015). Such representation and increased willingness to participate, alongside commitments made by the Liberals, NDP, and, to an extent, the Greens, demonstrated a significant shift in political parties' approaches to Indigenous peoples and likely boosted even further what would be the highest turnout of Indigenous peoples in a Canadian federal election.

In 2015, Canadians opted to elect a Liberal majority government, thus ushering in Justin Trudeau as Canada's next prime minister. Voter turnout among Canadians rose to 69.1%, an increase of 8% from 2011 (Grenier 2015). The highest jump in turnout, however, was that of Indigenous peoples: the number of Indigenous people casting a ballot in that election brought forth a double-digit increase, bringing Indigenous turnout to 61.5% (Dubois 2019). This boost reflected in part the focus relating to Indigenous peoples because of Idle No More and the willingness of the opposition parties to engage with Indigenous peoples unlike anything seen before. In some Indigenous communities, turnout increased by as much as 270 percent; a dozen First Nations communities ran out of ballots, leading to some community members being unable to participate (Puxley 2015).

The increase in both Canadian and Indigenous turnout not only brought forth a change in government but also the election of a record number of Indigenous representatives to the House of Commons. In total, 12 Indigenous MPs were elected, and media highlighted this result and the historic Indigenous turnout (Associated Press 2015). Although such turnout and the number of Indigenous MPs was historic, the reasoning for these phenomena relates little to feelings of duty as Canadian citizens.

DEMOCRATIC IMPLICATIONS: INDIGENOUS PARTICIPATION AS EQUAL CITIZENS OR A TOOL OF PROTECTION?

The trifecta of high turnout, participation, and representation of First Nations, Métis, and Inuit in the 2015 Canadian federal election occurred because of longstanding frustration over their treatment, which reached a tipping point with the Harper government. Like many prior Canadian governments, the Harper government approached Indigenous peoples with a unilateral and top-down mindset, which, following its formation as a majority government in 2011, led many Indigenous peoples to look at ways to counter such impact – with participation in the federal electoral process being one such option.

Since the 2015 Canadian federal election, there has been an increase in Indigenous representation within the House of Commons but also a downturn in Indigenous peoples casting a ballot. While researchers, commentators, media, and pollsters have given greater focus to Indigenous participation, with various pieces exploring such involvement and representation for both the 2019 and 2021 Canadian federal elections,[8] little attention has been paid to how Indigenous engagement has been approached, evolved, and come to reflect its current standing.

To understand Indigenous participation, it is important to explore the ways that participation and Canadian citizenship have been used by the Canadian state in relation to First Nations, Métis, and Inuit. Regarding First Nations, these aspects have continuously been used to disconnect Indigenous people not only from their own nations, but also from their own forms of citizenship until 1960. Since then, when First Nations were granted the right to vote without losing their identity, there has been a steady increase in recognition, representation, and input. In relation to the Métis, citizenship and participation have been used by the state not to treat Métis as equal citizens but to further access Métis homelands and to claim legitimacy and sovereignty over vast swaths of territory for Canada's national interest when related to resources and agriculture. A tyranny-of-the-majority approach was inflicted on the Métis, causing little to no recognition of Métis rights until the *Constitution Act, 1982.*

In relation to the Inuit, the granting of citizenship did not equate to equal rights or an ability to participate but instead served to further solidify Canadian interests, legitimacy, and sovereignty in the north. Thus, Indigenous participation until 1979, one could argue, reflected the Inuit more so as human flagpoles rather than equal citizens. The representation of Inuit in the House of Commons from 1979 on has had various impacts, such as Inuit being included in the *Constitution Act, 1982* and with it the establishment of a process for Inuit land claims and the eventual creation of the territory of Nunavut.

Following the upheaval in Canadian constitutional politics, the summer of 1990, and the push for the creation of the RCAP, Indigenous participation and representation continued to grow and with it the beginning of reflection of Indigenous voting and representation. The late 1980s, 1990s, and 2000s marked many firsts for Indigenous engagement, but turnout continued to be much lower than the Canadian public. With the return to a top-down and unilateral approach to Indigenous/Canadian relations and policy by the Harper government, especially after the 2011 federal election, many Indigenous peoples pushed back. This included the decision to participate in higher numbers, whether as a candidate or by casting a ballot in the 2015 federal election. The record high Indigenous turnout contributed to not only a change in government but also the approach the Liberals, NDP, and Greens took in engaging with and including Indigenous peoples. For some Indigenous peoples, the change expected has not been reached, and thus Indigenous turnout in favour of the current Trudeau government has not maintained its 2015 level. However, nor has the Trudeau government angered Indigenous peoples to the same extent as the Harper government and thus has not faced a similar rebuke to date.

NOTES

1 This is also referred to in Canada as the Red River Rebellion.

2 First Nation, for the purpose of this chapter, reflects those listed under Canadian Law as "Status Indian," those who are listed as "non-Status Indian," as well as those termed "Indian" in literature that historically discusses those who come from nations and communities that are referenced as "Indian" under section 27 of the *Indian Act*, 1876.

3 It is important to highlight that some Status First Nations women were able to vote when women obtained the right to vote federally in 1917 as a result of serving in World War I.

4 An exception was granted to First Nations veterans from World War I who also lived on reserve in 1924.

5 Michi Saagiig Nishnaabeg, in English, translates to Mississauga peoples. The Mississauga Nation is a member of the Anishinaabeg Confederacy.

6 For further explanation and understanding of this, please see Cowie 2024.

7 Note: The number for the LPC is actually 20. Randy Boissonnault was not listed by Fontaine, nor was Marc Sarre, who identifies as Métis.

8 See Cowie 2024; Cowie and Midzain-Gobin 2022.

REFERENCES

Associated Press. 2015. "Canada Elects Record Number of Indigenous Candidates to Parliament." *The Guardian*. October 22. https://www.theguardian.com/world/2015/oct/22/canada-elects-record-number-of-indigenous-candidates-to-parliament.

Barkwell, Lawrence. n.d.a. "Cyril Keeper, MP (b. 1943)." Report for the Louis Riel Institute. https://www.metismuseum.ca/media/document.php/14224.Cyril%20Keeper.pdf.

Barkwell, Lawrence. n.d.b. "Roger Teillet, MLA, MP, PC (1912–2002)." Report for the Louis Riel Institute. http://www.metismuseum.ca/media/db/12137.

Bell, Jim. 1997. "The Federal Election and Nunavut." *Nunatasiaq News*. April 25. https://nunatsiaq.com/stories/article/65674the_federal_election_and_nunavut/.

Chartrand, David. 2021. "The Métis People: An Inconvenient Nation." *Canadian Issues: Thémes Canadians* (Spring/Summer): 33–35.

Coates, Ken. 2015. *#IdleNoMore and the Remaking of Canada*. Regina: University of Regina Press.

Cowie, Chadwick. 2012. "Canada: It's Time to #IdleNoMore." *Indigenous Peoples Commission of the Liberal Party of Canada* (December). https://ipc-cpa.liberal.ca/blog/idle-no-more/.

———. 2013. "Validity and Potential: Dual-Citizenship and the Indigenous Vote in Canada's Federal Electoral Process." MA thesis, Department of Political Studies, University of Manitoba.

———. 2021. "A Vote for Canada or Indigenous Nationhood? The Complexities of First Nations, Métis, and Inuit Participation in Canadian Politics." *The Conversation*. November 1. https://theconversation.com/a-vote-for-canada-or-indigenous-nationhood-the-complexities-of-first-nations-metis-and-inuit-participation-in-canadian-politics-169312.

———. 2023. "Resurgence and Division: The Question of Indigenous Belonging and the Canadian State." In *Citizenship in Transnational Perspective: Australia, Canada, and Aotearoa New Zealand*, 2nd ed., edited by Jatinder Mann, 179–202. New York: Palgrave MacMillan.

———. 2024. "Does Indigenous Involvement Matter? Indigenous Political Participation and Representation in Canadian Electoral Institutions – Assessing the Forty Second Federal Election and Parliament." PhD thesis, Department of Political Science, University of Alberta.

Cowie, Chadwick, and Liam Midzain-Gobin. 2022. "Progress or Status Quo? Indigenous Peoples, Participation, and Representation," in *The Canadian Federal Election 2021*, edited by: Jon H. Pammett and Christopher Dornan, 220–45 Montreal: McGill-Queen's University Press.

DBpedia. n.d. "Wally Firth." *DBpedia.org*. https://dbpedia.org/page/Wally_Firth.

Dubois, Stephanie. 2019. "First Nations Vote Unlikely to Hit Levels Seen in 2015 Election, Says Experts." CBC. October 7. https://www.cbc.ca/news/canada/edmonton/on-reserve-votes-federal-election-1.5308087.

Fontaine, Tim. 2015. "An Indigenous Guide to the 2015 Federal Election." CBC. August 6. https://www.cbc .ca/news/canada/manitoba/an-indigenous-guide-to-the-2015-federal-election-1.3179421.

Geddes, John. 2019. "From Residential School Runaway to Trailblazing MP: Ethel Blondin-Andrew, This Year's Maclean's Lifetime Achievement Award Winner." *Maclean's*. December 4. https://www.macleans.ca /politics/ottawa/from-residential-school-runaway-to-trailblazing-mp/.

Gottardi, Francesca. 2020. "Sacred Sites Protection and Indigenous Women's Activism: Empowering Grassroots Social Movements to Influence Public Policy / A Look into the Women of Standing Rock and Idle No More Indigenous Movements." *Religions* 11 (8): 1–13. https://doi.org/10.3390/rel11080380.

Government of Canada. 1997. "Thirty-Sixth General Election 1997: Official Voting Results: Synopsis." *Elections Canada*. https://www.elections.ca/content.aspx?section=res&dir=rep/off/dec3097&document= res_ table12&lang=e.

Grenier, Éric. 2015. "Indigenous Voter Turnout Was Up – and Liberals May Have Benefited the Most." CBC. December 16. https://www.aptnnews.ca/national-news/mulcair-trudeau-make-lot-promises -annual-afn-meeting/.

Hicks, Bruce M. 1996. "Liberals Sweep Canadian By-Elections." *UPI*. March 25. https://www.upi.com /Archives/1996/03/25/Liberals-sweep-Canadian- by-elections/5252827730000/.

ICT Staff. 2011. "Former Prime Minister Paul Martin Honoured for Aboriginal Relations." *Indian Country Today*. September 15. https://indiancountrytoday.com/archive/former-prime-minister-paul-martin -honored-for-aboriginal-relations.

Jeffrey, Brooke. 2011. "The Disappearing Liberals: Caught in the Crossfire." In *The Canadian Federal Election of 2011*, edited by Jon H. Pammett and Christopher Dornan, 45–75. Toronto: Dundurn Press.

Kermoal, Nathalie. 2021. "Métis Lands in Western Canada: An Unresolved Issue." In *Canadian Issues: Thémes Canadians* (Spring/Summer): 44–48.

Kino-nda-niimi Collective. 2014. "Idle No More: The Winter We Danced." In *The Winter We Danced: Voices from the Past, the Future, and the Idle No More Movement*, edited by The Kin-nda-niimi Collective, 21–27. Winnipeg: ARP Press.

Kinew, Wab. 2014. "Idle No More Is Not Just an Indian Thing." In *The Winter We Danced: Voices from the Past, the Future, and the Idle No More Movement*, edited by The Kin-nda-niimi Collective, 95–98. Winnipeg: ARP Press.

Kirkby, Cole. 2019. "Reconstituting Canada: The Enfranchisement and Disenfranchisement of 'Indians' Circa 1837–1900." *University of Toronto Law Journal* 69 (4): 497–539. https://doi.org/10.3138/utlj.2018-0078.

Ladner, Kiera, and Michael McCrossan. 2007. "The Electoral Participation of Aboriginal People." *Working Paper Series on Electoral Participation and Outreach Practices,* 5–46. Ottawa: Elections Canada.

Marchand, Len, and Matt Hughes. 2000. *Breaking Trail*. Prince George: Caitlin Press Inc.

McAdam, Sylvia. 2014. "Armed with Nothing More Than a Song and a Drum." In *The Winter We Danced: Voices from the Past, the Future, and the Idle No More Movement*, edited by The Kin-nda-niimi Collective, 66–67. Winnipeg: ARP Press.

Milen, Robert A. 1991. "Aboriginal Constitutional and Electoral Reform." In *Aboriginal Peoples and Electoral Reform in Canada: Volume 9 of the Royal Commission on Electoral Reform and Party Financing*, edited by Robert A. Milen, 3–65. Toronto: Dundurn Press.

Nunavut Tunngavik. 2018. "NTI Expresses Condolences to the Family of Thomas Suluk." Nunavut Tunngavik – Media Centre. October 15. https://www.tunngavik.com/news/nti-expresses-condolences -to-the-family-of-thomas-suluk/.

Pammett, Jon H. and Christopher Dornan. 2011. "Appendix B: Results By Constituency." In *The Canadian Federal Election of 2011*, edited by John H. Pammett and Christopher Dornan, 333–61. Toronto: Dundurn Press.

Parliament of Canada. n.d. "Jack Iyerak Anawak, MP. Parliament of Canada: Parlinfo." https://lop.parl.ca /sites/ParlInfo/default/en_CA/People/Profile?personId=7084.

Puxley, Chinta. 2015. "Voter Turnout Up by 270 Per Cent in Some Aboriginal Communities." *Toronto Star*. October 25. https://www.thestar.com/news/federal-election/2015/10/25/voter-turnout-up-by-270-per-cent-in-some-aboriginal-communities.html.

Smith, Loretta. 2006. "Mending Fences: Increasing Aboriginal Representation in Canada." Research paper presented to the *Canadian Political Science*. June. Toronto.

Teillet, Jean. 2021. "Louis Riel and Canada: A New Relationship, 150 Years in the Making." In *Canadian Issues: Thémes Canadians* (Spring/Summer): 56–60.

Tester, Frank. 2017. "Colonial Challenges and Recovery in the Eastern Arctic." In *Inuit Quajimatuqangit: What Inuit Have Always Known to Be True*, edited by Joe Karetak, Frank Tester, and Shirley Tagalik, 20–40. Halifax: Fernwood Publishing.

Vongdouangchanh, Bea. 2004. "Meet Canada's First Innu MP, the Bloc's Bernard Cleary." *The Hill Times*. November 8. https://www.hilltimes.com/2004/11/08/meet-canadas-first-innu-mp-the-blocs-bernard-cleary/4273.

Wardhaugh, Robert. 2021. "Lament to Manitoba." In *Canadian Issues: Thémes Canadians* (Spring/Summer): 3–7.

Wootherspoon, Terry, and John Hansen. 2013. "The Idle No More Movement: Paradoxes of First Nations Inclusion in the Canadian Context." *Social Inclusion* 1 (1): 21–36. https://doi.org/10.17645/si.v1i1.107.

CHAPTER NINETEEN

Lavender Elections: 2SLGBTQ+ Candidates and Voters in Canadian Elections

Joanna Everitt and Angelia Wagner

INTRODUCTION

The past 20 years have resulted in dramatic changes in the opportunities for 2SLGBTQ+ individuals to participate in Canadian elections. Historically, stigmatization around sexual-minority, transgender, or gender-diverse individuals meant that 2SLGBTQ+ people kept their identities hidden in an effort to avoid the harmful spotlight that might be directed at them if they were to become politically involved. Some people who did run for election and won political office only came out as gay after leaving politics. Beginning in the late 1970s, other individuals bravely ran as out gay or lesbian candidates at the provincial level but were not elected. It was not until 1988 that an out gay candidate won a federal election campaign: Svend Robinson, a New Democratic Party (NDP) member of Parliament (MP), re-took his seat in Burnaby-Douglas (BC) a few months after he publicly announced that he was gay. It took nearly another decade for a second out candidate, Réal Menard of the Bloc Québécois (BQ), to be re-elected to the House of Commons (see Chapter 17 for a similar account of racialized MPs elected in Canada).

By the early 2000s things began to improve for 2SLGBTQ+ citizens with the increased awareness of 2SLGBTQ+ rights and growing public acceptance of 2SLGBTQ+ individuals. The opportunities to participate in electoral politics improved as well, with the rates of participation of out 2SLGBTQ+ candidates increasing ever since, giving researchers the ability to examine their political experiences, challenges, and media coverage. At the same time, increased willingness of 2SLGBTQ+ individuals to identify as such in public opinion surveys over the past decade means we are now able to measure differences in the participation rates, political interest, and vote choices of 2SLGBTQ+ voters and other Canadians. Through tracing the context and evolution of the participation and behaviour of 2SLGBTQ+ candidates and voters, this chapter highlights their past and current opportunities to fully engage in Canadian election campaigns.

IMPORTANCE OF THE STUDY OF 2SLGBTQ+ CANDIDATES AND VOTERS

Democracies are states that enable their citizens to participate in the decision-making process through their rights to vote in elections, be elected to political office, or to lead political parties. This participation legitimizes decisions that are made by elected governments and ensures these bodies remain responsive to citizens' interests and concerns. Since Confederation in 1867, the expansion of who is entitled to participate in Canadian politics has broadened, particularly in terms of the right to vote. From its original restriction to men age 21 or older who owned property, Canadian suffrage has expanded to include women who met the same eligibility criteria of men (1918), those who did not own property (1920), Asian Canadians (1948), First Nations women and men (1960), citizens with intellectual disabilities (1993), and incarcerated electors (2004).[1] However, access to voting rights has not always led to greater participation in terms of voting or running for elected office. For many years women, racialized Canadians, and Indigenous people have lagged behind white men in terms of voting turnout during election campaigns and were even slower to seek and win elected office.

While 2SLGBTQ+ individuals were never explicitly denied the right to vote, their sexual and gender identities have limited their opportunities for political engagement. The fact that homosexuality was illegal in Canada until 1969 meant that few individuals were comfortable being open about their sexual orientation or identities until the 1970s, as having a criminal record precluded them from seeking elected office (Everitt and Tremblay 2023). Even after homosexuality was decriminalized, the public was slow to show support for sexual relations between people of the same gender. A decade and a half after the emergence of the Gay Pride movement in the early 1970s, an Environics survey in 1987 found that only 10% of Canadians were prepared to indicate approval when asked "Do you personally strongly approve, somewhat approve, somewhat disapprove, or strongly disapprove of homosexuality?" with 55% indicating disapproval and 34% remaining neutral (Langstaff 2011, 51). In the last two decades, however, acceptance has grown more dramatically. A 2019 Pew Global Attitudes Survey found 85% of Canadians believed homosexuality should be accepted by society, up from 69% in 2002 (Poushter and Kent 2020). Another 2019 federally commissioned poll revealed that 91.8% of Canadians said they would be "comfortable" if a next-door neighbour was gay, lesbian, or bisexual, and 87.6% indicated they would be "comfortable" if a neighbour was transgender (Atkin 2019). Growing societal acceptance of 2SLGBTQ+ individuals and entrenchment of 2SLGBTQ+ rights in legislation has made Canada one of the top-ranked countries in the world on the LGBT Equality Index (equaldex.com/equality-index).

Yet even though Canadians have registered relatively strong support for the idea that homosexuals should be permitted to run for public office, especially when compared to the United States or Mexico (Everitt and Tremblay 2020), the number of 2SLGBTQ+ people who do and get elected remains small in comparison to other industrial nations. As Table 19.1 indicates, Canada still ranks behind many other Western democratic countries in terms of the presence of 2SLGBTQ+ actors at national levels of political office. This raises the question of why this is the case and what factors contribute to this result? To answer this question, we must first understand the experience of 2SLGBTQ+ politicians in Canada.

Table 19.1. Country Ranking by Percentage of National Lower House Legislators Who Are 2SLGBTQ+ as of January 2024

Country	# of 2SLGBTQ+ Elected	Total # of Legislators	% of Legislators Who Are 2SLGBTQ+
New Zealand	13	120	11.0
UK	53	650	8.2
Scotland	10	129	7.7
Israel	6	120	5.0
Wales	3	60	5.0
Sweden	14	349	4.0
Australia	5	151	3.3
US	11	435	2.5
Canada	8	338	2.4

Note: Calculations done by the authors.

EVOLUTION OF THE STUDY OF 2SLGBTQ+ CANDIDATES AND VOTERS

It is hard to study what one cannot easily identify. As noted earlier, it was not until relatively recently that politicians were prepared to publicly admit they were 2SLGBTQ+ people. Until Svend Robinson's revelation in 1988 and subsequent re-election, it was considered politically fatal or at the least seriously damaging to one's political career to come out as gay (Rayside 1998). Individuals like Heward Grafferty, Conservative MP for Brome-Missisquoi (1958–1980), and Ian Waddell, Liberal MP for Vancouver-Kingsway (1979–1993), did not publicly acknowledge their sexuality until after they left office. Others like Charles Lapointe, Liberal MP for Charlevoix (1974–1984), revealed their orientation only to certain individuals in their party caucus. For several years after Robinson's self-outing, MPs such as the BQ's Réal Ménard, the NDP's Libby Davies, and the Liberals' Scott Brison and Mario Silva continued to conceal their sexuality from the public in their election campaigns (Everitt and Camp 2014). While these politicians later came out during their time in office and were subsequently re-elected, Everitt and Camp (2014) argued that they were successful because they had already developed a public profile and were thus not hampered by negative stereotypes often attributed to gay or lesbian politicians (Golebiowska 2001; Golebiowska and Thomsen 1999).

Bill Siksay's election in 2004 was the first time that an openly gay man ran for office and was elected without having prior electoral experience. Siksay had worked as Robinson's constituency assistant and succeeded him as NDP MP in the Burnaby-Douglas riding when Robinson decided not to run again. Siksay's election was a turning point in Canadian politics: thereafter, all successful 2SLGBTQ+ politicians ran as out in their first elections. This included Raymond Gravell (BQ) in 2006; Rob Oliphant (Liberal) in 2008; Randall Garrison, Dany Morin, Craig Scott, and Philip Toone (all NDP) in 2011; Sheri Benson (NDP), Randy Boissonnault (Liberal), and Seamus O'Regan (Liberal) in 2015; Eric Duncan (Conservative) in 2019; and Blake Desjarlais (NDP), Melissa Lantsman (Conservative), and Pascale St. Onge (Liberal) in 2021. In total, Canada has had 19 2SLGBTQ+ MPs, yet at no point has there been more than eight holding office at the same time.

Figure 19.1. Number of 2SLGBTQ+ Candidates by Gender, 1988–2021

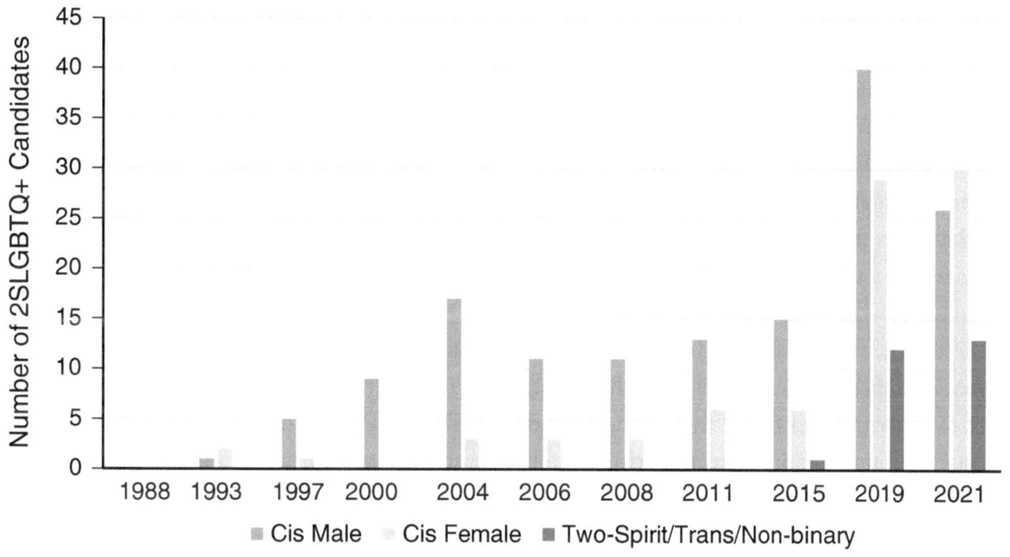

Note: Calculations based on 2SLGBTQ+ Candidate Data Set maintained by Everitt.

Although the percentage of elected 2SLGBTQ+ MPs is comparatively low, a far larger number of candidates have run for elected office. Until recently, the number of 2SLGBTQ+ candidates in any given election remained small, with a peak of 20 candidates running in 2004. Numbers dropped in subsequent elections before climbing again to 21 in 2015 and jumping dramatically in 2019 and 2021. In 2019, 81 2SLGBTQ+ candidates represented 5.65% of all candidates. In 2021, the 69 2SLGBTQ+ candidates comprised 5.1%.

Given the small number of out candidates running for office, researchers originally found little evidence that 2SLGBTQ+ candidates were run as sacrificial lambs (Everitt 2015). Sacrificial lambs are candidates whose chances of success are limited because support for their party in their riding is traditionally low. This can make these uncompetitive seats less attractive to potential candidates and lead nomination committees to search out candidates they might not otherwise have approached. In the past it was women who were sought out in these noncompetitive ridings; however, the dramatic rise in the number of 2SLGBTQ+ candidates running in recent elections suggests that parties are now running such candidates in non-winnable ridings in the same way (Baisley and Albaugh 2021; Thomas and Bodet 2013).

As Figure 19.1 demonstrates, early 2SLGBTQ+ candidates were primarily cisgender males, but more recent elections have seen an increase in the number of cisgender female, Two-Spirit, transgender, and nonbinary candidates.[2] Although it is possible that in the past the small number of 2SLGBTQ+ women who were elected could be attributed to the differences in the number of men and women who ran (Everitt and Camp 2014; Ashe 2020), other factors may now be coming into play.

One possible argument is that women, whether straight cisgender or queer, may be less willing to put themselves forward as political candidates (Lawless and Fox 2005 and 2010). A substantial body of work on political ambition suggests women in general are less interested than men in running for politics and perceive themselves as less qualified to do so. Furthermore, the differences in men's and women's responses to questions on these factors have not changed dramatically over the past 20 years (Lawless and Fox 2022).

Added to this, the increased toxicity of election campaigns, polarization of the electorate, and impact of social media and its ability to spread misinformation and violate the privacy of candidates all contribute to this lack of interest despite an increase in the number of eligible potential women candidates in the political pipeline. The result is that women often benefit from being approached by a figure in a political party or encouragement from their peer network to seriously consider running as a candidate, whereas men are more likely to be self-starters who seek party nominations without external encouragement.

These same factors are identified by 2SLGBTQ+ candidates as reasons they choose not to run for elected office. In her recent work based on interviews with candidates and potential candidates, Wagner (2019a) found that concerns about the loss of privacy, exposure to public scrutiny and public shaming, and increased criticism all factored into their decisions not to run. Added to this was the fear that negative judgments of their appearance along with moral judgments about their sexuality and/or gender identities would leave them vulnerable to negative campaigning (Wagner 2019b).

Despite these concerns, instead of waiting to be recruited, both women and men 2SLGBTQ+ candidates in Canada are more likely to be self-starters, often harbouring political aspirations from an early age (Wagner 2019b). This finding differs from that of Haider-Markel (2010), who found that lesbian and gay candidates in the United States in the early 2000s were more likely to require recruitment by party officials, sitting politicians, or political leaders. One reason 2SLGBTQ+ individuals might need to be self-starters is because of challenges that parties face in recruitment. Ashe (2020) found that the difference in the number of 2SLGBTQ+ cisgender women or trans/nonbinary and Two-Spirit candidates compared to 2SLGBTQ+ cisgender men candidates was because of parties' difficulty in finding these candidates.

Like other would-be candidates, 2SLGBTQ+ individuals are motivated to seek political office for many reasons, including a desire to be involved in political decision making, serving their community, and promoting changes or advancing specific policy goals (Wagner 2022). However, interviews with aspiring candidates or elected politicians seldom mention a specific desire to represent the 2SLGBTQ+ community and their issues of concern (Wagner 2019b; but see Tremblay 2019a, 2019b, 2019c). Instead, most candidates try to avoid the perception of being single-issue candidates (Everitt and Camp 2009a and 2009b; Lalancette and Tremblay 2019) by focusing on issues of broad concern such as education, the environment, or health care, deliberately downplaying policies focusing on equality or civil rights (Haider-Markel 2010; Wagner 2019b).

Recent work by Everitt and Tremblay (2023) examining the experiences of 2SLGBTQ+ candidates in the 2015, 2019, and 2021 federal elections has found that gender is a key reason that only four openly 2SLGBTQ+ cisgender females have been elected to federal office and why gay cisgender men are more successful.[3] Comparing the experiences of cisgender men, cisgender women, and gender-minority candidates, they argue that even with the continued challenges facing all 2SLGBTQ+ candidates, differences in electoral success rates can be attributed to the fact that cisgender gay or bisexual men have the advantage of being men. On the other hand, cisgender lesbian, bisexual women, and gender-minority candidates "continue to be nominated by parties with lower likelihoods of winning and within those parties relegated to ridings with less welcoming social and electoral contexts" and that as a result they have become the "new sacrificial lambs" in Canadian politics (Everitt and Tremblay 2023, 302; see also Baisley and Albaugh 2021).

Part of the explanation for the more limited success of 2SLGBTQ+ candidates can be attributed to the parties for which they are running. As many authors have noted, the NDP and, more recently, the Green Party have been most open to nominating and running 2SLGBTQ+ candidates (Ashe 2020; Everitt 2015; Everitt and Tremblay 2023; Everitt et al. 2019). Of the 69 candidates who ran for election in 2021, 41 ran for the NDP, 12 for the Liberals, 9 for the Greens,[4] 4 for the Conservatives, and 1 for the People's Party of Canada. No out 2SLGBTQ+ individual ran for the Bloc Québécois, a party that only runs candidates in the province of Quebec, while two others ran as independents or for a small minor party. Similarly, the NDP has often led with the highest number of racialized candidates in federal elections (see Chapter 17).

The larger number of 2SLGBTQ+ candidates running for left-wing parties can be attributed to these parties' ideological priorities that value and emphasize equality of traditionally underrepresented groups. In the case of the NDP, this commitment has led to internal structures such as a formal LGBT Commission and requirements at both the federal and provincial levels that promote affirmative action for 2SLGBTQ+ individuals and others who have traditionally been underrepresented in Canadian politics (Ashe 2000; Everitt 2015; Everitt et al. 2019). Parties on the political right, such as the Conservative Party or the People's Party of Canada, are less sympathetic to participatory pressures and do little, if anything, to recruit or support queer candidates. The Liberal Party has been slightly more strategic in their nomination of 2SLGBTQ+ candidates, typically doing so in ridings where the party has had strong support and that have substantial 2SLGBTQ+ populations (Everitt et al. 2019). Despite this, the last two federal elections have seen the party run more 2SLGBTQ+ candidates in places like Alberta, where they have limited chances of success (Everitt and Tremblay 2023). These patterns in party nominations are accentuated by differing levels of party competitiveness: despite running more candidates, the NDP and Green Party see a smaller proportion of their candidates elected because they are overall less electorally successful as parties. The success rates of the Liberal or CPC candidates is somewhat higher as, overall, candidates for those parties are more likely to be successful and the occasional 2SLGBTQ+ candidate is run in a party's stronghold, thus virtually guaranteeing that they will get elected.

2SLGBTQ+ candidates' success at the provincial level is not much better. Openly 2SLGBTQ+ politicians have held seats in all provincial or territorial legislative assemblies except Nunavut (Everitt, Tremblay, and Wagner 2019), although some were less forthcoming about their identities than others. Provinces such as British Columbia, Ontario, and Quebec, which have large metropolitan centres that are home to large 2SLGBTQ+ populations, have had higher levels of representation than others (Everitt and Camp 2014), although even in provinces with larger rural populations such as Alberta, the unexpected success of the NDP in 2015 saw three queer candidates elected (Everitt and Tremblay 2020). These patterns speak to the importance of factors such as constituencies' demographic profiles and parties' ideologies and success rates in contributing to changes in the number of 2SLGBTQ+ candidates elected to office.

Despite the relatively small number of 2SLGBTQ+ members of federal or provincial parliaments, Canada has been among the groundbreakers in the world in terms of having 2SLGBTQ+ individuals leading political parties and, on occasion, governments. While none of these individuals have actually held party leadership at the federal level,[5] several have run and been successfully elected at the provincial level. The most high profile of these was Kathleen Wynne, who was chosen as leader of the governing Liberal Party in Ontario in January 2013, and then led it until she resigned in 2018 after losing the election earlier that year. Wade MacLauchlan also served as Prince Edward Island's premier from 2015 to 2019, while others such as Allison Brewer, who led the NDP in New Brunswick (2006), and André Boisclair, who led the PQ in Quebec (2005–2007), campaigned as leaders but were unsuccessful. While rumoured to be gay and later acknowledged to be so by those who knew him, Richard Hatfield never publicly came out and instead governed New Brunswick from the 1970s to 1980s as a closeted gay man (Everitt and Tremblay 2023).

The study of 2SLGBTQ+ candidates and politicians in Canada has developed significantly since David Rayside's (1998) groundbreaking book *On the Fringe: Gays and Lesbians in Politics*, but much less work has examined 2SLGBTQ+ voters. The main reason is that, until recently, studies of citizen political behaviour have not included measures of sexual identity or gender identity beyond "man" and "woman." For example, questions measuring sexual orientation first appeared in the Canadian General Social Survey of 2008 and then again in 2013. However, it was not until 2019 that the Canadian Election Study used a question assessing voters' sex that included an "other" option (e.g., trans, nonbinary, Two-Spirit, genderqueer) and then also asked respondents "Do you consider yourself to be: Heterosexual/Homosexual/Bisexual/other?" This omission means little is known about the political engagement of 2SLGBTQ+ voters prior to the last 15 years. Canada is not unique in our inability to examine historical patterns of queer participation: the American National Election Study included an "other" option to the question measuring sex in 2016, and many studies in other countries around the world have yet to ask these questions.

However, evidence from more specialized surveys or experimental studies provides some sense of how 2SLGBTQ+ citizens have engaged with the political system. Interestingly, unlike other marginalized groups (such as women and Black, Latino, and Indigenous people) who have tended to be less politically engaged, this has not been the case for 2SLGBTQ+ individuals (Bowers and Whitley 2020; Turnbull-Dugarte and Townsley 2020). Instead, research suggests 2SLGBTQ+ people are more participatory and interested in politics than other members of the general population. For example, they are found to be more likely to contact government officials, work with others to solve a problem, donate money to a campaign, attend protests or rallies, write letters to the editor, or work for a campaign (Egan, Edelman, and Sherrill 2008). Turnbull-Dugarte and Townsley (2020) have found similar results in Western European democracies between 2002 and 2017, where lesbians, gays, and bisexuals scored higher than others on measures such as political interest, voter turnout, working for political parties, taking part in protests, signing petitions, boycotting products, and wearing political badges.

Research into 2SLGBTQ+ participation in Canada produces comparable findings. Gray and Desmaias' (2014) study of university students found that queer students were more likely to identify as activists. Likewise, Perrella, Brown, and Kay's (2019) analysis of the Canadian General Social Surveys of 2008 and 2013 found lesbian, gay, and bisexual voters to be more politically interested and

Figure 19.2. All Canadians versus 2SLGBTQ+ Canadians, Political Engagement

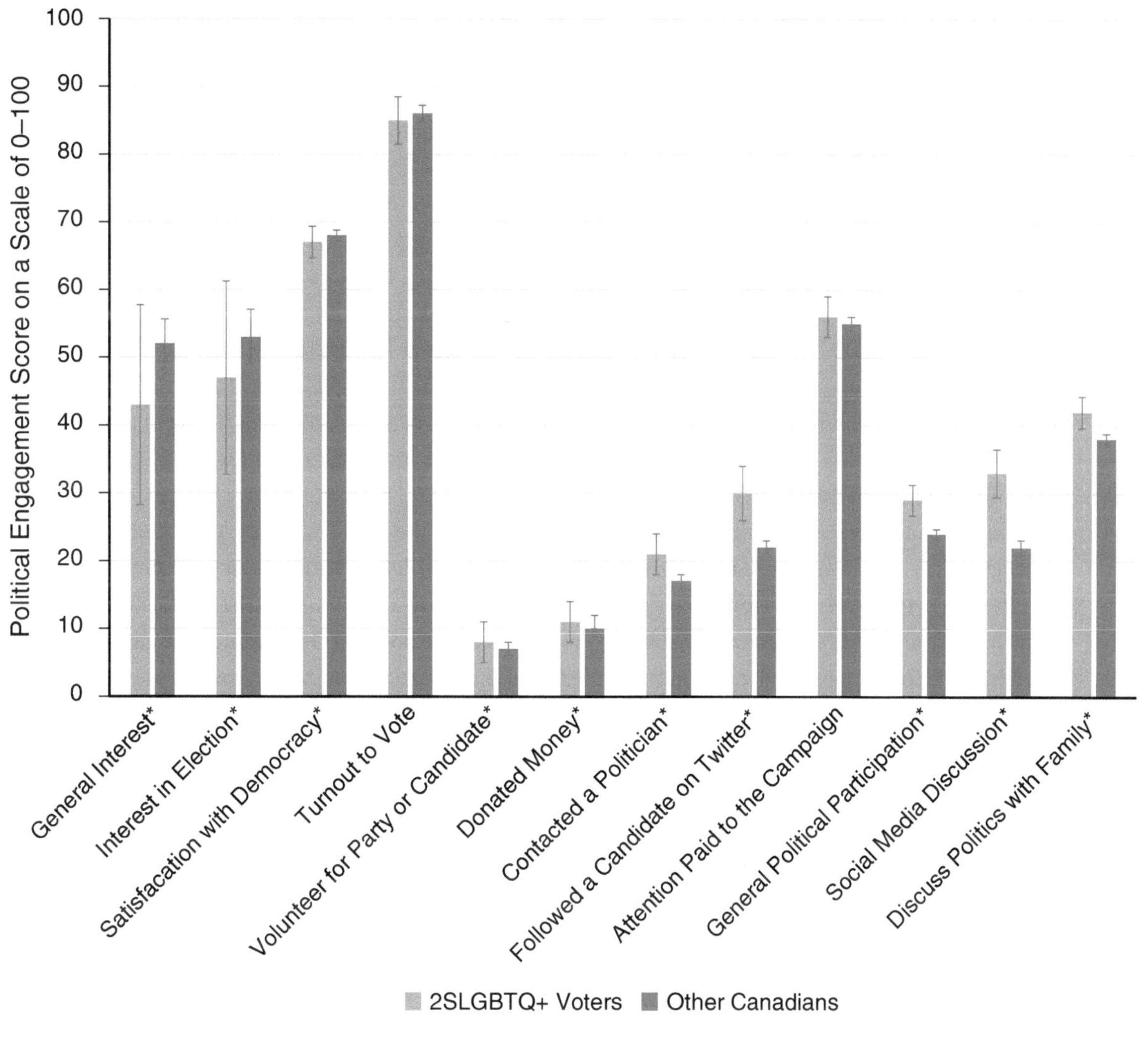

* p< .001
Note: Data from the 2021 Canadian Election Study.

active than other respondents, although their turnout rates were virtually the same.[6] More recent work by Everitt and her colleagues (forthcoming) based on the 2021 Canadian Election Study, however, finds slightly different results: 2SLGBTQ+ individuals scored higher than the average Canadian on activities such as donating money, contacting a politician, following a candidate on Twitter, engaging in non-campaign forms of participation, and discussing or sharing political information on social media, but lower on things such as having a general interest in politics or the election.

Figure 19.2 presents our analysis of the 2021 Canadian Election Study and illustrates the levels of political engagement of 2SLGBTQ+ Canadians compared to all Canadians. Political engagement involves interest and attitudes toward politics and the state of democracy along with activities that range from turning out to vote, discussing politics with others, volunteering for a political party, or donating money to a party. These results show that 2SLGBTQ+ voters differed little from other Canadians in terms of turning out to vote or paying attention to the campaign. Their willingness to engage in political discussion, particularly through social media, might be a reflection of younger Canadians who are more social media savvy being more willing to self-identify as 2SLGBTQ+ in a survey.

More academic attention has been paid to the voting behaviour of 2SLGBTQ+ citizens. Numerous American studies have shown that LGB voters predominantly support the Democratic Party and typically hold liberal positions on most issues (Hertzog 1996; Lewis et al. 2011; Strolovitch et al. 2017; Swank 2018a and 2018b). Closer study finds some variations among members of this community, with bisexual and asexual voters positioning themselves as less liberal than lesbian women or gay men (Lewis et al. 2011; Strolovitch et al. 2017; Worthen 2020) and pansexuals as more liberal (Worthen 2020). Turnbull-Dugarte's work finds similar patterns among 2SLGBTQ+ voters in the UK (2022) and Western Europe (2020, 2021), as they are more inclined to vote for left-of-centre parties and identify as more left-wing.

Canada's multiparty system makes it more complicated for groups to vote as blocks, but here too 2SLGBTQ+ voters tend to favour parties of the centre and left, splitting their vote between the Liberal Party, NDP, and Green Party and showing aversion to voting for the Conservative Party. Again, variations appear among different members of the 2SLGBTQ+ community: gay and bisexual men tend to support the Liberals while lesbians and bisexual women lean toward the NDP (Guntermann and Beauvais 2022; Perrella, Brown, and Kay 2012, 2019). Patterns in which lesbian/bisexual women are almost twice as likely as gay/bisexual men to place themselves on the left of the political spectrum (Perrella et al. 2019; Guntermann and Beauvais 2022) reflect more traditional gender gaps in the population at large. Albaugh and her colleagues (2024) found that trans and nonbinary voters are even more likely to support the NDP than others. It should be noted that candidate voter affinity effects might be at play here, since as noted, left-wing parties most frequently run 2SLGBTQ+ candidates (Everitt and Tremblay 2021; Baisley and Albaugh 2021).

IMPLICATIONS FOR CANADIAN DEMOCRACY

Canada has witnessed a sea change in attitudes toward 2SLGBTQ+ rights since same-sex marriage was legalized in 2005. Since then, policies addressing survivor benefits, adoption rights, age of consent to sexual activity, and protection from discrimination based on sexual orientation, gender identity, or gender expression have all been introduced. While transgender rights continue to lag behind those sought by gays and lesbians, achievements have been made. Since 2017 Canadian passports have been available with an "X" sex descriptor, and every province and territory allows for a change of name and legal sex without sex reassignment surgery. The result is that Canada is considered to be one of the most 2SLGBTQ+ friendly countries in the world.

Despite these policy successes, advocacy organizations called for more attention to 2SLGBTQ+ issues during the 2021 election campaign and invited representatives of the major parties to town halls and debates on these subjects. The major issues involved homelessness among queer people, affirmative health care for trans people, mental health services, the continued blood donation ban for gay men, ending conversion therapy, and the perpetual concern about hate crimes and discrimination, particularly against trans individuals (Woods 2021). However, little attention was paid to these issues during the campaign, even though 69 2SLGBTQ+ candidates ran for election in 65 ridings and eight were successful (up from four in 2019) or that these candidates ran for major and minor parties and in ridings in major metropolitan cities, mid-sized towns, and rural communities. Only a few policies were included in parties' platforms, and those were not new and often appeared more as token attempts to not appear homophobic than as real commitments to addressing 2SLGBTQ+ community needs (Johnstone 2021). Little media attention was given to these policies during the campaign, and despite advocacy groups' efforts no major campaign events specifically focused on the 2SLGBTQ+ electorate or politicians.

This lack of attention to 2SLGBTQ+ concerns is at odds with the increasingly active role that 2SLGBTQ+ individuals are playing in Canadian electoral politics. At the grassroots level, 2SLGBTQ+ voters are turning out to vote and engaging in other forms of political activity at rates that are higher than other previously oppressed groups within society. 2SLGBTQ+ individuals are no longer hesitant to step forward and seek party nominations to run for elected office. Parties are increasingly choosing them to run as candidates, and while many run as sacrificial lambs, the number of candidates who are running in party strongholds is increasing, as are the number who are getting elected federally and provincially. Even at the most elite levels of political officeholding – that of party leader – 2SLGBTQ+ individuals have had some demonstrated success. Nonetheless, as noted in Table 19.1, Canada continues to lag behind other Western democracies in terms of the percentage of seats held in parliament by 2SLGBTQ+ individuals. Without more research it is not clear why this is the case, but one contributing factor might be the generally accepting Canadian culture that could make it less imperative for 2SLGBTQ+ individuals to run for office to protect or advance their rights. Additional explanations include the first-past-the-post electoral system and the weakness of political party elites in controlling candidate selections at the constituency levels, which has resulted in many 2SLGBTQ+ candidates running as sacrificial lambs.

Furthermore, we might argue that the increased political presence of 2SLGBTQ+ people in legislatures has had more of a symbolic than substantive impact on the quality of Canadian democracy. That 2SLGBTQ+ politicians are taking their rightful place in government is seen as proof that Canada lives up to the democratic expectation of political equality, or the right of all adult citizens, regardless of background, to participate in political decision making. It also expands symbolic notions of who is a legitimate political actor, an important step toward the incorporation of this traditionally underrepresented group in Canadian democracy. But a focus on their *symbolic* representation has overshadowed, and perhaps even discouraged, their *substantive* impact on public policy. By heralding the growing *presence* rather than the growing *power* of 2SLGBTQ+ politicians, various actors use the descriptive representation of 2SLGBTQ+ people in our legislatures to reinforce national narratives of an inclusive Canada while leaving uninterrogated the reality that the 2SLGBTQ+ community remains marginalized in society. In other words, 2SLGBTQ+ politicians are tokenized as symbols of a mythical Canadian equality but deliberately not valorized as agents with the right to transform Canadian society for the betterment of the 2SLGBTQ+ community. Symbolism can thus be a tool of containment. Social conservatives might tolerate 2SLGBTQ+

politicians, but they actively work to prevent or unravel any 2SLGBTQ+ friendly policies advanced by these newly empowered legislators.

Strong party discipline in Canada also limits what 2SLGBTQ+ backbenchers can do, as they must work within a rigid party hierarchy to advance any policy proposals (Tremblay 2019a). 2SLGBTQ+ party leaders have the necessary institutional power, but they need to appeal to a broad electorate that includes voters who are ambiguous or blatantly hostile to 2SLGBTQ+ concerns, and they might moderate their party platforms and avoid discussions of these issues to improve their party's electoral viability (Everitt and Camp 2009a and 2009b; Everitt and Raney 2019).

In short, 2SLGBTQ+ politicians face enormous institutional, electoral, and societal constraints in promoting 2SLGBTQ+ friendly policies despite their growing numbers. This reality reduces the responsiveness of government to the needs of an important and distinct group of Canadians. But the growing political participation of 2SLGBTQ+ individuals in Canadian politics shows they are not deterred. Canadian democracy needs the active involvement of people from all walks of life and of life experiences, and 2SLGBTQ+ people are determined to bring theirs to the policymaking process. The quality of Canadian democracy will improve when 2SLGBTQ+ politicians see their policy impact match their political presence.

NOTES

1 See: https://electionsanddemocracy.ca/voting-rights-through-time-0/brief-history-federal-voting-rights-canada.
2 The Government of Canada (2019) uses "cis" as a short form of "cisgender" and "trans" for "transgender." A cisgender individual is defined as "a person whose gender identity aligns with their sex assigned at birth," a transgender individual is "a person whose gender does not align with their gender assigned at birth," a nonbinary individual is "a person whose gender identity does not align with a binary understanding of gender such as man or woman," and a Two-Spirit person is "a North American Indigenous person who embodies both female and male spirits or whose gender identity, sexual orientation or spiritual identity is not limited by the male/female dichotomy."
3 Blake Desjarlais became Canada's first Two-Spirit federal politician in the 2021 election.
4 The Green Party did not field a full slate of candidates in 2021, which is likely why their number of 2SLGBTQ+ candidates was lower than the 23 that they ran in 2019.
5 Amita Kuttneer, the interim leader of the Green Party after the 2021 federal election, identifies as nonbinary, transgender, and pansexual and uses they/them and he/him pronouns. They served as party leader from the resignation of Annamie Paul in November 2021 to the election of Elizabeth May and Jonathan Pedneault as co-leaders in November 2022.
6 The relationship between turnout and 2SLGBTQ+ identity becomes substantive and statistically significant with controls for demographic variables such as age, as younger generations are more likely to identify as 2SLGBTQ+. Age is also negatively correlated with political turnout.

REFERENCES

Albaugh, Quinn M., Allison Harell, Peter John Loewen, Daniel Rubenson, and Laura B. Stephenson. 2024. "From Gender Gap to Gender Gaps: Bringing Nonbinary People into Political Behaviour Research." *Perspectives on Politics*. https://doi.org/10.1017/S1537592724000975.

Ashe, Jeanette. 2020. "Canada's Political Parties: Gatekeepers to Parliament." In *Palgrave Handbook of Gender, Sexuality and Politics in Canada*, edited by Manon Tremblay and Joanna Everitt, 297–316. New York: Palgrave Macmillan Press.

Atkin, David. 2019. "Federal Government Asked Canadians if They're 'Comfortable' with LGBT People." *Global News*. December 28. https://globalnews.ca/news/6344287/canadian-government-asked -canadians-comfortable-lgbtq2/.

Baisley, Elizabeth, and Quinn M. Albaugh. 2021. "From Rainbow Sheep to Sacrificial Lambs: District Competitiveness and the Nomination of LGBTQ Candidates." Paper presented at the annual meeting of the Canadian Political Science Association. Virtual Conference.

Bowers, Melanie M., and Cameron T. Whitley. 2020. "Assessing Voter Registration Among Transgender and Gender Non-conforming Individuals." *Political Behavior* 42 (1): 143–64. https://doi.org/10.1007/s11109 -018-9489-x.

Egan, Patrick J., Murray Edelman, and Kenneth Sherrill. 2008. "Findings from the Hunter College Poll of Lesbians, Gays and Bisexuals: New Discoveries about Identity, Political Attitudes, and Civic Engagement." Hunter College, City of New York. https://www.yumpu.com/en/document/view/18581081/findings -from-the-hunter-college-poll-oflesbians-gays-and-.

Everitt, Joanna. 2015. "Gender and Sexual Diversity in Provincial Election Campaigns." *Canadian Political Science Review* 9 (1): 177–92. https://doi.org/10.24124/c677/20151208.

Everitt, Joanna, and Michael Camp. 2009a. "Changing the Game Changes the Frame: The Media's Use of Lesbian Stereotypes in Leadership Versus Election Campaigns." *Canadian Political Science Review* 3 (3): 24–39. https://doi.org/10.24124/c677/2009140.

———. 2009b. "One Is Not Like the Others: Allison Brewer's Leadership of the New Brunswick NDP." In *Opening Doors Wider: Women's Political Engagement in Canada*, edited by Sylvia Bashevkin, 127–44. Vancouver: UBC Press.

———. 2014. "In Versus Out: LGBT Politicians in Canada." *Journal of Canadian Studies* 48 (1): 226–51. https://doi.org/10.3138/jcs.48.1.226.

Everitt, Joanna, and Tracey Raney. 2019. "Winning as a Woman/Winning as a Lesbian: Kathleen Wynne and the 2014 Ontario Election." In *LGBT People and Electoral Politics in Canada*, edited by Manon Tremblay, 80–101. Vancouver: UBC Press.

Everitt, Joanna, and Manon Tremblay. 2020. "LGBT Candidates and Elected Officials in North America." *Online Oxford Research Encyclopedia of Politics*. New York: Oxford University Press.

———. 2023. "Are Openly LGBTQ2+ the New Sacrificial Lambs? Campaign Contexts and the Gendered Implications for LGBTQ2+ Candidates." *Canadian Journal of Political Science* 56 (2): 300–24. https://doi .org/10.1017/S0008423923000161.

Everitt, Joanna, Manon Tremblay, and Angelia Wagner. 2019. "Pathway to Office: The Eligibility, Recruitment, Selection, and Election of LGBT Candidates." In *Queering Representation: LGBTQ People and Electoral Politics in Canada*, edited by Manon Tremblay, 240–58. Vancouver: UBC Press.

Golebiowska, Ewa. 2001. "Stereotypes and Political Evaluation." *American Politics Research* 29 (6): 537–38. https://doi.org/10.1177/1532673X01029006001.

Golebiowska, Ewa A., and Thomsen, C. J. 1999. "Group Stereotypes and Evaluations of Individuals: The Case of Gay and Lesbian Political Candidates." In *Gays and Lesbians in the Democratic Process: Public Policy, Public Opinion, and Political Representation*, edited by Ellen D.B. Riggle and Barry L. Tadlock, 192–219. New York: Columbia University Press.

Government of Canada. 2019. *Gender and Sexual Diversity Glossary*. https://www.btb.termiumplus.gc.ca /publications/diversite-diversity-eng.html.

Gray, Amy, and Serge Desmarais. 2014. "Not All One and the Same: Sexual Identity, Activism, and Collective Self-Esteem." *Canadian Journal of Human Sexuality* 23 (2): 116–22. https://doi.org/10.3138/cjhs.2400.

Guntermann, Eric, and Edana Beauvais. 2022. "The Lesbian, Gay and Bisexual Vote in a More Tolerant Canada." *Canadian Journal of Political Science* 55 (2): 373–403. https://doi.org/10.1017/S0008423922000026.

Haider-Markel, Donald P. 2010. *Out and Running: Gay and Lesbian Candidates, Elections, and Policy Representation*. Washington, DC: Georgetown University Press.

Hertzog, Mark. 1996. *The Lavender Vote: Lesbians, Gay Men, and Bisexuals in American Electoral Politics*. New York: NYU Press.

Johnstone, Fae. 2021. "Another Federal Election that Fails LGBTQ2S+ Communities." *THIS Magazine*. September 15. https://this.org/2021/09/15/another-federal-election-that-fails-lgbtq2s-communities/.

Lalancette, Mireille, and Manon Tremblay. 2019. "Media Framing of Lesbian and Gay Politicians: Is Sexual Mediation at Work?" In *Queering Representation: LGBTQ People and Electoral Politics in Canada*, edited by Manon Tremblay, 102–23. Vancouver: UBC Press.

Langstaff, Amy. 2011. "A Twenty-Year Survey of Canadian Attitudes towards Homosexuality and Gay Rights." In *Faith Politics and Sexual Diversity in Canada and the United States*, edited by David Rayside and Clyde Wilcox, 49–66. Vancouver: UBC Press.

Lawless, Jennifer L., and Richard L. Fox. 2005. *It Takes a Candidate: Why Women Don't Run for Office*. New York: Cambridge University Press

———. 2010. *It Still Takes a Candidate: Why Women Don't Run for Office*. New York: Cambridge University Press.

———. 2022. "It Takes More than a Candidate: The Invincible Gender Gap in Political Ambition." Unpublished paper.

Lewis, Gregory B., Marc A. Rogers, and Kenneth Sherrill. 2011. "Lesbian, Gay, and Bisexual Voters in the 2000 US Presidential Election." *Politics and Policy* 39 (5): 655–77. https://doi.org/10.1111/j.1747-1346.2011.00315.x.

Perrella, Andrea M.L., Steven D. Brown, and Barry J. Kay. 2012. "Voting Behaviour Among the Gay, Lesbian, Bisexual and Transgendered Electorate." *Canadian Journal of Political Science* 45 (1): 89–117. https://doi.org/10.1017/S000842391100093X.

———. 2019. "Profile of the Lesbian, Gay, and Bisexual Electorate in Canada." In *Queering Representation: LGBTQ People and Electoral Politics in Canada*, edited by Manon Tremblay, 51–79. Vancouver: UBC Press.

Poushter, Jacob, and Nicholas O. Kent. 2020. *The Global Divide on Homosexuality Persists: But Increasing Acceptance in Many Countries Over Past Two Decades*. Washington, DC: Pew Research Center. https://www.pewresearch.org/global/2020/06/25/global-divide-on-homosexuality-persists/.

Rayside, David. 1998. *On the Fringe: Gays and Lesbians in Politics*. Ithaca: Cornell University Press.

Strolovitch, Dara Z., Janelle S. Wong, and Andrew Proctor. 2017. "A Possessive Investment in White Heteropatriarchy? The 2016 Election and the Politics of Race, Gender, and Sexuality." *Politics, Groups, and Identities* 5 (2): 353–63. https://doi.org/10.1080/21565503.2017.1310659.

Swank, Eric. 2018a. "Sexual Identities and Participation in Liberal and Conservative Social Movements." *Social Science Research* 74: 176–86. https://doi.org/10.1016/j.ssresearch.2018.04.002.

———. 2018b. "Who Voted for Hillary Clinton? Sexual Identities, Gender, and Family Influences." *Journal of GLBT Family Studies* 14 (1/2): 21–42. https://doi.org/10.1080/1550428X.2017.1421335.

Thomas, Melanee, and Marc André Bodet. 2013. "Sacrificial Lambs, Women Candidates, and District Competitiveness in Canada." *Electoral Studies* 32 (1): 153–66. https://doi.org/10.1016/j.electstud.2012.12.001.

Tremblay, Manon. 2019a. "Representation: The Case of LGBTQ People." In *Queering Representation: LGBTQ People and Electoral Politics in Canada*, edited by Manon Tremblay, 220–39. Vancouver: UBC Press.

———. 2019b. "Outing Representation: LGBTQ Politicians' Narratives." *European Journal of Politics and Gender* 2 (2): 221–36. https://doi.org/10.1332/251510819X15538597467765.

———. 2019c. "Political Representation and Emotions: The Case of Out Self-Identified LGB Representatives in Canada." *Representation* 55 (2): 125–39. https://doi.org/10.1080/00344893.2019.1604421.

Turnbull-Dugarte, Stuart J. 2020. "The European Lavender Vote: Sexuality, Ideology and Vote Choice in Western Europe." *European Journal of Political Research* 57 (3): 517–37. https://doi.org/10.1111/1475-6765.12366.

———. 2021. "Multidimensional Issue Preferences of the European Lavender Vote." *Journal of European Public Policy* 28 (11): 1827–48. https://doi.org/10.1080/13501763.2020.1804987.

———. 2022. "Who Wins the British Lavender Vote? (Mostly) Labour." *Politics, Groups, and Identities* 10 (3): 388–409. https://doi.org/10.1080/21565503.2020.1838304.

Turnbull-Dugarte, Stuart J., and Joshua Townsley. 2020. "Political Engagement and Turnout among Same-sex Couples in Western Europe." *Research and Politics* 7 (4). https://doi.org/10.1177/2053168020976952.

Wagner, Angelia. 2019a. "LGBTQ Perspectives on Political Candidacy in Canada." In *Queering Representation: LGBTQ People and Electoral Politics in Canada*, edited by Manon Tremblay, 259–78. Vancouver: UBC Press.

———. 2019b. "Avoiding the Spotlight: Public Scrutiny, Moral Regulation, and LGBTQ Candidate Deterrence." *Politics, Groups, and Identities* 9 (3): 502–18. https://doi.org/10.1080/21565503.2019.1605298.

———. 2022. "Motivations for Federal Candidacy." In *Inside the Local Campaign: Constituency Elections in Canada*, edited by Alex Marland and Thierry Giasson, 65–84. Vancouver: UBC Press.

Woods, Mel. 2021. "LGBTQ2S+ Candidates on the Issues that Matters Most This Federal Election." *XTRA Magazine*. September 15. https://xtramagazine.com/power/canada-election-lgbtq-candidates-208618.

Worthen, Meredith 2020. "A Rainbow Wave? LGBTQ Liberal Political Perspectives During Trump's Presidency: and Exploration of Sexual, Gender, and Queer Identity Gaps." *Sexuality Research and Social Policy* 17: 263–84. https://doi.org/10.1007/s13178-019-00393-1.

CHAPTER TWENTY

The Rural-Urban Divide in Canadian Politics

Clark Banack

INTRODUCTION

"In many advanced democracies," Armstrong and colleagues (2021, 2) have noted, "electoral division between urban and rural areas is one of the most striking features of contemporary politics." Importantly, in several of these countries, there is now clear evidence that rural voters, more than simply holding different political opinions than their urban counterparts, are playing an outsized role in powering the recent global conservative populist uprising, much of it containing a distinct authoritarian flavour. Indeed, seemingly sensing that they have been "left behind," both economically and culturally, and eager to significantly overturn "the establishment," rural citizens have overwhelmingly endorsed Donald Trump in the United States (Albrecht 2022; Monnat and Brown 2017), strongly supported the United Kingdom's exit from the European Union (Brooks 2019; Neal et al. 2021), and have served as key bulwarks for right-wing populist movements across Europe (Corradi 2022; Franquesa 2019) and South America (Scoones et al. 2021). As Rodríguez-Pose (2018) quipped in reference to this rurally based populist uprising, we may now be witnessing "the revenge of the places that don't matter."

What of Canada, a country whose politics have long been plagued with meaningful conflict structured around religious, linguistic, and regional cleavages but have rarely been analyzed through the lens of a potential divide between rural and urban? To what extent does a meaningful political divide exist on this front? On one hand, the answer is increasingly clear. In the 2021 federal election, the Liberal Party dominated urban ridings while the Conservatives were the party of preference for most rural Canadians. On the other hand, is it fair to assume that these electoral outcomes equate to a level of political polarization between rural and urban that has been witnessed elsewhere? In the wake of the 2021 federal election, news headlines bemoaned the "deep" (Alhmidi 2021) and "dangerous" (Thompson 2021) divide between rural and urban Canada, "two new solitudes … (that) now define the Canadian political landscape" (Wherry 2021). The broader societal divisions wrought by the COVID-19 pandemic have seemingly increased the concern that a vast gulf is opening between rural and urban Canadians, with the former demonstrating higher levels of vaccine hesitancy and opposition to public health restrictions compared to the latter (Yun 2021). To what extent is there legitimate potential for such divisions to lead to the emergence of a rurally supported right-wing populist movement similar to those witnessed elsewhere across the Western world? This chapter unpacks this question by investigating the political divide between urban and rural Canada: its historical roots, its evolution, and its contemporary context. Ultimately, I argue that the electoral divide between rural and urban Canada is growing, with important and problematic implications for our politics, but it seems unlikely that an electorally powerful right-wing authoritarian populist movement fuelled by "rural resentment" is imminent.

DEFINING THE RURAL-URBAN DIVIDE AND ITS IMPORTANCE IN CANADIAN ELECTIONS

The rural-urban divide in Canadian politics refers to the unique ideological positions, policy preferences, and voting patterns held by citizens who reside in rural as opposed to urban areas. In a country traditionally preoccupied by divisions between English and French or east and west (or perhaps centre and periphery), very little attention has traditionally been paid to "rural" as representing an important characteristic that can help us understand Canadian politics. There are studies that demonstrate a connection between living in a rural location and holding a more conservative political outlook than those in urban Canada (see Bittner 2007 and Cutler and Jenkins 2002), but it is only recently that a more sustained academic focus on the political divide between rural and urban Canadians has emerged. Before expanding on this recent work, however, it is necessary to take a short detour to explore what we are referring to when we point to "rural Canada," a label that has long been a point of contention among demographers, scholars, and policymakers.

According to Statistics Canada (2022), whose definition of rural equates to "an area with less than 1,000 inhabitants and a population density less than 400 people per square kilometre," just a hair over 6.6 million people, representing just under 18% of Canada's total population, live in rural communities. However, Statistics Canada (2017) also utilizes distinctions between "small" (populations between 1,000 and 29,999), "medium" (30,000–99,999) and "large" (100,000 and over) population centres. Perhaps a more accurate count of rural Canada would include those living in communities of less than 1,000 (traditional definition) *and* those living in small population centres? This would bring rural Canada's population to more than 11 million people, representing closer to 30% of Canadians. But is a city of 26,000, especially if it is within commuting distance of a large one, actually rural? Given this complication, several studies have thus embraced a tripartite urban-suburban-rural division (Roy et al. 2015; McGrane et al. 2016; Walks 2005), although it is still not clear how one is to draw a firm line between these categories.

To muddy the waters further, rurality can often be powerfully experienced as a subjectively defined identity more so than an objective measure, a fact that can make "rural" an important political characteristic while simultaneously making it impossible to define precisely. Given these challenges, most rural-focused scholars have abandoned attempts to draw a firm boundary between "rural" and "urban" and instead approach "rurality" as existing along a continuum, often along two separate dimensions: population density and "distance to density" (Bollman and Reimer 2019). These dual measures acknowledge that the lived experiences of people living outside of Canada's obvious metropolitan centres will be shaped considerably by both the size of their community *and* their proximity to a large urban centre. Of course, none of the above is meant to imply that "rural" is a meaningless descriptor in terms of understanding aspects of Canadian politics. It is, however, often a more complicated descriptor than most realize. With such caveats raised, on to the main course.

The Importance of the Rural-Urban Divide for Canadian Elections

As alluded to in the introduction, the political divide between rural and urban Canada has grown in ways that are now difficult to ignore. Antweiler (2019) has demonstrated that population density was strongly correlated with voter preference in the 2019 federal election, with highly dense ridings far more likely to be won by the Liberals and less dense ridings far more likely to go Conservative. In fact, the median population density of the ridings won by Liberal candidates was 38 times higher than for the ridings captured by Conservative candidates. The 2021 federal election was more of the same, with the Liberals capturing all of the 25 most urban ridings and 109 of the 150 most urban ridings across the country (Wherry 2021). Indeed, relying on an innovative measure of "urbanity," Armstrong and colleagues (2021, 19) have shown that Canada is "currently experiencing the most profound urban-rural divide in support for the major political parties in the country's history."

Of course, Canada's first-past-the-post electoral system routinely generates seat counts that overshadow the fact that wide swaths of urban Canadians vote Conservative just as decent-sized pockets of progressive-leaning voters reside in rural communities. Similarly, two recent public opinion reports suggest that the *perceptions* Canadians hold about the divide between rural versus urban citizens with respect to political values is often larger than the *actual* gulf that exists between voters in either location (Loewen et al. 2021; Speer and Loewen 2021). However, such qualifications do nothing to alter the contemporary composition of the caucuses of Canada's two main parties, which are looking increasingly more "urban" or "rural." This raises very serious questions related to representation and subsequent policy outcomes. Having caucuses that are either urban- or rural-centric will have significant consequences for the types of issues that are raised by either party, the issues that are deemed the most important, and especially the positions they take on those issues.

For instance, it is unlikely that a Liberal Party so constructed will have its finger on the pulse of issues pertinent to rural Canadian communities, for reasons rooted more so in a lack of familiarity rather than malice, let alone possess the capacity to generate policy that can meaningfully address them. This is especially problematic given that rural development scholars in Canada have long demonstrated that across several policy areas, assuming "what works" in urban areas is bound to work in rural communities is often a recipe for very poor outcomes in rural Canada. Indeed, there has been a strong push for policymakers to not only become more knowledgeable about the specific challenges rural communities face (and how these challenges can often be very different *across* rural communities) but to also routinely employ a "rural policy lens" to ensure legislation is not inadvertently placing additional negative pressures on rural communities and citizens, many of whom may already be struggling (OECD 2006).

Of course, the representational issues inherent in an urban-based Liberal Party are present, in reverse fashion, in a Conservative Party composed of mostly rural MPs. Can a party that is routinely shut out of Canada's most urban ridings plausibly claim to both understand and thus possess the capacity to address the key issues such ridings face? Or would a Conservative Party that finds itself in government automatically default to policy positions favoured by its heavily rural caucus? This is a slightly more complicated set of questions when compared to the policy preferences of a governing Liberal Party given that one of the surest paths to a Conservative electoral victory would necessitate overcoming the rural-urban divide to a degree. Indeed, the increasing rural-urban electoral divide places the Conservative Party in a perpetual state of playing "catch-up" to the Liberals given their sizable advantage in support in the more numerous urban ridings. This in turn raises the ever-present catch-22 for the contemporary Conservatives that has already toppled successive party leaders in the post-Harper era. Ought party leadership placate their heavily rural caucus by refusing to budge on issues such as the carbon tax, universal day care, or gun control, knowing full well such positioning will hurt them in urban Canada? *Or* ought they attempt to broaden the appeal of the party into urban (or at least suburban) Canada in search of the extra seats required to defeat the Liberals, but risk a rural caucus revolt that, at best, may cost the leader their job, or at worst lead to a literal fracturing of the party? No matter the strategic decision the Conservatives make, the broader issue related to representation in Canadian politics will persist and, given that party fundraising is reliant on individual donations, there is a strong incentive for both Liberal and Conservative parties to "play to their base," whether it be urban or rural, and thus further entrench this partisan division.

The Rural-Urban Divide and the Potential for Anti-Establishment Politics

Again, Canada is not alone in experiencing a stark partisan sorting between rural and urban citizens. Given the size of the rural-urban political divide that has emerged across several countries, scholars have turned their attention toward identifying the factors that are potentially driving it. As Taylor and colleagues (2024) note, traditional attempts to explain rural voter preference focus on either "composition effects" – the individual characteristics of rural populations such as age, class, level of education, and so on – or "contextual effects" – the broader social or economic context of a rural region, such as the longstanding cultural values of the region or its economic health. Yet in certain circumstances, such as when issues that rural and urban citizens disagree on become politically salient, composition and contextual effects may interact in ways that generate in individual members a cohesive place-based political identity, a strong social connection to a particular location. This in itself is not inherently dangerous, nor ought it be surprising – most people, rural or urban, form a particular connection to their home location and, for many, this connection will serve as a lens through which they see the world, including the political world.

However, scholars, especially in the United States, have been observing the growth of not just a rural, place-based *identity* but a rural, place-based *resentment*, a "hostility toward place-based outgroups perceived as enjoying undeserved benefits beyond those enjoyed by one's place-based ingroup" (Munis 2020, 1). Much of this scholarship follows the pathbreaking political ethnography work of Cramer (2016) in rural Wisconsin and her coining the phrase "rural consciousness" – the notion that rural citizens understand themselves to be both fundamentally different from urbanites *and* often ignored, and even looked down upon, by urban-focused decision makers. It is this form of place-based resentment that, Cramer demonstrates, has done much to generate in rural Wisconsin citizens a strong anti-government sentiment that is rooted not in a straightforward acceptance of the logic of "low tax" anti-government ideology but rather in a sense of resentment of urbanites and the politicians who seemingly act in their interests. Jacobs and Munis (2019), Trujillo and Crowley (2022), and Munis (2020) have all used quantitative techniques to further confirm the existence of a politically charged, place-based resentment in rural America that is steeped in a sense of being "underrepresented" and "looked down upon" and that frequently translates into political support for not just a conservative candidate but a thoroughly anti-establishment one. Importantly, Jacobs and Munis (2019) note that this placed-based resentment can be easily primed by politicians eager to consolidate political support in rural regions to a degree that traditional conservatism cannot, thereby creating clear incentives for political actors to further incite anti-urban (and broader anti-establishment) sentiments.

It is here, obviously, that the real danger for advanced democracies lies. This type of resentment is fertile soil for right-wing, authoritarian-leaning populist movements that promise to tear down "the establishment" or strike back at the "urban elites." It is thus not a coincidence that rural citizens have shown such strong support for such movements across multiple countries (Scoones et al. 2021). The question for Canada then becomes: will the emerging political divide between rural and urban voters noted above translate into growing rural support for an aggressive anti-establishment, and perhaps even authoritarian, movement similar to those witnessed elsewhere? As will be further unpacked in the following section, there is already evidence of a "rural resentment" in pockets of Canada, although it remains an open question the degree to which this political energy may be channelled in particularly problematic directions.

THE EVOLUTION OF THE RURAL-URBAN POLITICAL DIVIDE IN CANADA

The most obvious way in which the political divide between rural and urban has evolved over time is related to the fact that the proportion of Canadians living rural rather than urban lives has shrunk drastically. At the time of Confederation, more than 80% of Canadians were living in rural communities, and it was not until the mid-1920s that the populations of rural and urban Canada were evenly divided. Interestingly, Armstrong and colleagues (2021) note that it was between 1917 and the mid-1920s that the first evidence of a rural-urban divide in terms of voting preference emerged in Canada. This was most directly linked to the pinnacle of the agrarian revolt that began with a series of provincial "farmers' parties" winning office in the first decades of the twentieth century and culminated with the emergence of the pro-farmer federal Progressive Party that swept through western Canada and parts of Ontario on the back of strenuous opposition to the high tariffs of the National Policy. The party won 65 seats in the 1921 federal election but would suffer a slow demise over the next decade, ending the first period wherein a rural-urban political divide was observed.

As rural populations continued to dwindle relative to that of urban centres in tandem with the emergence of a more industrial economy throughout the middle of the twentieth century, it was inevitable that "rural issues" would not retain the significance they had held in previous decades. From today's vantage point, fully cognizant of the place-based resentment mentioned in the previous section, one could be forgiven for assuming that the emergence of "urban" issues as the focus of politics may have generated a political divide between rural and urban citizens mid-century, but there is little evidence that suggests this happened. Indeed, both the post–World War II boom as well as the corresponding building of the welfare state across Canadian provinces was largely inclusive of urban *and* rural communities and, aside from some predictable squabbles, there was little inherent in either major political party that would encourage either rural or urban citizens into unique political silos.

Armstrong and colleagues (2021, 17) do, however, note a reappearance of the rural-urban political divide in the early 1960s, with the Liberals in particular beginning to enjoy a significant advantage in urban areas. Although unable to pinpoint the exact reasons behind this emergence, they suggest that, due to both the criticisms of Canada's urban business and media elites by Progressive Conservative (PC) prime minister John Diefenbaker and the Liberal's embrace of highly educated urban professionals within their party apparatus, the Liberals essentially became the party of the "urban, well-educated 'knowledge workers'" at this point in Canadian history.

Interestingly, the Conservative Party's relationship with rural voters is not nearly as linear from the 1960s onward, due both to changes in party leadership and especially the eventual arrival of conservative-leaning third parties. As Armstrong and colleagues (2021, 14) demonstrate, the PCs enjoyed a clear electoral advantage in rural ridings under both Diefenbaker (1960s) and Mulroney (mid-1980s) but not under either Stanfield (1967–76) or Clark (1976–83). By the 1990s, wherein the PCs were nearly eliminated from the electoral map completely, it was the two new regional protest parties, the Reform (eventually Canadian Alliance) in western Canada and the Bloc Québécois in *la belle province*, that dominated rural ridings in their respective regions. However, the merger of the Canadian Alliance and the PCs in 2004, which created the contemporary Conservative Party, represents the moment wherein the current advantage they enjoy in rural ridings crystallizes. In fact, several additional studies have similarly noted the strong support that the Canadian Alliance (Blais et al. 2002) and the Conservative Party of Canada (Gidengil et al. 2006 and 2012) have garnered from rural citizens over the past two decades.

To note that rural voters are more likely to vote conservative, in Canada or elsewhere across the Western world, is certainly not a profound observation. However, Armstrong and colleagues (2021) highlight the importance of the 1990s as the point that rural voter support became especially concentrated, first among two regional protest parties and then in the contemporary Conservative Party, which essentially assumed the mantle of the key right-wing player going forward. For rural communities across Canada, the 1980s and 1990s represents a key period of transition toward the contemporary era. Urbanization, driven by both technological innovation and broader structural changes in the economy, was obviously nothing new. Between 1931 and 1961, Canada's rural population fell from 46% of the population to 30%. Yet from 1971 to 1991, it largely flatlined around 24% before again declining to 20% in 2001 (Statistics Canada 2011a). This decline in population mirrors a broader decline in the economic and social well-being of rural communities across Canada in the wake of the embrace of neoliberalism.

For the agricultural sector, the elimination of transportation subsidies demanded by newly crafted free trade deals – in addition to the shuttering of regional rail lines, the centralization of grain handling facilities, and the entrance of large multinational grain buyers and chemical man-ufacturers into the agricultural marketplace – fundamentally altered the economics of grain farm-ing, greatly reducing profit margins and leading to the demise of thousands of small-scale family farms (Statistics Canada 2011b; see also Epp and Whitson 2001). Rural communities buttressed by the forestry industry faced similar challenges due to the increased competition generated by a liberalized global trade environment, an increase in foreign ownership of mills by multinationals, and a more general "hands off" approach by governments when it came to the requirements of such companies to adhere to nonmarket considerations related to the environment, labour, or the well-being of the local community (McCarthy 2006; Young and Matthews 2007). Even Atlantic Canadian fisheries, so important to the small towns of the region, were negatively impacted by the introduction of neoliberal policies (Mansfield 2004). Overall, this period witnessed a noticeable "de-linking" between the profit generated by resource extraction occurring in rural areas and the broader well-being of communities. This in turn has led to increasingly uneven development trends between urban and rural Canada.

The economic impact of these changes on rural communities throughout the 1990s was com-pounded by the fact that they coincided with a significant reduction in government spending on various services across the country. For rural Canada, not only did this often entail the downsizing, if not outright closing, of key government institutions, from regional service offices to schools to hospitals to post offices, it also equated to both an offloading of costly responsibilities on un-derequipped municipalities and a significant reduction in spending on rural development efforts (Lauzon et al. 2015; Reimer and Markey 2013). Taken together, rural communities across Canada have subsequently suffered economic decline, capital flight, an outmigration of youth, and a decline of key government services and, as a result, today such communities are now older, less educated, and less diverse than urban areas (Halseth 2019).

Circling back to patterns of electoral support in rural Canada, it is not, I suggest, a coincidence that the populist right-wing Reform Party's emergence in western Canada (which was especially rooted in the *rural* west – see Flanagan 1995) aligns with this period of rural decline throughout much of the prairies and British Columbia. As Harrison (1995, 201–2) has noted, in 1991, essentially half of the Reform's membership was drawn from rural areas. Surely "western alienation," the notion that the political and economic interests of western Canada have been consistently overlooked by the federal government, was the raison d'être of the Reform Party. But it was also a party driven by a grassroots rage, so much of it rooted in rural areas, aimed not just at Ottawa or Quebec but at "political elites" in general and the overall direction of Canada in particular, in both economic and social dimensions. For instance, Harrison depicts Reform members as distinctly anti-government and anti–welfare state, skeptical about multiculturalism, and especially opposed to abortion or the advancement of the rights of what we today refer to as the 2SLGBTQ+ community (Harrison 1995, 205–6). Such issue positions have long been noted by scholars of rural public opinion, especially those related to social conservatism, which multiple studies have identified as being consistently higher in rural rather than urban regions (Bittner 2007; Cutler and Jenkins 2002; McGrane et al. 2016).

Harrison (1995, 208), to his credit, notes the connections between a surging Reform Party dis-proportionately rooted in rural areas, the broader transformation of the farming economy ("a way of life slipping under the wheels of seemingly irresistible modernity"), and the changing mores of a liberalizing society and, just briefly, raises the prospect of "a sense of social dislocation" as being the prime motivator for so many rural supporters of the party. Epp (2001) similarly notes a connection between the declining health of rural communities, the growing resentment across the rural west in the 1990s, and support for the Reform Party – and eventually the Canadian Alliance. This is an important connection that is frankly underdeveloped within the scholarly literature but is a key point in the evolution of the rural-urban political divide in Canada – a point, perhaps the first since the rise of the Progressive Party in the 1920s, wherein a distinct set of largely rural grievances, both economic and social, finds a national-level political voice. Granted, these rural concerns were part of a larger political stew containing both western alienation and neoliberal economics as key ingredients. However, it seems clear that the rise of Reform foreshadowed the potential rise of a rural-specific resentment in contemporary Canada.

The Rural-Urban Political Divide Today

How divided are rural and urban (and suburban?) Canadians on contemporary policy issues? There is a surprising dearth of extensive academic work on this question. In general, it remains true that on most key issues, rural citizens sit to the right of urban (and suburban) citizens. Lucas (2022), relying on the same measure of "urbanity" developed by Armstrong and colleagues (2021), has shown that this is true with respect to the importance of addressing climate change, the importance of traditional family values within society, the question of increasing immigration, and the importance of the energy sector. That said, there are meaningful provincial variations in terms of how far "right" rural respondents sit on such questions, with rural Albertans consistently sitting further to the right than other rural Canadians.

Loewen and colleagues (2021), using the most recent Canadian Election Study data and defining rural Canada as the 20% of federal ridings (84 in total) with the lowest population density in the country, note that there is a definite partisan divide between urban and rural Canada (with the latter preferring the Conservative Party), but that there are also a number of areas where a neat "right versus left" dichotomy between rural and urban does not fit. In fact, there are several areas of convergence wherein sizable majorities of both urban and rural residents agree, including on the benefits of free trade, the redistributive role of government to address income inequality, the implementation of higher taxes on high-earning corporations and individuals, and the need to increase spending on law enforcement and criminal justice. Interestingly, rural and urban Canadians even largely agree that obtaining abortions should be "very easy" or "somewhat easy" (Loewen et al. 2021, 10–11). However, the authors identify a handful of key issues where a clear divide does exist, including on perceptions related to the state of the economy, the environment and climate change, immigration policy, traditional values, and trust in government. That rural Canadians are pessimistic about the economy in rural communities and frequently express a sense that the government "does not care about people like them" is especially alarming given that such views appear to be essential ingredients in the type of rural resentment that has fuelled right-wing populism elsewhere across the Western world. So what of rural Canada?

Again, there is limited research on the existence of "rural resentment" in Canada, although the studies that do exist suggest there are elements present. Banack (2021) replicated Cramer's (2016) political ethnographic method in rural Alberta and unearthed clear evidence of a rural resentment that is motivating political behaviour in a single province. In a series of "coffee shop" conversations with groups of rural citizens, Banack noted a deep-seated sense of rural identity serving as a lens through which many rural individuals were making sense of a variety of political issues. Similar to the "rural consciousness" noted by Cramer (2016), Banack describes an identity rooted in (1) an adherence to a particular set of values and a broader "way of life" that is perceived to be fundamentally different from that experienced by urban (or suburban) dwellers *and* (2) a strong sense that rural issues were routinely ignored by governments and rural citizens themselves were frequently "looked down upon" by their urban counterparts. This in turn generated a sense of resentment that subsequently coloured the ways in which rural Albertans interpreted other issues, including their preference for anti-establishment politics and their sense that newcomers to Canada and Indigenous peoples were unjustly favoured by governments.

Borwein and Lucas (2023), in an attempt to quantitively measure place-based resentment among urban, suburban, and rural citizens across Canada, note that members of *each* group hold some level of such resentment, but it is highest among rural citizens and is, interestingly, aimed at both urban and suburban Canadians in equal measure. Relying on the same survey, Lucas (2022), has demonstrated that, although rural place-based resentment is higher than urban or suburban resentment in every single Canadian province, its actual score varies across provinces, with rural residents in western Canada expressing the highest levels of resentment while rural residents of Quebec appear to be the least "resentful." However, there is clearly more work to do to tease out both the size and nature of "rural resentment" in Canada, its unique appearance across provinces and regions, and its potential political implications.

DEMOCRATIC IMPLICATIONS OF THE RURAL-URBAN DIVIDE FOR CANADIAN ELECTIONS

At this point it is likely that the broader democratic implications of the rural-urban political divide that has emerged in recent Canadian elections are largely evident. On one level, we have entered an era of national politics wherein the two major parties have essentially become either urban- or rural-centric. The policy implications of such an outcome, namely the increasing lack of capacity of either party to meaningfully engage with "the other side," were discussed above. That structural factors like party fundraising rules and the importance of "getting out the vote" further incentivize each party to play to their respective bases will likely further entrench this division going forward. More broadly, increasingly "safe seats" in very urban or very rural parts of Canada may further depress voter turnout in such ridings and perhaps even decrease an engagement with politics more generally (Cutler et al. 2022). Whether or not this happens, for the foreseeable future it seems that the federal government will likely suffer from a meaningful lack of representation of either rural or urban Canadians. Given the policy consequences of this trend, especially for rural communities already struggling with myriad challenges rooted in broader structural changes to the economy, this may very well lead to a growth in the type of place-based resentment that has been on the rise elsewhere.

This leads to a second, albeit related, set of implications for Canadian elections and politics more generally. I have already discussed the emerging evidence of a place-based "rural resentment" across Canada. Although both moral traditionalism (Trujillo and Crowley 2022) and racism (Nelsen and Petsko 2021) have been shown to be linked to rural resentment in the United States, the strongest factors underlying its emergence tend to be rooted in the declining economic prospects of rural communities (Scoones et al. 2021). As noted, the economic prospects of most rural communities across Canada have declined. Although thoroughly underdeveloped in the scholarly literature at this point, there seems to be a connection between the concentration of the rural vote in western Canada behind the populist right-wing Reform Party in the 1990s, and the declining prospects of rural communities hit hard by the embrace of neoliberal policies throughout the 1980s and 1990s. Sifting through more recent data, Speer (2019) has noted that, in general, rural communities across Canada continue to generate both employment rates and labour force participation rates that are lower than those in urban Canada. Somewhat ominously, Speer further warns that the rates between rural and urban locations are especially uneven for working-age males, a scenario that has been highlighted by scholars as having the potential to generate especially problematic economic and social consequences in rural regions (Eberstadt 2018). Indeed, it is often underemployed working-age males that are most susceptible to the messaging of emerging right-wing populist and authoritarian movements.

Is it thus simply a matter of time before more extreme right-wing parties emerge out of rural areas, powered by a growing place-based resentment, in Canada? At this point, the evidence is decidedly mixed. Some have speculated that the so-called "Freedom Convoy" that overtook downtown Ottawa in February 2022 was an especially "rural" reaction to COVID-19 restrictions in particular and, more broadly, to an "urban" Liberal government led by the cosmopolitan Justin Trudeau, although the scholarly evidence is thin at this point (Lett 2022). One admittedly imperfect attempt to measure rural support for an emerging far-right movement would be to explore voter support for the federal People's Party of Canada. They have advocated for a set of policies similar to the upstart right-wing populist parties of Europe, including blatant anti-immigration and anti-multiculturalism stances, opposition to climate change initiatives, and a repealing of all public health restrictions related to the COVID-19 pandemic. Using Loewen and Speer's (2021) definition of rural Canada as the least-dense 84 ridings across the country, a quick calculation shows that, in the 2021 federal election, People's Party candidates garnered an average of 7.13% of the votes cast in these "least dense" ridings, slightly better than their overall total of 4.94% nationwide. Interestingly, People's Party support jumps to an average of 9% across the rural ridings of the four western provinces and 10.5% in Alberta's rural ridings. There is clearly more support for the People's Party in rural, rather than urban, Canada, and this increases as we move west (a finding that corresponds with the rural west's support for the Reform Party in the 1990s *and* mirrors Lucas' contemporary observation that rural resentment is currently the highest in western Canada). However, these numbers are hardly overwhelming and, again, support for the People's Party is not a perfect measure of an outbreak of "rural resentment."

More research is needed to better understand the political implications of rural resentment in Canada but, at this point, it seems unlikely that the emergence of a powerful, rural-based authoritarian populist movement is imminent. What makes Canada seemingly unique on this point? Again, acknowledging more research is required on this topic, I'll close with two observations. First, the Conservatives have, especially under current leader Pierre Poilievre, attempted to "corner the market" in a certain sense by demonstrating sympathy for the Freedom Convoy and by staking out clear positions on issues like climate change and gun control that are very popular in rural regions, perhaps even to the determent of their broader electoral fortunes in urban and suburban Canada. This must go some distance toward dampening a sense of being "overlooked" for rural Canadians, even if the Conservatives are taking these positions from the opposition benches. Second, recall that place-based resentment – especially in rural regions suffering economic decline or feeling increasingly dislocated socially or culturally – is something that can easily be primed by political actors to great effect. In Canada, neither the Conservatives nor the People's Party have, as of yet, moved in this direction in any meaningful way compared to the actions of certain American politicians. Again, further research is required to better understand this pattern but, if asked to speculate, I suspect that the electoral maps of the United States, often heavily gerrymandered in favour of rural regions across several states at the congressional level and constitutionally mandated to overrepresent rural regions in national Senate elections, go some way to creating strong incentives to prime rural resentment in America. In Canada, the electoral math is quite different and, to be frank, the incentives to incite rural resentment are not nearly as strong. In short, it is likely a losing strategy to play the rural resentment card too forcibly.

REFERENCES

Albrecht, D.E. 2022. "Donald Trump and Changing Rural/Urban Voting Patterns." *Journal of Rural Studies* 91: 148–56. https://doi.org/10.1016/j.jrurstud.2022.03.009.

Alhmidi, Maan. 2021. "Election Results Show Deep Divide between Rural and Urban Canadians: Experts." *Global News*. September 25. https://globalnews.ca/news/8220649/canada-election-results-urban-rural-divide/.

Antweiler, Werner. 2019. "Canada's Growing Urban-Rural Divide." Blog. https://wernerantweiler.ca/blog.php?item=2019-10-23.

Armstrong, David A., Jack Lucas, and Zack Taylor. 2021. "The Urban-Rural Divide in Canadian Federal Elections, 1896–2019." *Canadian Journal of Political Science* 54 (2): 84–106. https://doi.org/10.1017/S0008423921000792.

Banack, Clark. 2021. "Ethnography and Political Opinion: Identity, Alienation and Anti-establishmentarianism in Rural Alberta." *Canadian Journal of Political Science* 54 (1): 1–22. https://doi.org/10.1017/S0008423920000694.

Bittner, Amanda. 2007. "The Effects of Information and Social Cleavages: Explaining Issue Attitudes and Vote Choice in Canada." *Canadian Journal of Political Science* 40 (4): 935–68. https://doi.org/10.1017/S000842390707117X.

Blais, Andre, Elisabeth Gidengil, Richard Nadeau, and Neil Nevitte. 2002. *Anatomy of a Liberal Victory: Making Sense of the Vote in the 2000 Canadian Election*. Peterborough: Broadview Press.

Bollman, Ray D., and Bill Reimer. 2019. "What Is Rural? What Is Rural Policy? What Is Rural Development Policy?" In *The Routledge Handbook of Comparative Rural Policy*, edited by M. Vittuari, J. Devlin, M. Pagani, and T.G. Johnson, 9–26. London: Routledge.

Borwein, Sophie, and Jack Lucas. 2023. "Asymmetries in Urban, Suburban, and Rural Place-Based Resentment." *Political Geography* 105: 1–10.

Brooks, Sally. 2019. "Brexit and the Politics of the Rural." *Sociologia Ruralis* 60 (4): 790–809.

Corradi, Valerio. 2022. "Right-Wing Rural Populisms: Comparative Analysis of Two European Regions." *Rural Sociology* 87 (S1): 715–32. https://doi.org/10.1111/ruso.12396.

Cramer, Katherine. 2016. *The Politics of Resentment: Rural Consciousness in Wisconsin and the Rise of Scott Walker*. Chicago: University of Chicago Press.

Cutler, Fred, and Richard W. Jenkins. 2002. "Where One Lives and What One Thinks: Implications of the Rural-Urban Cleavage for Canadian Federalism." In *Canada: The State of the Federation 2001*, edited by Hamish Telford and Harvey Lazar, 367–90. Montreal and Kingston: McGill-Queen's University Press.

Cutler, Fred, Alexandre Rivard, and Antony Hodgson. 2022. "Why Bother? Supporters of Locally Weaker Parties Are Less Likely to Vote or to Vote Sincerely." *Canadian Journal of Political Science* 55 (1): 208–25. https://doi.org/10.1017/S0008423921000755.

Eberstadt, Nicholas. 2018. "Men without Work: America's Quiet Catastrophe … The Collapse of Work – for Men." American Enterprise Institute. January 30. http://www.aei.org/publication/men-without-work-2/.

Epp, Roger. 2001. "The Political De-skilling of Rural Communities." In *Writing Off the Rural West: Globalization, Governments, and the Transformation of Rural Communities*, edited by R. Epp and D. Whitson, 301–24. Edmonton: University of Alberta Press.

Epp, Roger, and Whitson, Dave, eds. 2001. *Writing Off the Rural West: Globalization, Governments, and the Transformation of Rural Communities*. Edmonton: University of Alberta Press.

Flanagan, Thomas. 1995. *Waiting for the Wave*. Toronto: Stoddart Publishing.

Franquesa, Jaume. 2019. "The Vanishing Exception: Republican and Reactionary Specters of Populism in Rural Spain." *Journal of Peasant Studies* 46 (3): 537–60.

Gidengil, Elisabeth, André Blais, Joanna Everitt, Patrick Fournier, and Neil Nevitte. 2006. "Back to the Future? Making Sense of the 2004 Canadian Election Outside Quebec." *Canadian Journal of Political Science/ Revue Canadienne de Science Politique* 39 (1): 1–25. https://doi.org/10.1017/S0008423906060069.

Gidengil, Elisabeth, André Blais, Joanna Everitt, Patrick Fournier, and Neil Nevitte. 2012. *Dominance & Decline: Making Sense of Recent Canadian Elections*. Toronto: University of Toronto Press.

Halseth, G., ed. 2019. *Transformation of Resource Towns and Peripheries: Political Economy Perspectives*. London: Routledge.

Harrison, Trevor W. 1995. *Of Passionate Intensity: Right-Wing Populism and the Reform Party of Canada*. Toronto: University of Toronto Press.

Jacobs, Nicholas F., and B. Kal Munis. 2019. "Place-Based Imagery and Voter Evaluations: Experimental Evidence on the Politics of Place." *Political Research Quarterly* 72 (2): 263–77. https://doi.org/10.1177/1065912918781035.

Lauzon, A., Bollman, R., & Ashton, B. 2015. "Ontario." In *The State of Rural Canada*, edited by S. Markey, S. Breen, R. Gibson, R. Mealy, & L. Ryser, 1–8. Canadian Rural Revitalization Foundation / Fondation canadienne pour la revitalisation rurale. http://sorc.crrf.ca.

Lett, Dan. 2022. "Convoy Protests Drive into Rural-Urban Divide." *Winnipeg Free Press*. February 14. https://www.winnipegfreepress.com/breakingnews/2022/02/14/convoy-protests-drive-into-rural-urban-divide.

Loewen, Peter, Sean Speer, and Stephanie Bertolo. 2021. "Fault Lines and Common Ground: Understanding the State of Canada's Urban-Rural Divide." Public Policy Forum. https://ppforum.ca/publications/fault-lines-and-common-ground/.

Lucas, Jack. 2022. "Urban-Rural Divides in Alberta: Issues, Identities, and Ideology." Presentation to the Parkland Institutes Conference. Edmonton. November 19.

Lucas, J., D.A. Armstrong, and R. Bakker. 2024. "The Development of the Urban-Rural Cleavage in Anglo-American Democracies." *Comparative Political Studies* 57 (8): 1339–74.

Mansfield, B. 2004. "Neoliberalism in the Oceans: 'Rationalization,' Property Rights, and the Commons Question." *Geoforum* 35 (3): 313–26. https://doi.org/10.1016/j.geoforum.2003.05.002.

McCarthy, James. 2006. "Neoliberalism and the Politics of Alternatives: Community Forestry in British Columbia and the United States." *Annals of the Association of American Geographers* 96 (1): 84–104. https://doi.org/10.1111/j.1467-8306.2006.00500.x.

McGrane, David, Loleen Berdahl, and Scott Bell. 2016. "Moving beyond the Urban/Rural Cleavage: Measuring Values and Policy Preferences across Residential Zones in Canada." *Journal of Urban Affairs* 39 (1): 17–39. https://doi.org/10.1111/juaf.12294.

Monnat, Shannon M., and David L. Brown. 2017. "More than a Rural Revolt: Landscapes of Despair and the 2016 Presidential Election." *Journal of Rural Studies* 55: 227–36. https://doi.org/10.1016/j.jrurstud.2017.08.010.

Munis, B. Kal. 2020. "Us Over Here Versus Them Over There … Literally: Measuring Place Resentment in American Politics." *Political Behavior* 44 (September 14): 1057–78. https://doi.org/10.1007/s11109-020-09641-2.

Neal, Sarah, Anna Gawlewicz, Jesse Heley, and Rhys Dafdd Jones. 2021. "Rural Brexit? The Ambivalent Politics of Rural Community, Migration and Dependency." *Journal of Rural Studies* 82: 176–83. https://doi.org/10.1016/j.jrurstud.2021.01.017.

Nelsen, Matthew D., and Christopher D. Petsko. 2021. "Race and White Rural Consciousness." *Perspectives on Politics* 19 (4): 1205–18. https://doi.org/10.1017/S1537592721001948.

OECD (Organisation for Economic Co-operation and Development). 2006. *Reinventing Rural Policy*. October. https://www.oecd.org/regional/37556607.pdf.

Reimer, Bill, and Sean Markey. 2013. *Dismantling of Rural Institutions*. Canadian Rural Revitalization Foundation Annual Report 2013–2014.

Rodríguez-Pose, Andrés. 2018. "The Revenge of the Places That Don't Matter (and What to Do about It)." *Cambridge Journal of Regions, Economy and Society* 11 (1): 189–209. https://doi.org/10.1093/cjres/rsx024.

Roy, Jason, Andrea M.L. Perrella, and Joshua Borden. 2015. "Rural, Suburban and Urban Voters: Dissecting Residence Based Voter Cleavages in Provincial Elections." *Canadian Political Science Review* 9 (1), 112–27. https://doi.org/10.24124/c677/20151203.

Scoones, Ian, and Marc Edelman, Saturnino M. Borras Jr., Lyda Fernanda Forero, Ruth Hall, Wendy Wolfod, and Ben White, eds. 2021. *Authoritarian Populism and the Rural World*. London: Routledge.

Speer, Sean. 2019. "Forgotten People and Forgotten Places: Canada's Economic Performance in the Age of Populism." Macdonald-Laurier Institute. August. https://macdonaldlaurier.ca/files/pdf/MLI_Speer_ScopingSeries1_FWeb.pdf.

Speer, Sean, and Peter Loewen. 2021. "Perceptions and Polarization: Measuring the Perception Gap Between Urban and Rural Canadians." Public Policy Forum. February 2. https://ppforum.ca/publications/perceptions-and-polarization/.

Statistics Canada. 2011a. "Canada's Rural Population since 1851." https://www12.statcan.gc.ca/census-recensement/2011/as-sa/98-310-x/98-310-x2011003_2-eng.cfm.

———. 2011b. "Snapshot of Canadian Agriculture." http://www.statcan.gc.ca/pub/95-640-x/2011001/p1/p1-00-eng.htm.

———. 2017. "Population Centre." https://www12.statcan.gc.ca/census-recensement/2016/ref/dict/geo049a-eng.cfm.

———. 2022. "Population Growth in Canada's Rural Areas, 2016 to 2021." https://www12.statcan.gc.ca/census-recensement/2021/as-sa/98-200-x/2021002/98-200-x2021002-eng.cfm.

Taylor, Zack, Jack Lucas, David A. Armstrong, and Ryan Bakker. 2024. "The Development of the Urban-Rural Cleavage in Anglo-American Democracies." *Comparative Political Studies* 57 (8) 1339–74. https://doi.org/10.1177/00104140231194060.

Thompson, Allan. 2021. "The Dangerous Divide Between Rural and Urban Canadians." *iPolitics*. September 22. https://ipolitics.ca/2021/09/22/the-dangerous-divide-between-rural-and-urban-canadians/.

Trujillo, Kristin Lunz, and Zack Crowley. 2022. "Symbolic Versus Material Concerns of Rural Consciousness in the United States." *Political Geography* 96: 102658. https://doi.org/10.1016/j.polgeo.2022.102658.

Walks, R. Alan. 2005. "The City-Suburban Cleavage in Canadian Federal Politics." *Canadian Journal of Political Science* 38 (2): 383–414. https://doi.org/10.1017/S0008423905030842.

Wherry, Aaron. 2021. "Two New Solitudes – Rural and Urban – Now Define the Canadian Political Landscape." CBC News. October 3. https://www.cbc.ca/news/politics/2021-election-rural-urban-conservative-liberal-1.6197095.

Young, Nathan, and Ralph Matthews. 2007. "Resource Economies and Neoliberal Experimentation: The Reform of Industry and Community in Rural British Columbia." *Area* 39 (2): 176–85. https://doi.org/10.1111/j.1475-4762.2007.00739.x.

Yun, Tom. 2021. "Vaccine Hesitancy Higher Among Rural, Low-Income Communities: Study." *CTV News*. March 30. https://www.ctvnews.ca/health/coronavirus/vaccine-hesitancy-higher-among-rural-low-income-communities-study-1.5368415.

PART FIVE

Landmark Canadian Elections

CHAPTER TWENTY-ONE

Landmark Canadian Elections: People, Players, and Processes in Action

Royce Koop and Tamara A. Small

INTRODUCTION

To date, Canada has had 44 general elections. Some of those elections have more significance than others. In this final section of *Elections in Canada*, we put our approach to elections as a process in practice. This chapter consists of short reflections on seven key elections throughout Canadian history that have had particularly notable consequences for the future and direction of the country.

In focusing on certain elections over others, we follow in a long tradition of Canadian political scientists who have focused on "critical" elections (LeDuc et al. 2016). According to Blake (1979), critical elections are those where there are significant shifts in the nature of voter support, whether those shifts represent temporary alterations or permanent realignments. The notion of "critical" elections tracks with the notion of party system change, with some transformational elections representing a dealignment from the old patterns of competition and others a realignment into new forms of competition. Such periods of transformation have happened several times throughout Canadian history; as Carty and colleagues (2000) note, "Long periods of rather predictable political alignments and party life have suddenly been overturned, and then rebuilt in new ways in the matter of a few years." Nor is this related only to competition between parties. In their conception of change across Canadian history, Carty and colleagues take a richer view of party systems, which encompass questions of party organization, campaign financing, how elections are fought, the ways parties and candidates communicate with voters, and even how parties see their own representational responsibilities.

This approach complements our own approach to the study of individual elections. We expand on the 1917, 1921, 1958, 1988, and 1993 elections because we believe each of these elections held consequences for the development of Canadian democracy and the future conduct of Canadian elections. In some cases, this was party system change. In others, these consequences included institutional innovation. In still others, the election being studied provides a stark illustration of some of the crucial themes in the study of Canadian politics and elections. In each case, we employ the broad knowledge developed in previous chapters to better understand these pivotal elections in Canadian history. Our final vignette differs somewhat from the others in that it covers two elections, held in 2011 and 2015, together. Our rationale for doing so is because it is potentially hazardous to draw broad conclusions from a single election that is still not very far back in Canada's history. By looking at the 2011 and 2015 elections together, we hope to draw more reliable conclusions and emphasize implications for the future of Canadian politics.

We approach each election in the same way, corresponding to the four themes of the book. Each election begins with a discussion of the context of the election with a focus on the institutional setting. The key players are highlighted next by providing a summary of the major parties and their leaders. We move on to highlight what happened in the campaign. Each election concludes with a discussion of the people – how and why Canadians voted the way they did in that election. While we take a similar approach to each election, it will be clear that what makes one election significant varies. In one election, changes to election law may be important while in another it is the introduction of new players.

Figures 21.1, 21.2, 21.3, and 21.4 provide at-a-glance overviews of the landmark elections discussed in this chapter.

Figure 21.1. Landmark Elections: Length of Campaign (Days)

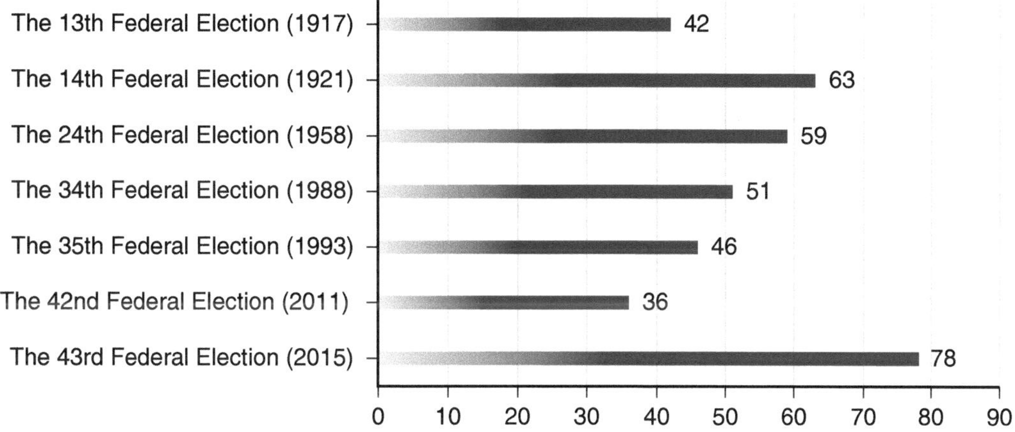

Figure 21.2. Landmark Elections: Redistribution of Seats

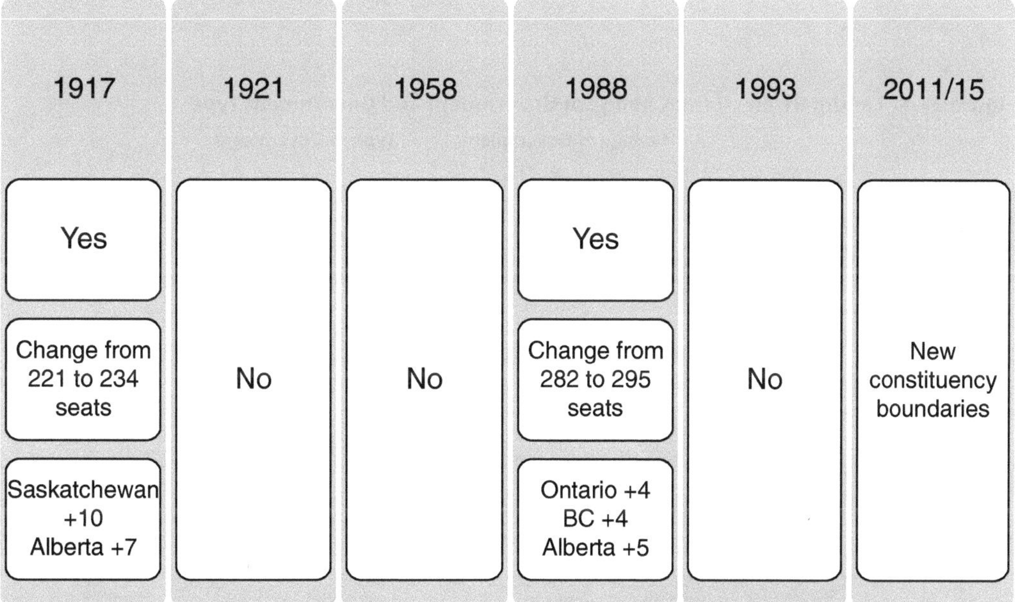

Figure 21.3. Landmark Elections: Voter Turnout (Percentage of Population)

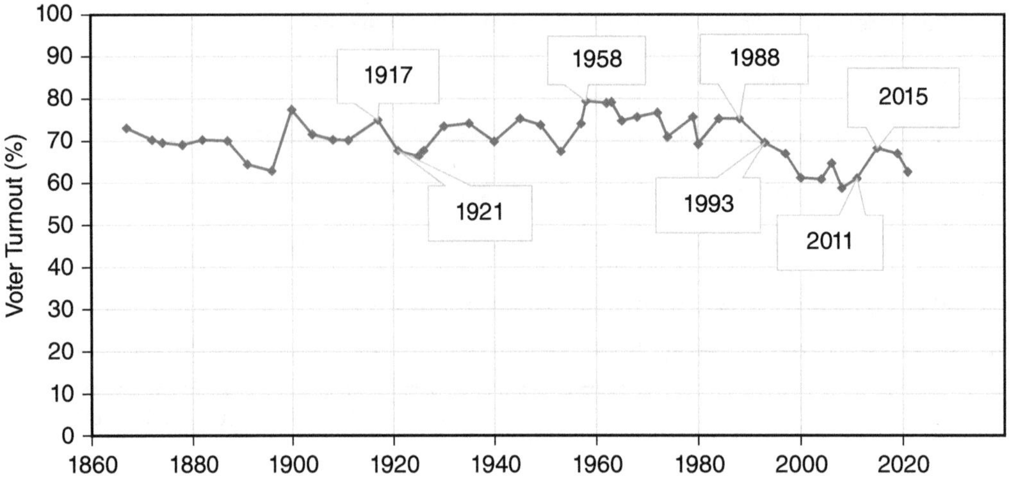

Source: Adapted from Elections Canada data: https://electionsanddemocracy.ca/elections-numbers-0/graph-voter-turnout-federal-elections.

Figure 21.4. Landmark Elections: Change of Government and Government Type

	Change of Government	Type of Government
1917	No	Earned majority
1921	Yes	Minority
1958	No	Earned majority
1988	No	Manufactured majority
1993	Yes	Manufactured majority
2011	No	Manufactured majority
2015	Yes	Manufactured majority

THE 13TH FEDERAL ELECTION
DECEMBER 17, 1917

THE FACTS

- **Length of campaign:** 42 days
- **Redistribution of seats prior to election:** Yes. In 1914, the seat total increased from 221 to 234. Both Saskatchewan and Alberta were added to the confederation. Saskatchewan received 10 seats and Alberta 7. In 1915, the seat total increased to 235. PEI received a new seat.
- **Turnout:** 75%
- **Change of government:** No, the Conservative government of Robert Borden remained in power. However, this government was a coalition formed of Conservative and some Liberal MPs.
- **Type of government:** Earned majority

CONTEXT AND INSTITUTIONAL SETTING

The 13th federal election is a fascinating election for what happened *before* the election than during the campaign itself. The 13th election should have taken place in 1916 at the very latest. Section 50 of the then *British North America Act* (1867) states that no parliament can last longer than five years.[1] However, the delay was caused by World War I, which began in 1914. Canada, as a Dominion of the British Empire, joined the war when Great Britain did, on August 4, 1914. Initially, politicians on both sides of the aisle supported the war effort; Liberal leader Wilfrid Laurier, former prime minister and now the leader of the opposition, agreed to the extension of Parliament for a year. By 1917, the political truce between Laurier and Conservative prime minister Robert Borden had broken down. The death toll of Canadian soldiers was very high; this resulted in Borden's turnabout on conscription or compulsory military service. In the fall, Borden passed the *Military Service Act*, making men ages 20 to 45 eligible for conscription. Laurier refused to extend Parliament, making an election necessary by the end of the year.

A bitter ethnolinguistic divide shaped this election (Duffy 2002). French Canadians, particularly those in Quebec, had less of an attachment to Britain and were against fighting for a "distant imperial cause" (Brookfield 2008, 484). Indeed, one of the reasons for conscription was that so few men from Quebec had volunteered in the first place. This divide made its way into party politics. Borden attempted to enter a coalition with Laurier and the Liberals, but Laurier refused. Within the Liberals, discord on conscription led the party to fragment. Almost half of Liberal English-speaking MPs broke ranks by voting in favour of the *Military Service Act*. Eventually, 2/3 of non-Quebec Liberals joined Borden's Union government in October 1917, with nine Liberals as cabinet ministers.

Perhaps more than any other, the rules of the game profoundly shaped this election. To outflank the Laurier Liberals, Borden introduced two of the "most controversial pieces of electoral legislation in Canadian history" (Courtney 2004, 115). First was the *Military Voters Act,* which defined a "military elector" as any British subject, male or female, who was an active or retired member of the Canadian Armed Forces. This meant that some women, First Nations persons, and persons below the voting age were able to vote. Second, a military vote could be assigned to any riding in which they had previously resided, or it could be assigned by the party of the voter's choice to the riding. Finally, military votes would be counted 31 days after the election. The second law, the *Wartime Elections Act,* was even more "draconian" (Dutil and MacKenzie 2017, 124). It gave any qualified female British subject the right to vote provided she was a "wife, mother, sister, or daughter of any person, male or female, living or dead, who was serving or had served in the war" (Elections Canada 2020, 81). At the same time, conscientious objectors, including the Mennonites and Doukhobors, were disenfranchised, as were "enemy aliens," those born in an enemy country who had become a naturalized British subject after March 31, 1902. While the obvious result of the two laws was to increase the number of voters sympathetic to the Borden government (Elections Canada 2020), this election is also remembered as the first time *some* women could vote in a federal election. Around 450,000 women, including 2,000 "Bluebirds" or military nurses, gained the franchise; at the same time approximately 60,000 potential male voters lost the vote, particularly on the Prairies, where many new immigrants had settled (Brookfield 2008; Elections Canada 2020). According to Brodie and Jenson (1988), disenfranchisement on the enemy alien clause was about five times more likely in the west than in the eastern provinces.

THE PLAYERS

Prime Minister Robert Borden

- Unionist or government
- Leader since 1901
- Won in 1911 with a majority government; first Conservative government since 1886

Sir Wilfrid Laurier

- Laurier Liberals or opposition
- Leader of the opposition since 1911
- Served as Canada's 7th prime minister; 15-year tenure as PM remains the longest unbroken term in Canadian history

As mentioned, the traditional party system was in disarray in this election. Conscriptionists, both Conservative and Liberal, ran under the banner of Unionists. The Unionists were sometimes referred to as the government. Those against conscription, including francophone MPs, were known as the "Laurier Liberals" (Bosc and Gagnon 2017) or the opposition.

THE CAMPAIGN

The 1917 election was relatively long at 42 days to allow for voting of service people. The Laurier Liberals attempted to make this campaign about more than just the war. The Liberal platform, released a month into the campaign, focused on Borden's performance in office, including railway policy, tariffs, corruption, and patronage (Dutil and MacKenzie 2017). With regard to the war, Laurier campaigned against the new election laws and promised voluntary war recruitment. Prior to the war, the government had been unpopular – as such, the Liberals attempted to appeal beyond anti-conscriptionists to labour and farmers, particularly in western Canada, who also had concerns about economic policy. Not surprisingly, the war effort dominated the Unionist platform. Given the broader English-French/conscription–anti-conscription divide, Dutil and MacKenzie (2017) suggest the Unionists were flush with resources, including political organization, money, and press support, compared to the Laurier Liberals. The Unionist campaign focused on moving beyond party politics by putting patriotism and the national interest front and centre. Much attention was given to targeting Quebec "slackers" who were not doing their part in the war effort. The biggest slackers were Laurier and Henri Bourassa, a former Quebec politician and editor of the newspaper *Le Devoir*; Bourassa featured in Unionist posters and pamphlets despite not being an active politician. The press in English Canada was very supportive of conscription and the Unionists. Moreover, the Canadian Press, a newswire service that still exists today, was established in 1917 with a grant from the Borden government to ensure "Canadian unity" (Nolan 1981). Unionist advertising, posters, and pamphlets, along with the English press, were rife with anti-Quebec and anti-Laurier rhetoric (Duffy 2002). For instance, one poster reads: "Are the Slackers in Quebec to rule Canada? A vote against the government means YES. A vote for the government means NO."[2] Perhaps not surprisingly, Quebecers were hostile to Borden and Union candidates. Candidates were threatened with violence, and Borden did not campaign in Quebec (Brodie and Jenson 1988).

Women and suffrage were also an important part of this campaign. To be sure, 1917 was far from the universal suffrage for which the women's movement had been calling for decades. In fact, women in five provinces already had the right to vote in provincial elections. Nevertheless, both parties attempted to appeal to this newly enfranchised class of voters. Laurier critiqued Borden for not introducing universal suffrage. However, many anglophone women's groups supported limited suffrage on nationalistic grounds (Brookfield 2008; Dutil and MacKenzie 2017). Borden framed conscription as a women's issue, and the campaign made emotional appeals to women voters (Brookfield 2008). For instance, the "Canadian Mother" poster reads: "Good bye and God bless you my boy! While you are away I will do *my* duty to cast my ballot for the Union government which will stand by you. *You will not be deserted*" (emphasis in original).

The 1917 campaign did not only take place in Canada. Campaign propaganda from both parties made its way to the front lines in Europe (Morton 1975). The parties even had people on the ground to speak to soldiers. One of the Unionists' key messages to soldiers was to encourage them to vote for the government rather than a particular candidate (Dutil and MacKenzie 2017), thus allowing the Unionists to benefit from the rules in the *Military Voters Act*.

Table 21.1. 1917 Federal Election Results

Party Name		1911	BC	AB	SK	MB	ON	QC	NB	NS	PE	YT	1917 Total
UP	Seats	**131**	**13**	**11**	**16**	**14**	**74**	**3**	**7**	**12**	**2**	**1**	**153**
	Vote	48.0	68.4	61.0	74.1	79.7	62.3	24.7	59.4	48.4	49.8	54.3	56.9
LPC	Seats	**85**	–	**1**	–	**1**	**8**	**62**	**4**	**4**	**2**	–	**82**
	Vote	45.8	25.6	30.6	23.4	20.3	32.1	73.4	40.6	45.5	50.2	45.7	38.8
Other	Vote	6.2	6.0	8.5	2.6	–	5.6	2.0	–	6.1	–	–	4.2
Total Seats		**221**	**13**	**12**	**16**	**15**	**82**	**65**	**11**	**16**	**4**	**1**	**235**

Legend: UP: Unionist Party; LPC: Liberal Party of Canada.

THE PEOPLE

The Unionist Party was elected with the biggest majority government in Canadian history. It is one of the rare earned majorities as well, as Table 21.1 shows.

The Unionists won 65.1% of the seats in the House of Commons with 56.9% of the vote (Morton 1975). The ethnolinguistic divide that structured the campaign was evident in the results. The Unionists won only three seats in Quebec, mainly in anglophone ridings, while 75% of the Liberal caucus was elected from Quebec. The government that was created was technically a coalition government; 10 of the 18-man cabinet were from the old Liberal Party.

Perhaps not surprising, more than 90% of service persons voted Unionist compared to just over 50% of civilian voters. Military votes mattered to the outcome. Duffy (2002) notes that the initial vote tally was 141 for the Unionists and 96 for the Laurier Liberals. Recall that within the *Military Voters Act*, service people could select a party rather than a candidate as the ballot structure was different.[3] The party could then distribute those votes to whatever riding the party wished, "thus tipping the balance to the Union side in a number of close races" (Duffy 2002, 102). While the military was decisive, many suggest that the Unionists would have won without the two laws (Brookfield 2008; Dutil and MacKenzie 2017), as support for conscription was so high.

Some footnotes to this election; First, World War I ended in November 1918, ending the need for conscription and the Union Party. Unionist MPs began to defect to the Liberals or to new parties such as the Progressives (see 14th Federal Election). Second, women received the right to vote in federal elections in 1918. This would make Canada the sixth jurisdiction to do so. However, First Nations women would not receive the right to vote without giving up their status until 1960 (see Chapter 18).

THE 14TH FEDERAL ELECTION
DECEMBER 6, 1921

THE FACTS

- **Length of campaign:** 63 days
- **Redistribution of seats prior to election:** No
- **Turnout:** 67.7%
- **Change of government:** Yes. The LPC under W.L. Mackenzie King defeated the incumbent Unionist Party of Robert Borden.
- **Type of government:** Minority

CONTEXT AND INSTITUTIONAL SETTING

Like the previous election, the Great War also shaped the 14th federal election. With World War I coming to an end, the glue holding together the Union government began to unravel. Robert Borden resigned as prime minister in 1920, weary from governing through a war but also from poor health (Bone 1922). He was replaced by Arthur Meighen, who had served in Borden's cabinets. Meighen had been the solicitor general during the war and the architect of the *Conscription Act, Military Voters Act,* and *Wartime Election Act* (LeDuc, Pammett, and Turcotte 2016). Beyond the war, the Union government had no real base of support or ideological connection to hold members of Parliament together. If the 1917 election was notable for changing of the rules of the game, the 1921 election was about the players – political parties. Canada's traditional two-party system of the Conservatives versus the Liberals was "shattered" by the National Progressive Party (Bickerton, Gagnon, and Smith 1999). The success of a new party was unprecedented in Canadian politics. More significantly, starting with this campaign, the Conservatives and Liberals would *always* fight elections against other political parties; some, like the Progressives, would have strong bases of support in western Canada.

It is worth highlighting two important institutional changes prior to this election. First, while some women got the franchise under the *Military Voters Act* and *Wartime Election Act,* all Canadian women, subject to age and property requirements, received the right to vote in 1918. One year later, women won the right to be candidates in a federal election. Four women ran in 1921. Finally, in establishing federal control of election law, the *Dominion Elections Act, 1920* removed property ownership as a requirement of the vote.[4] Thus, the electorate effectively doubled in size (Courtney 2004). However, there were still several racial disqualifications to the franchise, such as Indigenous people and Canadians of Asian origin. Second, as was discussed in Chapter 2, Elections Canada was ostensibly created with the *Dominion Elections Act*, as it established the office of chief electoral officer. Given the partisan nature of the 1917 election, the creation of a nonpartisan office to administer federal elections was significant progress toward independent administration of elections in this country.

THE PLAYERS

Prime Minister Arthur Meighen

- Conservatives
- Succeeded Robert Borden as Conservative leader and prime minister in 1920
- First elected to the House of Commons in 1908
- Served in cabinet

W.L. Mackenzie King

- Liberal Party of Canada
- Leader since 1919
- First elected to the House of Commons in 1908 and served as minister of labour
- Lost seat in 1911 and did not run in 1917

Thomas Crerar

- Progressive Party
- Leader since 1920
- Appointed as an unelected minister of agriculture in Borden's Union government
- First elected to the House of Commons in 1917

As mentioned, the players are central to understanding the 1921 election. In addition to changes within the Conservatives, the Liberals also had a new leader. When Wilfrid Laurier died in 1919, he was replaced by W.L. Mackenzie King. Of interest to students of party politics, King is the first federal leader selected by convention rather than by caucus. However, the Progressive Party is at the heart of this election story. The Progressives were part of the broader agrarian/farmers' movement that had been around since before the turn of the century. While much of this movement operated outside of legislative politics, many agrarian parties were established in the provinces. Indeed, the United Farmers of Ontario formed a government in 1919, as did United Farmers of Alberta in 1921. The agrarian movement challenged the historical dominance of the Conservatives and the Liberals all over Canada (Morton 1946).

The Progressives were formed in 1919 when Thomas Crerar, Union minister of agriculture, resigned in protest of inadequate reductions in the national tariff in the budget (McMenemy 1976). Ten other Union MPs, mainly from western Canada, also defected (Morton 1946). Even though Crerar had ties to the Liberals, the eleven sat as independents due to King's position on the tariff (McMenemy 1976). In 1920, "Canada's first authentic federal third party had been born" (Duffy 2002, 104) when the dissidents designated themselves the National Progressive Party with Crerar as their leader. Although economic issues were central policy planks of the Progressives, they were also a protest movement concerned with reforming the political system along populist lines (Morton 1946). The Progressives presented voters with a very different option than the two traditional parties. The Progressives ran 137 candidates (out of a possible 235) in the 1921 election, mainly contesting rural ridings in the Prairie provinces and southwestern Ontario (Johnston 2017).

THE CAMPAIGN

Discussions of the 1921 campaign are scant in the literature as it is generally focused on the Progressives' impact on party politics. However, the presence of the Progressives did mean that economic issues were important in the campaign, especially tariff policy. The Conservatives presented themselves "as the saviour of protection" while King resurrected the Liberals' policy of free trade with the US, which had led to their defeat in 1911 (Bone 1922, 577). Free trade was certainly an attempt to appeal to western and Ontarian farmers. Whereas Meighen positioned himself in opposition to the Progressives, King regarded the farmers as allies (LeDuc, Pammett, and Turcotte 2016).

With regard to campaigning techniques, little had changed from previous elections. Campaigning by train was still the main method, as was the campaign pamphlet. Leduc and colleagues (2016) note that King gave speeches all across Canada during two lengthy train trips from the Maritimes to the west. Meighen made some 250 speeches during the campaign. Products of their political times, both Meighen and King are described as effective orators.

THE PEOPLE

Table 21.2 presents the results of the 1921 federal election. First, after losing power in 1911, the Liberals returned to government. A key factor in their success was that they won every seat in Quebec, with 70% of the vote. The war may have been over, but the legacy of the conscription crisis was clearly in the minds of Quebecers. As the author of conscription, Meighen was a "pariah" in Quebec (Duffy 2002, 105); less than 20% of Quebecers voted Conservative. Despite winning seats in every province except Alberta, the Liberals were one seat shy of a majority government. The 1921 election marked the first minority government in Canada.

The Progressives won the second-most seats in the House of Commons with 58. It was the most successful party in western Canada, taking 66% of all seats there. To be sure, Canada's electoral system of single-member plurality matters here. As Chapter 4 notes, parties with "regionally concentrated support – typically parties of regional protest – tended to be rewarded much more generously by the electoral system than parties whose appeal is diffuse and natural." As Table 21.2 shows, the Progressives received a lower percentage of the vote than the Conservatives despite winning nine more seats. One notable Progressive who was elected was Agnes Macphail. She was the first woman elected to the House of Commons.

The results were disastrous for the Conservatives, as they went from the largest majority in Canada to the third party in Parliament. The Conservatives won the most seats in Ontario but were shut out of six provinces, including the entire Prairies. Leader Arthur Meighen lost his seat, giving him the dubious honour of being the first sitting Canadian prime minister to lose their seat in an election (though he did return to Parliament in a by-election the following year).

In some ways, the impact of the National Progressive Party on Canadian politics was short-lived. Despite being the second largest parliamentary party, they opted out of being the Official Opposition due to their ideological commitment to anti-partyism (LeDuc, Pammett, and Turcotte

Table 21.2. 1921 Federal Election Results

Party Name		1917	BC	AB	SK	MB	ON	QC	NB	NS	PE	YT	1921 Total
LPC	Seats	**82**	**3**	–	**1**	**3**	**21**	**65**	**5**	**16**	**4**	–	**118**
	Vote	38.8	29.8	15.8	18.7	18.9	30.1	70.2	50.2	52.4	45.7	47.6	41.2
NPP	Seats	–	**3**	**8**	**15**	**11**	**20**	–	**1**	–	–	–	**58**
	Vote	–	11.7	39.6	61.7	41.9	25.6	3.1	8.7	10.2	12.3	–	21.1
CPC	Seats	–	**7**	–	–	–	**36**	–	**5**	–	–	**1**	**49**
	Vote	–	47.9	20.3	16.3	24.4	38.8	18.5	39.4	32.3	37.2	51.1	30.0
LP	Seats	–	–	**2**	–	**1**	–	–	–	–	–	–	**3**
	Vote	1.8	6.8	11.1	0.8	5.7	2.3	0.7	–	3.5	4.8	–	2.7
UFA	Seats	–	–	**2**	–	–	–	–	–	–	–	–	**2**
	Vote	–	–	12.9	–	–	–	–	–	–	–	–	0.7
UFO	Seats	–	–	–	–	–	**1**	–	–	–	–	–	**1**
	Vote	–	–	–	–	–	0.3	–	–	–	–	–	0.1
Independent	Seats	–	–	–	–	–	**4**	–	–	–	–	–	**4**
	Vote	1.0	3.5	–	–	7.4	5.4	6.9	1.7	–	–	1.3	3.5
Other	Vote	–	0.4	0.2	2.4	1.8	0.2	0.6	–	1.6	5.2	–	1.2
Total Seats			**13**	**12**	**16**	**15**	**82**	**65**	**11**	**16**	**4**	**1**	**235**

Legend: LPC: Liberal Party of Canada; NPP: National Progressive Party; CPC: Conservative Party of Canada; LP: Labour Party; UFA: United Farmers of Alberta; UFO: United Farmers of Ontario.

2016), and the Conservatives took up the role. By the next election, the Progressives had become the third-place party in Parliament and had all but disappeared by 1935. Many MPs were absorbed into the Liberals, including Crerar, who eventually served as a Liberal cabinet minister and senator (Johnston 2017). That said, the Progressives are very important to understanding party politics in Canada. Most scholars see the 1921 election as the beginning of the second-party system (Carty 1996; LeDuc, Pammett, and Turcotte 2016), which is, as Carty (1996) notes, characterized by the dominance of the Liberal Party and the presence of a third party that generally receives a much smaller share of the vote than the other two parties. Even though the Progressives did not last, they were followed by the Co-operative Commonwealth Federation (CCF)/NDP and Social Credit. Also of significance, starting in 1921, we begin to see the west as a distinctive political electoral region (Carty 1996). Until this time, the main divisions were French/English and Catholic/Protestant, but the west added a new regional dimension to Canadian electoral politics. While the Progressives should not necessarily be conceived of as a western-based party (Morton 1946), the results of this election can lead to this interpretation (Bickerton, Gagnon, and Smith 1999). The Progressives are the first in a line of parties, including the Social Credit, the CCF, and the Reform Party, where a regional base of support in western Canada has been crucial to electoral success. The continual persistence of regionally based minor parties, even today, means that the vagaries of the SMP electoral system have always been in play in Canadian elections.

THE 24TH FEDERAL ELECTION
MARCH 31, 1958

THE FACTS

- **Length of Campaign:** 59 days
- **Redistribution of seats prior to election:** No
- **Turnout:** 79.4%
- **Change of government:** No. The Progressive Conservatives, under John Diefenbaker, went from a minority government (in 1957) to a majority (one of the largest majority governments in Canadian history).
- **Type of government:** Earned majority

CONTEXT AND INSTITUTIONAL SETTING

The 1958 federal election came only nine months after the 1957 election. Headed into the latter campaign, longtime Liberal cabinet minister and later prime minister Louis St. Laurent was confident of victory. Every indication was the longtime Liberal dynasty would continue in power (Regenstreif 1965, 26). But Liberal confidence aside, the government grappled with public perceptions of both arrogance and incompetence in the lead-up to the 1957 campaign. While the Tories were led by George Drew, he became ill and was replaced by Saskatchewan MP John Diefenbaker, who energetically toured the country and made impressive and compelling appearances on television; in contrast, St. Laurent was unenthusiastic about the new medium and declined to make many appearances. When the dust settled on election night, the Liberals were defeated for the first time in a quarter of a century.

While Diefenbaker won in 1957, he was held to a minority government: 112 seats out of 265 to the Liberals' 105 seats. The balance of power was held by both the Co-operative Commonwealth Federation (CCF) (25 seats) and Social Credit (19 seats). In the PC Party, there was a sense that the government would soon fall and that Diefenbaker was well positioned to trounce the Liberals and win a majority government. Accordingly, with a new cabinet in place, the government opened the faucets of public spending, including boosting benefits, increasing salaries, and delivering money to government agencies to pass along to voters (Courtney 2022, 132–33).

Meanwhile, St. Laurent resigned as Liberal leader and was replaced by Lester "Mike" Pearson with a convincing 77.8% of ballots cast at the 1958 Liberal leadership convention. Pearson had impressive credentials as a former diplomat and recipient of the Nobel Peace Prize in 1957 for his work organizing the United Nations Emergency Force in the midst of the Suez Canal Crisis. But would Pearson perform well in the rough and tumble of domestic politics? A preliminary answer was provided when the new Liberal leader gave his maiden speech in the House of Commons in which he called on the new Tory government to resign in order to make way for him and the Liberal Party to take office without an election. Diefenbaker responded in the House by tearing Pearson apart for his and the Liberals' arrogance. With this excuse in hand, a few days later, Diefenbaker requested a dissolution and the 1958 election campaign began (Courtney 2022, 138).

The 1958 election, paired with the 1957 election, is noteworthy for three reasons. First, it well and truly ended a very long period of Liberal dominance and suggested the pattern that would characterize Canadian party politics for some time: long periods of Liberal dominance characterized by explosions of Tory support producing oversized Tory majority governments. Just under 30 years later, the pattern would repeat itself as PC leader Brian Mulroney, following a long period of Liberal rule, would win a massive, oversized majority government in the 1984 election.

Second, the 1957 and 1958 elections introduced Canadians to a new medium of campaigning in the form of television, a new type of charismatic leader, and a new type of politics. Catch-all politics came to Canada in the 1950s.[5] In 1957, Diefenbaker's charisma and campaign skills, particularly on television and in contrast to a dour Liberal leader, defeated the seemingly unbeatable Liberal Party.

Finally, the 1958 election in particular illustrates some of the dynamics and distortions created by Canada's single-member plurality electoral system, as the Tories' impressive result was translated into an overwhelming majority government and the smaller parties were essentially crushed by first past the post.

THE PLAYERS

Progressive Conservative Party: John Diefenbaker

- Prime minister leading a minority government. Won in June 1957
- Selected as PC leader in 1956 on the first ballot
- First elected as an MP from Saskatchewan in 1940

Liberal Party: Lester Pearson

- Leader of the Official Opposition
- Selected as Liberal leader in January 1958, succeeding former Liberal prime minister Louis St. Laurent
- Had previously been a diplomat, serving as Canadian ambassador to the United States and president of the United Nations General Assembly

Cooperative Commonwealth Federation: M.J. Coldwell

- Leader of the CCF, selected as leader at the 1942 CCF convention
- Influential in the development of the Canadian social safety net under Liberal governments
- First elected as an MP from Saskatchewan in 1935, was previously a Regina city councillor

Social Credit Party: Solon Earl Low

- Leader of the federal Social Credit Party, having been acclaimed as the party's first leader in 1944 – Low would remain as Social Credit leader until 1961

- Previously a member of the Alberta legislature, first elected in the Social Credit sweep under leader William Aberhart in 1935. Low served as treasurer and as minister of education.
- Member of the Church of Jesus Christ of Latter-day Saints.

THE CAMPAIGN

The 1958 election campaign was dominated by Diefenbaker. The prime minister sought a dissolution because both he and almost everyone in the party believed the opportunity would produce a Tory majority government. In the campaign, Diefenbaker again used his public-speaking skills to draw large audiences to raucous rallies and to his television appearances. His spellbinding speeches consisted of exhortations to Canadians to join his "crusade" and to send a message to the arrogant Liberal Party. As a charismatic public speaker, Diefenbaker had little trouble creating an emotive bond with his audiences. As PC strategist Dalton Camp mused following a Diefenbaker rally, "It is a little like watching a nightly miracle, the recurrent chemistry between Diefenbaker and his audiences" (1970, 334).

Diefenbaker campaigned on themes that have informed Conservative thought in Canada since 1957 and 1958. When not castigating the Liberal Party, Diefenbaker presented an individualistic and egalitarian vision of "One Canada" that was particularly appealing on the Prairies and among communities of new Canadians who had not felt traditionally accommodated in Canadian politics. Diefenbaker helped to build the party by bringing these communities within the Tory tent, where many would remain. But his philosophy directly contradicted the myth of Canada as consisting of two founding peoples, and Diefenbaker could not easily accommodate Quebec exceptionalism. This did not weigh down Diefenbaker during the 1958 campaign, but it would following the election.

Pearson was not well suited for television or to counter Diefenbaker's onslaught of charisma. Further, the Liberal Party in the 1950s was grappling with its own organizational problems, the result of decades of intermingling between state and party that left the latter desiccated the moment the Liberals fell from power (Whitaker 1977). Further, the Liberal Party could not count on provincial affiliates or regional ministers to provide a foundation for a strong campaign, as had been the case in the past. The defeats in 1957 and 1958 would create the impetus for significant organizational reform in the party.

The CCF and Social Credit held the balance of power in Parliament following the 1957 election, but Diefenbaker's growing popularity meant this would not last. Both parties lacked resources at the beginning of the 1958 campaign, having spent on the previous election. Coldwell suffered from health problems and had to call on his colleagues to stand in for him at campaign events. Social Credit suffered from internal divisions over both leadership and party ideology. Wisely, the party turned its attention to protecting its incumbent seats in Alberta and British Columbia, but even in this modest task, the party failed.

THE PEOPLE

Table 21.3 illustrates the results of the campaign. Ultimately, Diefenbaker scored a majority of the vote, 53.7%, which is very rare in modern Canadian history. The Chief's vote share was impressive,

Table 21.3. 1958 Federal Election Results

Party Name		1957	BC	AB	SK	MB	ON	QC	NB	NW	PE	NL	YT	NT	NU	1958 Total
PC	Seats	112	18	17	16	14	67	50	7	12	4	2	1	–		208
	Vote	38.5	49.4	59.9	51.4	56.7	56.4	49.6	54.1	57.0	62.2	45.2	54.5	42.8		53.7
LPC	Seats	105	–	–	–	–	14	25	3	–	–	5	–	1		48
	Vote	40.5	16.1	13.7	19.6	21.6	32.1	45.6	43.4	38.4	37.5	54.4	43.3	57.2		33.4
CCF	Seats	25	4	–	1	–	3	–	–	–	–	–	–	–		8
	Vote	10.6	24.5	4.4	28.4	19.6	10.5	2.3	1.8	4.5	0.3	0.2	–	–		9.5
LL	Seats	–	–	–	–	–	1	–	–	–	–	–	–	–		1
	Vote	–	–	–	–	–	0.5	–	–	–	–	–	–	–		0.2
Other	Vote	9.3	10.0	22.1	0.5	2.2	0.6	2.1	0.7	–	–	0.2	2.3	–		3.2
Total Seats		265	22	17	17	14	85	75	10	12	4	7	1	1		265

Legend: LPC: Liberal Party of Canada; PC: Progressive Conservatives; CCF: Co-operative Commonwealth Federation; LL: Liberal-Labour.

but the electoral system transformed that vote share into an overwhelming majority: 208 seats, or 78%. This was the largest majority government in Canadian history, only to be surpassed by Mulroney's majority government in the 1984 election. The Liberals' vote share plummeted to 33.4%, and the party elected only eight candidates. The CCF and Social Credit fared worst, their vote shares declining and seat shares decimated.

Diefenbaker's success was in part a result of Tory resurgence in Quebec. Since the Conscription Crisis of 1917, in which Robert Borden's government conscripted servicemen to fight in World War I, Quebec had turned its back on the Tories. Indeed, Quebec had become the Liberal Party's foundation for election success for the quarter century prior to the 1957 election. But 1958 broke the Liberals' grip on Quebec. In part this was because Quebec premier Maurice Duplessis threw his support behind Diefenbaker, and the Tories benefited mightily from the support of Duplessis' Union Nationale organization. Diefenbaker scored 50 Quebec seats, double the number the Liberals won, in 1958, demonstrating that Quebec, when in play, could help decide the outcome of Canadian elections.

The 1958 election reinforced the enduring impact of television in Canadian election campaigns. Just as in 1957, the energetic and charismatic Diefenbaker outperformed a Liberal leader who was not adapted to the new medium. Despite his many accomplishments, Pearson did not project well on television, and this contributed to his defeat in 1958. Just as radio changed Canadian election campaigns, so too did television, and new forms of communication via the internet would change the nature of campaigning in the future.

Diefenbaker's massive majority government was a dream on election night that would eventually become a nightmare as he struggled to reconcile the various factions and interests within his government and mollify a veritable army of egos. As with Mulroney, Diefenbaker would learn that large majority governments introduce challenges that are not present when governments are smaller.

The 1958 election also provides a stark illustration of Canada's electoral system at work. The system gave a massive boost in seats to the winning party. But the other three parties were penalized, including the Liberals. The CCF dipped to 9.5% of the vote but managed to elect eight candidates. Social Credit, in contrast, scored only 2.6% of the vote and was wiped out. Both parties would make comebacks in different ways, but 1958 was nevertheless a consolidating election, reducing the number of small parties in the face of Diefenbaker's onslaught.

THE 34TH FEDERAL ELECTION
NOVEMBER 21, 1988

THE FACTS

- **Length of campaign:** 51 days
- **Redistribution of seats prior to election:** Yes. In 1987, seat total increased from 282 to 295. Ontario gained 4 seats, BC 4, Alberta 5.
- **Turnout:** 75.3%
- **Change of government:** No. The Progressive Conservatives formed a second majority government.
- **Type of government:** Manufactured majority

CONTEXT AND INSTITUTIONAL SETTING

The 34th federal election differs from most other federal elections given that it was fought largely on a single issue: free trade. In October 1987, Prime Minister Brian Mulroney negotiated the Canada-US Free Trade Agreement (FTA) with American president Ronald Reagan. Scheduled for implementation on January 1, 1989, the FTA was subject to parliamentary approval. The Progressive Conservatives held a majority in the House of Commons, but the Senate was dominated by the Liberal Party. Liberal leader John Turner publicly instructed Liberal senators to hold approval for the FTA until after an election. This action was highly unusual in Canada given that the appointed Senate normally demonstrated "considerable deference" to the elected lower chamber (Macfarlane 2021, 16). One rationale was because Mulroney had not campaigned on or "even hinted at" such an agreement in the 1984 election (Campbell 1989, 2). Though not a referendum per say, the 1988 election sought to "let the people decide" the FTA (LeDuc 1989). The 1988 election has ties to two other twentieth-century elections: free trade with the United States was central to the 1911 election, while the 1917 election, as just discussed, was another single-issue campaign. It is worth noting that the 1988 election took place on a newly redrawn electoral map; 13 new electoral districts had been established in 1987, resulting in a House of Commons with 295 seats.

THE PLAYERS

Progressive Conservative Party: Brian Mulroney

- Prime Minister
- Won largest majority in Canadian history in 1984
- Leader since 1983

Liberal Party: John Turner

- Leader of the opposition
- Canada's second shortest-serving prime minister
- Leader since 1984

NDP: Ed Broadbent

- Leader since 1975
- First elected to the House of Commons in 1968
- The most successful NDP leader until Jack Layton in 2011

THE CAMPAIGN

The 1988 campaign took place in a "highly competitive party" environment (Erickson and Carty 1991). All three parties hovered between 30% to 40% in the polls in the lead-up to the election and each party had a stint in last place. Canada's party system looked like a three-party system going into this campaign. The PCs had won one of largest majority governments in Canadian history in 1984 by combining their historical dominance in western Canada with more than 3/4 of the seats in Quebec, which for several decades had been a Liberal stronghold. However, the PCs' polling numbers going into the campaign were soft due to several scandals, including eight ministerial resignations. Indeed, in the year before the election the PCs were polling lower than the two opposition parties (LeDuc, Pammett, and Turcotte 2016). The Liberals were not faring better. While they had only won 10 more seats than the NDP in the 1984 election, the Liberals led in many polls in the years before the 1988 election (Johnston et al. 1992). This advantage had all but evaporated by the election. Moreover, the party had financial problems and there were serious questions about the leadership of John Turner (LeDuc 1989). The New Democrats, on the other hand, had reason for optimism. The NDP were polling at similar numbers as the other two parties, which was about 10% higher than their historical support. This was due in part to the personal popularity of NDP leader Ed Broadbent. Broadbent consistently polled ahead of Mulroney and especially Turner. The New Democrats, for the first time in their history (and not again until 2011) were serious contenders in a Canadian election. Indeed, the first couple of weeks of the campaign focused on the "Liberal deathwatch" (Duffy 2002, 330).

The two opposition parties were against free trade. Duffy (2002) notes that while the Liberals were against the specifics of the agreement rather than the idea of free trade, the NDP were adamantly against it. Though nuance was probably not evident to voters as such, the PCs were able to own the pro–free trade position while the opposition parties shared the anti–free trade position.

The 1988 debates are seen by many scholars as crucial to this election (Johnston et al. 1992). As was typical during the period of regularization of debates, as discussed by McKay in Chapter 12, there were two televised debates, one in each official language. The French debate took place on October 24, followed by the English one the next day. The two debates were formatted identically; they were divided into three one-hour slots that consisted of one-on-one interactions between two leaders. Each hour began with a question from a panel of journalists followed by a free debate by the two leaders involved. Both debates began and ended with statements from all three leaders. According to Blais and Boyer (1996, 162), the 1988 debates had an "enduring" effect on the voting behaviour of Canadians. This is due to John Turner's "electrifying" performances in both debates, which elevated free trade from a minor issue to the major one (Campbell 1989, 4). In one of the most dramatic moments, Turner quipped to Mulroney in the English debate, "I happen to believe that you've sold us out. With one stroke of a pen … you have thrown us into the North-South influence of the United States. And, when the economic levers go, political independence is sure to follow." The soundbite was later used in Liberal advertising (LeDuc 1989). Several post-debate polls indicated that Turner won the debates. Research suggests that the Liberals gained at the expense of both the Progressive Conservatives and the NDP because of Turner's performance (Blais and Boyer 1996).

Another element in the 1988 campaign was third parties. A third party is a person or group other than a candidate, registered political party, or an electoral district association that participates in an election. Advertising by pro– and anti–free trade groups was central to the discussion of free trade in this campaign. The interventions of third parties in 1988 are important for two reasons. First, it has been suggested that the Progressive Conservatives benefited from the extra pro-free trade advertising beyond the party's own ability to advertise. One important group of advertisers were business groups, which have tended to not be players in Canadian election campaigns (Campbell 1989). However, it is reported that business groups spent $13 million on print advertising in support of free trade while groups opposing free trade only spent $1 million (Gauja and Orr 2015). Not surprising, much of this business advertising came in the aftermath of the two televised debates. Anti–free trade forces included unions, women's groups, artists, and farm organizations concerned with Canada's political and economic sovereignty (Denton 1988). Given that the PCs were the only party supporting free trade, this business spending gave them a perceived unfair advantage (Hiebert 2006). While there is no conclusive evidence to suggest that third–party interventions affected voter choice, some have suggested that "it would be unwise to reject altogether the possibility of such effects" (Bakvis and Smith 1997, 173). The second reason that third–party activity in 1988 is important relates to the institutional context of campaign finance. As Beange notes in Chapter 9, the federal government had been trying to regulate third-party spending for some time. The 1988 election operated without any third-party regulations due to the ruling in *National Citizens' Coalition Inc. v. Canada* (1984), which found that the rules violated section 2 of the Charter. Thus, the ability for business groups to spend so much in the first place is related to the lack of legislation.

The People

As Table 21.4 shows, Mulroney and the Progressive Conservatives were returned to the government benches with a reduced yet comfortable majority. The PC victory ensured the passage of the free trade agreement; it was approved by the House of Commons on Christmas Eve, and the Liberal-dominated Senate approved it six days later. The voter turnout in 1988 was near identical to the previous election at 75.3%. It is worth noting that this was the last election where the turnout was in the seventies.

Table 21.4. 1988 Federal Election Results

Party Name		1984	BC	AB	SK	MB	ON	QC	NB	Ns	PE	NL	YT	NT	NU	1988 Total
PC	Seats	211	12	25	4	7	46	63	5	5	–	2	–	–		169
	Vote	50.0	35.3	51.8	36.4	36.9	38.2	52.7	40.4	40.9	41.5	42.2	35.3	26.4		43.0
LPC	Seats	40	1	–	–	5	43	12	5	6	4	5	–	2		83
	Vote	28.0	20.4	13.7	18.2	36.5	38.9	30.3	45.4	46.5	49.9	45.0	11.3	41.4		31.9
NDP	Seats	30	19	1	10	2	10	–	–	–	–	–	1	–		43
	Vote	18.8	37.0	17.4	44.2	21.3	20.1	14.4	9.3	11.4	7.5	12.4	51.4	28.3		20.38
Other	Vote	3.1	4.8	16.5	–	3.3	1.4	1.4	4.3	–	–	–	2.0	–		4.6
Total Seats		282	32	26	14	14	99	75	10	11	4	7	2	1		295

Legend: LPC: Liberal Party of Canada; PC: Progressive Conservatives; NDP: New Democratic Party.

This election is an example of what Harold Jansen in Chapter 4 calls the inconsistent translation of votes into seats under Canada's electoral system, single-member plurality. The PCs won 57% of seats in the House of Commons with only 43% of the vote. The PCs' electoral success was due to the maintenance of the coalition between western Canada and Quebec that brought Mulroney to power in 1984; the PCs took 67% of seats in the Prairies and 84% in Quebec in 1988. Free trade as a public policy was popular in both regions. Nevertheless, this meant that a majority of Canadian voters actually supported a party that opposed free trade. As Campbell (1989, 4) puts it, the 1988 election at best created "an alleged mandate for free trade" for the Tories.

Despite the "deathwatch," the Liberals were returned as the Official Opposition, winning 43 more seats than they did in the previous election. As mentioned, the debates were politically significant for Turner and the Liberals; "[h]ad there been no debates or had John Turner not won the debates, the Liberals and the NDP would have been involved in a close race for second place and it is not even certain that the Liberals would have formed the official opposition" (Blais and Boyer 1996, 161). Nevertheless, given that post-debate polling for the party showed the Liberals in a minority government position, the result was still a disappointment (Duffy 2002).

The same can be said for the NDP. Despite the 1988 election being the most successful election in the New Democratic Party's history, with its highest seat total and percentage of the vote, the optimism of an electoral breakthrough for the party did not pan out in 1988. They were clearly still the half party in the two-and-a half system. To be sure, the SMP electoral system is also at play here: the NDP received 14.5% of seats in the House of Commons with 20.1% of the vote.

Unsurprisingly, free trade was the most important issue in the 1988 campaign. Data from the Canadian Election Study shows that at the beginning of the campaign, more than half of respondents picked free trade as the top issue (Johnston et al. 1992). That number increased after the two debates, and by election day, it was hovering at around 3/4. In terms of support, Gidengil (1995) finds a sizable gender gap. By the end of the campaign, 3/5 (60%) of the men supported the FTA compared to less than half (44%) of Canadian women.

THE 35TH FEDERAL ELECTION
OCTOBER 25, 1993

THE FACTS

- **Length of campaign:** 46 days
- **Redistribution of seats prior to election:** No. The 1993 federal election was fought in the 295 seats introduced prior to the 1988 federal election.
- **Turnout:** 70.9%
- **Change of government:** Yes. The PC government was defeated, reduced to a mere 2 seats, and replaced by a Liberal majority government.
- **Type of government:** Manufactured majority

CONTEXT AND INSTITUTIONAL SETTING

The 35th federal election took place in a roiling, volatile political environment due to both failed constitutional negotiations and regional discord under Brian Mulroney's PC government. Mulroney's first government, elected in 1984, included substantial numbers of MPs from both Quebec and western Canada – it was, to use Johnston and colleagues' (1992, 110) memorable phrase, a coalition of francophones and francophobes, and thus intrinsically unstable. Mulroney soon learned that balancing the competing interests of these regions would be extremely challenging.

Mulroney's desire to bring Quebec into the constitution led to two failed constitutional deals – the Meech Lake Accord and the Charlottetown Accord. Canadians outside of Quebec (particularly in western Canada) were tired of the constitutional wrangling and talk about Quebec's distinctiveness, while the failure of these accords was seen as a rejection of Quebec within that province. Regional dissatisfaction in the west and Quebec would have consequences for the structure of the party system following the 1993 federal election. Two new regional parties, the Bloc Québécois and the western-based Reform Party, were well positioned to exploit regional discontent, and both parties benefited from increased profiles following their participation in the successful "No" campaign in the Charlottetown Accord referendum in 1992 (Carty et al. 2000).

The PC government's popularity plummeted under Mulroney and so he resigned, paving the way for Kim Campbell to become PC leader and prime minister in 1993. Despite the government's deep unpopularity, Campbell's perceived fresh approach as prime minister succeeded in boosting support for the PC Party; in fact, the 1993 federal election campaign began with Campbell's PC Party close behind the Liberals in popular support, a remarkable recovery (Flanagan 2022). While the campaign promised to be competitive, the eventual very lopsided result reminds us once again that, in Canadian elections, *campaigns matter*.

THE PLAYERS

Progressive Conservative Party: Kim Campbell

- First female prime minister of Canada
- Became PC leader and prime minister after winning the 1993 Progressive Conservative Party leadership contest
- Minister in PC government under Brian Mulroney, including as minister of justice and attorney general and minister of national defence

Liberal Party: Jean Chrétien

- Leader of the opposition
- Succeeded John Turner in the 1990 Liberal Party of Canada leadership election
- Longtime politician, having first been elected in the 1963 federal election; served as a minister in Pierre Trudeau's Liberal governments

NDP: Audrey McLaughlin

- Became NDP leader following the 1989 NDP leadership election
- The first female leader of a major Canadian political party
- MP for Yukon, first elected in a 1987 by-election

Bloc Québécois: Lucien Bouchard

- The first leader of the sovereigntist Bloc Québécois, assuming the position in 1990
- A former minister in Brian Mulroney's PC government who left the PC Party after disagreements with Mulroney over Quebec's place in Canada
- Was a leader of the sovereigntist forces in the 1995 Quebec independence referendum and would go on to become premier of Quebec from 1996 to 2001

Reform Party of Canada: Preston Manning

- Son of the longtime Social Credit premier of Alberta, Ernest Manning
- One of the founders and the first leader of the Reform Party of Canada, becoming leader in 1987
- Ran unsuccessfully as a Reform candidate against former prime minister Joe Clark in the 1988 federal election

THE CAMPAIGN

The PC Party was seriously damaged by years of constitutional wrangling under Mulroney, but the selection of Campbell as leader in 1993 suggested that Canadians were willing to give the party a second look. The new leader chipped away at her deficit in the polls in the months leading up to the 1993 campaign. By the time she visited the governor general on September 8, Campbell had managed to boost her standing among Canadians and was just behind the Liberals in terms of popular support; indeed, subsequent polls showed the Tories with a slight lead or as even ahead of the Liberals. Meanwhile, support for the new regional parties seemed to have evaporated in the lead-up to the campaign, with Reform and the Bloc in single digits in the polls.

The 1993 election campaign illustrates the importance of leadership in this process. Of all the leaders, Chrétien was the most experienced, with a political career dating back decades. In contrast, Campbell and McLaughlin had relatively little experience. In particular, Campbell was selected as leader with only months until she was constitutionally required to face the electorate. While Campbell used the time to boost the PC Party's standing in the polls, she was deprived of time to build experience and a confident grasp of the party.

This difference in experience manifested itself during the campaign. Despite expectations, Chrétien maintained discipline throughout the campaign and stuck to the party's "Red Book" platform, refusing to be goaded. The Liberal leader had to calm down "nervous nellies" in his party as Campbell's polling numbers increased. In contrast, Campbell's shoot-from-the-hip instincts became a liability during the campaign as her advisors struggled to clarify her remarks. In one example, Campbell argued that election campaigns were the wrong time to discuss weighty, substantive issues with voters, creating the impression that she was elitist.

Regional discord in the lead-up to the campaign as well as the presence of two regionalist parties ensured that the 1993 campaign took on a partially regional tone. The Bloc Québécois ran candidates and campaigned exclusively in Quebec. Bouchard and his candidates stoked discontent with Canada during the campaign and presented Quebecers with a genuinely sovereigntist alternative to the mainstream parties. During the leaders' debate, Bouchard took every opportunity to bring discussion back to the needs and concerns of Quebecers, much to the annoyance of some Canadians. Meanwhile, the Reform Party, which had run candidates only west of Ontario in the 1988 election, ran candidates in every region of the country except Quebec. While Manning skillfully employed a range of tactics during the campaign, his use of the "Party of the West" tactic, as Flanagan (1995) terms it, paid dividends for the party.

In contrast, the three older parties ran largely national campaigns. Regional campaigning, especially following the results of the 1993 election, would become a feature of Canadian election campaigns for a time (Bickerton et al. 1999). A major issue that arose during the campaign was the debt and deficit. Several credit downgrades had pushed the issue to the forefront of public consciousness in the lead-up to the campaign. In response, Chrétien promised to prioritize new public investments and spending in order to kickstart the economy and generate additional revenue to tackle the deficit. The Liberals ran an old-fashioned campaign with Chrétien promising "jobs, jobs, jobs!" In contrast, Manning took a hardline approach to the deficit, promising to reduce it to zero in three years through deep cuts. The Reform Party's "Zero in Three" promise received substantial media attention. Chrétien and Manning offered clear alternatives to voters. Campbell, in contrast, promised to reduce the deficit but was vague in how she would go about doing so. The PC campaign also lacked credibility on the issue as the deficit had grown while Mulroney was prime minister. Ultimately, squeezed between Chrétien and Manning's detailed proposals, Campbell could not find traction on the issue.

Leadership took on a different tone in the final days of the campaign. When it became evident that Campbell was likely leading her party to an election loss, the PCs unveiled a negative advertising campaign that focused on Chrétien. The ads were intended to call into question Chrétien's competence and raise doubts about whether he was up to the challenge of being prime minister. In their execution, the ads displayed pictures of Chrétien's face in ways that seemed designed to highlight the facial paralysis he had suffered as a child due to Bell's Palsy. Together with a voice asking viewers "Is this a prime minister?," many viewers thought the PCs were mocking Chrétien's paralysis.

Chrétien responded to the advertisement. "They tried to make fun of the way I look. God gave me a physical defect and I've accepted that since I was a kid. It's true that I speak out of one side of mouth. I'm not a Tory, I don't speak out of both sides of my mouth." Campbell immediately encountered backlash over the ad, and the party soon saw a rebellion of PC candidates against the leader. Campbell soon withdrew the ad and apologized to Chrétien, but the damage was done. The infamous ads left a warning to strategists that negative ads, while potentially useful and effective, could also explode in the hands of the party that was deploying them.

THE PEOPLE

Table 21.5 illustrates the results of the 1993 election. The Liberals came in first with 41.3% of the votes. This produced a manufactured majority government, with Chrétien scoring 177 seats out of 295. The two new regional parties came in second and third, with the Bloc winning 54 and the Reform Party 52. In contrast to this success, the NDP and the PCs were decimated. The NDP, which had won 43 seats in the 1988 election, dropped to just 9. But it was the PCs who received the result for the history books. In 1988, Mulroney won 169 seats and formed a majority government as a result. In 1993, Campbell won just 2 seats and lost her own.

PC failure in the 1993 election represents one of the biggest wipeouts in the history of democratic politics. Campbell resigned as leader, and the disastrous result would help to define party politics in Canada for at least another decade, as the PC Party struggled to survive against the resilient Reform Party and, later, the Canadian Alliance. This split between Tories and Reformers would benefit Chrétien's Liberals as the two centre-right parties split each other's votes, allowing Liberal candidates to win in traditionally Conservative seats.

The success of the regional parties would also mark Canadian party politics. Both parties won by representing and articulating regional interests, and they would continue to do so from the opposition benches. By doing so, both Reform and the Bloc were able to concentrate their vote in enough seats to win a healthy number; in contrast, support for the NDP and PCs was spread across the country so thinly that both parties could barely put together enough support in a single seat to win. In this way, Canada's single-member electoral system cast a long shadow over the results of the 1993 election and reinforced the strength of regionalism in the years to come.

In addition to Reform and the Bloc, there was a proliferation of minor parties in 1993: 14 registered parties in total. These included the reputable National Party led by Mel Hurtig, but also contenders like the Natural Law Party, which advocated yogic flying. None of these small parties had the concentrated regional support that Reform and the Bloc enjoyed and, accordingly, the electoral system obliterated them.

Table 21.5. 1993 Federal Election Results

Party Name		1988 Total	BC	AB	SK	MB	ON	QC	NB	NS	PE	NL	YT	NT	NU	1993 Total
LPC	Seats	**83**	**6**	**4**	**5**	**12**	**98**	**19**	**9**	**11**	**4**	**7**	–	**2**		**177**
	Vote	31.9	28.1	25.1	32.1	45.0	52.9	33.0	56.0	52.0	60.1	67.3	23.2	65.4		41.3
BQ	Seats	–	–	–	–	–	–	**54**	–	–	–	–	–	–		**54**
	Vote	–	–	–	–	–	–	49.3	–	–	–	–	–	–		13.5
RPC	Seats	–	**24**	**22**	**4**	**1**	**1**	–	–	–	–	–	–	–		**52**
	Vote	2.1	36.4	52.3	27.2	22.4	20.1	–	8.5	13.3	1.0	1.0	13.1	8.4		18.7
NDP	Seats	**43**	**2**		**5**	**1**	–	–	–	–	–	–	**1**	–		**9**
	Vote	20.38	15.5	4.1	26.6	16.7	6.0	1.5	4.9	6.8	5.2	3.5	43.4	7.7		6.9
PC	Seats	**169**	–	–	–	–	–	**1**	**1**	–	–	–	–	–		**2**
	Vote	43.0	13.5	14.6	11.3	11.9	17.6	13.5	27.9	23.5	32.0	26.7	17.7	16.2		16.0
Independent	Vote	–	0.3	0.4	1.0	0.1	0.8	1.1	1.3	2.1	–	–	–	–		0.8
Total Seats			**32**	**26**	**14**	**14**	**99**	**75**	**10**	**11**	**4**	**7**	**1**	**2**		**295**

Legend: LPC: Liberal Party of Canada; PC: Progressive Conservatives; NDP: New Democratic Party; BQ: Bloc Québécois; RPC: Reform Party of Canada.

While Chrétien was fond of saying the Liberal Party was now Canada's only national party, this was far from true. In fact, the Liberals were able to form a majority government largely on the basis of a strongly regionalized vote centred in Ontario and Atlantic Canada. In Ontario, Chrétien scored a striking 98 out of 99 seats. Just as Reform and the Bloc won in large part due to regional concentration of their votes, so too did the Liberals. And regionalization of the government had consequences for the way Chrétien governed, with complaints emerging that the government was well attuned to the needs of Ontario but less so to other regions where the Liberals had only a few MPs.

In 1993, after a period of very substantial unrest, Canadian politics came apart, torn primarily along regional lines. At the time, it was unclear whether the results represented a fundamental realignment of Canadian politics or a temporary blip. And 30 years later, the answer to that question is still not entirely clear.

THE 42ND AND 43RD FEDERAL ELECTIONS
MAY 2, 2011, AND OCTOBER 19, 2015

THE FACTS

- **Length of campaign:** 36 (2011) and 78 days (2015)
- **Redistribution of seats prior to election:** New constituency boundaries came into effect for the 2015 election, which meant the 2011 and 2015 elections were conducted using different boundaries.
- **Turnout:** 61.1% (2011) and 68.3% (2015)
- **Change of government:** In 2011, Prime Minister Harper's Conservative Party was re-elected. In 2015, Harper was defeated by Justin Trudeau and the Liberal Party.
- **Type of government:** Manufactured majorities in both elections

CONTEXT AND INSTITUTIONAL SETTINGS

The idea of a *party system* is simply that democratic politics tends to have relatively stable patterns of party competition over time, but that systems can end (dealignment) and give rise to new ones (realignment) (Blondel 1968). The 1993 federal election was significant because it set off a period of Canadian political history that Carty, Cross, and Young (2000) described as Canada's fourth party system. This system, they argue, was characterized by – and was distinguished from previous systems by – new parties, regionalization, segmentation of voter appeals, ideological and organizational diversity among the parties, and internal party democracy. Was Carty, Cross, and Young's fourth Canadian party system the new normal for Canadian politics? Would pre-1993 politics eventually make a comeback? Or would something new arise?

As Canadian politics trundled into the new century, several developments suggested that what Carty, Cross, and Young had observed might be coming to an end. The most important development was the reunification of Canada's centre-right parties. The creation of the Canadian Alliance in 2000 was meant to subsume both the Reform Party and the Progressive Conservatives, but the PC Party remained, staffed by stubborn mostly red Tories who wanted nothing to do with the Reformers and their new party. Real unification came in 2003 when Alliance leader Stephen Harper and PC leader Peter MacKay – both of whom had won leadership of their parties promising no merger between their parties – signed a deal that led to the creation of the new Conservative Party of Canada. A leadership race saw Harper clinch the leadership of the party, and the new CPC performed well (but failed to win) in the 2004 election as centre-right vote splitting came to an end.

The departure of the Reform Party as a result of reunification meant that one of the crucial regionalist parties that had emerged in 1993 was removed from the system. The Bloc Québécois did not disappear, stubbornly continuing to win roughly 50 seats in each of the elections between 2004 and 2008. But 2011 saw the party decimated: leader Gilles Duceppe won only 4 seats, and the party could only elect 10 candidates in the next election. The decline of the Bloc – together with the disappearance of the Reform Party – suggests that the regionalism that characterized Carty, Cross, and Young's fourth party system had come to an end.

The 2000s also ended Liberal dominance and seemed to usher back in competitive party politics. Harper won the 2006 election but, unlike Mulroney and Diefenbaker's massive majority governments, he was held to a minority. In 2008, Harper won again but still with a minority government. Minority governments lent Canadian politics in the 2000s a chaotic character, and it ushered in the phrase "permanent campaigning" to describe the constant vigilance and discipline that characterized this period, when parties were always prepared for an election that was potentially just around the corner (Marland, Giasson, and Esselment 2018).

So, by 2011, Canadian politics seemed to have emerged from the patterns of pathologies of the party system that appeared in 1993. But this period had many quirks of its own. Ultimately the 2011 and 2015 elections would help clarify some aspects of the new Canadian party system while muddying others.

THE PLAYERS

Conservative Party (2011 and 2015): Stephen Harper

- Prime minister from 2006 to 2015
- Selected as leader of the Canadian Alliance in 2002 and then as leader of the Conservative Party in 2004
- Served as the Reform Party's first director of research and was first elected as a Reform MP in the 1993 election

Liberal Party (2011): Michael Ignatieff

- Selected as Liberal leader in 2009
- First elected as the MP for Etobicoke-Lakeshore in 2006
- Formerly a high-profile public academic, author, and journalist before entering politics

Liberal Party (2015): Justin Trudeau

- Selected as Liberal leader following Ignatieff's resignation in 2013
- First elected as the MP for Papineau in 2008
- Son of former prime minister Pierre Elliott Trudeau

NDP (2011): Jack Layton

- Selected as NDP leader in 2003 and elected as MP for Toronto–Danforth in the 2004 election
- Served as a Toronto city councillor from 1982 to 2000
- Announced in 2010 that he had been diagnosed with prostate cancer; Layton died in August 2011

NDP (2015): Thomas Mulcair

- Selected as NDP leader in 2012 following Layton's death
- Leader of the Opposition from 2012 to the 2015 election
- Was previously a minister in Quebec's provincial Liberal government under Jean Charest

THE CAMPAIGNS

By 2011, Stephen Harper and the Conservatives had been in power for roughly five years and won two minority governments. The 2011 campaign began with Harper's exhortation to bring the chaos of minority governments in the 2000s to an end by electing a "strong, stable, Conservative majority government." The Liberals had selected Michael Ignatieff as their leader after the 2008 campaign; the NDP and Bloc were led by their longtime leaders, Jack Layton and Gilles Duceppe, respectively. Polling at the outset showed Harper with a comfortable lead over Ignatieff and the Liberals, with Layton and the NDP in third place.

In the 2008 campaign, the Conservatives had effectively targeted Liberal leader Stephane Dion with a negative advertising campaign, claiming Dion was not an effective leader. The campaign was effective and so, in 2011, the Tories unleashed a new campaign against Ignatieff, claiming the former Harvard professor was "just visiting" Canada and would return to the US if he lost the election. As with Dion, the ads hit their mark, and Ignatieff was quick to blame the ads for his subsequent defeat (Ignatieff 2013). The Liberal leader was further clobbered in the leaders' debate when Layton pointed to the Liberal leader's poor attendance record in Parliament, arguing that "you know, most Canadians, if they don't show up for work, they don't get a promotion."

As the campaign wore on, the attacks took a toll on the beleaguered Ignatieff, and Liberal support dropped as NDP support rose. About 3/4 of the way through the campaign, Layton's NDP passed the Liberals in popular support and didn't look back. Ultimately, the NDP received 31% of the vote to the Liberals' 19%.

The results of the 2011 election were notable for two reasons. First, Harper finally secured a majority government. This was the first time a majority government had been elected in Canada since the 2000 election. Harper also won three times in a row, an unfamiliar historical pattern for the Conservatives. Second, and perhaps most importantly, the NDP finished in second and formed the Official Opposition, consigning the Liberals to third place. This "orange wave" was built in part on NDP success in Quebec, and the Bloc was decimated. For the first time since the founding of the NDP in 1961, it appeared that the party was successfully challenging the Liberals and would become the country's left-of-centre alternative to the Liberal Party.

In office between 2011 and 2015, Harper was increasingly beset by scandals that are inevitable for a long-surviving government. In particular, Harper was caught up in an ongoing scandal involving Conservative senator Mike Duffy, who was personally paid $90,000 by Harper's chief of staff to cover the senator's expenses. In addition, the government began to dip its toes into cultural conservatism, such as by banning the wearing of the niqab during citizenship ceremonies. On the opposition benches, Layton, who had led his party to unprecedented success, died of cancer and was subsequently replaced by former Quebec cabinet minister Thomas Mulcair. Ignatieff resigned as Liberal leader and, following a leadership election, was replaced by Justin Trudeau, the son of former prime minister Pierre Elliot Trudeau.

The total number of seats contested in the 2015 election increased to 338 as a result of the 2012 redistribution. In total, new seats were given to British Columbia (6), Alberta (6), Ontario (15), and Quebec (3). This meant that the 2011 and 2015 elections were fought on different electoral maps.

As in 2008 and 2011, the Tories prepared a negative advertising campaign to deploy against their opponents, particularly Justin Trudeau. The ads condemned Trudeau as a celebrity and declared the Liberal leader was "just not ready," although the Tories did take the opportunity to compliment Trudeau's hair. The Tories also, if re-elected, promised to create a tip line where people could report instances of "barbaric cultural practices," a follow-up to government legislation introduced a year earlier promising to convey to immigrants that "harmful and violent cultural practices are unacceptable in Canada," promises seen by the Tories' opponents as unfairly targeting Muslims.

Trudeau distinguished himself during the campaign by making numerous uncosted spending promises, a position that was criticized by both Harper and Mulcair. Trudeau soon admitted he would have to run deficits to pay for his spending promises, although he promised these would be small and for only three years. These changing positions drew mockery from Harper, but Trudeau was successful in distinguishing himself from his two opponents.

Both Harper and Mulcair were very experienced politicians and campaigners, whereas Trudeau was an upstart in his first campaign as Liberal leader. Given the parties' standings, most observers felt that Mulcair's NDP would be the primary challenger to the Tory incumbents. Early polling in the campaign confirmed this. Nevertheless, the Liberals soon passed the NDP in popular support. It seemed clear that the Tories and NDP had underestimated the new Liberal leader, who represented a fresh face that contrasted with the sometimes grumpy personas of both Harper and Mulcair. Trudeau ran an energetic campaign and was seemingly unaffected by the Conservative attack ads. On election night, the Liberals rebounded from their 2011 drubbing, winning a majority government.

THE PEOPLE

Table 21.6 shows the outcome for both the 2011 and 2015 national elections. In 2011, the Conservatives scored a comfortable majority: 166 out of 338 seats. In 2015, the Liberals finished in roughly the same situation: 184 out of 338 seats. The 2011 election was remarkable for switching the fortunes of the Liberals and NDP, with Layton's NDP winning 103 seats to the Liberals' 34, and forming the Official Opposition as a result. But by 2015, it appeared that 2011 had been a blip, with the NDP returning to its traditional place as the third-place party in Parliament.

In both 2011 and 2015, the electoral system cast a long shadow over the results. SMP has, for most of Canadian history, produced single-party majority governments that have alternated between the Liberals (mostly) and the Conservatives (occasionally). But throughout the 2000s,

Table 21.6. 2011 and 2015 Federal Election Results

Party Name		2011 Total	BC	AB	SK	MB	ON	QC	NB	NS	PE	NL	YT	NT	NU	2015 Total
LPC	Seats	**34**	**17**	**4**	**1**	**7**	**80**	**40**	**10**	**11**	**4**	**7**	**1**	**1**	**1**	**184**
	Vote	18.9	35.2	24.6	23.9	44.6	44.8	35.7	51.6	61.9	58.3	64.5	53.6	48.3	47.2	39.5
CPC	Seats	**166**	**10**	**29**	**10**	**5**	**33**	**12**	–	–	–	–	–	–	–	**99**
	Vote	39.6	30.0	59.5	48.5	37.3	35.0	16.7	25.3	17.9	19.3	10.3	24.0	18.0	24.8	31.9
NDP	Seats	**103**	**14**	**1**	**3**	**2**	**8**	**16**	–	–	–	–	–	–	–	**44**
	Vote	30.6	25.9	11.6	25.1	13.8	16.6	25.4	18.3	16.4	16.0	21.0	19.5	30.8	26.5	19.7
BQ	Seats	**4**	–	–	–	–	–	**10**	–	–	–	–	–	–	–	**10**
	Vote	6.0	–	–	–	–	–	19.3	–	–	–	–	–	–	–	4.7
GPC	Seats	**1**	**1**	–	–	–	–	–	–	–	–	–	–	–	–	**1**
	Vote	3.9	8.2	2.5	2.1	3.2	2.9	2.3	4.6	3.4	6.0	1.1	2.9	2.8	1.5	3.4
Other	Vote	0.4	0.1	0.8	0.2	0.6	0.2	0.1	0.1	0.3	0	2.9	–	–	–	0.2
Total Seats		**308**	**42**	**34**	**14**	**14**	**121**	**78**	**10**	**11**	**4**	**7**	**1**	**1**	**1**	**338**

Legend: LPC: Liberal Party of Canada; CPC: Conservative Party of Canada; NDP: New Democratic Party; BQ: Bloc Québécois; GPC: Green Party of Canada.

Canadians were governed by minority governments, with substantial consequences for the conduct of our politics. In part, the Bloc was largely responsible for this: with a small party depriving the major parties of roughly 50 Quebec seats, it became much more difficult for the major parties to win enough seats to form a majority government. But 2011 and 2015 returned Canada to majority governments, although future elections would once again produce minorities.

The results of the 2011 election seemed to have major implications for our understanding of the Canadian party system. The decimation of the Liberals and rise of the NDP suggested that Canadian politics was moving closer to the politics of the United Kingdom or Australia, characterized by clear competition between a party of the centre-left and a party of the centre-right. The Liberal Party on this view could only ever hope to be a minor party of the centre, squeezed between the primary competitors. The longstanding pattern of Canadian politics – an often-dominant party of the centre – seemed to come to an end, and some predicted that this was sure to be a lasting realignment of Canadian politics (Koop and Bittner 2013).

But it was not to be. The 2015 election dashed that expectation, with the Liberal Party roaring back into a majority, the Conservatives as the Official Opposition, and the NDP as the third party. This is a very familiar pattern in Canadian history, and it appeared that 2015 had returned Canada to its traditional form of politics. But did it? Subsequent elections, in which the Liberals retained power but fell to a minority government and the Bloc returned to the scene in force, suggest not.

What is the future of Canadian politics? The 2011 election reminds us of the dangers of assigning broad consequences and implications to a single election. But Canadian politics seems unsettled; unmoored from the traditional alignments and patterns that provided structure for almost the entirety of the twentieth century (Johnston 2017). We suspect that the authoritative account of recent Canadian politics – particularly the remarkable period that included the 2011 and 2015 elections – has yet to be written.

NOTES

1 The *BNA Act* becomes the *Constitution Act, 1867* in 1982 with patriation. A similar clause is in section 4.1 of the *Charter of Rights and Freedoms.*

2 A copy of this poster and others can be found on the Library and Archives Canada website: https://library -archives.canada.ca/

3 See Morton (1975) for a copy of this military ballot.

4 Most elections held between 1867 and 1917 were run using provincial laws that varied from province to province (except between 1885–88). The *Dominion Elections Act* finally established federal control of election law.

5 See Kirchheimer (1966) or Carty (2013) for a discussion of catch-all and brokerage politics in Canada.

REFERENCES

Bakvis, Herman, and Jennifer Smith. 1997. "Third-Party Advertising and Electoral Democracy: The Political Theory of the Alberta Court of Appeal in Somerville v. Canada (Attorney General) [1996]." *Canadian Public Policy* 23 (2): 164–78. https://doi.org/10.2307/3551483.

Bickerton, James, Alain-G. Gagnon, and Patrick J. Smith. 1999. *Ties that Bind: Voters and Parties in Canada.* Don Mills: Oxford University Press.

Blais, André, and M. Martin Boyer. 1996. "Assessing the Impact of Televised Debates: The Case of the 1988 Canadian Election." *British Journal of Political Science* 26 (2): 143–64. https://doi.org/10.1017 /S0007123400000405.

Blake, Donald E. 1979. "1896 and All That: Critical Elections in Canada." *Canadian Journal of Political Science* 12 (2): 259–79. https://doi.org/10.1017/S0008423900048113.

Blondel, J. 1968. "Party Systems and Patterns of Government in Western Democracies." *Canadian Journal of Political Science* 1(2): 180–203. https://doi.org/10.1017/S0008423900036507.

Bone, John R. 1922. "Canada's Liberal Landslide." *Current History (1941)* 15 (4): 576–79. https://doi.org /10.1525/curh.1922.15.4.576.

Bosc, Marc, and André Gagnon, eds. 2017. *House of Commons Procedure and Practice.* 3rd ed. Ottawa: House of Commons. https://www.ourcommons.ca/procedure/procedure-and-practice-3 /index-e.html.

Brodie, Janine, and Jane Jenson. 1988. *Crisis, Challenge and Change: Party and Class in Canada Revisited.* Montreal: McGill-Queen's University Press.

Brookfield, Tarah. 2008. "Divided by the Ballot Box: The Montreal Council of Women and the 1917 Election." *Canadian Historical Review* 89 (4): 473–501. https://doi.org/10.3138/chr.89.4.473.

Camp, Dalton. 1970. *Gentlemen, Players and Politicians.* Toronto: McClelland and Stewart.

Campbell, Robert Malcolm. 1989. "Post-Mortem on the Free Trade Election." *Journal of Canadian Studies* 24(1): 3–165. https://doi.org/10.3138/jcs.24.1.3.

Carty, R. Kenneth. 1996. "Three Canadian Party Systems: An Interpretation of the Development of National Politics." In *Party Politics in Canada,* 8th ed., edited by Hugh G. Thorburn and Alan Whitehorn, 16–31. Scarborough, ON: Prentice Hall Canada.

———. 2013. "Has Brokerage Politics Ended? Canadian Parties in the New Century." *Parties, Elections, and the Future of Canadian Politics,* edited by Amanda Bittner and Royce Koop. Vancouver: UBC Press, 10–23.

Carty, R. Kenneth, William P. Cross, and Lisa Young. 2000. *Rebuilding Canadian Party Politics.* Vancouver: UBC Press.

Courtney, John C. 2004. *Elections.* Vancouver: UBC Press.

———. 2022. *Revival and Change: The 1957 and 1958 Diefenbaker Elections.* Vancouver: UBC Press.

Denton, Herbert H. 1988. "Canada's Senate Approves Free-Trade Pact." *Washington Post*. December 31. https://www.washingtonpost.com/archive/business/1988/12/31/canadas-senate-approves-free-trade-pact/2a90d97b-6e5f-4cd4-84b7-b37f97e06e31/.

Duffy, John. 2002. *Fights of Our Lives: Elections, Leadership and the Making of Canada*. Toronto: HarperCollins Canada.

Dutil, Patrice, and David MacKenzie. 2017. *Embattled Nation: Canada's Wartime Election of 1917*. Toronto: Dundurn.

Elections Canada. 2020. *A History of the Vote in Canada*. 3rd ed. https://www.elections.ca/content.aspx?section=res&dir=his&document=index&lang=e.

Erickson, Lynda, and R. Kenneth Carty. 1991. "Parties and Candidate Selection in the 1988 Canadian General Election." *Canadian Journal of Political Science/Revue Canadienne de Science Politique* 24 (2): 331–49. https://doi.org/10.1017/S0008423900005114.

Flanagan, Tom. 1995. *Waiting for the Wave: The Reform Party and Preston Manning*. Don Mills: Stoddart.

Flanagan, Tom. 2022. *Pivot or Pirouette? The 1993 Canadian General Election*. Vancouver: UBC Press.

Gauja, Anika, and Graeme Orr. 2015. "Regulating 'Third Parties' as Electoral Actors: Comparative Insights and Questions for Democracy." *Interest Groups & Advocacy* 4 (3): 249–71. http://dx.doi.org/10.1057/iga.2015.2.

Gidengil, Elisabeth. 1995. "Economic Man – Social Woman?: The Case of the Gender Gap in Support for the Canada-United States Free Trade Agreement." *Comparative Political Studies* 28 (3): 384–408. https://doi.org/10.1177/0010414095028003003.

Hiebert, Janet. 2006. "Elections, Democracy and Free Speech: More at Stake than an Unfettered Right to Advertise." In *Party Funding and Campaign Financing in International Perspective*, edited by Keith Ewing and Samuel Issacharoff, 269–90. Portland: Bloomsbury Publishing.

Ignatieff, Michael. 2013. *Fire and Ashes: Success and Failure in Politics*. Toronto: Random House Canada.

Johnston, Richard. 2017. *The Canadian Party System: An Analytic History*. Vancouver: UBC Press.

Johnston, Richard, André Blais, Henry E. Brady, and Jean Crete. 1992. *Letting the People Decide: Dynamics of a Canadian Election*. Montreal: McGill-Queen's University Press.

Kirchheimer, Otto. 1966. "The Transformation of Western European Party Systems." In *Political Parties and Political Development*, edited by J. LaPalombara and M. Weiner, 177–200. Princeton: Princeton University Press.

Koop, Royce, and Amanda Bittner. 2013. "Parties and Elections after 2011: The Fifth Canadian Party System?" In *Parties, Elections, and the Future of Canadian Politics*, edited by Amanda Bittner and Royce Koop, 308–331. Vancouver: UBC Press.

LeDuc, Lawrence. 1989. "The Canadian Federal Election of 1988." *Electoral Studies* 8 (2): 163–67. https://doi.org/10.1016/0261-3794(89)90033-4.

LeDuc, Lawrence, Jon H. Pammett, and André Turcotte. 2016. *Dynasties and Interludes: Past and Present in Canadian Electoral Politics*. 2nd ed. Toronto: Dundurn.

Macfarlane, Emmett. 2021. *Constitutional Pariah: Reference Re Senate Reform and the Future of Parliament*. Vancouver: UBC Press.

Marland, Alex, Thierry Giasson, and Anna Lennox Esselment, eds. 2018. *Permanent Campaigning in Canada*. Vancouver: UBC Press.

McMenemy, John. 1976. "Fragment and Movement Parties." In *Political Parties in Canada*, edited by Conrad Winn and John McMenemy, 29–49. McGraw-Hill Ryerson Series in Canadian Politics. Toronto: McGraw-Hill Ryerson.

Morton, Desmond. 1975. "Polling the Soldier Vote: The Overseas Campaign in the Canadian General Election of 1917." *Journal of Canadian Studies* 10 (4): 39–58. https://doi.org/10.3138/jcs.10.4.39.

Morton, W. 1946. "The Western Progressive Movement, 1919–1921." *Report of the Annual Meeting / Rapports Annuels de La Société Historique Du Canada* 25 (1): 41–55. https://doi.org/10.7202/290017ar.

Nolan, Michael. 1981. "Political Communication Methods in Canadian Federal Election Campaign 1867–1925." *Canadian Journal of Communication* 7 (4): 28–46. https://doi.org/10.22230/cjc.1981v7n4a260.

Regenstreif, Peter. 1965. *Parties and Voting in Canada: The Diefenbaker Interlude*. Don Mills: Longmans Canada.

Whitaker, Reginald. 1977. *The Government Party: Organizing and Financing the Liberal Party of Canada 1930–58*. Toronto: University of Toronto Press.

Editors and Contributors

EDITORS

Royce Koop is a professor in the Department of Political Studies at the University of Manitoba.

Tamara A. Small is a professor of political science at the University of Guelph.

CONTRIBUTORS

Christopher Adams is the rector of St. Paul's College and adjunct professor in the Department of Political Studies at the University of Manitoba.

Keith Archer was British Columbia's chief electoral officer from 2011 to 2018 and was previously professor in the Department of Political Science at the University of Calgary.

Clark Banack is an assistant professor of political studies and the director of the Alberta Centre for Sustainable Rural Communities at the Augustana campus of the University of Alberta.

Pauline Beange is a sessional lecturer in the Department of Political Science at the University of Toronto.

Ian Brodie is a professor in the Department of Political Science at the University of Calgary.

Chadwick Cowie is an assistant professor in the Department of Political Science at the University of Toronto.

Brooks DeCillia is an assistant professor in the School of Communication Studies at Mount Royal University.

Joanna Everitt is a professor in the Department of History and Politics at the University of New Brunswick – Saint John.

Holly Ann Garnett is an associate professor in the Department of Political Science and Economics at the Royal Military College of Canada.

Asif Hameed is a PhD candidate in the Department of Political Science at Carleton University.

Allison Harell is a professor in the Department of Political Science at the Université du Québec a Montréal.

Harold J. Jansen is a professor in the Department of Political Science at the University of Lethbridge.

Andrew J.A. Mattan is a PhD candidate in the Department of Political Science at Carleton University.

Spencer McKay is a sessional lecturer in the Department of Political Science at the University of British Columbia.

Kelly Saunders is a professor in the Department of Political Science at Brandon University.

Anthony M. Sayers is a professor of political science at the University of Calgary.

Christian Schimpf is a postdoctoral research fellow in the Department of Political Science at the University of British Columbia.

Laura B. Stephenson is a professor of political science at the University of Western Ontario.

Melanee Thomas is a professor of political science at the University of Calgary.

Erin Tolley is Canada Research Chair in Gender, Race, and Inclusive Politics and an associate professor of political science at Carleton University.

Angelia Wagner is an assistant lecturer of political science at the University of Alberta.

Stephen E. White is an associate professor of political science at Carleton University.

Lisa Young is a professor of political science at the University of Calgary.

Index

Page numbers in italics indicate tables.